MAHMOOD MONSHIPOURI

In the Shadow of Mistrust

The Geopolitics and Diplomacy of
US–Iran Relations

HURST & COMPANY, LONDON

First published in the United Kingdom in 2022 by
C. Hurst & Co. (Publishers) Ltd.,
New Wing, Somerset House, Strand, London, WC2R 1LA
© Mahmood Monshipouri, 2022
All rights reserved.

A Cataloguing-in-Publication data record for this book
is available from the British Library.

ISBN: 9781787387119

This book is printed using paper from registered sustainable
and managed sources.

www.hurstpublishers.com

Printed in Great Britain by Bell and Bain Ltd, Glasgow

CONTENTS

ACKNOWLEDGMENTS

Over the past four decades, I have written about US–Iran relations from different perspectives and have had the opportunity to present my ongoing research at conferences in the United States, Europe, and the Middle East. I recently decided to put my thoughts together in a systematic and much broader conceptual framework to shed some light on the dynamics and complexity of this relationship. While unpacking the multitude of factors affecting the relations between the two countries, I argue that ending the lingering hostility that has long characterized US–Iran relations will have positive consequences for stability in the region and beyond. In undertaking this project, I have been fortunate to benefit from the writings of so many regional experts. There is no way to adequately thank all these scholars whose writings have enlightened me throughout all these years. I wish to thank Dr. Mehran Kamrava, whose support and feedback on this project helped me to bring the volume to fruition. I would like to extend special thanks to Professors William V. Dunlap, Jonathan Whooley, and Burcu Ellis, whose invaluable ideas and suggestions enabled me to successfully complete this project. I am especially grateful to Dr. Javad Heiran-Nia for providing me with numerous Iranian sources throughout the course of writing this volume. My special thanks to Steve Barr for his invaluable editorial assistance throughout this project. I am also so thankful to Dr. Amir Nadimi, Susan Nadimi, Yousef Moslehi, and Taylor Myers for sharing their indispensable thoughts and reflections with me. Finally, I wish to express my deep gratitude to anonymous external reviewers for their

ACKNOWLEDGMENTS

insightful remarks on an earlier version of this manuscript. The responsibility for the veracity and validity of the information and arguments offered here, however, rests with me.

Mahmood Monshipouri
October 21, 2021

PART I

INTERNAL CONTEXT

1

INTRODUCTION

CHECKERED US–IRAN RELATIONS

Present and potential future US–Iran relations cannot be understood apart from the past. Neither can the current trends and developments in US–Iran relations be properly understood without an understanding of what has underlined their roller-coaster relations throughout much of the twentieth century. Following the 1979 Iranian Revolution, normalization of relations between the two countries has appeared unrealistic if not inconceivable, given that the Iranian state has vigorously pursued an anti-American ideology since that time. The Obama presidency, however, marked a rare moment in US–Iran relations as negotiations between the two countries and several great powers produced an unprecedented nuclear deal officially known as the Joint Comprehensive Plan of Action (JCPOA).

Historically, US–Iran relations can be traced back to the 1830s, when Americans traveled to Iran as the first missionaries. During the Naseredin Shah period, direct contacts with Americans helped to create a navy force for Persia in the Bushehr port. Later, in the 1870s, a group of American physicians helped establish Urmia University's College of Medicine. By the early twentieth century, relations between the two countries became a major force in the modernization of Iran's economy, helping to liberate it from British and Russian influences.

During the Persian Constitutional Revolution (1905–11), Morgan Shuster was appointed Treasury General of Persia, in a bid to counter Russian and British interests in Iran. Under pressure from both Russia and Great Britain, Shuster resigned. The British proved instrumental in carrying out the 1921 coup that brought Reza Pahlavi to power. World War II and the emergence of the United States as the dominant player on the global scene marginalized the British role in Iran. The abdication of Reza Shah and his son's ascension to power in the early 1940s heralded a new era in US–Iran relations, one that was marked by fast-paced modernization and political ebbs and flows.

The checkered history of US–Iran contacts was aptly captured by a keen analyst of Iranian politics as "a fraught enterprise with a long history of false starts, missed opportunities and failures to communicate."[1] These lost opportunities were due to each country's domestic politics, and also due to regional and international contexts. As some observers have reminded us, "no Iranian leader has ever permanently ruled out a relationship with the United States."[2] Similarly, successive US administrations since 1979—some democrats and some republicans—have either sought rapprochement with Iran or have actually tested Iranian leaders' appetite for moving toward normalizing relations between the two countries. With the exception of the Trump administration, as other analysts remind us, no administration has persistently taken the position that a working relationship with the Islamic Republic is unacceptable or inappropriate.[3]

In each case, Iran's ruling elites have gauged the risks and rewards of negotiations and rapprochement with the United States before making any move. In most cases, the risks have been greater than the potential rewards. Iranian hard-liners have warned about different and contrasting aspects of the cooperation with the United States. They have held a Janus-faced view of US–Iran history. Uncertainty and mistrust have long permeated the foreign policy conduct of both countries, poisoning relations between the two. Had Washington and Tehran looked at diplomacy seriously in each context, both countries would be at a different place today. Instead, US–Iran relations have been shaped by a cascade of counterproductive policies marked by sanctions that escalated tensions and failed to yield any sustainable outcome, or any long-term vision to transform the relations between the two countries.

INTRODUCTION

A confrontational relationship between the two countries is not necessarily carved in stone nor is a dramatic improvement in US–Iran relations realistic for the foreseeable future. That is why working toward an incremental and measured diplomatic solution entails considerably lower risk for Iranian ruling elites. From the US standpoint, there is no simple military solution to the challenge of Iran. There are nearly 60,000 US soldiers deployed throughout the Middle East and North Africa. The US military is overextended and cannot afford another massive military commitment. The Trump administration lacked a coherent strategy toward Iran, and its maximum pressure policy failed to produce the desired results. Instead, this policy pushed Iran further into a theater of Chinese and Russian exploitation.[4] Under such circumstances, pursuing overlapping interests is the only wise and realistic option for any progress in the relationship.

Despite their political rhetoric, Iran and the United States seem to have been involved in an inescapable relationship since the outbreak of the Cold War. Both states have mutual geostrategic interests. In the face of growing uncertainty resulting from the gradual US pullout from the region, the current state of relations between Tehran and Washington assumes a different dynamic while facing even higher stakes. Today, however, neither Iran nor the United States appears serious about engagement. The most viable option to de-escalate regional tensions is to foster more cooperation between Iran and its Arab neighbors. Ultimately, sustainable resolution to the region will not come from US–Iran negotiations alone, but because of agreement among regional countries. Working toward this goal is potentially far more rewarding for Iran than imagining new avenues of reconciliation with Washington.

Given the gradual US disengagement from the region, the general mood of unease around the potential return of extremist groups and factions, such as the Islamic State in Iraq and Syria (ISIS), is understandable. In the face of this ongoing threat, cooperation between key regional actors has never been more urgent. These new and dynamic political realities have necessitated the search for a diplomatic solution that can effectively address Tehran's and Riyadh's political differences over regional issues, including but not limited to the status of Yemen.

Throughout this book, I argue that the key to negotiations—and ultimately, rapprochement—lies in perceived or actual gains. These gains, however, are only one side of this equation. Risks involved in such endeavors are simultaneously the great constraining force that could prevent further progress toward the contemplation of diplomatic solutions. When the rewards of negotiations outweigh its risks, rapprochement wins over antagonism and estrangement. Negotiations leading up to the signing of the Iran nuclear deal (JCPOA) were signs of a growing rapprochement between the two countries. Yet the Trump administration's strategy of maximum pressure made the negotiations with the United States virtually devoid of any potential political gains for Iran. The result has been no major change in Iran's foreign policy behavior.

Moreover, the maximum pressure strategy has alienated Europe and has thrown the region into more uncertainty. If nothing else, it has rendered the return to regional and domestic politics all the more imperative for the region's peace and stability. Given US reluctance to engage militarily in the region, and absent negotiations between Iran and the United States, the "maximum-pressure" campaign has backfired, as Iran's ruling elites have come to view adding uncertainty to an already unstable region as politically rewarding, while also operating through their regional network of allies to enhance the risk of wars and economic isolation.

In the sections that follow, we first explain the reasons for why relations between Iran and the United States since the 1979 Iranian Revolution have been overshadowed by more risks than rewards. In most cases since 1979, striking a proper balance between risks and rewards of negotiations has been stymied by either domestic or international forces. After exploring the reasons for the gradual US disengagement from the region, we turn to the viability of regional and domestic solutions, while arguing that the Trump administration's strategy of maximum pressure failed to bring Iran to the negotiating table, much less forced it to change its foreign policy behavior.

It is safe to conclude that, ultimately, sustainable resolution to the conflicts in the region will come from US–Iran negotiations. Historically, the détente between Iran and the United States has almost always led to the reduction of tensions between Iran and its Arab neighbors. Working toward achieving reconciliation with Washington has potentially been rewarding for Iran, rendering reaching a regional détente with Iran's neighbors all the more plausible. As to which theoretical framework best explains US–Iran relations since the 1979 Iranian Revolution, I argue that a combination of neorealism, liberal institutionalism, constructivism, and securitization of the Copenhagen School seems to be the best path forward for analysis in this book.

Brief History: Contemporary Iran

The twentieth century bore witness to a myriad of key moments in the contentious relations between Iran and outside powers. Perhaps the most dramatic one came earlier in the century when progressive political forces coalesced around the establishment of a parliament in Persia during the Qajar dynasty. What came to be known as the 1906 Constitutional Revolution smoothed the path for a cataclysmic change in Persia, ushering in a modern era filled with hopes and aspirations for building a democratic polity.

During the Persian Constitutional Revolution (1905–11), William Morgan Shuster was appointed treasury general of Persia, in a bid to counter Russian and British interests in Iran. Shuster and his American team represented the first significant involvement of the United States in Iran, albeit as an essentially private initiative. Prior to that, the US presence in Iran had been confined to a few non-governmental areas, including American Presbyterian missionaries who had been active in northwestern Iran among the Nestorian Christians since the 1830s.[5]

Shuster was committed to the task of creating a viable administrative apparatus to collect taxes by helping to increase public revenue despite domestic and foreign opposition. In the countryside, Shuster also played a crucial role in creating the Iranian Gendarmerie as an effective arm of the state, replacing the older Qajar rural police. Both of these attempts were regarded as vital components of a sovereign government capable of resisting imperialism.[6] As a result, Shuster and his administrative assistants became the direct targets of the Russian invasion of the country in 1911–12. Under pressure from both Russia and Great Britain, Shuster resigned. The British proved instrumental in carrying out the 1921 coup that brought Reza Pahlavi to power. World War II and the emergence of the United States as the dominant player on the global scene marginalized the British in Iran. The subsequent abdication of Reza Shah and his son's ascension to power in the early 1940s heralded a new era in US–Iran relations, one marked by fast-paced change, economic development, and modernization.

However, Iran's occupation before World War I, and before and after World War II exposed the country's ongoing vulnerability to outside incursion. United States and British support for the Pahlavi dynasty as the linchpin of their presence in the region only lasted for a short period before the charismatic Prime Minister Mohammad Mossadeq spearheaded the anti-colonial movement to expel the foreign powers who had exploited Iran's national wealth and resources for too long.[7] The ensuing Pahlavi era, the 1953 coup against Mohammad Mossadeq, the dramatic events of the 1979 Iranian Revolution, and the Iran—Iraq War, as Ervand Abrahamian notes, provided common experiences that have intensified a sense of national identity for Iranians to an unprecedented level. History has turned "subjects, peasants, and often non-Persian speakers into full-fledged Iranian citizens."[8] By and large, this national identity has only been questioned in the exterior Sunni regions inhabited by Kurds, Turkmans, and Baluchis. "Unlike many states in the region," writes Abrahamian, "Iran is not the product of imperial map-making."[9]

The 1979 Iranian Revolution, which toppled a pro-West monarchical regime, set the country on a different foreign policy course, radically different from the previous pro-US position. The Islamic Republic, no longer acting as a pillar of stability critical to the maintenance of the status quo, found itself diametrically opposed to the United States, whose presence in the Persian Gulf was seen by the new regime in Tehran as a direct threat to Iran's regional policies.[10] In the ensuing years, Iran's resurgence as a regional power has brought it into a collision course with the United States, especially in the aftermath of the latter's invasion of Afghanistan and Iraq, and in light of its numerous military bases throughout the region, including the Caucasus, Central Asia, Turkey, Qatar, and Bahrain. For its part, Iran's influence on Shi'a empowerment in Iraq, Afghanistan, and Lebanon has dramatically increased, raising concerns in Washington that Iran is bent on becoming a "hegemonic" power throughout the region.

INTRODUCTION

Tehran has responded to Washington's policy of containment with a strategy of deterrence. This approach is the result of both Iran's perception of its own vulnerabilities and Iran's perception of the restrictions that the international community has imposed on the country. A better approach would be a strategy of engagement. Washington must recognize that there is no diplomatic magic stick and switch that can fix its "Iran problem" overnight, as any normalization of US–Iran relations will be a long and difficult process. Unless Tehran and Washington make a strategic choice to normalize relations, the many forces that continue to drive them apart are likely to obstruct the process.[11]

Iran's foreign policy and practice are understandable in terms of its security needs. It is possible, though, to resolve tensions without resorting to war or precipitating the creation of a nuclear Iran. This would require disentangling policies on contentious issues, such as Iran's regional policies and its missile program, while keeping the focus on re-entering the Iran nuclear deal and preventing Iran from becoming a nuclear-armed state.[12] Ultimately, the US–Iran rivalry is not a notoriously difficult problem to resolve. Washington and Tehran face three alternatives: concession by one side or the other; a negotiated compromise (diplomacy) in which the two countries can find a way to coexist in the same perilous region; or an ongoing brinkmanship that could just as easily escalate into a long-term disaster.[13]

The Revolutionary Zeal

Intent on restoring power to the common person and reinstating the social solidarity of early Islamic communities to urban life, neo-Islamic populism under the Khomeini regime aimed to terminate foreign economic and cultural domination. In the early years of the revolution, and during a chaotic and troubling era, the government of Mehdi Bazargan struggled to define its foreign policy. Bazargan's attitude toward the West was a mix of admiration and disgust. While admiring the West for its technical and scientific civilization, he severely criticized Christianity for being unable to give believers directives for pragmatic, social, and political life.[14]

On November 1, 1979, Carter's National Security Adviser Zbigniew Brzezinski met Prime Minister Bazargan in Algiers. Bazargan tried to open a channel of communication with the United States, an act which was heavily criticized at home by the clergy. Militant students in Tehran feared their government was again cozying up to the United States, and that Washington was plotting to reinstall the Shah. The attacks against the US Embassy in Tehran in late 1979, which led to a lingering hostage-taking drama for months, effectively disrupted and even terminated any diplomatic relations that existed between the two countries.

Having broken diplomatic relations with Iran, President Carter secretly approved of a rescue plan. The limited rescue mission, which took place in an Iranian desert some 200 miles from Tehran, failed when two US aircrafts burst into flames, killing eight US servicemen. For Iran, the fallout from this episode was costly. The United States froze Iranian assets on deposit in the West—estimated to be around $12 billion. The massive arms purchase started under the Shah was also frozen, and several weapons systems, including major warships, were canceled or sold to other parties.

A diplomatic standoff took place between the United States and Iran when fifty-two American diplomats and citizens were held hostage after a group of Iranian students belonging to the Muslim Student Followers of the Imam's Line, who supported the Iranian Revolution, took over the US Embassy in Tehran. This episode, which lasted for 444 days from November 4, 1979, to January 20, 1981, brought tensions between the United States and Iran to boiling point. The magnitude of humiliation caused by the hostage crisis and the enormity of change resulting from the revolution shaped the US relationship with Iran for decades thereafter. The financial cost and the enormous loss of international legitimacy, which have haunted Iran since, suggest that the hostage episode was an exercise in futility.[15]

The ensuing Iran—Iraq War (1980—88) further challenged US–Iranian relations. Many Iranian experts hold the view that the Iraqi invasion of Iran was largely instigated by the United States. In 1986, the Reagan administration "reflagged" Kuwaiti and other tankers that shipped oil from the Middle East to the West, establishing that the tankers would be defended by the US Navy. In 1988, as the war drew to a close, the *USS Vincennes* mistakenly shot down an Iranian airliner, killing all 290 people on board.

In a secret deal in 1987, the United States arranged for Iran to purchase missiles and other arms to win a trade for the release of American hostages held in Lebanon, as well as to provide funds for the Contras fighting a civil war in Nicaragua—funding that the US Congress had banned.[16] When this deal, which came to be known as the Iran—Contra Affair, became public, President Reagan rationalized it in the name of building support for the moderates within the Iranian regime.[17] The challenge of revolutionary Iran in the Persian Gulf became a central preoccupation of US foreign policy. Several factors contributed to the establishment of the Gulf Cooperation Council (made up of representatives from Bahrain, Kuwait, Oman, Qatar, Saudi Arabia, and the United Arab Emirates) in the early 1980s: the Iranian Revolution, the Soviet invasion of Afghanistan, superpower competition, and the threat of spillover violence from the Iraq—Iran war.[18]

The publication of Salman Rushdie's novel *The Satanic Verses* in 1989 gave Khomeini the necessary ammunition to criticize the West as well as to unify the nation during a period strained by the losses incurred in the war with Iraq. Khomeini issued a death *fatwa* (religious edict) against Rushdie, effectively putting a bounty on his head. The moderates in Iran were unprepared for dealing with the furor that erupted in the Muslim community more generally (and in Iran more particularly) in response to the publication of *The Satanic Verses*.[19]

During the 1990s, however, Iranian officials frequently maintained that their government had no plans to track down Rushdie and carry out the execution. On September 24, 1998, Iran's foreign minister, Kamal Kharrazi, announced the lifting of the death decree against Rushdie. Speaking at a press conference at the United Nations, Kharrazi stated: "The government of the Islamic Republic of Iran has no intention, nor is it going to take any action whatsoever to threaten the life of the author of *The Satanic Verses* or anybody associated with his work, nor will it encourage or assist anybody to do so."[20]

Although the *fatwa* remained in force, it had no official backing. In his visit to the United Nations in late September 1998, Mohammad Khatami, Iran's president at the time, distanced himself from the *fatwa* by declaring the case against Rushdie "completely finished." Internationally, Khatami's decision was seen by many as part of his emphasis on civilizational dialogue to bring Iran into the international fold. Internally, however, his position was not shared by conservative factions within Iran, revealing the jockeying for power among different factions. While many hard-liners continued to insist that the death sentence against Rushdie be carried out, Khatami, who sought to improve ties with the West, seemed determined to lay the *fatwa* to rest.

During the presidency of Ronald Reagan, US policy was influenced by several events, of which the three salient ones were: the Iran—Iraq War (1980–88), the Israeli invasion of Lebanon in 1982 (known as "Operation Peace for Galilee"), and the abduction of American hostages in Beirut. US military aid to Iraq with the aim of defeating Iran was fragmentary, and backfired. Iran's victory was thwarted, but Iraq emerged more belligerent than anticipated. Two years after the ceasefire with Iran, Saddam Hussein invaded Kuwait, provoking a major war with a US-led coalition with devastating consequences for Iraq.[21] In response to the Israeli invasion of Lebanon, Iranians fostered the birth of Hezbollah—a Shi'ite resistance movement. Armed and financed by Iran, Hezbollah became a potent army while acting as Tehran's main proxy force in the region. Hezbollah consolidated its power in Lebanon and waged a low-intensity guerrilla war against the Israeli occupation of southern Lebanon—a war that continued for the next eighteen years. The high number of casualties incurred in this war sparked an increasing debate within Israel about the wisdom of the Israeli invasion of Lebanon. In May 2000, the then Israeli Prime Minister Ehud Barak authorized a unilateral withdrawal from Lebanon.

In 1983, during the presidency of Ronald Reagan, a US Marines barrack in Lebanon was attacked, resulting in 307 deaths, of which 241 were US service personnel and fifty-eight were French soldiers. According to US officials, Iran was implicated in these attacks. However, no evidence was produced to that effect. White House National Security Adviser Robert C. McFarlane and four other Americans went to Tehran in May 1986 to seek normalization of ties between the two countries. Revelation of the meeting undermined Ali Akbar Hashemi Rafsanjani, speaker of the Iranian parliament at the time, who wanted some form of normalization of relations with America in the eyes of the Iranian people.

At around the same time, as part of the Iran—Contra deal, Israel delivered weapons to Iran while they were at war with Iraq. The money paid to Israel by Iran for these weapons was passed on to the Nicaraguan Contras by the Israelis. In return, Iran used its influence to bring about the release of the American hostages being held by pro-Iranian groups in Lebanon (the central figure on the Iranian side being Hashemi Rafsanjani).[22] On July 3, 1998, Iran Air Flight 655, which was a passenger flight from Tehran to Dubai, was shot down by a surface-to-air missile fired from the *USS Vincennes*—a guided missile cruiser of the US Navy. As a result of this attack, 290 civilians—including sixty-six children and several non-Iranians—were killed. This incident seriously undermined any possibility of rapprochement between the two countries.

Back to Pragmatism

On several occasions in the post-Khomeini era (1989–present), Iranian reformists have offered a positive strategic overture to US presidents. These gestures have been either marginalized or left without any reconciliatory moves on the part of the US in response. The result was forcing these reformist leaders on the defensive in their competition for power with the hard-liners at home.

With the passing away of Khomeini, factional disputes and the primacy of the economy over Islamic ideology came to characterize Rafsanjani's two-term presidency (1989–97). President Rafsanjani helped obtain the release of the American hostages from Lebanon in 1992. Incoming US President Bill Clinton failed to reciprocate. Quite the contrary, since the mid-1990s, US sanctions became a principal instrument for pressuring Iran as part of a declared policy of "dual containment" intended to contain both Iran and Iraq. The results were mixed. The immediate effect of Clinton's executive order banning trade and investment with Iran from May 8, 1995 was a sudden fall in the value of the Iranian currency and, subsequently, a formal devaluation of the *rial*. US allies in the West supported efforts to contain Iraq, but also criticized the confrontational approach held by the US toward Iran. These allies generally declined to cooperate with the US efforts to isolate Iran, leaving the US standing alone with its unilateral sanctions against Iran.

The 1996 Iran—Libya Sanctions Act (ILSA) put in place under President Clinton continued the sanction policy on Iran's petroleum exports. The aim of this act was to impose secondary sanctions on any country that intended to invest in the Iranian oil and gas by cutting off Tehran's access to US markets and finance.[23] Such unilateral sanctions proved ineffectual, as they pulled Iran and Russia together, and drove the United States and its European and Asian allies apart. In 1995, when US corporation Conoco's deal was canceled under the embargo, the French oil company Total replaced Conoco to develop the Sirri offshore oil fields in the Persian Gulf.

Failed Reformist Attempts at Rapprochement

In a decisive electoral victory on May 23, 1997, Mohammad Khatami became Iran's new reformist president. US–Iran relations entered a relaxed phase when US Secretary of State Madeleine Albright met with Iran's deputy foreign minister at the Six-Plus-Two talks during the 1998 UN General Assembly. It was the highest-level US–Iran contact since the 1979 Iranian Revolution. In April 2000, Albright acknowledged the United States' role in overthrowing Mossadeq and described previous policy toward Iran as "regrettably shortsighted." Although the United States failed to explicitly apologize for the US intervention in Iran's internal politics, some sanctions against Iran were lifted.[24]

Throughout Khatami's two-term presidency, conservative clerics trumped his efforts to appoint a more open and democratic government or to pursue much-needed reform. Constrained by domestic Iranian politics, Khatami could not have initiated a rapprochement with the United States. Meanwhile, Clinton sought to build a relationship with Khatami after his landslide victory in the 1997 election, but was thwarted by the Khobar Tower bombings (1996) in which nineteen US Air Force personnel and one Saudi local were killed. Although the Clinton administration initially named members of Hezbollah Al-Hejaz (Party of God in the Hijaz) as responsible, a decade later a US court accused Iran and Lebanese Hezbollah of being the main culprits behind these attacks.

Clinton offered to set up a direct dialogue without conditions, but Iran refused. The Clinton administration approached the normalization talks with a two-track strategy. On the one hand, the administration continued to insist that if ILSA was to be suspended, Iran must end its efforts to gain access to nuclear weapons, terminate its support for terrorism, and forgo denouncing the Middle East Peace Process. On the other hand, the administration repeatedly expressed its readiness to enter into state-to-state talks with Iran.

Meanwhile, according to the National Security Archive, the United States, in attempting to contact President Khatami exclusively, entirely misunderstood Iran's leadership dynamics. Powerful constituencies within the Islamic Republic—such as the Iranian Islamic Revolutionary Guard Corps (IRGC) and Iran's Supreme Leader Ayatollah Khamenei—fell far short of backing Khatami's move toward détente with the United States. For its part, Iran responded with demands such as ending the US military presence in the Persian Gulf, releasing the Iranian assets the United States had frozen from the time of the revolution, repaying Iran the money under dispute at the Hague, and stopping attempts to overthrow Iran's Islamic regime. These issues were only compounded by a lack of political determination and a lack of commitment on either side to address how the barriers to normal diplomatic ties between the two countries could be overcome. All of this hindered any further progress toward normalization.

The 9/11 Attacks

Khatami's second term (2001–05) coincided with the presidency of George W. Bush. The September 11, 2001 attacks on the United States significantly altered US foreign policy toward the region. These attacks provided yet another unique opportunity for Tehran and Washington to cooperate on overlapping interests. At the Bonn Conference (January 2002), Iran played an instrumental role in the formation of a new government in Afghanistan and the repatriation of Afghan refugees in the post-Taliban era, as well as collaborating with the newly established Karzai government in order to create a "sphere of influence" in Kabul.

Despite these positive diplomatic overtures by Iran, President George W. Bush placed Iran alongside Iraq and North Korea in the

"Axis of Evil," as defined in his 2002 State of the Union address, and bolstered his anti-Iranian rhetoric, especially regarding Iran's nuclear programs and its alleged ties with Hezbollah, Hamas, and Islamic Jihad. Khatami and his reformist camp never recovered from that characterization. It seemed as though any possibility of rapprochement between the United States and Iran was lost. Following a multilateral effort to edge North Korea toward a nuclear non-proliferation treaty, the Islamic Republic of Iran ranked high on the agenda of US foreign policy.

In retaliation for the September 11 terrorist attacks, the United States invaded Afghanistan and Iraq. The latter invasion placed Iranian rulers in a far better position to bargain with the United States. The toppling of the Taliban regime with assistance from Iran and other regional countries, including Pakistan, raised the possibility of an opening in US–Iran relations. Likewise, the Iraqi war brought Iran and the United States closer in the sense that stability in Iraq served both countries' interests, and Iran could be a stabilizing factor in the postwar reconstruction, as had been the case in Afghanistan. Yet at the same time, Iranians genuinely feared—and continue to fear—encirclement by the United States. Rapprochement between the two countries could prove to be a vexing problem for US policymakers. Winning trade and investment concessions from the West would almost certainly reinforce the rule of the clerics. Without genuine democratic reforms, these trade ties could further deepen the rift between the Iranian state and Iranian society. US–Iran rapprochement was likely to bypass Iranian civil society, which was one of the most vibrant, explosive, and developed examples of its kind in the Middle East.

The Return to Radicalism

In the 2005 presidential elections, Mahmoud Ahmadinejad, Tehran's former mayor, became Iran's new president. Iran's Islamic hardliners swept into power after thousands of pro-reform candidates were barred from running in disputed parliamentary elections. The Bush administration seemed unenthusiastic about pushing for regime change in Iran, even as conservative Iranian clerics consolidated political control at home. Although, some observers insisted that Iran remained the next target of a US preemptive strike.

When the conservatives won a new majority, the real question became: "would Iran and the United States work toward improving their relations?" Undoubtedly, for many Iranians, the sham parliamentary elections further deepened their discontent with clerical rule. In the disputed 2009 presidential elections, an opposition movement dubbed the Green Movement challenged the veracity of the election results that had seen the re-election of President Ahmadinejad. This grassroots movement presented a new threat—not only to the electoral legitimacy of the Islamic Republic, but also to its identity.

Since its inception, the Islamic Republic of Iran has guaranteed its political longevity by defending itself against real and imagined external enemies, thereby garnering nationalist support. This time, however, Iran faced a new challenge: a green wave reminiscent of the post-Communist "color revolutions" that transpired in Georgia (Rose Revolution—2003), the Ukraine (Orange Revolution—2004), and Kyrgyzstan (Tulip Revolution—2005). These revolutions demonstrated that political opposition groups, together with civil society, can successfully use nonviolent strategies to topple governments. The Green Movement presented a similarly homegrown and popular threat to the Iranian regime. The reach of social networking and digital interactions diminished the effectiveness of the regime's "external enemy" narrative that had been a convenient foil in previous conflicts.

US foreign policy faced a classic dilemma: to prioritize the geopolitical context or to prioritize the promotion of democratic values. President Obama threw only his moral support behind the Green Movement. Any other form of intervention in favor of the movement would have run the risk of tainting his internally motivated and genuine pursuit. And yet no Iranian politician was under any grand illusions that considerations of power politics and the regional balance of power would be subordinated to the democratic values enunciated in US foreign policy. In fact, pragmatic conservatives signaled that they were ready to bargain with the United States when the time came. Likewise, the Bush administration found it necessary—if not desirable—to deal with Iran's power-wielding elites who could deliver on the Non-Proliferation Treaty (NPT), the stabilization of Iraq, the reconstruction of Afghanistan, narco-terrorism, Al-Qaeda, and Israeli—Palestinian tensions.

Regarding Iran's nuclear program, it was evident that the central problem, rather than nuclear technology, was Iran's foreign policy as a revolutionary state, with nuclear ambitions that collided with the interests of its neighbors and the West.[25] The persistence of the Bush administration in asserting a pragmatic agenda alone was particularly damaging to youth, women, and reform-minded journalists and activists—in essence, the human capital essential to any democratic reform in Iran. No dramatic breakthroughs in US–Iran relations seemed likely unless US policymakers were willing to consider a major role for Iran in the new regional security structure as imperative to preventing Iraq from descending into chaos and partition.

Moderates at the Helm

Hassan Rouhani's victory in Iran's 2013 presidential election opened the door for a new start to US–Iran relations. Many in the US foreign policymaking establishment welcomed the change in leadership in Iran, and many in Washington saw a unique opportunity to solve international and regional problems through pragmatic and diplomatic engagement for the first time in thirty years. Rouhani's commitment to ending the nuclear stalemate between Iran and the world powers was aptly captured in his campaign slogan: "centrifuges should spin, but so should people's lives."[26] Rouhani's first term coincided with the US presidency of Barack Obama. A phone conversation between President Obama and President Rouhani set the stage for a new path. This was the first diplomatic contact between the heads of state since the sustained diplomatic contact between Tehran and Washington ended in 1979.

Sensing an opening, President Obama pursued the old policy of keeping sanctions, while at the same time opting for an "Open Hand" policy toward Iran—a strategy that eventually led to the 2015 nuclear deal that included the permanent five members of the UN Security Council (Britain, China, France, Russia, and the United States), plus Germany, the EU, and Iran. These negotiations came to be known as the P5+1 talks. It should be noted this deal was initially facilitated in

February 2013 by secret bilateral talks in Oman through back-channel negotiations with Iran. These talks were based on the broader understanding that it was not the policy of the United States to seek regime change in Iran, but rather Washington was determined to prevent Iran from acquiring a nuclear weapon.[27] Another key message conveyed to the Iranians was that the Obama administration was prepared to "explore the possibility of a limited domestic enrichment program as part of a comprehensive agreement."[28]

For the first time, President Rouhani, Supreme Leader Ayatollah Khamenei, and the IRGC were on the same page. They all believed that the rewards of negotiations (regime preservation and legitimacy) surpassed the risks, largely because this agreement laid to rest the notion of regime change. Rouhani and his foreign minister Mohammad Javad Zarif found themselves aligned with their US counterparts: the Obama-Kerry team. Because of this agreement, President Obama moved Iran from enemy status to that of unfriendly adversary, which was the best-case scenario for foreseeable cooperation in overlapping areas.[29]

Within the nuclear deal framework, Iran's enrichment program continued, but was to be capped at 3.67 percent for the next fifteen years. This cut Iran's capacity to enrich uranium by about two-thirds. Monitoring and verification methods were installed to block any covert pathways. The breakout period of two to three months was increased to twelve months, and robust and intrusive inspections were initiated to ensure that the process of enrichment remained focused on the exclusive generation of nuclear energy for civilian purposes. All Iranian nuclear facilities were open to inspection by the International Atomic Energy Agency (IAEA), demonstrating maximum transparency and openness on Iran's part. Some inspections were scheduled to go on for twenty to twenty-five years. In exchange, Iran was allowed relief from some of the sanctions that had crippled its economy. By signing the JCPOA, the Obama administration hoped that Iran, as a state, would become normalized over time, rather than remain a revolutionary government bent on exporting radical ideas to the region. The reward for Tehran would conceivably be that it would be treated as a normal, legitimate actor by the rest of the world, thus alleviating much isolation and tension.

Domestically, while support for Rouhani's election was consistent with Iran's reformist inclinations of the recent past, in the United States there was a shift in American public opinion away from any military intervention. The single greatest explanatory factor as to why only diplomacy was possible between Iran and the United States was because many Americans had grown wary of military intervention by the United States. Playing "world's policeman" had lost its allure to the American public. International cooperation and multilateral diplomacy increasingly supplanted the call for military intervention. US foreign policymakers, tired of wars (Afghanistan and Iraq), hesitant about the use of force to address regional security issues, unable to contain the unbridled sectarian tensions in Syria, Iraq, and Bahrain, and crippled with an ailing economy at home, came to the realization that cooperation with Iran could be timely and instrumental in meeting some of the lingering challenges in the region.

Under the pressure of war, and ethnic and sectarian conflicts in the region, US policymakers seemingly concluded that resolving their tensions with Iran would have a positive impact throughout the Persian Gulf region, which would otherwise likely face further tumult. When the French and British foreign ministers specifically noted that the Syrian crisis could not be resolved through diplomatic means without Iran's presence at the table, it became clear that the EU would be opposed to any further isolation of Iran at a time when the latter's active participation seemed crucial to resolving some of these regional conflicts. Under such circumstances, Washington needed little persuasion to follow suit.

Increasingly aware of the fact that the Syrian crisis could adversely affect the outcome of sectarian tensions in Iraq and Lebanon, some US policymakers asserted that Iran could be part of the solution. Likewise, Iranians, under ferocious economic sanctions, turned their attention to the benefits of a dialogue with the United States over resolving the nuclear issue. Would the balance of power in the region be tilted toward Iran rather than its Arab neighbors if relations with Iran were further normalized? In short, the answer proved to be "no." Iran's support for Hezbollah in Lebanon and for the Palestinians under Israeli occupation offers a difficult challenge to any long-term relations between Iran and the United States. Both President Obama and

President Rouhani were hamstrung by domestic political consider-ations that could confine their ability to maneuver.

Paradoxically, but understandably, Iran found its interests overlap-ping with the United States in a different context. Without coopera-tion between the United States and Iran, the Islamic State of Iraq and Syria (ISIS) could have captured a large swath of Iraq. That was a scary proposition for Iran's Arab neighbors especially, and the Arab world more generally, at a time when they suffered from a lack of a center of gravity and strategic leadership, with Egypt's hands tied down in regard to its own domestic politics for years to come, and with the Saudis' new and uncertain military venture in Yemen, executed with US-supplied aircraft and ordinance, causing unforeseen difficulties for them further down the road.

The Trump Administration

The Trump administration pursued a policy of maximum pressure, which meant levying sweeping economic sanctions against Iran in an attempt to coerce it into accepting strict restrictions on their nuclear program and military capabilities. This confrontational approach has entrapped the United States and Iran in the current no-win situation they still face by injecting a new element of uncertainty into an already volatile region. President Trump's pullout from the JCPOA in May 2018—despite zero evidence of Iranian non-compliance—was part of an effort to renegotiate rules-based world order through sanctions and economic domination. US allies (France, Germany, and the UK), as well as China and Russia, considered this move contrary to the existing world order's norms and values—having guaranteed the JCPOA's sustainability through approval by the UN Security Council (UNSC).

Furthermore, US Secretary of State Mike Pompeo laid out twelve conditions for negotiating with Iran. Those included—among oth-ers—ending Iran's ballistic missiles development, halting support for Lebanese Hezbollah and Palestinian groups (including Hamas), allow-ing nuclear inspectors "unqualified access to all sites throughout the country," shutting down Iran's uranium enrichment program, ending involvement in Syria and Iraq, and disarming Shi'ite militias.

Pompeo's claim that these demands were broadly shared by Washington's European allies was widely misleading. Perhaps the most glaring flaw in Pompeo's announcement was that the conditions he laid out failed to add up to a clear strategy. The US unilateral abrogation of the nuclear deal and its list of impossible demands astronomically increased the obstacles to negotiation, seriously undermining any realistic possibility of rapprochement. The sanctions regime also adversely affected several vulnerable segments of the Iranian population, including medical patients who were unable to afford medication[30] and students who could no longer pursue their studies outside the country.

Under such circumstances, the Iranians equated the negotiation with abandoning the nuclear deal—a deal in which they had painstakingly invested much political capital. If they did, they would give up the hard-won right to their civilian nuclear program recognized in the accord.[31] Trump's repeated dismissiveness toward Iran while scuttling the 2015 nuclear deal by imposing war-like sanctions on Iran undermined any possibility of negotiation with Iran.[32] Similarly, his policy of sanctioning Iran's supreme leader and foreign minister, as well as designating the country's Revolutionary Guards as a terrorist organization, upended any chance of breaking the current political impasse. Absent sanctions relief, President Rouhani was left with no incentive to continue negotiating with the United States. The result was the emergence of a strategic dilemma marked by the Trump administration's pursuit of so-called maximum pressure in contrast to the Rouhani administration's reaction of adopting a maximum resistance policy.

On June 13, 2019, two oil tankers were attacked near the Strait of Hormuz. Washington blamed Iran for these attacks, with Trump ordering the deployment of one thousand additional troops to the region in response. The tension between the two countries further intensified when the IRGC shot down a US surveillance drone on June 20, 2019. Having blamed Iran, the United States seized an Iranian vessel sailing near the British territory of Gibraltar.[33]

The massive protests throughout Iran that followed a government decision to increase fuel prices in November 2019 demonstrated that the Islamic Republic faced an unprecedented budget crunch fueled largely by US sanctions. The country's ongoing economic crisis and the resulting bloody crackdown against protesters weakened President Rouhani's hands, but they were highly unlikely to bring Iran to the negotiating table—in part because the Islamic Republic mainly views the unrest as a foreign, and especially US-inspired plot, thus refusing to negotiate from a position of weakness. That explains the current standoff.[34]

A Theoretical Commentary

The question of what the most applicable theory is to explain Iran's foreign and security policies in the aftermath of the 1979 Iranian Revolution has invited divergent views. I would argue that in order to explain the complexity of US–Iran relations, a synthesized theoretical approach is more effective than a single paradigm approach (which is often used in international relations). For example, neorealists emphasize power distributions as the most important factor in international relations.[35] This sheds some light on Iran's foreign policy conduct in terms of its regional activities and proxies. Neorealism on its own, however, would fail to fully account for domestic agendas, constituencies, or armed groups like the IRGC. Some analysts argue that under neorealism, states are like billiard balls, in that they only change in size and weight relative to their level of material power.[36]

Following the revolution, Iran's foreign policy behavior has largely been explained and even rationalized by two theoretical approaches: realism and constructivism. The exclusion of Iran from regional security arrangements has left Tehran with no other option than to seek allies beyond its immediate borders, while also reinforcing its defensive and deterrence systems by relying on its own ballistic missile program. For the most part, Iran's place in the regional and global balance of power has informed its foreign policy behavior.

In some cases, identity, ideology, and soft power have also served as guiding principles of Iran's foreign policy.[37] In other cases, the country's foreign policy has been chiefly motivated by pragmatic considerations. One observer has maintained that "the dictate of circumstances has forced Iranian foreign policymakers to interpret their religious ideology pragmatically in order to advance the state interest."[38] Iran's attempt to strengthen and expand its proxy ties throughout the region is, in the most direct sense, a reaction to the formation of the anti-Iran bloc—the United States, Israel, and Saudi Arabia—and also serves to offset its inferior conventional military budget compared to those of these countries.

However, in the post-revolutionary era (1989–present), Iran's foreign policy has entertained the possibility of engagement with the United States and its Gulf Arab neighbors. In this period, Iranian reformists' attempts to move toward a regional détente have frequently been contained or blocked by both domestic and external forces. The draconian economic sanctions and political isolation, however, forced a change in Iran's foreign policy conduct at the beginning of Obama's second term.

Iran's compliance within the context of the 2015 nuclear deal has also proven consistent with liberal institutionalism and its emphasis on the NPT and a nuclear-free zone in the Middle East.[39] The securitization of Iran's nuclear program as part of an attempt to contain and deter Iran from posing an existential threat to the United States and its regional allies in the Persian Gulf has gained much traction as a new theoretical method.[40] This theory may, in part, explain how discussions surrounding nuclear militarization in the Middle East tend to securitize the potential nuclear arsenal of Iran rather than the actual arsenal of Israel. This also explains why securitization is often conceptualized in terms of targeting Iran as a source of destabilization in the region.[41]

In essence, Iran's nuclear program, especially its domestic enrichment and power generation, is viewed by the United States as a manifest security threat. Any belligerence on the part of Iran (resistance to inspections, testing of missiles, or conventional harassment of shipping in the Gulf) supports this narrative. That Iran is a hostile power in pursuit of nefarious ends is taken as a given, because according to our Copenhagen colleagues, Iran has been functionally securitized in the minds of most American foreign policy actors.

In this book, while I adopt an integrated method of applying these theoretical frameworks in a bid to put US–Iran relations in their proper context, I also argue that cooperation within the context of the nuclear deal noticeably reduced Iran's international viewpoint of their own insecurity. The mutual compromises and concessions made in the nuclear talks served the interests of both Iran and the United States. Iran's military strategy is arguably based on defensive realism. As a result, its nuclear program is largely geared toward having a nuclear ability, not a nuclear weapon. Much of Iran's military capability is aimed at resistance and balancing, as opposed to invasion or conquest.[42] On balance, liberal institutionalist theories offer a far greater insight into analyzing the JCPOA as a work of US foreign policy. This makes sense given that treaties, deals, and negotiations are the province of the liberals, as realists continue to be largely dubious of any accord or trust-building activity, characterizing it as a short-sighted and doomed endeavor. The nuclear deal marked a shift in US foreign policymaking away from the realist tradition.[43]

The Trump administration pulling out of the JCPOA broke with such a mindset and returned US foreign policy to unilateralism and coercive diplomacy—without any clear strategy—by reimposing further sanctions on Iran while the latter was in full compliance with the deal. The outcome was an absolute failure, as Trump's hard-line policy failed to produce a reduction in the perceived threat of Iran's nuclear program by brokering a deal superior to the JCPOA. In one fell swoop, Trump's policy pushed both countries to the brink of military confrontation. The Biden administration later reversed this course, fostering multilateralism and the revival of the JCPOA. While it is too early to predict what lies ahead, it is clear that the tensions between the two countries have drastically lessened just as swiftly as the rift between Washington and its European allies.

A different theoretical approach called the English School (also known as the International Society tradition) can be useful in addressing US–Iran relations. This approach, which underscores the importance of historical understanding and context, as well as how the global order is regenerated through complex patterns of socialization and resistance,[44] is likely to shed some light on the tensions in US–Iran relations within the context of the emerging international order. Iran's support for a multipolar world order has been a major source of normative bonding with China and Russia, while also adding to frictions with the United States. While Iran's persistent criticisms of North Atlantic Treaty Organization (NATO) and US military interventions, such as the Iraq War, the Kosovo War, the Libya debacle, the Syrian Civil War, and the Taliban's re-occupation of Afghanistan has a regime security and geostrategic impetus, it also has an ideational component. Fundamental ideational disagreements over the global order render dialogue and engagement with the United States over wide-ranging issues much harder, if not impossible.

The English School's theoretical strength lies in its ethic of pluralism and detailed attention to ideational forces, yet it takes little account of transnational activities, complex global relations, domestic aspects of foreign policy, and international economics. The maximum pressure strategy employed by the Trump administration (2018–20) to bring the Islamic Republic to the negotiating table failed to accomplish its stated goal, but it had a devastating impact on Iran's economy. Similarly, a closer look at domestic factors in Iran demonstrates that, according to one expert, what brought Iran to the negotiating table in 2013 was not necessarily the economic distress caused by the Obama administration's sanctions. Rather, it was a popular longing on the part of Iran's middle class for economic growth through access to the global economy, if not through improved relations with the West.[45]

The English School's weakest link, as noted above, is its neglect of domestic aspects of foreign policy. Its strongest link lies in the way it teaches us about the interpretive mode of inquiry, arguing that there is no escape from values and ideational forces. In politics and international relations, according to the English School, values are often irreconcilable, and difficult choices have to be made.[46] Over the past four decades, several US administrations have taken a more confrontational stance toward Iran, widening the gulf between Tehran and Washington. This helps explain why the resiliency of populism in Iranian politics since the 1979 Iranian Revolution cannot be fully understood by focusing on internally driven variables alone.[47]

Structure and Scope of the Book

The book is divided into three parts. Part I focuses on the internal context of Iranian politics since the 1979 Revolution. Chapter One provides an overview of contemporary US–Iran relations, explaining the checkered relationship between the United States and Iran. Chapter Two examines the impacts and consequences of the Iranian Revolution, as well as the struggle for power among reformists, populists, and moderates. The 2009 Green Movement and the urban unrest during the 2018–19 period have highlighted the weaknesses of the Islamic Republic.

Chapter Three explains how US security concerns and economic interests have historically undermined the long-term human rights objectives of its foreign policy.[48] Following the 1979 Iranian Revolution, Washington has repeatedly used human rights to delegitimize the Islamic Republic. Several US administrations, however, have also chosen to refrain from supporting Iranian political dissents, including the student protests (1999) and the Green Movement (2009), for largely geopolitical reasons. In the meantime, political rights and civil liberties in Iran have deteriorated. Today, human rights violations occur frequently, as the authorities continue to suppress the rights to freedom of expression, association, and assembly. Security forces systematically engage in lethal crackdowns to crush public gatherings, arbitrarily detaining thousands of protesters. Women continue to face inequality and mistreatment just as ethnic and religious minorities encounter discrimination. Torture and other ill-treatment remain endemic. There are widespread systematic denials of fair trials. The state routinely invokes repressive tactics to suppress street unrest, blaming external intrusion as the main cause of this turmoil.

Part II puts the spotlight on the regional context, expounding on Iran's foreign policy and how it straddles ideological and geopolitical spheres. This situation is attributed in part to Iranian internal politics but is also largely due to Iran's long-term foreign policy goals, which are predicated on strictly geopolitical interests. Chapter Four explores this evolving context in light of the US military presence in the region—a presence that has failed to promote regional security.

The failure of Washington and Tehran to seriously engage in negotiations has escalated tension between the two countries, complicating Iran's relations with its neighboring countries and blocking its entry into the global markets. A combination of miscommunication with Iran and misperceptions of its intentions and capabilities has damaged relations between the two countries, rendering it very difficult, if not impossible, to reduce the tensions diplomatically. Chapter Five examines several hotbeds of regional conflicts: Syria, Yemen, and the South Caucasus. These regional conflicts have deepened the rivalries between Iran, Saudi Arabia, and Turkey. Their ideological and geopolitical causes and the way in which they have invited outside intervention deserves considerable exploration.

Part III turns to the international context, examining US–Iran relations over the past two decades. More specifically, Chapter Six takes a closer look at the Iran nuclear deal, which was signed on July 14, 2015, and came to be known as the P5+1 (the United States, UK, China, Russia, France and Germany—with EU participation) agreement. Subsequently, it was officially named the Joint Comprehensive Plan of Action (JCPOA). The agreement, which emerged after nearly two years of excruciating negotiations, significantly scaled back Iran's nuclear program for a period of ten–fifteen years, in return for the lifting of sanctions against Iran. The United Nations Security Council (UNSC) unanimously approved a resolution that conferred legitimacy on the deal, constituting a basis for lifting UN sanctions against Iran. In this chapter, I also demonstrate the important role that the Obama administration played in striking this deal.

Chapter Seven investigates how President Trump's decision to pull out of the JCPOA unraveled the key foreign policy achievement of his predecessor, Barack Obama, and isolated the United States from its Western allies. The decision left the 2015 agreement in tatters. The United States proceeded to impose a new set of stringent sanctions on Iran, even as Iran remained in full compliance with the deal even though the new sanctions were crippling its economy. France, Germany, and Britain criticized the Trump administration for such a unilateral move. Likewise, China and Russia—also signatories to the deal—blamed President Trump for violating the accord. The resulting tensions in the Persian Gulf region have strengthened the hand of the hard-liners in Iran, bringing Iran to the brink of confrontation with the United States and driving Iran further into the arms of China and Russia.

Chapter Eight discusses the prospects of the Biden administration returning the United States to the JCPOA, and why engaging Iran will prove to be a sensible course of action. How Biden can revive the Iran nuclear deal remains the key question. Iran's domestic politics is likely to pose serious challenges to negotiating a new nuclear deal. The "moderate" administration of President Hassan Rouhani lost much credibility in the face of a slew of economic problems. Ebrahim Raisi, a hard-liner who captured the presidency in a carefully engineered election in the June 2021 election, is likely to present new challenges to President Biden's Iran policy. While pledging to return to the JCPOA and engagement with the West in order to lift sanctions on Iran, Raisi is expected to take a much harder line on the negotiation. Regardless, there is a broad consensus among experts that Raisi will most likely be prepared to pursue P5+1 negotiations—in large part because Iran's economy is in desperate need of resuscitation.[49]

Chapter Nine advances the argument that current trends and developments in US–Iran relations cannot be appreciated without understanding what has underlined such roller-coaster relations through much of the twentieth century and beyond. The Trump administration's maximum pressure strategy posed the biggest impediment to any possible future negotiations. The most viable option to de-escalate the existing tensions is to pursue diplomacy while simultaneously fostering more cooperation between Iran and its Arab neighbors. Ultimately, a sustainable resolution in the region will come from successful US–Iran negotiations, because the current strategic standoff between the two countries, if left unresolved, is likely to push Iran further into the arms of China and Russia.

Finally, Chapter Ten concludes that Iran should take full advantage of the opportunity to break this impasse by negotiating with the United States, largely because an agreement with Washington will render reaching a regional détente with its Arab neighbors more plausible in light of the conceivable gradual US withdrawal from the Persian Gulf region. The best course of action is to follow tested paths that have been proven effective in the past when diplomatic initiatives have allowed such attempts.

2

REVOLUTION AND ITS AFTERMATH

THE STRUGGLE FOR POWER

Throughout history, revolutions have been associated with a radical change in the established order, in political systems, and in social institutions. They have profoundly altered public belief while also promoting new (if not always sustainable) ideologies, along with social change over time. Broadly known as an instrument of change for the sake of equality, social justice, and human dignity, revolutions have also been a major source of disruption. In 1979, the normal course of events in Iran, as well as the Persian Gulf region more generally, was disrupted by a particularly abrupt and dramatic change. A period of political unrest between 1977 and 1979 highlighted the serious economic and political challenges that would leave Iran paralyzed.

The Iranian Revolution of 1979 had a profound impact within Iran as well as beyond its borders, affecting not only the Middle East but also Islamic states throughout the world. It also captured the attention of external powers that had particular interests in the Middle East. Within Iran, the revolution came to be known as "a cataclysmic event" that profoundly transformed the country's political, socioeconomic, and legal structure. A product of a series of impetuous, largely unorganized strikes and demonstrations, the Iranian Revolution is generally described as a spontaneous rebellion with little advance planning, and one that began with haphazard, unorganized acts of protest.[1] The revolution overthrew the monarchy of Mohammad Reza Shah and led to the establishment of a republic; it replaced secular laws with Islamic law (*Shari'a*); and it ousted the Shah's favored political and military leaders and set up a new elite.[2]

The Iranian Revolution led to several profound regional and global impacts. One of the most important consequences of the revolution, as Ali Ansari and Kasra Aarabi note, was geopolitical and regional. For much of the twentieth century, they argue, Iran was a principal Western ally, serving as the vanguard of regional security. Iran was anchored to Turkey (a member of NATO) and was part of the US twin pillar strategy with Saudi Arabia in the Persian Gulf. As a result, Iran became a status quo power seeking further integration into the global economy.[3] While the revolution inherited the Pahlavi state, it rejected its worldview: the first foreign leader to visit Tehran after the revolution was Yasser Arafat, leader of the Palestine Liberation Organization (PLO). The seizure of the US Embassy in Tehran on November 4, 1979, manifested Iran's anti-Western political ideology, while Tehran called for an Islamic revolution of the oppressed throughout the world.[4]

The Iranian Revolution, Mehrzad Boroujerdi aptly notes, was the first revolution in which the dominant ideology, government organization, and leadership were religiously driven; the first contemporary revolution that led to the establishment of a theocracy; and the only modern social revolution in which peasants and rural guerrillas played a negligible role.[5] From 1960–70, the percentage share of GDP contributed by the agricultural sector in Iran dropped from twenty-nine percent to nine percent—the largest decline of any Middle Eastern country during that period. High economic growth rates during the 1960s and the 1970s resulted in a narrow distribution of income. The continued reliance of the Shah's regime on oil revenues made such growth rates possible.

At the same time, social mobilization in Iran contributed to higher levels of education, literacy, communication development, and urbanization. The newly mobilized, politically active segments of the population had a high propensity for political participation. These social strata were composed of elements of the middle class, the urban working class, and the jobless labor forces in cities. The latter proved to be highly politicized during the 1979 Iranian Revolution.[6]

The Shah's state had reduced the spheres of influence of religious authorities and culminated in a crisis of legitimacy that weakened the Shah's regime in the late 1970s. This regime deprived the clerics of their control of the two areas in which their social influence had been dominant—law and education—as well as of their economic and ideological status. The only opposition group allowed to operate was a secular group, the Committee for Defense of Freedom and Human Rights. Established in Tehran in 1977, this committee was the first independent human rights organization in Iran's history. Its membership included Shahpur Bakhtiar and Mehdi Bazargan. The latter became Iran's first prime minister in the Islamic Republic of Iran.[7]

The widespread public discontent and climate of fear sowed the seeds of the monarchy's demise. "The crown, and more specifically the person of the Shah," as aptly summarized by Mehran Kamrava, "became the state."[8] The Shah's political and economic plans, according to Mohsen Milani, suffered from several flaws. To begin with, the Shah's modernization programs led to the creation and superimposition of a modernized system on an old and flimsy order, resulting in a socioeconomic dualism. Although the economic system became modernized, the political system remained archaic. The country saw the unfolding of two contradictory trends: economic growth on one side, and political underdevelopment on the other. Ultimately, the political system lacked a robust legitimizing ideology and thus failed to generate a broader popular base of support.[9]

The Shah's notorious security apparatus, SAVAK, in the absence of any viable secular opposition, caused deep resentment against the regime among the vast majority of Iranians. This, along with the failure of urban guerrillas to develop a large enough base to promote an effective guerrilla war, gave the clergy a unique opportunity to direct the revolution. By the late 1970s, the Shah's violent attempts to curb revolutionary fervor had proved ineffective. The conservative forces, spearheaded by Ayatollah Rouhollah Khomeini, overwhelmed pro-Shah forces and toppled the monarchy.[10]

In this chapter, I examine the Iranian Islamic Revolution and its aftermath in light of the ongoing power struggle between and among hard-liners, reformists, and moderates. I argue that the dynamic interplay of domestic power struggles and foreign influence in the region has shaped Iran's foreign policy. Both regional actors and patrons—most predominantly, the United States—have shaped the region's security landscape. Aside from larger structural causes of insecurity, it should be noted that disregard for human security concerns has given rise to sectarianism, identity politics, and regional political rivalries, all of which have been manipulated by states for their own political gains.[11] With the gradual US withdrawal from the Persian Gulf and its declining dependence on the region's oil, the most realistic hope to maintain stability is through a regional security structure that aims to achieve détente through diplomacy—not through threats posed by outside powers in the region.

The Pahlavi Dynasty

The Pahlavi dynasty (1925–79) was founded by Reza Khan Pahlavi in 1925. A former brigadier-general of the Persian Cossack Brigade who ruled Iran until 1941, he was forced to abdicate by the Allies after the Anglo-Soviet invasion of Iran. On December 12, 1925, the newly convened constituent assembly unanimously voted for the new Pahlavi monarchy. Shortly thereafter Reza Khan was sworn in as the new shah. This marked the end of 150 years of rule by the Qajars. During his first decade in power, as Abbas Amanat reminds us, Reza Shah and his military and civilian supporters sought to fulfill the much-anticipated national aspirations for sovereignty and development. The variegated experiments with constitutional democracy over the previous two decades, foreign interventions, a selfish political elite, and the inexorable disarray that came first with the Constitutional Revolution (and then with World War I) had convinced most urban Iranians of the urgency of the alternative offered by Reza Shah.[12]

Reza Khan Pahlavi came from a humble background. He rose up the ranks from soldier to military leader to oust the last ruler of the Qajar dynasty, which had initially consolidated power in the late 1780s. In 1921, Reza Khan led a coup against the incumbent government. Over the next four years, he defeated tribal forces, packing the parliament (*Majles*) with cronies. At his instructions, the *Majles* deposed the last Qajar shah and named Reza Khan the shah. A modernizing despot, Reza Shah followed the path of his Turkish contemporary, Mustafa Kemal Ataturk, by developing a robust infrastructure made possible by the earnings from its rapidly growing oil industry. His repressive rule reflected the very *modus operandi* of local authoritarian orders in Iran, forbidding political parties and other civil society institutions while marginalizing the Shi'a clergy and religious foundations and practices.[13]

During World War II, Britain and the USSR became fearful of Reza Shah's friendly relations with Germany. In 1941, the two countries invaded and occupied large swaths of Iran, with the British occupying the south and the Russians controlling the north. They forced Reza Shah to abdicate in favor of his son, Mohammad Reza (1919–80), who assumed the throne at only twenty-two years old. The new Shah's reign began against a backdrop of socioeconomic disarray, political instability, and food shortages. Mohammad Reza Shah Pahlavi ruled Iran from 1941–79 and maintained a pro-Western foreign policy. He continued the reform policies of his father, but soon encountered a domestic challenge posed by his prime minister, Mohammad Mosaddeq, a charismatic and shrewd secular democrat whose nationalist credentials were undisputed.

Facing a parliamentary government spearheaded by a strong and legitimate prime minister, the new Shah had limited powers. He frequently found himself opposed not only by secular nationalist leaders such as Mohammad Mossadeq, but also by the clerics who constantly questioned the legitimacy of his rule as well as his close connection with the West. The Shah relied more on the army and the security apparatus for his power, making sure that they would remain royal to him. Lacking a broad social base, he banned all political parties, including the Russian-inspired Tudeh Party.

During the early 1950s, Iran's democratically elected prime minister, Mossadeq, rose to an unprecedented level of popularity, forcing Shah Mohammad Reza Pahlavi into exile. Mossadeq's rise to power and parliament's approval of the nationalization of the Anglo-Iranian Oil Company (AIOC) thrilled Iranians and outraged British leaders.[14] Mossadeq was removed from power in 1953 by a CIA—MI6 engineered coup (known as Operation Ajax) conducted mainly from the US Embassy in Tehran. US officials helped organize street demonstrations and protests to overthrow Mossadeq and returned the Shah to power from his brief exile. The 1953 coup ended Iran's fledgling attempts at democracy, giving rise to a modernizing, royal dictatorship that, a quarter of a century later, would set off an anti-American revolution bringing militant Islamic groups to power. The Shah restored his absolute power by eliminating all constitutional obstacles in his way. He repressed opposition newspapers, political parties, trade unions, and civic groups.[15]

The real tragedy of US–Iran relations stems from the fact that US policymakers depended solely upon the Shah's view of the situation and overlooked obvious signs of popular disenchantment and unrest, which ultimately led to the Islamic Revolution. Many US foreign policymakers were caught off guard by the Khomeini revolution, and by the extent of the hatred toward the United States. In the long run, US intervention in Iran paved the way for the eventual rupture of US–Iran relations and the 1979 Islamic Revolution.[16]

US–Iran relations were premised largely on maintaining stability in the Persian Gulf. The Shah received unconditional US support as a pillar of US foreign policy in the region. US President Richard Nixon developed a strategy of cooperation with dictators such as the Shah, positioning them as guarantors of US regional interests. Despite the pressure on the Shah to open up the country's political space, the Jimmy Carter administration viewed the Shah as an ally (and thus a source of stability) that had to be backed by US foreign policy.

The Shah's aggressive modernization and Westernization projects alienated cultural and religious elites in a country where religious values held a tight grip on cultural traditions. Moreover, modernization under the Shah was intimately linked to economic growth and industrialization. Oil-induced growth boosted Iran's GNP per capita from $108 in 1957 to $1,660 in 1978.[17] The pace of economic growth reached its peak between 1970 and 1978, when the annual average growth rate of GNP was 13.3 percent—by far the world's highest.[18] Meanwhile, the agricultural sector faced many setbacks as a result of the Shah's program of industrialization at any cost. The Shah's land reform programs, initiated under pressure from the Kennedy administration in the early 1960s, altered the class structure in Iran's countryside, creating a new rural bourgeoisie, a new rural propertied class, a new proletariat, and a new landless class that relied on its labor for survival.

Prelude to the Iranian Revolution

During the 1960s, Iran's agricultural sector faced a significant decline, as agriculture as a share of GDP fell from twenty-nine percent to nine percent. High growth rates during the 1960s and 1970s, fueled by oil imports, resulted in a narrow distribution of income. The Shah's lack of attention to civilian politics and his close ties to the army (and the United States) alienated him from certain segments of the Iranian population. The legitimacy crisis facing the Shah regime, as Mehrzad Boroujerdi rightly points out, emanated from Iran's rentier state, a state that derived all or at least a significant portion of its national revenues from the rent paid by foreign individuals, companies, concerns, or governments, rendering it completely independent of income tax. This led to the "gradual erosion of the bonds linking the state and civil society."[19]

At the same time, however, social mobilization led to higher rates of education, literacy, development, and urbanization. A newly mobilized social strata composed of elements of the middle and working classes became engaged politically. The Shah's Iran saw a decline in the status and control of the clerics, especially in their formerly dominant areas of law and education. The Shah's close ties to the army, as well as to the United States, alienated him from segments of the population. His aggressive security apparatus and their clampdown on any viable secular opposition led to deep resentment among most Iranians. This absence of any legitimate secular opposition left the clergy with a unique opportunity to direct the revolution. By the late 1970s, the Shah's violent attempts to curb revolutionary fervor had proved ineffective. Ayatollah Khomeini led the conservative forces that were able to topple the Shah's monarchy.

Since the 1979 Iranian Revolution, over forty years of tension with Iran has, ironically, brought the US government face to face with a new reality—that they must deal with Iran through diplomatic means rather than confrontation. Perhaps the single most important explanation for this new reality was the resurgent Iranian power in the region in the aftermath of the George W. Bush administration's gross miscalculations and unsuccessful ventures in Iraq and Afghanistan. As a result, the choice for US policymakers is clear—either confront Iran, with all of its attendant consequences, or negotiate.

Increasingly, the complexities of regional politics and military interventions have convinced US policymakers that the alternative to negotiation with Iran would be costly for the United States and destabilizing for its allies in the region. This chapter aims to explain how the US–Iran relationship has gone through several phases: from estrangement, to impasse, to limited pragmatic engagement, to direct negotiations over the nuclear deal, and to a view of Iraq in the aftermath of the US invasion. The Trump administration's exit from the Iran nuclear deal (JCPOA) dealt a fatal blow to the rule of moderates such as Hassan Rouhani and his foreign minister, Javad Zarif, who sought normalizing ties with the United States. Inevitably, Iran's stabilizing role in the region—especially in Afghanistan and Iraq—has enhanced its position in shaping the region's geopolitics. Iran's influence can no longer be marginalized given that it is pulling the strings in the southern part of Iraq and Lebanon, has ties to Hamas and Syria, and is playing a significant role in Afghanistan and the broader Persian Gulf region.[20]

The Post-Khomeini Era

The popular unrest that toppled the Pahlavi dynasty and led to the birth of the Islamic Republic was initially (and profoundly) influenced by Ayatollah Khomeini. As the leader of the revolution, Khomeini introduced a new brand of clerical populism to Iran—one that effectively used populist rhetoric in mobilizing the masses.[21] Khomeini promoted the extension of basic services and welfare measures such as building infrastructure in rural areas and poor urban neighborhoods. He oversaw the construction of housing projects for the urban poor, and his populist agenda underscored the importance, for millions of poor households, of providing electricity, safe drinking water, basic health services, and schools. The tensions and contradictions between the elitist conception of ruling elites and the egalitarian conception of justice, however, undermined clerical populism as well as Khomeini's legacy more generally, resulting in ongoing authoritarianism and widespread popular discontent as the country faced US sanctions in the coming years.[22]

Khomeini's tumultuous tenure as the spiritual leader of the revolution saw the ensuing hostage crisis, the Iran—Iraq War, and growing tensions with Iran's neighboring countries. With Khomeini's death in 1989 came a long-anticipated power struggle among the conservative factions and remaining factions. That, along with more formal power centers, including the Supreme Leader, the Guardian Council, the *Majles*, the judiciary, and the Revolutionary Guards, formed a prelude to tense and highly contentious political tides.

Iran has experienced long-term processes of cumulative social change that have fostered various kinds of reactions and adjustments, including contentious politics and a wide variety of social movements bent on transforming the social realm. Internal challenges to long-held ways of defining power have intensified relations among different factions vying for control and access within the Islamic Republic. The striking intensity and speed with which change is occurring in Iran and outside of it has far surpassed the ability of even the most entrenched institutions and leadership factions to come to grips with it.

Struggles for power among the competing factions within and outside of the governing institutions, especially in the post-Khomeini era, have completely overshadowed any systematic and meaningful focus on the economic, cultural, religious, and technological changes taking place in Iran. The persistent reliance of Iranian leaders on ad hoc and improvised policy decisions has led to gross miscalculations and mismanagement. More broadly, these factors have led to cumulative uncertainties and policy failures in the wake of the dramatic changes that the country has undergone, making it increasingly necessary to define and understand the broader contours of social and cultural change in Iran.[23]

It is crucially important to remember that Ayatollah Khomeini depicted the 1979 Revolution as an Islamic one rather than an exceptionally Iranian one, conferring further legitimacy on it as an anti-imperialist and anti-Western movement capable of spreading. Both symbolically and substantively, this move fueled pan-Islamism throughout the region, and led to an increased disdain toward foreign influence. The subsequent Iran—Iraq War (1981–88) was rooted in the belief of the Saddam Hussein regime that revolutionary Iran was attempting to trigger a Shi'ite uprising in Iraq, and derailed the direction of the nation's socioeconomic and cultural change. Had the war with Iraq not taken place, one expert notes, religious populism could have faded away more quickly in the immediate aftermath of the revolution, and the society would have moved toward adopting more pragmatic measures. The war, however, facilitated the populist-Islamist authority to mobilize the ideologically overburdened masses and to repress political opponents on the pretext of defending "the land of Islam."[24]

The war allowed little space for normal life as most Iranians were badly hit by the economic stagnation and sociocultural restrictions it engendered. The long-term effects of that bloody and devastating conflict cast a dark shadow over many Iranians for the ensuing years. Khomeini's death in 1989 led to a new era with a new emphasis for Iranian politics. Revolutionary fervor was replaced by a desperate and urgent need for national reconstruction and economic development.

Thus, the post-Khomeini era has been marked by profound changes in the sociopolitical landscape of Iran. Since 1989, the internal dynamics of change in Iran—encompassing a panoply of socioeconomic, cultural, institutional, demographic, and behavioral factors—have led to a disruptive transition in both societal and governmental structures of power. These factors have also caused a transition in the ways in which Iranians have come to deal with the changing conditions of their society. Global trends in communication and information expansion have hastened burgeoning demands for women's rights and individual freedoms, and exacerbated festering tensions over cultural politics. These realities have rendered Iran a country of unprecedented—and at times paradoxical—changes. But more importantly, and of particular relevance to this chapter, the post-Khomeini era has fueled an internal power struggle that continues to this day.

While the first decade of revolution came to be closely associated with the consolidation phase of revolutions, post-Khomeini Iran

entered into an adaptation phase in which reformists tried to recon-
cile Iran's revolutionary spirit with the global resurgence of democracy and economic reform. The return of populists to power at the
beginning of the twenty-first century placed a brake on this evolution-
ary trajectory, initiating a reversal toward the earlier revolutionary
principles and practices of the new republic. In 2013, the rise of
moderates to power led full circle to Iranian politics becoming again
bound for a new phase of integration into the international community. Trump's presidency disrupted this renewed cycle of evolution
by pulling out of the nuclear deal and reimposing a new set of harsh
sanctions on Iran, thus undermining the credibility and staying power
of the moderates. After analyzing the immediate fallout of the Iranian
Revolution, we turn to the nature and consequences of this power
struggle, with an eye toward demonstrating the core domestic drivers
shaping Iran's foreign policy.

The Consolidation Phase: Wars and Sanctions

Shortly after the 1979 Revolution, the Iran—Iraq War aided the
political survival of the regime for nearly a decade (1980–88), as the
ruling elites of the Islamic Republic portrayed Saddam Hussein as a
US lackey bent on containing the spread of the Islamic Revolution to
the rest of the region. During this time, the strategic goals of the
United States in the region were twofold: to isolate and punish the
Islamic Republic, and to prop up the Mujahedeen resistance movement inside Afghanistan, dislodging Soviet troops from there. The
pro-Western monarchies of the Persian Gulf supported these two
strategic goals. But these strategies had far-reaching implications, and
led to new complications for the US presence in the region.

In 1988, Ayatollah Khomeini conceded that the cease-fire was a
harsh reality with which the Iranians must come to grips. This ended
the Iran—Iraq War. In the post-Khomeini era (1989–present), Iran
has encountered continued sanctions, boycotts, and political isolation
by the United States (and some of its allies) in the West—policies that
have pushed the Islamic Republic to violence, while exploiting ongoing propaganda and an ongoing conspiracy to prolong its political
longevity. The ensuing Iraqi invasion of Kuwait in 1990, which, in a

subtle way, was the result of unconditional US support for Saddam's regime in its war with Iran in the preceding decade, led to a temporary US–Iran tactical cooperation to defeat the Saddam Hussein regime and liberate Kuwait.

The Adaptation Phase: Pragmatists and Reformists

With the passing away of Khomeini from the Iranian political scene, inter-factional disputes and the primacy of the economy over Islamic ideology came to characterize Ali Akbar Hashemi Rafsanjani's two-term presidency (1989–97). Reform of foreign trade and correction of the exchange rate were crucial elements of Rafsanjani's liberalization programs. The outside world's encouragement of the expansion of the private sector and economic liberalization, however, failed in large part because Iran's mercantile elites were themselves part of the country's semi-authoritarian state, and they shied away from the creation of an industrialized economy with closer ties to the outside world. Instead, they favored a system that allowed them to maintain their economic control over trade and commerce within the country.

As a result, the Rafsanjani administration failed to transfer wealth from the public to the private sector. These protectionist proclivities only caused the boundaries between the two sectors to become even more blurred.[25] In the March 1996 parliamentary elections, the Council of Guardians excluded nearly half of the more than 5,000 candidates for parliament on the basis of discriminatory and arbitrary criteria. This practice obstructed access to the political process and blocked citizens' freedom of choice.

Iran's foreign policy of independence—known as "neither East nor West"—notwithstanding, it was Rafsanjani who began to open the door to moderation toward the United States. Rafsanjani believed that US–Iran relations would improve only if the United States would release frozen Iranian assets as a gesture of goodwill. By taking a position of neutrality during the 1991 Gulf War, Rafsanjani was attempting to send a sign to US policymakers that he was willing to deal with the United States.[26] This politically expedient collaboration was terminated in 1996 when the Clinton administration adopted a "dual containment" policy toward Iran and Iraq. The Iranian half of dual containment was based on a "five-part challenge" that Iran posed to the United States and the international community: support for "terrorism and assassination across the globe," opposition to the Arab-Israeli peace process, efforts to subvert pro-Western governments, a military buildup aimed at dominating the Persian Gulf region, and a quest to acquire nuclear weapons.[27] Dual containment drove a wedge between the US foreign-policy consensus with Europe and Japan.

US unilateral sanctions against Iran continued, as President Clinton signed the Iran—Libya Sanction Act (ILSA) in August 1996 to punish Iran and Libya for alleged state-sponsored terrorism. ILSA required the US president to impose sanctions against any company, foreign or domestic, that invests $40 million or more a year in oil and gas projects in either Iran or Libya. The law was questioned by Canada, the EU, Australia, and Japan—all US allies—on the grounds that it violated international law.[28] Washington's Iran policy was crafted by a pro-AIPAC (American Israel Public Affairs Committee) Congress in the Clinton era, and to the detriment of Iranian interests. Likewise, George W. Bush's Iran policy was significantly influenced by anti-Iran resolutions passed by the US Congress.[29]

Some experts have systematically traced the roots of the policy of dual containment of Iran and Iraq, the problems with the exact aims of this policy, and its negative and contradictory effects. They have argued that the policy has been in existence for over a quarter century without much to show in the way of accomplished goals. In the 1980s, for both the United States and Israel, dual containment meant helping Iran and Iraq destroy one another in a long and costly war of attrition.[30] After the war, and particularly during the Clinton administration, attention shifted to imposing sanctions on these two countries, and dual containment became synonymous with imposing economic hardship on them in the hope of overthrowing the two regimes. During the George W. Bush administration, neoconservatives used the events of 9/11 to launch a destructive war against Iraq, and subsequently a regime change in Iran. But thus far neither the pain of sanctions nor the death and destruction of wars in the region have been able to bring about the desired change.[31]

At around the same time, the Taliban regime took over a good portion of Afghanistan with military assistance and training from

Pakistan (a long-time US ally in the region) and financial backing from Saudi Arabia and the United Arab Emirates (UAE). The core contradiction in this flawed policy was that while the United States contained one Islamic movement in Iran, it chose to turn its back on another movement in Afghanistan, where a far more fundamentalist regime than the one in Iran took over the country.

In a decisive victory on May 23, 1997, Mohammad Khatami became Iran's new reformist president, winning seventy percent of the vote. He went on to liberalize the press, establish new political parties, and initiate a "dialogue of civilizations" with the West.[32] His presidency became equated with the expansion of civil society and the enhancement of women's rights. In women's rights, women's participation in sports saw a dramatic increase, involving more women and girls than in the pre-revolutionary period.[33] Women have embraced such social openings.[34] Jane Mary Howard explains how the atmosphere changed with the election of the reformist President Khatami, and how Iranians dared to demand more freedom and discuss their problems more openly.[35]

The dramatic social and political opening during the Khatami presidency is best illustrated by the increase in the number of political associations in the country—from thirty-five in 1997 to 130 by 2001. The number of professional and advocacy NGOs, including those focusing on women's rights and issues, increased to 230 by 2000, and 330 two years later. Youth and environmental organizations exceeded 2,500 after 2001. The Student's Office of Consolidation and Unity, an active organ of civil society and of the democratic ethos of changing times in Iran, began a news agency, Iranian Students' News Agency (ISNA), and published a national newspaper called *Azar* along with some 700 local newspapers, while also sponsoring some 1,437 cultural, scientific, and social associations. As a backlash to these openings, between 1997 and 2002, 108 newspapers and periodicals were banned.[36] A contrasting view argues that despite the rise of reformists to power, restrictions on individual liberty, rampant corruption, and soaring unemployment further increased the gap between the clerical ruling elite and the emerging civil society.[37]

It should be noted that US–Iran relations entered a relaxed phase when in 2000 US Secretary of State Madeleine Albright apologized for past US actions in Iran, opening the door for rapprochement. Throughout Khatami's two-term presidency, conservative clerics trumped his efforts to appoint a more open and democratic government or to pursue much-needed reform. Constrained by the conservative establishment, Khatami could not have initiated a rapprochement with the United States. His rhetoric of normalization of ties with the United States never went far. The Clinton administration approached the normalization talks with a two-track strategy. On the one hand, it continued to insist that if the 1996 Iran-Libya Sanctions Act was to be suspended, Iran must end its efforts to gain access to nuclear weapons, must terminate its support for terrorism, and must forgo denouncing the Middle East Peace Process. On the other hand, it repeatedly expressed its readiness to enter into state-to-state talks with Iran.[38]

For its part, Iran responded with demands of their own, including ending the US military presence in the Persian Gulf, releasing Iranian assets the United States had frozen from the time of the revolution, repaying Iran the money under dispute at the Hague, and stopping attempts to overthrow its Islamic regime. These issues, along with the lack of political determination and commitment on either side to genuinely address how the barriers to normal diplomatic ties between the two countries could be overcome, have hindered any further progress toward normalization.

President Khatami pursued a regional détente and greatly reduced tensions between Iran and its Arab neighbors. Nevertheless, areas of friction and deeply rooted mistrust continued to characterize Iran's relations with other states of the Persian Gulf. Much of this mistrust can be attributed to the early years of the Iranian Revolution, when Iran was viewed as bent on exporting its brand of Islamic revolution throughout the region. By the early 2000s, it was Iran's nuclear program that became a major concern of its neighbors.[39]

In the aftermath of the 9/11 terrorist attacks on the United States in 2001, relations between Washington and Tehran warmed up in an unprecedentedly rare moment, as Iran offered cooperation with and support for the US campaign against the Taliban regime in Afghanistan. In November 2001, the then Secretary of State Colin Powell shook hands with his Iranian counterpart, Kamal Kharrazi, at a UN meeting—a gesture seen by some observers as a potential start-ing point for rapprochement between the two countries, unheard of since the 1979 Revolution and the ensuing hostage crisis.

In a staggering contrast to this expectation, President George W. Bush, in his 2002 State of the Union address, labeled Iran, along with Iraq and North Korea, as part of an "Axis of Evil" bent on threat-ening world peace. Khatami's efforts to introduce more democratic reforms within Iran, along with a major shift in foreign policy directed at ending Iran's diplomatic isolation and building bridges with its Arab neighbors, EU member states and, if possible, the United States, suf-fered a major blow by President Bush's labeling Iran as such. Overall, writes Jack Straw (British Foreign Secretary from 2001–06), the hard-liners reaped a long-term dividend from Bush's apparent threat of military action against Tehran, shifting the domestic debate in Iran by completely dismissing the possibility of dialogue with the US gov-ernment. Khatami offered an opportunity that Washington could have converted to its own interests but instead turned its back on. Had Khatami been able to achieve his aim of breaking the logjam between the two countries, re-establishing decent relations with the United States, and showing the Iranian people the dividends, then it is highly unlikely that the hard-liner Mahmoud Ahmadinejad could have been elected in 2005 and again in 2009.[40]

In the end, Khatami's government got very little from the Bush administration for the constructive role it played in the military cam-paign to topple the Taliban rule and combat Al-Qaeda in Afghanistan. Hopes of minimizing the tensions between the United States and Iran, and more broadly between the West and the Muslim world, proved to be naïve, and were jeopardized by the Bush administra-tion's antagonistic policies toward Iran, prompting the return of populism with a vengeance to the Iranian political scene.[41] Some experts construed this to mean that the Bush administration's inten-tion was to delegitimize the Iranian Revolution and overthrow the regime.[42] This lurking danger—perceived or real—significantly diminished the agenda of the reformists in Iran to resolve differences with the United States and calcified the deep-seated hard-liner mis-trust of the United States.

REVOLUTION AND ITS AFTERMATH

The US Invasion of Iraq and Its Implications

The US invasion of Iraq in 2003 raised serious concerns both domestically and internationally. Concern about a US invasion of Iran grew at home—especially regarding the lack of any apparent endgame. There was good reason to be concerned. Building an indigenous Iraqi army had not undercut the guerrilla insurgency there. Occupation bred insurgency, and the latter, in turn, made any reasonable assessment of war impossible. Preventive war doctrine as applied to Iraq was a failure, as the Bush administration's poorly calculated campaign demonstrated. The continuing insurgency in Iraq and the so-called War on Terror made American troops more vulnerable. The United States turned the secular country of Iraq (with Saddam Hussein, a contained dictator, at its helm) into an epicenter of fundamentalist-inspired insurgency that was hard to control.

Moreover, the Iraq War damaged the US' image immensely in the Arab and Muslim worlds, both of which tended to see US intervention as "perverse" and typically called into question the Bush administration's motives to civilize and democratize—if not Christianize—the rest of the world. Increasingly, the US vision of remaking the world in the image of the United States and that of its European allies, who tend to put their faith in international institutions and law, stood in sharp contrast to the worldview of the region's populations. The importance of the Iraq War in relation to combating global terrorism also came under heavy criticism as US intelligence utterly failed to break into the insurgent networks. Under such circumstances, the effectiveness of the Iraqi 2005 elections was difficult to gauge. Some intelligence reports warned that the process of building democracy in Iraq would be a long, drawn out, and uncertain prospect that could very well entail civil war.

Like Afghanistan, Iraq became frontline for cooperation and competition between Iran and the United States. There were (and are) some common goals, such as order and stability, support for the country's constitution, and the elimination of Al-Qaeda in Iraq—however, there are many more diverging objectives. Iran also vehemently opposed the establishment of permanent US bases in Afghanistan and Iraq. But perhaps the major difference stemmed from the fact that Iran seemed to operate from the assumption that its existing influence in southern Iraq—the country's predominantly Shi'ite zone—would transform the region into a kind of proxy region, like southern Lebanon, creating a mini-state within a state.[43] That the administration of Prime Minister Nouri al-Maliki was a close ally of both Tehran and Washington offered a unique opportunity for those two governments to secure their interests in Iraq.[44] Meanwhile, the US presence in Iraq coincided with the resurgence of populists in Iran.

The Reversal Phase: The Return of Populism

The promise of economic liberalization backfired in the form of resistance. There were ethical problems with pushing for pro-market policies within the context of Iranian politics—who does privatization or an unbridled free market serve? And who should shape its development? The runoff election, in which both poor and middle-class people rejected Ali Akbar Hashemi Rafsanjani as the embodiment of a privileged political class and as the ultimate insider, illustrated that there were enormous cultural and economic gaps in Iranian society.

Despite their flaws, these elections demonstrated that reformists had failed to come to grips with the realities on the ground. Mahmoud Ahmadinejad's victory in the presidential election was equivalent to another revolution within the Islamic Republic, one in which a new generation of hard-liners were keen on returning Iran to the fundamentals of the 1979 Islamic Revolution, when the dispossessed and underprivileged were given hope for a better life. Twenty-six years later, the Islamic Revolution had gone awry, privileging clerical rulers who had become far removed from the struggles of average Iranians, who suffered from double-digit unemployment rates and rampant inflation. This is why Ahmadinejad presented his mandate as a return to the origins of the revolution, and to the populist tendencies of Khomeinism.[45]

Those who participated in elections sent a strong signal to the religio-political establishment that there were serious cultural and economic gaps in Iranian society, and that some civil and political rights must take a backseat to the people's overall economic security.

As in the rest of the world, the economy proved to be a deciding factor in elections, and many Iranians voted with their pocketbooks. Insofar as a cultural gap was concerned, this fissure stemmed from the fact that Islamic traditions have always placed social justice above civil and political rights. Both class and religion mattered in these elections, as the poor and the pious largely voted for Ahmadinejad. This demonstrated why Ahmadinejad's key slogan ("Islam without justice is not Islam") struck a chord with many Iranians tired of corruption and economic decay.

Ahmadinejad's populist message of economic equality won over other candidates who espoused promises of neoliberal economic projects. Populism and revolt against the ruling elites returned to the forefront of Iranian politics. Ahmadinejad's discourse, conduct, and appearance expressed a carefully crafted and politically shrewd message of pious populism.[46] This was indeed a reversion to the Islamic Revolution of Ayatollah Khomeini. The notion of liberal democracy and its related reforms failed to resonate deeply with the Iranian people, of which nearly forty percent lived below the poverty line. Eighty percent of the economy was state controlled. All presidential candidates (with the exception of Ahmadinejad) talked about privatization without even mentioning the corrupting influence that oil revenues had had on the management of oil resources. Many demanded that the country's national wealth be redistributed in the form of subsidies for the poor and tangible economic benefits in their lives.

President Ahmadinejad faced many challenges, but none more formidable than the domestic economy and Iran's nuclear program. One key problem regarding the domestic economy persisted—how to promote the privatization of state-owned industries, redistributing the wealth in shares of stock to each Iranian family, while simultaneously pushing for subsidies and welfare packages, such as health insurance and low-interest loans. Ahmadinejad's protectionist policies proved to be costly if not disastrous for an economy hungry to join the globalizing world. Quite understandably, the same populist campaign platform that had brought him to power spelled trouble for him, as his policies failed to narrow Iran's existing economic divide— a daunting task that no president, in the short history of the Islamic Republic, had successfully undertaken.

Iran's nuclear program presented a deeper challenge. Unlike Khatami, Ahmadinejad was part of a system that had a complete monopoly over all levers of powers, including executive, judicial, and legislative branches that were all but controlled by the hard-liners. This monopoly gave him more maneuverability with regards to the West. However, this card was limited, and could not be over-played. While emphasizing Iran's fundamental right to the peaceful use of nuclear energy and technology, he failed to make a compelling case before the country's Supreme Security Council for resolving the nuclear standoff with the West. The failure to do so led to the refer-ral of the Iranian case to the UN Security Council (UNSC), pitting Iran against an international consensus that was hard to ignore or defeat. The resultant UN resolution led to harsh economic sanctions against Iran which would prove to have grave diplomatic costs in the coming years.

In the end, Ahmadinejad failed to break Iran's relative isola-tion from the United States and more generally from the West. Ahmadinejad's populist rhetoric and confrontational posture toward the United States left no space for restoring US–Iran diplomatic rela-tions. The ensuing gestures offered to Iran by the Bush administra-tion—supporting Iran's entry into the World Trade Organization, selling Iran its aircraft spare parts, and agreeing that Iran could develop the capacity to enrich a limited amount of uranium—fell on deaf ears in Tehran.

The next (and major) challenge to the Ahmadinejad administration came in the form of a local opposition movement dubbed the "Green Movement," which assumed a popular and widespread resistance to Ahmadinejad's reelection in 2009. History has shown that revolutions or counterrevolutions tend to destroy their own ideals and descend into chaos when recourse to violence becomes their sole method of govern-ing.[47] The Islamic revolutionaries or counterrevolutionaries of 1979 attacked what was the postwar zeitgeist: the deeply held conviction that the secular political order was progressive, rational, egalitarian, and just. Some experts argue that modern theocracy failed to "solve the problems that brought it to power. It has increased inequalities between genders and among religious communities and has brought about its own backlash and counter-mobilization."[48] Clearly, the regime of the

Islamic jurists in Iran increasingly resembled the one they aspired to destroy: corrupt, cynical, starkly opposed to popular yearnings for reform, and concerned first and foremost with retaining power.[49]

It is worth noting that the record of post-revolutionary regimes (Bolivia, Cuba, Iran, and Nicaragua) in the developing world serves as a grim reminder that typically these regimes have vacillated between repression and accommodation, while failing to attain internal cohesion.[50] Uprisings have occurred with some regularity in Iran since the late nineteenth century, when unpopular concessions on tobacco sold to the British led to nationwide strikes that forced the Iranian government to nullify the concession in 1892. Subsequent uprisings occurred in 1905 (constitutional revolution), 1953 (anti-Shah uprisings), 1979 (Iranian Revolution), 1999 and 2003 (student protests), and 2009 (disputed presidential elections). Some of these uprisings failed because of government crackdown. Others succeeded in spite of it.[51]

Since its inception, the Islamic Republic of Iran has almost always guaranteed its political longevity by defending itself against real or perceived enemies. Iran has frequently attempted to use its oil power, as experts maintain, to push back against Washington's hostile approach toward Tehran. Furthermore, Ahmadinejad used the nuclear issue and tension with the United States and its regional allies to fuel nationalist fervor and to safeguard the regime against potential external military threats.[52] Arguably, the Islamic Republic, as in many other countries, owes its political survival to constructing an enemy and imagining an external threat. Historically, anti-imperial sentiments, as well as reactions to neocolonialism, have been an integral part of Iran's complex political culture. Suspicion of meddling by outside powers—Great Britain, Russia, and the United States—is deeply ingrained in the minds of many Iranians. This time, however, the Islamic Republic faced a new challenge: the green wave reminiscent of the "color revolutions" in Ukraine and Georgia, which posed a popular homegrown threat to the country's revolutionary power structure. As a result, fissures between and among the clerical establishment, the military, and the Revolutionary Guards deepened.

Additionally, significant ruptures within the clerical state that were likely to affect Iran's political landscape emerged. Several resignations and dismissals in Ahmadinejad's inner cabinet early in his second term complicated efforts to form a new government. The discontent among the clerics and their opposition to the way in which the elections were manipulated marked a noticeable shift in power away from the clerical establishment and toward the Revolutionary Guards and the military.[53] On the street, the use of brute force to quell spiraling unrest continued, rendering the Ahamadinejad administration fragile, fractured, challenged, and belligerent in the ensuing months and years.[54] Leaving aside the issue of elite fragmentation, it was evident that the clerical regime had ruled a society that in many respects had grown even more secular.[55]

One major takeaway from the Green Movement was the fact that the mobilization against "outside" threat or intervention, which has often been exploited and abused by repressive regimes, was no longer viable, as actual or potential threats of an outside conspiracy failed to account for the unrest and protests in the street. Instead, it was the reach of social networking and digital communication that enormously diminished the effectiveness of the narrative of an "external" enemy as recourse to avoiding intractable internal problems. Just as the show of popular will and resistance through street protests brought down the Shah's regime in 1979, so the Green Movement and its widespread protests cast a shadow of perpetual doubt over the divine authority of the Islamic Republic.

The Sanctions Policy

Iran's leaders, including conservative forces in control of both the Iranian parliament (*Majles*) and the presidency, seemed to have equated promoting nuclear energy with the country's national security. After a long period of negotiation with the EU-3 (Britain, France, and Germany), Iran chose to restart uranium enrichment in 2007. The EU-3 negotiations, however, were stymied. In large part this was because they failed to effectively recognize and confer legitimacy on Iran's peaceful nuclear activities. European countries also fell short of persuading Washington to negotiate with Tehran in order to promote regional stability, especially given the ongoing turmoil in Afghanistan and Iraq. The ensuing UNSC resolutions (1737 and 1747)—which imposed further sanctions on Iran during the 2006–07 period for its failure to suspend its enrichment program—targeted both Iranian assets abroad and certain individuals within the country for their participation in upgrading Iran's nuclear and missile programs.[56]

Meanwhile, the Iranian government claimed that it had suspended its activities on a voluntary basis, and that it had a legal right to develop its nuclear program for peaceful purposes according to Article 4 of the Non-Proliferation Treaty (NPT). US and Israeli officials continued to claim that Iran was assembling an atomic bomb and yet did not provide evidence to implicate Iran.[57] Some experts echoed a similar sentiment, arguing that American and Israeli accusations in this regard were based on Tehran's presumed intentions as opposed to its actual capabilities. It should be noted that Iran's Shahab-3 and Shahab-4 missiles, with a range of 1,300–1,500 km respectively, were the only weapons in Iran's arsenal that could have been regarded as nuclear-capable delivery vehicles.[58]

Regardless, according to one study, the United States and Israel in fact achieved what they had worked for systematically, namely "the imposition of UN sanctions against Iran." As a result, Iran became the new target of containment policy. The Bush administration supported a media propaganda campaign aimed at vilifying Iran under the assumption that Iran was trying to become a nuclear power.[59] US–Iran relations grew more intense than ever, as the Bush administration continued to display similar signs of enmity and suspicion toward Iran after the tragedy of September 11, 2001.

The pervasive negative perception of Iran in Washington, along with the consequences of the 2004 parliamentary election and the 2005 presidential election that introduced a new era of hard-line politics to post-revolutionary Iran, went to show how perceptions and realities of nuclear politics have shaped US–Iran relations over the years.[60] A different view stressed that the key problem with the Islamic Republic was never its nuclear technology but rather its foreign policy conduct as a revolutionary state, and one with ambitions that more often than not collided with the interests of its Arab neighbors and the West.[61]

The US military fiasco in Iraq at the same time awakened some policymakers in the Bush administration to the fact that a military approach toward Iran was invariably risky—especially at a time when the United States was largely preoccupied with reconstructing Iraq and Afghanistan.[62] The Obama administration, by contrast, relied on sanctions rather than military threats. Some experts noted that even though President Obama came to office promising to engage Iran, in reality, his administration followed the policy of "coercive diplomacy," which included imposing crippling sanctions on Iran. This approach, according to one expert, was designed mostly by those associated with Israeli lobby groups in the United States, who intended to give an ultimatum to Iran, offering the option of either accepting US-Israeli demands or facing aggression, all the while creating the illusion of engaging Iran in order to gain international support for the imposition of tough sanctions and aggressive actions.[63]

Under the Trump administration, as one expert notes, the neoconservatives abandoned both containment and multilateralism in favor of compellence in advancing US foreign policy objectives in the broader Middle East and North Africa (MENA) region. Sanctions became the main vehicle with which to pursue this policy. Yet the reimposition of new sanctions failed to limit Iran's missile program. Quite to the contrary, sanctions "made Iran's national missile program more attractive from an economic standpoint than buying foreign advanced fighter jets."[64] Unilateral sanctions have had little impact on Iran's defense programs and spending and are unlikely to alter Iran's defense approach.[65] Understandably, unilateral sanctions along with Trump's maximum pressure strategy against Iran have provided the impetus for the encouragement of a non-dollar based international economic trading system.[66]

The Integration Phase: The Victory of Moderates and Diplomacy

Hassan Rouhani's startling victory in Iran's presidential election on June 14, 2013, was a clear protest vote against the Ahmadinejad administration's mismanagement of Iran's relations with the Western world, including the nuclear issue. It also opened the door to a new start for US–Iran relations.[67] Many in the US foreign policymaking establishment welcomed the change in leadership in Iran, and many in Washington saw an opportunity to solve international and regional problems through diplomatic engagement for the first time in thirty years. Obama's congratulatory phone call on Rouhani's re-election set the stage for a new path.

While support for Rouhani's election was consistent with Iran's recent reformist inclinations, in the United States there was a shift in American public opinion away from military intervention. International cooperation and diplomacy had increasingly supplanted the call for military intervention. Weary of wars (Afghanistan and Iraq); hesitant about the use of force to address regional security issues; unable to contain the unbridled sectarian tensions in Syria, Iraq, and Bahrain; and crippled with an ailing economy, US foreign policymakers came to the realization that cooperation with Iran could meet some of the lingering challenges in the region.

When the French and British foreign ministers specifically noted that the Syrian crisis could not be resolved through diplomatic means without Iran's presence at the table, it became clear that the EU would be opposed to any further isolation of Iran at a time when the latter's active participation seemed crucial to resolving some of these regional conflicts. Under such circumstances, Washington needed little persuasion to follow suit.

Increasingly aware of the fact that the Syrian crisis could adversely affect the outcome of sectarian tensions in Iraq and Lebanon, some US policymakers asserted that Iran could be part of the solution. Likewise, Iranians, under ferocious economic sanctions, turned their attention to the benefits of a dialogue with the United States over settling the nuclear issue. Needless to say, there were huge impediments, both regional and international, that made progress difficult. Neoconservatives in Congress as well as the Israeli lobby appeared wary of any compromise. Likewise, the Israeli government was clearly rattled by diplomatic initiatives taken up by President Rouhani, who Prime Minister Benjamin Netanyahu labeled a "wolf in sheep's clothing."

Economic hardships under the sanction regime made Iranians very eager for the country to establish and maintain a good relationship with the United States. However, even though both countries were in favor of diplomatic relations, there were many domestic and international factors that made progress difficult. Examples include resistance from Israeli lobbyists, conservatives in Congress, and Washington think tanks. Meanwhile, in the US, many republicans stated that they were in favor of more sanctions on Iran, while the democrats leaned toward trusting Rouhani's presidency and his determination to maintain diplomatic negotiations with the United States.

Iran's support for Hezbollah in Lebanon and the Palestinians under the Israeli occupation would offer a difficult challenge to any long-term relations between Iran and the United States. Both President Obama and President Rouhani were greatly restricted by domestic economic and political considerations that confined their ability to maneuver. Internally, Rouhani's support for broader social freedoms, his criticism of the securitization of Iranian society, and his strong advocacy for women's rights rendered him a favorite candidate for change. Economic insecurity—largely caused by the imposition of economic sanctions by the Western world in reaction to Iran's nuclear program—was a central factor in his victory. Public discontent was rooted in Iran's broken economy.[68]

Calling US–Iran enmity "an old wound that must be treated," Rouhani hinted at improving relations between the two countries. With the Syrian crisis deepening, and with NATO forces preparing to withdraw from Afghanistan in 2014, Iranian leadership was crucial. Ending the nuclear stalemate with the West in the immediate future was the most important challenge facing the Rouhani administration because of the direct link between sanctions and the country's economic difficulties.[69]

Some experts questioned the effectiveness of the sanctions regime, arguing that states that impose sanctions despite the knowledge that they will fail to coerce the target state increase the costs and risks for themselves by increasing the probability that the sanctioning state will ultimately resort to force.[70] Warnings that a successful US air strike would halt Iran's nuclear program for at least five years remain questionable.[71] Arguably, a nuclear deal with Iran could alleviate Iranian security concerns, prompt Iranian recognition of the rights and interests of Arab regimes in the Persian Gulf, and eventually promote a gradual political evolution in Iran.[72]

A contrasting view held that if the United States kept sanctions against Iran in place, preservation of the status quo would be a significant economic and diplomatic boost for the Arab countries of the Persian Gulf, especially the UAE. While political and economic crises in the region were not welcomed, a weakened Iran served the interests of the Persian Gulf states.[73] Some analysts saw an opportunity for rapprochement between Iran and the United States, asserting that given that anti-Americanism has been a key part of the identity of the Islamic Republic's foreign policy since 1979, such unprecedented open discussion in Iranian society regarding reaching a deal with the United States demonstrated that the country might have been on the verge of a shift in its strategic thinking.[74]

The challenge of degrading and ultimately defeating the Islamic State in Iraq and Syria (ISIS) raised the stakes, with the unexpected effect of injecting some common sense into diplomacy with Iran. Some experts, such as Nader Entessar, took a pessimistic view, arguing that Iran's strategic loneliness and the history of US–Iran relations since the 1979 Iranian Revolution indicated that the path toward normalizing relations between the two countries was replete with barriers on both sides. Amid these new uncertainties, the failure to reach a deal with Iran was marked by strategic blunders and missed opportunities to work with Iranians in areas of mutual interest.[75] In contrast, others, like Trita Parsi, provided an optimistic outlook, noting that the odds of resolving the nuclear standoff were much more favorable than in the past and that resolving this issue was far more feasible compared to a whole host of intractable problems that the MENA region encountered at the time.[76]

In July 2015, US–Iran relations entered a new phase, as the nuclear agreement, formally known as the Joint Comprehensive Plan of Action (JCPOA), became a landmark accord reached between Iran and several world powers, including the United States, China, Russia, Great Britain, France, and Germany. Under its terms, Iran agreed to dismantle much of its nuclear program and open its facilities to more intrusive UN inspections in exchange for sanctions relief. While the United States committed to lifting its nuclear-related sanctions on Iran, it continued to impose many other sanctions, including those related to Iran's ballistic missile program, regional activities, and human rights abuses. Similarly, the United States, which had committed to lifting its sanctions on oil exports, kept its restrictions on financial and banking transactions by blocking international trade with Iran.

No sooner had Iran's economy recovered from the lifting of these sanctions when President Trump withdrew the United States from the deal in 2018, claiming it failed to curb Iran's missile program and expanding regional reach and activities. The imposition of new sanctions on Iran throttled its economy, sparked dramatic inflationary impacts, and caused *currency depreciation* of cataclysmic proportions. The Rouhani government faced a colossal challenge in attempting to stay the course.

The Triumph of Hard-liners

The Trump administration's punitive sanctions on Iran were revealed to be conducive to the victory of a hard-liner in the June 2021 Iranian presidential elections. The grim state of the Iranian economy—in part due to the COVID-19 pandemic but also because of government mismanagement and endemic corruption on top of the sanctions—enhanced the hard-liners prospects of winning the presidency, while also bringing many questions regarding the future of US–Iran relations to the fore. Low turnout—the lowest for a presidential election in the Islamic Republic's history, at forty-nine percent—clearly favored Raisi, who won with nearly eighteen million votes out of just under twenty-nine million votes overall. Raisi's victory assumed a different meaning as the *Majles*, the judiciary, and the presidency—all fell firmly in the hands of hard-liners.[77]

US–Iran relations, according to one observer, will be transactional and revolve primarily around security concerns in the coming years. The seductive appeal of a broader rapprochement will likely lose much of its traction in Tehran and Washington. The policy potential of a "grand bargain" between the two countries is unlikely to materialize.[78] Raisi has advocated engagement with the rest of the world if not an outright integration into the global economy. He also has made clear that he has no major objections to the nuclear deal, only to the specific aspects of the accord that have allowed the United States to violate it with impunity. Having criticized the JCPOA in the past, Raisi now supports it, as long as Washington honors its obligations.[79]

This is understandable given that Supreme Leader Ayatollah Ali Khamenei, who often plays a key role in major foreign policy decisions, has given the green light to return to negotiating the JCPOA. This decision is partly due to Iran's need for sanctions relief to salvage its ravaged economy.[80]

Meanwhile, the US strategy of pivoting away from the Middle East brought regional détente and new tensions into sharper focus. The Biden administration's recent decision to disengage from Afghanistan has raised the issue of strategy, expectations, and more importantly, logistics. Twenty years of US military intervention under multiple US administrations, and $83 billion spent on building the Afghan army, have failed to build a reliable fighting and security force—leaving one whose soldiers merely had the will to fight. In the end, Afghan security forces were revealed to be hollow, collapsing impotently in the face of the Taliban assault and occupation of the capital city, Kabul.

With the return of the Taliban to power in Afghanistan in mid-August 2021, several questions have resurfaced. What strategic leverage does the United States have on the Taliban? Could Al-Qaeda find a new foothold in Afghanistan? What are the regional implications of the Taliban's return to power in Afghanistan? Many experts believe that the United States will have little or no strategic leverage over the Taliban. The resurgence of terrorism and the triggering of an influx of refugees will have dire consequences for its neighboring countries, especially for Iran, which is already home to millions of Afghan refugees, and Pakistan, which has served as a safe haven for Taliban members that fled the country some two decades ago.

It should be noted, however, that many Iranian hard-liners have long viewed Taliban control of Afghanistan as the only feasible political option—or, at least, the only viable option for a friendly Islamic state in the region. The hard-liners in Tehran respect the Taliban's resilience if not its popularity, and despite their ideological differences, have a lot in common, including their revisionist views and hostility toward the United States.

It should be noted that well before the Taliban took complete control of Afghanistan, hard-liners in Iran sought to paint a polished and presentable picture of the Taliban as a movement rooted in the Afghan people. The most direct comment in this regard was made by Ahmad

Naderi, a member of *Majles* (Iranian parliament) and Professor of Anthropology at the University of Tehran, whose views on the Taliban are still heavily criticized by critics. Referring to Taliban as a legitimate political force to be reckoned with, on December 3, 2016, Naderi noted: "Working with them can promote stability in Afghan society and prevent the infiltration of groups such as ISIS. We should not fall into the trap of misrepresenting them in the American media."[81]

This sympathy—or better yet, tactical affinity—could smooth the path toward future strategic cooperation between Iran and Afghanistan, provided that the Taliban would be willing to protect the interests of Afghan Shi'a.[82] It is in this context that Iran's President Ebrahim Raisi's comments in the aftermath of the Taliban's takeover of the country should be understood: "America's military defeat and its withdrawal must become an opportunity to restore life, security and durable peace in Afghanistan."[83] Raisi went on to say: "Iran is committed to its neighborly relations with Afghanistan by closely monitoring developments in this country."[84] In yet another statement, while equating the Taliban's takeover of Afghanistan with the rule of Afghan people over their country, Raisi pointed out: "The rule of the will of the oppressed people of Afghanistan has always been security-building and stabilizing."[85]

The Taliban's takeover of the country has increasingly demonstrated that US counterinsurgency efforts to upend the Taliban's presence and influence in Afghanistan have all but failed. Counterinsurgency was in the end not a military solution—only the means for creating a political settlement. The swift and immediate collapse of the Afghan army is proof of the failed long-term viability of expensive and complicated counterinsurgency operations. The return of the Taliban to power in Afghanistan will inject new uncertainties in the region in more ways than one—a region that is already reeling from the unexpectedly rapid collapse of healthcare infrastructure in the face of the COVID-19 pandemic, climate change consequences, unemployment, and a refugee crisis—not to mention terrorism and sectarian strife. The lasting impact of this failed US mission should instruct future leaders about the viability of imposing foreign governance regimes on target states and the notion of creating pockets of stability and control while the vast majority of the state is left to a faithful oppositional fighting force.[86]

Conclusion

The 1953 coup infiltrated the consciousness of Iranian political elites. Perhaps more importantly, it fundamentally altered the country's domestic power balances on the ground. In many respects, the 1979 Iranian Revolution was a backlash to the lingering effects of that coup. In terms of foreign policy, the revolution posed a real menace to secular nationalism in the region, both symbolically and from a political standpoint, while also disrupting the balance of power in the Persian Gulf region with far-reaching implications. The hostage ordeal (1979–81) signified a symbol of defiance, becoming integral to the continuity of the revolution. It also set in motion a new power struggle in the coming years between hard-liners, reformists, and moderates.

With the large Shi'ite population in his country, Iraqi President Saddam Hussein felt threatened by the prospect of destabilizing impacts that the Iranian Revolution could have had on his country. His desire to eliminate the threat from Iran drove him to do the unthinkable: he invaded Iran in September 1980. This led to a bloody war that lasted until August 1988, when both countries finally agreed to a UN-brokered cease-fire. The war galvanized the nation, gave hard-liners and the Revolutionary Guards renewed life, and consolidated the revolution against its enemies at home and abroad. It bears remembering that the lifeblood of every revolution is the existence of an enemy—perceived or real.

The enhanced US military presence in the Persian Gulf region in the 1980s influenced political debate within Iran, obviating the rationale for any negotiations with Washington, while also giving hard-liners in Tehran an alibi to maintain their hold on the country's domestic politics and foreign policy. The power struggles between and among reformists, populists, and moderates became front and center of Iranian politics since the death of Khomeini. The consolidation of the earlier phase of the revolution was gradually replaced by the adaptation to a globalizing world of the late twentieth century, especially after the Iran—Iraq War.

Under crippling sanctions and in a long war with Iraq, Iran moved toward forging a network of proxies throughout the region, none more effective than the Lebanese Hezbollah. The formation of the

Gulf Cooperation Council (GCC) in 1981, partly due to the 1979 Iranian Revolution and partly due to the Iran—Iraq War, brought the Gulf Arab states together. They were not united by common interests and by similar perceptions of the threat from Iran and Iraq, coming together largely out of fear of the violence and insurrection spreading through the region.

The Iraqi invasion of Kuwait in August 1990 put the final nail in the coffin of pan-Arabism, prompting the resurgence of Islamists throughout the region. Both the US liberation of Kuwait, achieved by dislodging Iraqi troops from that country in 1991, and the US invasion of Iraq in 2003, which led to the killing of Iraqi President Saddam Hussein, rendered Iran the most likely beneficiary. Yet the Bush administration's refusal to seriously consider any possibility of rapprochement with the reformist government of Khatami undermined the latter's strategic vision and power. This rather hostile approach toward Iran dealt a fatal blow to reformists' position, who saw the populists take control of the presidency in 2005.

Opinions vary as to why reform has repeatedly failed in Iran. Some experts, such as Kazem Alamdari, a sociologist at California State University, Northridge, write that after the 1979 Revolution, regressive religious forces, along with the absolute powers of the *velayat-e faqih* (rule by the jurisconsult), dominated society, making the state's survival largely contingent upon its security and military apparatus—institutions that were utterly inhospitable to any social reforms. Today, independence and socio-political reforms are a prerequisite for the exercise of popular sovereignty—not breaking off the relationship with developed countries of the West or pursuing global isolation in the name of independence. The Islamic Republic's initial mantra, "neither East nor West," and their hostile reactions to Western modern values, have portrayed Iran's global status in lockstep with the authoritarian regimes in China and Russia.[87]

The Green Movement of 2009, however ill-fated, challenged this trend. The massive protests in reaction to the disputed 2009 elections suggested a growing anti-establishment sentiment that provided a rich reservoir of energy. The political energy unleashed as a result refused to be wasted as it culminated in the victory of moderates in 2013 who promised a new phase in internal Iranian politics—one that was directed at integrating Iran's economy into the international community. The Iranian moderates' major achievement of striking a nuclear deal with key international players in order to lift most foreign economic sanctions, in exchange for allowing stringent limits on Iran's nuclear program, was severely undermined by the Trump administration's decision to unilaterally withdraw from the deal and impose harsh new sanctions on Iran.

The US military presence in the Persian Gulf has failed to control the security narrative as the region "is likely to remain both heavily militarized and highly insecure for the foreseeable future."[88] More attention must be given to non-military security threats, including religious and secular identity, economic aspirations, demographic pressures, and ecological degradation.[89] A new strategic calculation has emerged in which a US military presence in the region is no longer seen as strictly necessary. The old-fashioned strategy of acting as an external balancer has lost its luster in Washington, rendering diplomacy and dialogue between Iran and its Gulf Arab neighbors all the more essential.[90] Taken together, these developments have reflected and shaped a new paradigm of security in the Persian Gulf.

With the reformist movement fully contained, the economy largely stagnant, and domestic tensions brewing, Iranian politics suffered yet another setback. The country saw frequent outbursts of ethnic unrest and labor discontent among young people and the urban middle class. This growing disenchantment was prompted by the reformists' way of dealing with the country's problems in 2018 and 2019. This culminated in Ebrahim Raisi's 2021 election victory following the lowest voter turnout in the history of the Islamic Republic.

Raisi's cabinet was largely approved by the Iranian parliament shortly after he was elected, with several of its members being former Islamic Revolutionary Guard Corps (IRGC) members and subject to US sanctions. Raisi's choice of foreign minister was the 57-year-old Hossein Amirabdollahian, who has served in Iraq, Bahrain, and Syria as Iran's top diplomat, and is believed to have close ties with Lebanon's Iran-backed Hezbollah and the IRGC. He appears to have been hawkish on relations with the West and intends to form an "Asia-centric" foreign policy.[91]

Whether the Raisi administration will be able to tackle challenges facing the country in terms of oil, economy, and the COVID-19 pandemic—not to mention tough foreign policy issues ahead—remains to be seen. Increasingly, a broader understanding of security in terms of national security and the balance of power dynamics has been the subject of an intense debate. Critics argue that human security and human rights have often been placed outside of this narrowly defined conception of security. Unsurprisingly, a new perspective has challenged today's national security state, seeking to foster the value of human security as a path to a more stable society. We turn to this perspective in the next chapter.

3

REFORM AND THE HUMAN RIGHTS CAMPAIGN

The 1979 Iranian Revolution led to a break in relations between the United States and Iran. The Carter administration's efforts to build a relationship with the new regime in Iran were effectively terminated after the takeover of the US Embassy in Tehran by extremist pro-Khomeini "Students in the Line of the Imam" on November 4, 1979. Fifty-two American diplomats and citizens were held hostage for 444 days, and released pursuant to the January 19, 1981, Algiers Accords. The United States broke diplomatic relations with Iran on April 7, 1980, just two weeks prior to the unsuccessful US military attempt to rescue the hostages in an operation called "Desert One."[1]

US–Iran relations since have largely been influenced by broader issues, including geopolitics, regional political stability, opposition to terrorism, and nuclear and chemical proliferation. These issues have long troubled the region. The primacy of these issues has in turn affected the domestic politics of Iran so deeply that Iranian officials have rarely—if ever—conferred any legitimacy on human rights as a top foreign policy issue. The issues of reform and human rights have been relegated to such a low priority, at times even outside the realm of direct negotiations, that both parties have regarded them as marginal to other first-order and security-related agenda items. The reluctance of US officials to prioritize human rights over geopolitical considerations—as part of pursuing "realist" thinking—has often been attributed to a fear that giving primacy to human rights would be tantamount to imposing Western values on Iran.

While Washington has promoted human rights values consistent with its geopolitical goals in certain contexts, time and again it has been motivated solely by a desire to take US–Iran relations to a level where problems are solved through diplomacy rather than unilateral intervention. The 2015 nuclear deal (Joint Comprehensive Plan of Action—JCPOA) was exclusively linked to Iran's nuclear capacity, with no mention made of human rights issues in the agreement. It also did not deal with Iranian regional policy, among other issues. This was the only way to reach an agreement on the regulation of nuclear weapons. The Trump withdrawal from the nuclear deal and his pursuit of a maximum pressure campaign put the nuclear weapons issue once again front and center, with further unsettling implications for the human rights situation in Iran. It is with these views in mind that I attempt to contextualize the status of the overall human rights situation and reform movements in Iran with an eye toward understanding the conundrum of US–Iran relations.

In this chapter, I will take a deep look at the ongoing debate over the tension between security and human rights and the way in which it affects government policies. I next turn to the state of human rights in the Islamic Republic of Iran with a particular focus on social change in the post-revolutionary era. In the ensuing sections, I examine women's rights, student unrest, the Green Movement protests, the status of religious minorities, and the recent protests that erupted in small cities, rural areas, and remote villages, before spreading to other parts of the country. In all these cases, it is evident that while the Islamic Republic idealizes the struggle against poverty and promotes the working-class lifestyle, the country's economic and labor conditions have deteriorated. Similarly, the country's human rights conditions have also worsened as protests have broken out and the regime has responded in a heavy-handed way. Clearly, the imposition of a new round of sanctions by the Trump administration made living conditions for the vast majority of Iranians excruciatingly difficult.

Security vs. Human Rights

Human rights struggles are fought and won on national turfs. Yet the role of external support and influence cannot be overlooked. From both an intellectual and a practical perspective, as one prominent human rights scholar once reminded us, human rights have a permanent but ambivalent status in US foreign policy. American exceptionalism and nationalism have led to considerable unilateralism in contemporary US foreign policy, resulting in attempts to either pursue or avoid human rights issues. When involvement has occurred, it has been combined with liberalism or realism. These traditions have meant that human rights issues have been effectively addressed or totally disregarded; pursued unilaterally or multilaterally; treated as immensely significant or clearly secondary to US self-interest. This self-interest has been defined in terms of power, traditional norms of security, and the preeminence of state sovereignty.[2]

While human rights continue to be a fixture on the agenda of contemporary US foreign policy, the precise content and application of human rights in different contexts requires a careful, case-by-case analysis. The end of the Cold War, for example, made no fundamental difference to the ambivalent US approach to international human rights in general. While the decline of the Soviet Union permitted a NATO intervention in defense of Albanian Kosovars, and allowed more attention to the promotion of democracy, it ultimately generated no consistent global liberalism in Washington's approach, much less a curbing of US unilateralism.[3] During the Cold War, the United States frequently referred to human rights to discredit the Soviet Union. Likewise, the Trump administration used human rights to discredit states such as Iran and China.

The selective support for human rights reflected in the great powers' foreign policies is often a function of their geostrategic interests.[4] Prioritizing security over human rights in selective contexts has been a consistent part of US foreign policy. Conspicuously absent has been a definitive resolution of the complexities of blending and balancing human rights concerns with other foreign policy priorities.[5] US foreign policy toward Iran has followed the same pattern. Successive US administrations have failed to genuinely support reformists and moderates in Iran, perpetuating the hard-liners' power grab. In the process, indigenous and legitimate human rights struggles and movements have been abandoned in the name of geopolitical considerations.

Sanctions have their own limits and are highly questionable, especially if lacking multilateral support. Other forms of outside intervention or support—material or moral—can be equally controversial. President Obama limited US support for the 2009 Iranian Green Movement to verbal encouragement on the grounds that any outside intervention would have likely delegitimized that indigenous, grassroots movement and damaged its credibility.

Some experts have sought a remedy in technological domains, calling for the United States to support greater openness by simply providing Iranians with improved access to information technology. On May 30, 2013, the US Departments of State and Treasury announced the lifting of sanctions on companies that sought to sell cell phones, laptops, encryption technology, and other equipment to Iranians who wished to dodge government media restrictions.[6] This may be an effective way to empower activists; at the end of the day, real change and progress toward realizing human rights must occur at both the governmental and societal levels.

The State of Human Rights

Over the past four decades, the human rights situation in Iran has noticeably deteriorated with the exception of certain periods in which restrictions on the rights of freedom of expression and peaceful assembly were lifted. Social and political protests have often been met with illegal detention. Torture and other ill-treatment have remained endemic. There are widespread systematic denials of fair trials. The state routinely invokes repressive measures and tactics to suppress street unrest, blaming external intervention as the chief source of this turmoil.

The lingering concerns about repressive measures and human rights violations more generally, which were significant at the height of the 1979 Iranian Revolution, have since been subordinated to the protection of the Islamic Republic. Human rights violations in Iran before and after the advent of the Islamic Republic have raised concerns and friction between Iran and the West. International bodies and nongovernmental organizations (NGOs) have repeatedly reported that Iran's human rights situation is poor and likely to further regress. As noted above, the United States has often glossed over human rights abuses in the Middle East and North Africa (MENA) region when faced with geopolitical considerations. Human rights are at risk of being trivialized or lost in light of the priority afforded to security and commercial interests.

The revolutionary zeal of the time, however, faced multiple challenges, as new socioeconomic and political problems aggravated the Islamic Republic's attempt to advance its ideological goals. Several problems, including the population explosion, the Iran—Iraq War, and the emigration of some three million Iranians, created numerous problems that weakened the ruling elites' revolutionary pursuit. By the late 1990s, over nine million urban dwellers lived below the official poverty line.[7]

In Iran, however, widespread corruption and domestic political uncertainty have contributed to the staying power of autocrats. The exertion of ill-advised foreign pressures has played into the hands of the ruling elites, who have blamed external actors for the country's deplorable performance. Harping on outside dangers, risks, and threats to the country's security, economy, and cultural traditions, Iranian ruling elites have repeatedly resorted to repressive tactics and methods to not only stay in power but also to perpetuate their rule while deferring genuine reform and opening up.[8]

Since its inception, the Islamic Republic of Iran has seen several major upheavals: the 1999 student protests, the 2009 Green Movement, and the period of 2018–19 unrest. While the Islamic Republic has survived these upheavals, the most recent events have exposed the regime's vulnerability and ineffectiveness. In each case, Iran's crackdown has successfully curbed, if not entirely eliminated, the domestic political threats to the regime's survival. Several days of protests in small and large cities around Iran in the recent eruption of political unrest (2018–19) served as yet another grim reminder that Iran has failed to keep its lower and middle classes content. The ongoing isolation of the country in the wake of mounting sanctions, and the consequent refusal of international banks to do business with Iran, has brought this issue into sharper focus.

Unlike the revolts of the 1990s and the 2009 Green Movement, according to Asef Bayat, a sociologist at the University of Illinois, Urbana-Champaign, the 2018 unrest came from a disenfranchised middle class that took to the streets in order to lead and organize nationwide revolts. The vast majority of those detained in these unrests were under the age of twenty-five and likely educated. This was the revolt of the middle-class poor who, although the product of a large youth cohort, broadened educational opportunities, and urbanization, were hostile to economic liberalization.[9]

Following the 1979 Revolution, Iran saw itself as the vanguard of the Muslim world in confronting Western values, ideals, and institutions. The Islamic Republic viewed human rights as a tool of external intervention, or more specifically Western imperialism, that had to be contained. Internally, however, the universal appeal of human rights was irresistible, as the populace often used it to stake their claims against the government. The human rights situation in Iran since the 1979 Revolution and its aftermath have been portrayed as problematic at best and bleak at worst.

Revolutionary leaders and successive governments have increasingly engaged in repressive policies reminiscent of the Shah's rule. Human rights violations under the Islamic Republic were (and continue to be) attributed to political, legal, and cultural sources. To secure their power base, the clerical elite have created a hierarchical structure of power that has denied equal opportunity to the individuals in the society. They have also maintained the mechanisms of social control in such a way as to trample upon the human rights of opposition forces, especially when such forces pose a direct threat to the vested interests of the Islamic Republic.[10]

The authoritarian Islamic Republic has consistently precluded the formation of any "power blocs" or an "alternative political force" among women, labor unions, students, intellectuals, professionals, or ethnic or religious minorities. Beyond political explanations, human rights violations can be attributed to the Islamic Republic's legal system. Islamic law has been widely used as a device to camouflage the clerical establishment's pervasive political powers.[11] Similarly, a closer examination of the causes of gender-biased abuses, in both legal and economic terms, points to the country's deeply entrenched patriarchal culture and social practices.

REFORM AND THE HUMAN RIGHTS CAMPAIGN

The leadership of the Islamic Revolution has regularly relied on several quasi-official and parallel institutions (such as the *Basiji*—a volunteer paramilitary group) in crushing opposition forces arising from civil society and other democratic and social movements. Under the control of the Office of the Supreme Leader, such groups have confronted student protests and progressive social and cultural elites. They have also disrupted academic conventions as well as intellectual and progressive forums. The *Basiji* have on many occasions committed violent crackdowns on activists celebrating International Women's Day in Tehran. Similar attacks have been perpetrated against reformist academics and journalists, creating a climate of intimidation and fear.

The clerics have also established their monopoly over crucial state institutions, such as the judiciary, the revolutionary guards and the Pasdaran, the national broadcasting media, and the quasi-governmental organizations known as *bunyad-e mostazaffin* ("foundations for the oppressed"). During the 1980s, the war against moral and economic corruption (*mufsid fil-arz*, or "corruption on earth") involved brutal punishment prescribed by revolutionary tribunals. During this time, a prison system emerged in which instruction and persecution were concomitantly administered. In the Evin Prison workshop, for example, prisoners chanted revolutionary slogans while working or changing shifts, and posters exhorted prisoners to change their ways.[12] Political prisoners continued to receive unfair trials before special courts, such as the Special Court for the Clergy, which fell far short of international standards of fairness. Amnesty International has regularly called upon the Iranian government to ensure impartial and thorough investigations into allegations of torture, disappearances, and extrajudicial executions.

In the early years of the revolution, concepts of Islamic government *velayate-e faqih* (rule by the jurisconsult) and the primacy of Islamic law were enshrined in Iran's constitution. These changes gave the clerics ultimate authority in managing and guiding the state. Under the de facto leadership of Ayatollah Khomeini, the revolutionary government of Mehdi Bazargan struggled during a chaotic and troubling era. In July 1988, Khomeini ordered the mass execution of political prisoners, many of whom were members of leftist parties that belonged to a very broad spectrum of socialism.[13]

To maintain stability and security, the Iranian state has been forced to come to grips with several critical issues, including tensions over ethnic minorities (especially the Kurds), US–Iran relations, the Iran—Iraq War, antigovernment guerrilla forces, and the Salman Rushdie affair. In 1989, Khomeini issued a death *fatwa* (religious edict) against Rushdie because his novel, *The Satanic Verses*, derided Muslims' sacred values. Since the 1990s, however, several successive Iranian governments have refused to enforce the death ruling.

Following Khomeini's death in 1989, factional infighting and competition permeated all aspects of the Iranian political process. Through a national referendum in 1989, the post of prime minister was abolished and replaced with a popularly elected president as head of the government. The president, therefore, did not need to be approved by the *Majles*, the sole chamber of parliament. At the time, this was taken to mean that the *velayate-e faqih* (rule by the jurisconsult) would no longer dominate the political sphere. Consequently, the president emerged as the most powerful figure of the state.

In September 1992, four Kurdish opposition leaders were assassinated at the Mykonos Café in Berlin. The German media pointed to the direct involvement of the Iranian Ministry of Intelligence in these violent acts. In March 1996, a German court went as far as to issue an arrest warrant for Minister of Intelligence Ali Fallahian for his role in the Mykonos case. In April 1997, the court stated that the government of Iran had pursued a deliberate policy of eliminating the regime's opponents living outside of Iran, including leaders of the opposition Kurdish Democratic Party of Iran (KDPI). The judge implicated the most senior levels of the Iranian government in the Mykonos murders.

During the 1980s, political liberalization in Iran came to a standstill. The press law, passed in 1985 and still in effect, allows the Ministry of Culture and Islamic Guidance to ban any publication that insults leading religious elites. The courts have closed many periodicals. Under the press law the government repeatedly charged journalists with espionage for activities that were routine practices in journalism elsewhere around the world. The works of the best-known Iranian film directors, including Bahram Beizai and Mohsen Makhmalbaf, were frequently censored.

In 1994, public discontent over economic and political conditions resulted in riots in several Iranian cities. Violent confrontations between demonstrators and security forces were reported in several cities, including Tehran, Tabriz, Zahedan, Qazvin, and Najafabad. Officially sponsored vigilantism became widespread in 1995 as Hezbollah directed its attacks against people critical of state corruption, such as Abdol-Karim Soroush. Domestic human rights organizations—including the Parliamentary Human Rights Committee, the Organization for Defending Victims of Violence, and the Human Rights Commission—were not allowed to operate effectively.

In the March 1996 parliamentary elections, the Council of Guardians excluded nearly half of the more than 5,000 candidates for parliament on the ground of discriminatory and arbitrary criteria. This practice impeded access to the political process and citizens' freedom of choice. In the same month, Maurice Copithorne, the UN human rights rapporteur, argued that the social atmosphere in Iran had become unbearable, and that the Islamic Republic harassed and abused the rights of Baha'is as a religious minority, and routinely assassinated dissidents living abroad.[14]

The Rise and Fall of the Reform Movement (1997–2005)

The landslide victory of Mohammad Khatami and his tenure as president (1997–2005) underlined the republican—and not the Islamic—side of the Islamic Republic. By 1999, Iran had become a party to the International Covenant on Civil and Political Rights; the International Covenant on Economic, Social, and Cultural Rights; the UN Convention on the Rights of the Child; the International Convention on the Elimination of All Forms of Racial Discrimination; the Convention Relating to the Status of Refugees; and the Protocol Relating to the Status of Refugees. Although human rights conditions did not improve considerably during the 1990s, for the first time since 1979 charges of torture were filed against active military officers and personnel.[15]

President Khatami made a valiant effort to promote human rights and their monitoring mechanisms in Iran. Certain trends were encouraging. The open debate about human rights subsequently became a notable aspect of Iran's nascent civil society and free press. Many intellectuals, including prominent writers, journalists, female novelists, scholars, activists, and government officials openly spoke against the ongoing abuses of civil-political rights. Although Human Rights Watch was able to send its researchers to Iran, other representatives of international human rights NGOs were denied permission to visit the country.

That said, pledges of reform in some areas fell far short of internationally recognized standards, and hopes of further openings in both social and political spaces were dashed. Torture and executions remained widespread in Iranian prisons. The human rights committee of the UN General Assembly, which had expressed discontent with the prevalence of torture, executions, and amputations, called on Iran to respect the due process of law. The committee voted on November 9, 2000, by a vote of fifty-eight to fifty-three, with forty-eight abstentions, for a resolution calling on the Islamic Republic of Iran to "ensure that capital punishment will not be imposed for crimes other than the most serious."[16] The committee also requested that the Iranian government live up to internationally recognized normative and legal standards for stemming torture of and discrimination against minorities.

Amnesty International reported that during 1999 scores of people were executed and several extra-judicial executions had occurred.[17] Since the 1979 Islamic Revolution, international human rights organizations have frequently criticized Iran's judiciary for holding unfair and closed trials, jailing and executing political prisoners without due process, and violating international norms for granting defendants access to attorneys and basic information about charges against them. During the Khatami presidency, the judiciary, which is accountable to Supreme Leader Ali Khamenei rather than the elected president, was at the center of many human rights violations.

Many abuses were carried out by the so-called parallel institutions (*nahad-e movazi*)—the plainclothes intelligence agents and paramilitary groups that violently attacked peaceful protesters, students, writers, and reformist politicians. These institutions also refer to the illegal secret prisons and interrogation centers run by the intelligence services. Groups such as Hezbollah and the *Basiji*, working under the Office of the Supreme Leader, are examples of such organizations.[18]

Khatami's reluctance to challenge the legitimacy of such organizations and the theocratic constitution of the Islamic Republic increasingly undermined his support for civil society and the rule of law. Because of this, Khatami's rhetoric, as one expert notes, "went no further than advocating better management of the government."[19] This compromised leadership severely limited Khatami's ability to spearhead the popular demand for democracy and the promotion of civil society that his own election had unleashed.

The conservative judiciary shut down about thirty reformist newspapers and magazines and jailed more than twenty-five reformist journalists, intellectuals, and political activists during the Khatami's first term. Almost all of the seventeen reformist writers and activists who attended the Berlin conference, organized by the German Green Party (Heinrich Böll Foundation) in April 2000, on the subject of "Iran after the Elections" went to prison. Some of them were tortured.[20] Akbar Ganji, one of the journalists on trial, whose exposés had linked government officials to murders of secular intellectuals, revealed in court the names of senior ultra-conservative clerics who had allegedly been behind a spate of political murders and extra-judicial killings between 1990 and 1998.

It should be mentioned, however, that in the first two years of Khatami's presidency, Iranian parliament enacted several laws significant to women. A law was passed that permitted women civil servants to retire after twenty years of service. For the first time, some 5,000 women were given a chance to run for 220,000 local council seats in cities, towns, and villages across the country. Nearly 300 women were elected to local city councils. Many NGOs actively promoted women's rights in both rural and urban areas. Increasing numbers of Iranian women were drawn less to the political arena and more to the practical control of their lives within political, social, and economic institutions, irrespective of the ideological configuration of these institutions. Khatami's administration proved incapable of curbing the repressive security apparatus, as the latter continued to act independently of the executive branch.

The slaying in late 1998 of five prominent secular critics of the Islamic government's conservative faction renewed fears of long-anticipated ideological and political turmoil and further related violence throughout the country. The killing of former Labor Minister Dariush Foruhar and his wife, Parvaneh Eskandari, who belonged to the outlawed National Iranian People's Party and who were living under house arrest, spread shock waves among the reformists. In the ensuing weeks, the kidnapping and slayings of writers and social critics who had been openly critical of the ruling clerical establishment fueled fears of broader violence and further chilled open dissent.

Several structural obstacles continue to stand in the way of building a civil society in Iran. For these barriers to be removed, there needs to be a balance between civil society and state organs. Such a balance requires the existence of an independent judiciary, separation of powers, and a free press. The absence of these standards in Iran is further confounded by the fact that ideological loyalties and commitments continue to inform the identity of political groups and the degree to which they can effectively operate within a safe context. While Iranian society was exposed to and imbued with modern ideas and paradigms, Iranian politics continued to straddle autocratic and democratic tendencies. The result was an intensified power struggle between different factions of the clerical regime with masses of ordinary people, secularists, and Islamic revisionists caught in the middle.

The Student Protests and the Free Press

Iran has a long tradition and political history of student protests and activism. Students have consistently challenged state authorities and state institutions, becoming an integral part of the country's modern history of anti-state contestation. A recurring feature of the post-revolutionary period, student protests have continued to flare up and are unlikely to disappear in the near future. Access to university education has led to the rise of a new generation that is highly critical of the unfulfilled promises of the 1979 Revolution.

The student demonstrations of July 8–14, 1999, were driven mainly by a protest against the closure of *Salaam*—a reformist and left-leaning Islamic daily newspaper that had begun to release critically significant information regarding the fall 1998 killings of secular reformists, including writers and journalists. The protests made clear that students were willing to voice their dissent over the suppression of the news media. Controlled by the conservatives, Tehran's Public Court 1410, commonly known as the Press Court, which hears most cases relating to journalists and publications based in Tehran, banned several pro-reform dailies. In one issue, it called for an end to the death penalty, while questioning Iran's law of retribution (*qasas*). The daily suggested that Iranian law replace "using violence" against criminals with the "modern" approach of reforming rather than punishing criminals. The closure of *Neshat* set off a new battle between the reformers and the conservatives, with the former arguing that the closure lacked a legal basis.

The press—in the absence of legitimate political parties, and given the myriad obstacles it faced—became not only a bastion of the struggle against the conservatives but also a driving force behind the country's political development. In many respects, the press—especially the elements of it supporting reform—took the place of political parties in Iran, a prospect that frightened the right-wing clergy and their supporters.

Many experts held that the students' demands were more broadly popular in nature and signified the cumulative resentment of the public against the suppression of the press and the restriction of other fundamental civil liberties and universal rights—and as such, were by no means particular to the university students alone. Indeed, the students' demands—transparency, accountability, integrity, and fairness in government—reflected broader societal demands. Another perspective advanced in press reports was that Iranian politics, highly complex and evolving, had to come to terms with the country's new political realities. The religio-political establishment used excuses such as the "foreign-inspired" demonstrations and the country's imminent political chaos to stop rallies, sabotaging the trend toward political liberalization and social reform.

Another view held that the student protests, which revolved around the curbs on press freedoms, "were hijacked by hard-liners determined to foment violence in order to prove President Khatami was incapable of controlling the country." Perhaps the most obvious message to emerge from these protests was the existence of a crisis of legitimacy and a crisis of confidence in the ruling conservative establishment. The ensuing pro-regime demonstration, organized by the conservative establishment to counter the student protests, failed to restore lost confidence.[21] The government finally quelled the protests by placing a ban on rallies.

The Clinton administration, having painted terrorism as one of the most important security challenges to the United States, was keen on maintaining strong sanctions against states such as Iran, Iraq, Libya, and Sudan. In 1996, Clinton signed legislation imposing tough new sanctions on companies that invested in Iran and Libya—nations considered to be state sponsors of terrorism.[22] The Clinton administration sought to build a relationship with President Khatami after his surprise 1997 election, but was shackled by the 1996 Khobar Towers bombing—in which nineteen US service members were killed and 500 people were injured—as well as by Iranian domestic politics.

Looking for compromise, the Clinton administration sent a letter to Khatami indicating that Washington had clear evidence that the Islamic Revolutionary Guard Corps (IRGC) had a direct hand in the Khobar Towers attacks. Washington insisted that Tehran hold accountable those responsible for the attacks and sought Khatami's assistance in ending Iranian support for terrorism. The message clearly pointed out that the United States wished to work toward better relations with Iran, noting that the attacks preceded Khatami's election. Both Clinton and Khatami urged face-to-face informal exchanges to reduce enmity and prepare the groundwork for improved relations.

Increasingly, however, the US intelligence community came to the realization that they might have overestimated Khatami's ability to deliver on his own, without having to consider the views of other key Iranian leaders, such as Supreme Leader Ayatollah Khamenei.[23] Subsequently, the Clinton administration adopted a neutral position vis-à-vis the 1999 student protests and remained silent as the nationwide student protests were violently suppressed. Although the student protests failed to achieve their goals, they nevertheless laid the foundation for the Green Movement that emerged almost a decade later.

The tragic attacks on the United States on September 11, 2001, brought Iran and the United States into close cooperation over the future of Afghanistan. The Khatami administration shared intelligence with Washington regarding the presence of Al-Qaeda in Afghanistan, and cooperated with the Bush administration in the ensuing years over the future of that country. Subsequently, however, President George W. Bush characterized Iran, along with North Korea and Iraq, as part of the "Axis of Evil" in his State of the Union address on January 29, 2002—a move generally regarded as an outright US denouncement of Iran's expanding reach in the region. This undermined the Khatami administration beyond repair, catapulting a populist—Mahmoud Ahmadinejad—to the top of Iran's political slate in the next presidential election. Like his predecessors, President Bush chose geopolitics over Khatami's reformist agenda.

The Green Movement

In 2009, Iran experienced a unique and dramatic social movement that came to be known as the "Green Movement." This movement posed a serious challenge to the Islamic Republic, gaining an unprecedented traction and popularity in urban areas nearly three decades after the country had witnessed such massive demonstrations and street protests. The movement embodied aspirations of the disaffected youth as well as the disenchanted public who have long advocated democracy and social change enthusiastically.

The dramatic 2009 post-election protests in Iran, which arose in reaction to disputed election results that declared Ahmadinejad president for another term, shook the foundation of the Islamic Republic. On June 13, 2009, Islamic Republic officials announced that incumbent president Mahmoud Ahmadinejad had won a landslide victory. His opponent, Mir Hossein Moussavi, accused Ahmadinejad's camp of rigging the results. After the announcement, Moussavi supporters took to the streets to vehemently protest the election. The so-called "Green Movement," reminiscent of the "color revolutions" in Ukraine and Georgia, posed a homegrown and popular threat to the country's power structure.

The reach of social networking and digital communication diminished the effectiveness of the usual narrative of the conservative leadership, which blamed an externally directed conspiracy for the protests. Riot police and *Basiji* paramilitary forces suppressed the demonstrations immediately following the election. Despite the fact that the street protests in Tehran and other provinces of Iran faded away in the face of the government crackdown, the political cleavages within the ruling establishment remained. Moreover, the credibility of the Ahmadinejad administration sank so low that a cloud of doubt would hang over Ahmadinejad's presidency for the next four years.

Initially, President Obama avoided making any public remarks about these developments in Iran. Later, however, he took a much tougher stance. On June 15, 2009, Obama commented: "It is up to Iranians to make decisions about who Iran's leaders will be," adding that "we respect Iranian sovereignty and want to avoid the United States being the issue inside of Iran."[24] Obama went on to assert: "I am deeply troubled by the violence that I have been seeing on television. I think that the democratic process—free speech, the ability of people to peacefully dissent—all those are universal values and need to be respected."[25] Behind Obama's cautionary and measured response to the riots in Iran lay an openness to the idea of a détente with Iran. Geopolitical considerations of reaching a nuclear deal kept Obama on the sidelines. This came as no surprise, as too often political leaders argue that national security concerns must take precedence over human rights considerations.[26]

The resurgence of an Islamic moderate in the 2013 presidential elections carried the promise of upending human rights regression and of normalization of relations with the West. Many Iranians hoped, given the Iranian political context, that Islamic moderates could play a more effective role in shaping the future than Islamic populists, although no swift or radical change was expected. Hassan Rouhani's victory in Iran's 2013 presidential election was a clear protest vote against his predecessor's mismanagement of Iran's relations with the Western world. It also demonstrated that many Iranians still prefer reform to revolution, because the latter more often than not produces chaos, instability, uncertainty, and despotism.[27] The Rouhani administration engaged in serious negotiations with the West and reached an interim deal with them over Iran's nuclear program. Rouhani prioritized Iran's economic recovery and the general well-being of the Iranian people over the ongoing enmity with the United States and Iran's political isolation.

Emphasizing that diplomacy with the Western world was the key to breaking Iran's isolation and that it was a "win-win" situation for both Iran and the West, the Rouhani administration took the view that beyond routing the Islamic State in Iraq and Syria (ISIS), Iran and the United States shared regional interests, including containing the spread of sectarianism, stability in Iraq and Afghanistan, and a possible rapprochement between Iran and its Arab neighbors and Turkey. Those regional relationships had been negatively impacted by disagreements over the Syrian crisis, with Iran supporting the Bashar Assad regime and the others vehemently opposing it.[28] Rouhani's presidency provided the perspective necessary to break away from Ahmadinejad's outdated and futile approach.[29]

The 2016 victory of Donald Trump in the US presidential election ended this optimistic trend in Iran, as the new president pulled out of the nuclear deal (JCPOA) and imposed a new set of sanctions on Iran even as Iran remained in full compliance with the deal. The relationship between Washington and Tehran deteriorated into a new cold war. These new sanctions had a chilling effect on Iran's economy and financial dealings with international banks. Iran also suffered badly under a severe shortage of supplies to fight the COVID-19 pandemic. These sanctions were a major setback to the Rouhani administration and its economic agenda.

Iranian Feminism on the Rise

Having gone through a tumultuous trajectory, the women's movement in Iran has gradually grown into a skillful and inspiring feminist model for those seeking equal rights and gender justice under authoritarian Islamist regimes, writes Nayereh Tohidi, Professor and founding Director of the Middle Eastern and Islamic Studies Program at California State University, Northridge.[30] While the 1979 Islamist Revolution led to profound socio-political changes and societal mobilization of both men and women, it soon implemented many retrogressive and discriminatory laws and policies against women, such as the enforcement of the mandatory wearing of hijabs, and gender segregation. The reformist era under President Khatami (1997–2005) triggered some relatively important socio-political openings and an upsurge of civil society discourse. More than anything, however, the chief distinguishing characteristic of this era was the emergence of a feminist press.

Women's press outlets, such as *Farzaneh* and *Zanan*, to which secular women regularly contributed, provided feminists a valuable forum for social and political protest.[31] This trend was reversed when President Ahmadinejad (2005–13) took office, implementing populist policies and repressing free media and civil society organizations, including women's groups. With the Rouhani ascendancy to power in 2013, Iranian women have seen some openness and improvements in the defense of their human rights, but improvement of their overall status has been blocked by hard-liners, who still held sway over the moderate president.[32]

Secular feminists continue to fight against unjust laws and restrictions. Divorce laws are no longer enforced under the authority of secular family courts where wives and husbands could enjoy comparable rights to divorce. Under the law, only husbands have a unilateral right of divorce. A husband has absolute rights over his wife, including her sexual availability, and he can forbid her from working outside the home.[33] Gender equality, Ziba Mir-Hosseini ruefully notes, is a notion to which Iranian male intellectuals, secular as well as religious, still do not subscribe. They seem to concur with the gender model embedded in *Shari'a* legal rules. For them, gender is only part of a larger problem that will go away when their political vision is realized.[34]

Some Iranian women within government circles, such as the former Representative Elaheh Koolaee, have predicted that Iranian officials should anticipate an emerging gender crisis in the future and warned of its consequences. While pointing to the gap between the ideals of the Islamic Republic and the reality of women's rights and status on the ground, Koolaee argues that the problem for Iranian women emanates largely from "the influence of traditional Islam" on the state's conservative forces.[35]

Feminists in Iran have generally framed their grievances and demands in Islamic jargon and have relied on cultural assets to press for women's rights and equality. For example, Valentine Moghadam writes about a group of women parliamentarians that petitioned Islamic clerics in October 2002 to demand that blood money compensation paid to the family of a murdered woman to be the same as that paid for a man. They justified the proposed change on the ground that women were now working and supporting their families.[36] In other cases, women have increasingly relied on Islamic arguments to limit polygamy.[37]

Islamic and secular women alike have begun to reject their confinement to the home and have managed to participate in the public sphere through their socioeconomic activities.[38] In doing so, they have contributed significantly to the development of civil society access for women in Iran. Some Islamist women have argued that "the ideals of the revolution cannot be attained unless women are present in the public sphere."[39] Thus, weaponizing the goals of the revolution itself in the process of attaining their particularized rights. Many NGOs have actively promoted women's rights in both rural and urban areas. The Iranian Islamic Women's Institute, headed by Azam Taleghani, was one such NGO. Its aim was to improve women's status by providing literacy classes, informing women of their rights, offering them free legal advice, and bolstering their financial independence with training in diverse activities, including carpet weaving, pottery making, and sewing.[40] Like the second wave of feminism in the West, economic empowerment is as important as equal access to the courts or political rights.

Many of Iran's experts, such as Ziba Mir-Hosseini, have argued that in order to achieve sustainable and deep-seated change, cooperation, dialogue, and consensus between Islamic and secular feminists is imperative. Such dialogue is key to coping with injustices that stem from patriarchal customs and laws based on archaic interpretations of the *Shari'a*. Far from mutually opposed, there exists a strong synergy between and among perspectives from Islamic studies, feminism, and broader human rights. This is especially noteworthy in launching an effective campaign against gender discrimination in Muslim contexts where the links between religious and political aspects of identity are particularly strong. Islamic feminists have increasingly become part of this new trend of reformist movement and thought.[41]

Similarly, Valentine M. Moghadam has underlined the need for a more inclusive and cross-cultural understanding of feminism and the global women's movement. Islamic feminists, according to Moghadam, clearly engage with transnational feminism.[42] Feminist movements of all kinds—secular and Islamic—"contribute to dialogue, knowledge, coalition building, and collective action."[43] This sentiment is echoed by Nayereh Tohidi, who argues that Islamic feminists have been willing to collaborate with their non-Islamic counterparts around women's common demands within frameworks consonant with the UN Convention on the Elimination of All Forms of Discrimination Against Women (CEDAW). Thus, Islamic feminists should not be seen as a rival force, but rather as a welcome addition to the diverse spectrum of global feminist movements, granted that they recognize as valid the diversity and plurality of feminist status for equal rights.[44]

The Iranian reform movement received a significant boost in 2003 when Shirin Ebadi, an Iranian lawyer, became the first Muslim woman to win the Nobel Peace prize. It is worth noting that Ebadi was also Iran's first female judge in 1969 under the Shah's regime; she lost her job as a lawyer after the Iranian Revolution. Ebadi continued her legal practice by devoting her time to courageously protecting the rights of women and children, working in a restrictive environment until massive street protests, in reaction to the disputed 2009 presidential elections, erupted. She was forced to live in exile because of her support for those protesters.

The Nobel Prize further mobilized a resurgent and animated women's rights movement that was already one of the country's most striking features.[45] The so-called "One Million Signatures Campaign," led by Noushin Ahmadi Khorasani and Parvin Ardalan and aimed at ending the regime's discriminatory laws against women, activated a grassroots feminist movement. Ebadi under-scored the importance of this movement, noting that despite the state's fierce repression—everything from laws that permitted ston-ing and polygamy to morality police who harassed women on the street for not dressing modestly—Iran has maintained a proliferating and vibrant women's movement.[46]

As a result, many Iranian women see an opportunity to play a greater role in the global movement for civil society. They regard global institutions and conventions, such as CEDAW, as major ave-nues to protect and promote their rights. Human rights activists and experts in and outside of Iran, however, have consistently noted that the international focus on Iran's nuclear program has hindered efforts to advance human rights reforms. Ebadi echoes the same sentiment: "Unfortunately, the nuclear energy issue has stalemated many issues in Iran, the most important being the issue of human rights."[47] The deadlock around the reality of Iran's nuclear enrichment, and its acknowledged legitimacy by the Western world, has been an effective tool of distraction and sleight of hand played by the regime. The pursuit of women's rights, however, will not be deterred or distracted from forever and the diligent activists who have propelled this movement forward, despite pain and frustration, will eventually see the fruits of their struggle.

It is worth noting, however, that the Trump administration's sanctions on Iran have invariably hurt the women's movement in Iran. Many Iranian observers maintain that if the external pressure was intended to advance women's rights, there is little to no evidence that this goal was achieved. The pervasive debate among women activists in Iran now revolves largely around terrifying and ongoing threats to the country's security and the people's well-being. Women have not just suffered economically, but also by losing that liberating force that enabled them to be financially autonomous.[48] The gargantuan challenges that Iranian women face in contesting their government's discriminatory laws and repressive measures are difficult enough without the paralyzing impact of sanctions. If they could have sent one central message to the Trump administration, it might have been a quote from the thirteenth-century Persian poet, Sa'adi, who stated: "I do not expect any favors from you. Just do no harm."[49]

Women in Post-revolutionary Iran

In the post-Green Movement era, opinions vary regarding the status of women's progress toward achieving their rights. Some argue that the women's struggle against religious oppression rages on and that those who now imagine women as immutably subjugated have a very short-sighted view of history.[50] Others warn that women's rights activism and social movements inside the country more generally have been forced to retreat. More specifically, press freedom has significantly diminished, with the state's tight grip on journalists leading to the decline of a sector that in the past has successfully led the reform movement. Several reformist publications—such as *Mardom Emrooz* and *Zanan-e Emrooz*, both of which promoted women's rights—have been shut down. These and similar publications served as a foundation for rights activism in post-revolutionary Iran. In the face of these restrictions, expression of political dissent and rights demands have increasingly moved online. Social media, including Facebook and Viber, is likely to serve as an important medium for exposing the regime's human rights abuses.[51]

On balance, however, it is important to realize that Iranian women have played a significant role in nudging along social change in post-revolutionary Iran. More specifically, many experts mention the role of women in pushing for reforms in law, engaging in struggles for political freedoms through culture and the arts, and facing a profound transformation in the family structure brought on by socioeconomic change. Although Iranian women face many obstacles in their attempts to achieve gender equality, they have achieved a degree of self-awareness unprecedented in modern Iran.

Some experts, such as Arzoo Osanloo, point out that Iranian women have played a critical role in changing archaic laws. Osanloo points to the codification of laws derived from Islamic principles, noting that the process has been flexible, fluid, and accommodating, discrediting the notion that a law is unchangeable solely because it is based on a *Shari'a* understanding of Islamic principles. Legal scholars and activists have increasingly voiced their opinions through scholarship and public awareness campaigns, in part because of the role that the post-revolutionary state has assigned to women as signifiers of morality. The state, Osanloo argues, has enhanced women's issues to a level where Iranian women can question the state's legitimacy with regards to how it treats them. The broader debates between legislators seeking a face-saving way to prohibit stoning without overreaching into the domain of Islamic jurists, as well as closing the gender gap in *diya* (blood money) serve as good examples here. In short, women's negotiating power has increased.[52]

Another gender studies expert, Farzaneh Milani, examines the evolution of women's social context through extant literary movements, an important way in which Iranian women have expressed their identities and their claims. She describes an unprecedented flourishing of women's literature as an unexpected benefit of the 1979 Revolution. The Islamic Republic failed to silence prominent women writers and poets for a long time, although it banned most of them in the immediate aftermath of the revolution, and succeeded in driving others into exile.

Despite a myriad of problems that women poets and writers face—such as gender resegregation, socioeconomic hardships, the eight-year war with Iraq, censorship, and conformity to the Islamic Republic's interpretation of morality—they have attained a stature previously reserved solely for men. Comparing the writings of the older generation, such as the works of Simin Behbahani and Forugh Farrokhzad, to those of the younger generation, such as Fariba Vafi's *My Bird* (2003), Milani demonstrates the pioneering role that women have played in redesigning and reimagining the family unit.[53]

One of the most significant changes since the 1979 Revolution is the transformation of the social structure of the Iranian family. Djavad Salehi-Isfahani looks at the past three decades and argues that Iranian families have seen a profound transformation. At the time of the Islamic Revolution in 1979, Salehi-Isfahani notes, the average family lived in a rural area in a home with no running water and no accessible school beyond the primary grades. Neither husband nor wife could read or write. The wife would give birth to six or seven children on average, as her main roles were confined to cooking, cleaning, and struggling to keep her children alive.[54]

The three decades of transformation since the revolution, Salehi-Isfahani maintains, have resulted in a narrowing gap between urban and rural residents and between men and women. The most striking aspect of this change is the narrowing gender gap in education. A generation ago, women had less than half the education of their husbands. Today, urban women are on average more educated than urban men, and in rural areas women have about the same level of education as men. Equality in education, coupled with a lower burden of fertility, has improved women's power within the family, helping channel family resources in the direction of child education.[55] Despite lower fertility and higher education leading to more balanced families, women still largely lack the earning opportunities enjoyed by male Iranians. Women account for only one-fourth of the income-earning labor force, and their rate of unemployment is twice that of men. Barriers to women's employment are due in part to the lack of appropriate jobs for women, but there is also a powerful ideological barrier. Women's struggle for political power is by no means assured.[56]

A recently amended family law requiring men to seek their wife's permission before taking a second wife has resulted in a conservative pushback on a number of fronts. Prior to the enactment of the Family Protection Law in 1967, there was no prohibition on polygamy for men, but for the first time, according to the Article 14 of this law, remarriage of men became subject to the court's permission, allowing the latter to inquire about whether or not the men under review have proper financial assets. As a result of the 1974 Family Protection Law, and more specifically its Article 16, the remarriage of men without the consent of the current wife was declared unconstitutional. Following the 1979 Revolution, the Family Protection Law remained intact—that is, the court approved the same guidelines regarding the men's conditional remarriage. Several attempts to remove this condition have thus far been unsuccessful. Similarly, in the new Family Protection Law (2012) under the Islamic Republic, a man's second marriage continues to be a choice contingent upon obtaining permission from his current wife.[57]

Religious Minorities

According to an annual US State Department report (2019 Report on International Religious Freedom: Iran), the Iranian government has continued to imprison, harass, and intimidate people based on their religious beliefs. In 2019, religious minorities, such as Sunni Muslims and Sufis, as well as Baha'is, Christians, Jews, and Zoroastrians, encountered all kinds of discrimination, including government and societal discrimination. The government "convicted and executed dissidents, political reformers, and peaceful protesters on charges of enmity against God and anti-Islamic propaganda."[58] The constitution defines the country as an Islamic republic and specifies Twelver Ja'afari Shi'a Islam as the official state religion. Approximately ninety percent of Iran's population is Shi'ite.

Iran's constitution renders it abundantly clear that all laws must be based on "Islamic criteria" in lockstep with an official interpretation of Shari'a. Thus, citizens shall enjoy human, political, economic, and other rights, "in conformity with Islamic criteria."[59] The constitution views Zoroastrians, Jews, and Christians as the only recognized religious minorities permitted to conduct their own worship and form their own religious societies within the confinement of the law. Human rights NGOs have frequently reported the disproportionately large number of executions of Sunni prisoners, especially Kurds, Baluchis, and Arabs. On numerous occasions, the government has harassed, interrogated, and arrested Baha'is, non-Armenian Christians (especially converts), Sunni Muslims, and other religious minorities.[60]

It is important to realize that the problems raised by minority group rights are many, varied, and complex. Some observers have defended a comprehensive pluralism as the best framework to address the minorities issue. In this framework, "human rights are neither strictly universal nor purely particular. Rather, they ought to be shaped by a dynamic and evolving tension caused by a simultaneous pull toward the universal and toward the particular."[61] The discussion of comprehensive pluralism stands against the failure to treat all humans with respect and dignity.

Others have noted that there are few legally binding provisions concerning minority rights, and those that do exist tend to convey contested meanings. Furthermore, there is no definition of a minority under international law, in part because of the diversity of factual situations in which minorities live.[62] To this day, legal experts add, "the effective measures for the protection of minorities are still lacking."[63] For the most part, the protection of minority rights is directly linked to the state's goodwill. That explains why "purely legal issues cannot be successfully resolved until states accept the proposition that the protection of minorities is essentially in their own interests."[64]

The preceding arguments compel an investigation of factors that are often invoked cynically to mask religious intolerance. Historically, the treatment of non-Muslim minorities in Iran has been influenced by the states' nationalist politics, local clergy's manipulation of events, anti-Western attitudes, and tension between secular and Islamic elites. Thus, it is wrong to argue that the issue of religious minorities was created by the Islamic Republic.[65] Yet what is a unique byproduct of the theocratic state since the 1979 Iranian Revolution is the institutionalization of segmentation: "*aqaliate*" (minority), "the other," "the marginal," and "the separate from us."[66]

Although expressions of coexistence, tolerance, and cooperation in the 1990s were many, improvements in the conditions of recognized religious minorities have been minimal. The penal code remained unchanged. Discrimination in employment continued. The situation of the Baha'is and Iranian Christian converts progressively deteriorated.[67] It is worth noting that, as Nazila Ghanea asserts, the Iranian Baha'i community has never sought territorial autonomy or self-determination. Rather, they have asked for the full respect of their individual human rights as enjoyed by other Iranian citizens as well as the recognition of their group rights, and that their community is allowed to enjoy its rights and privileges collectively. Yet Baha'is, who remain outside the legal realms of tolerance and engagement, represent an unresolved challenge to the Islamic Republic.[68]

Rouhani's Reformist Agenda

Rouhani's first term saw some progress in the country's human rights situation. In his early days in office, in a carefully crafted, symbolic move, Rouhani freed eighty political prisoners, including a prominent human rights lawyer and activist, Nasrin Sotoudeh, who had been imprisoned following protests over the disputed 2009 presidential elections. This clearly led to a more relaxed social and political atmosphere under the presidency of Rouhani. That said, Rouhani could not play a sustained role in enhancing human rights conditions in the aftermath of the Trump administration withdrawal from the nuclear deal. The imposition of new sanctions on Iran dramatically undermined Iran's economic conditions, giving rise to widespread public discontent and street protests.

In Rouhani's second term, on at least two occasions the low-income classes took to the streets to protest their worsening economic conditions. The 2017–18 protests, which initially broke out in the northern city of Mashhad, were spurred on largely in reaction to the country's stunted economy and the high prices of basic goods such as rice, meat, eggs, and cooking oil. The protests turned into an open rebellion against the political regime. Among the major participants in these protests were working-class Iranians who sought higher wages and an end to rampant unemployment. They were frustrated that the economy has been glacially slow to grow despite the lifting of sanctions in the aftermath of the 2015 nuclear deal. The unemployed and low-income young people expressed similar grievances.

In a sudden announcement on November 15, 2019, the Rouhani administration increased gas prices by approximately 300 percent, while introducing a new rationing system.[69] The government's plan was to prevent gas smuggling to neighboring countries and to raise funds to subsidize programs directed toward assisting the poor. The protests swept around several cities, with demonstrators openly chanting anti-government slogans. The regime used tear gas, water cannons, and live ammunition to disperse the protesters. The government also nearly completely shut down the internet for five days to prevent images of the protests and crackdown from spreading over social media.

In both cases, the protesters' demands had nothing to do with democratic aspirations or the state of civil society and much to do with their ongoing economic grievances. The Iranian media frequently reported layoffs and strikes by workers who had received no wages for months. In both cases, the government's reactions were much harsher—as evidenced by the number of protesters killed by riot police—than those intended to contain the spread of the 1999 student protests and the 2009 Green Movement.

It is essential to underscore the importance of the unintended consequences of US sanctions, including reinforcing the authoritarian impulses of the ruling elites. The fact remains that demands for democratic values—and human rights more generally—are unlikely to flourish during difficult economic times, but they remain strikingly relevant as a legitimate tool for empowering both the educated and voiceless sectors of the population. US sanctions on Iran have weakened the country's middle class, and, with that, have dramatically undercut the voices of globalization and political moderation.[70] Today, Iran's middle class has lost its appetite for political development as it struggles to maintain some modicum of economic security. While US sanctions are not the direct cause of this attitudinal reorientation, they have contributed greatly to feelings of indifference and poor motivation.

Raisi's Rise to Power

Raisi's record on crackdown and human rights has faced massive criticism, both internal and external. In the 1980s, writes Hadi Ghaemi, founder and Executive Director of the Center for Human Rights in Iran, Ayatollah Ruhollah Khomeini issued an order that any prisoner who still held to his or her political beliefs should be executed. He appointed four men, including Raisi, to the so-called "Death Committee" to implement his order.[71] It should be also noted that the United States imposed sanctions on Raisi in 2019 for human rights violations, including the 1980s executions and his role in the suppression of protesters in the 2009 Green Movement protests.[72]

The young Raisi, a 28-year-old prosecutor at the time, was reportedly instrumental in planning and organizing the massacre. Raisi was subsequently promoted to Prosecutor General of Tehran, a position he held until 1994. Between 1994 and 2021, as the elected president of the Islamic Republic, he served as the Director of the National Inspection Organization, the most potent oversight body under the judiciary, and became the first deputy under the chief of the judiciary, and later Iran's General Prosecutor, while also serving as head of the Astan Quds Foundation, an economically powerful religious institution. Before being elected as the country's president, he also served as head of the judiciary.[73] His record as Iran's judiciary chief from 2019–21 invited heavy criticism from the legal community and beyond. In this capacity, he led a campaign of repression, rendering the judicial system heavily involved in security and intelligence agencies.[74]

Crucially, many human rights organizations have raised red flags about Raisi's background as the head of the Iranian judiciary. His long career in Iran's judicial system has been blatantly marked with executions and prison sentences, as well as repression and a suffocating political environment, all of which has been on the rise in recent years under his watch as the country's chief of judiciary. The Center for Human Rights in Iran as well as many human rights activists have called for accountability for Raisi's human rights abuses. More specifically, Amnesty International's Secretary General Agnès Callamard has asked for an investigation into Raisi's crimes.[75]

Conclusion

The US criticism of Iran's human rights record has often been grounded in geopolitics, rather than genuine concerns for the well-being of the Iranian people. Equally confounding but understandable has been Washington's strategic reticence to castigate Iran's poor human rights record in pursuit of broader national interest. The only constant in the US foreign policy agenda has been its inconsistent attempt to foster human rights in different political contexts. Historically, US security concerns and economic interests have undermined long-term human rights objectives of its foreign policy.[76]

Following the 1979 Iranian Revolution, Washington has repeatedly used human rights to delegitimize the Islamic Republic. Several US administrations, however, have also chosen to refrain from supporting Iranian political dissents, including the student protests (1999) and the Green Movement (2009), largely for geopolitical concerns. The Trump administration reiterated the language of human rights to attack adversaries like China and Iran, but deliberately refrained from criticizing Saudi Arabia when the latter recklessly killed, dismembered, and destroyed the remains of dissident journalist Jamal Khashoggi, a legal resident of the United States and a staff writer of the *Washington Post*, in its consulate in Istanbul.[77] The Biden administration fell short of applying sanctions as a viable option against the powerful Saudi figure Crown Prince Mohammad bin Salman, known to be responsible for the murder of Khashoggi, even though Biden promised to punish senior Saudi leaders during his election campaign.

The last four years, Karen Kramer points out, have been devastating for human rights in Iran. Several serious protests over economic grievances and political repression have been crushed by security forces. The judiciary has meted out harsh prison sentences to human rights lawyers and activists as well as death sentences to protesters and dissidents. Imprisoned lawyers and activists, such as the defense attorney Nasrin Sotoudeh and the recently released activist Narges Mohammadi, have successfully voiced their messages against suppression. Their letters from prison continue to circulate widely on Iranian social media. Voicing support for these courageous activists while denouncing their prosecution in international forums is both morally and strategically warranted.[78] A holistic approach to security that places human rights on an equal footing with other strategic issues is ultimately the most effective way to promote peace, stability, and political and economic development in the troubled Middle East.[79]

The history of the last forty years demonstrates that the authorities of the Islamic Republic have vigorously restricted human rights and continue to suppress expression, association, and assembly. Security forces systematically engage in lethal crackdowns to crush public gatherings, arbitrarily detaining thousands of protesters. Women continue to face inequality and mistreatment, just as ethnic and religious minorities encounter discrimination. Torture and other ill-treatment remain endemic. There are widespread systematic denials of fair trials. The state routinely invokes repressive tactics to suppress street unrest, blaming external intrusion as the main cause of this turmoil.

The fear of uncertainty and political instability inside Iran plays into the hands of Iran's authoritarian regime. According to Abbas Amanat, Professor of History and International Studies at Yale University and Director of the Yale Program in Iranian Studies at the MacMillan Center for International and Area Studies, the Islamic Republic, for nearly four decades since 1979, and despite a barrage of domestic and international challenges, has been able to provide Iran with security at its borders and a notable degree of internal stability. This at a time when the entire region has experienced domestic conflict, civil war, military interventions by superpowers, and prolonged and brutal occupation. Such stability, however, has come at the price of domestic repression, social divisions, and fervent discontent that periodically have exploded and are likely to explode again.[80]

Amanat goes on to cite the renowned Iranian thinker Mohammad Ghazzali (1058–1111), who, almost nine centuries ago, said "a hundred years of oppression is better than a day of chaos."[81] A contrasting view is offered by Bhikhu Parek, who argues that history suggests that economic development, national unity, and social solidarity, while valuable goals, are rarely a good rationale for the denial of internationally recognized human rights.[82] One major question emerges: What is the most effective way to promote human rights around the world? Is it relying on treaty-based bodies to engage states? Supporting local and global social movements? Protecting and expanding civic space? Supporting non-state actors? Supporting national human rights institutions? Educating the public about human rights? Or applying punitive measures such as sanctions and trade embargos? While there may be agreement on the feasibility and desirability of some of these, there is no consensus on how sanctions could create an environment conducive to human rights.

As the Islamic Republic of Iran has faced more sanctions and economic hardship, it has tightened its grip on civil society organizations and human rights activists. Several Iranian presidents since the 1990s, including Rafsanjani, Khatami, and Rouhani, promised to extricate human rights from national security matters, treating them as bona fide dignity-related issues that deserve fair attention. Yet, domestic factors having to do with the incompetency and mismanagement on the one hand, and external pressures aimed at isolating Iran on the other, have contributed to the longevity of a repressive regime.

PART II

REGIONAL CONTEXT

4

IRAN'S FOREIGN POLICY

NAVIGATING IDEOLOGICAL AND GEOPOLITICAL SPHERES

The victory of the Iranian Revolution electrified Islamists the world over. In fact, there were several manifestations of the resurgent Islamist ideology.[1] The immediate impact of Islamism was felt in the takeover of the Grand Mosque in Mecca (November–December 1979) following the riots by Shi'ites in eastern oil fields in Saudi Arabia. The 1980s saw the formation of an elite revolutionary military force. Iraq's invasion of Iran on September 22, 1980, not only failed to dissuade the Iranians from pursuing their revolutionary goals but also led them to double down on these efforts. Ironically, it was in the midst of that war that the Iranian revolutionaries came up with the idea of forming the Islamic Revolutionary Guard Corps (IRGC) Quds Force, tasking it with "liberating" Palestine and exporting the revolution beyond Iran's borders.[2]

In the ensuing decades, the IRGC Quds Force operated covertly throughout the Middle East. Israel's invasion of Lebanon in 1982 to drive the Palestine Liberation Organization (PLO) out of southern Lebanon provided the grounds for one of the Islamic Republic's key foreign policy objectives—namely the creation of Hezbollah. Founded by Iranian revolutionaries within the IRGC, Hezbollah fundamentally altered the nature of Islamic insurgency through its ideological culture of martyrdom. By throwing their support behind Hezbollah and Palestinian Islamists, the Islamic Republic claimed a direct stake in the Israel—Palestine conflict. Since attaining this stake, Tehran has focused on calling for Israel's destruction, while simultaneously arming Palestinian Islamists and Hezbollah. The successful Hezbollah operations throughout the region became emblematic of Islamist ideology as the key ideological driver of Iran's foreign policy.[3]

How Islamic ideology shapes Iran's foreign policy can be traced to colonial and post-colonial contexts. Given the complex and evolving security challenges that Iran faces, no consistent foreign policy patterns can be discerned, as the country's ruling elites have often chosen to navigate sharply contrasting patterns, alternating between ideological and geopolitical considerations. Islamic ideology and symbols have often been deployed in the campaign against foreign military intervention in the Middle East. Iranian ruling elites, by contrast, have turned to rational calculations of the country's national interests in other circumstances. While the country's conservative elites have utilized Shi'ism as the vehicle of political legitimation, what has driven Tehran's foreign and regional policies has been, by any reckoning, the factual calculation of national interest.[4] Iran's relations with the six Arab monarchies of the Gulf Cooperation Council (GCC), for example, have been largely based on geopolitical considerations.[5]

This chapter intends to demonstrate how the Islamic Republic of Iran has managed to maintain a balance between the ideological and geopolitical imperatives of its foreign policy. Given the fast-changing political contexts and domestic constraints of Iranian politics, this equilibrium has been difficult to sustain. The core takeaway of this chapter is that religion remains only one of several key factors that contribute to national identity and Iranian foreign policy. Like any other state, the Islamic Republic makes hard-nosed and calculated policies in pursuit of its national security interests.[6]

In the sections that follow, I will first examine Iran's foreign policy in the first decade of revolution, including the Iran—Iraq War, the Israeli invasion of Lebanon, and the Salman Rushdie controversy. Next, I will shift our attention to the evolution of Iran's foreign policy in the post-Khomeini era by explaining recent developments in the Persian Gulf region in an attempt to understand the shifting security paradigms in the Persian Gulf, the downsizing of US military presence in the region, the cold war between Riyadh and Tehran, and the Abraham Accords and their implications. A closer look at these developments illustrates the expansion of Iran's influence as well as its limits. On balance, however, a geopolitical and pragmatic agenda—not ideological, cultural, or historical—have influenced Iran's foreign policy decisions. The idea that Iran's foreign policy is driven largely by ideology (and ideology alone) is a myth, as the following cases demonstrate. The perennial question persists—can the Islamic Republic follow a pragmatic foreign policy without sacrificing its ideological consistency and its integrity?

In considering the many complexities that Iran's foreign policy faces, perhaps the key challenge for Tehran has been its anti-US and anti-Israeli propaganda. In both cases, Iran's ideological positions and activities in the region have strengthened the hands of conservative hawks in Washington and right-wing hard-liners in Tel Aviv by providing an excuse for militarized responses based primarily on heated rhetoric. The Islamic Republic's hostile ideological position vis-à-vis the United States constitutes the major barrier to normalization of relations with Washington. Nor has the ongoing rhetoric of destroying Israel used by some ultra-conservative factions within Iran gained much traction in the region and beyond—especially as no actual destruction seems to have ever been planned or attempted.

The Iran—Iraq War

Iraqi forces invaded Iran on September 22, 1980, when Iran was undergoing profound revolutionary changes and its army was in disarray. In Iraq, the secular and Sunni Ba'athist ruling party of Saddam Hussein viewed Iran's 1979 Islamic Revolution as both a threat and an opportunity. The revolution created a threat in that a majority of the Iraqi population was Shi'a and thus susceptible to revolutionary messages aimed at overthrowing a regime that was neither appropriately religious nor sufficiently representative. But at the same time, it was an opportunity, in that Iran was seen as vulnerable due to domestic unrest in the aftermath of the revolution as the parties that formed the coalition opposed to the Shah were engaged in a violent power struggle. This division was seen by Iraqi leaders as a sign of weakness, convincing them that the time was opportune to launch a massive military attack against Iran.[7]

Known as the First Persian Gulf War, this war turned out to be most devastating because of its duration (1980–88), and the massive loss of human life and material destruction that it caused. As noted above, the most widely shared explanation for the Iraqi invasion of Iran was that Saddam Hussein's regime felt threatened by the spill-over of the Islamic Revolution into Iraq. This perception of threat was understandable, given that Iraq was a Shi'a-majority country under minority Sunni rule. According to this view, Saddam decided to preempt further unrest in Iraq's Shi'a-majority areas.[8] For others, however, this war was one of the most unnecessary wars in the history of the Middle East, as it occurred largely because of the rhetorical exaggerations of Iran's traditional threat perceptions in the Sunni Arab world.[9]

In the early years of the war, the Islamic Republic defined and justified its duel with Iraq in religious terms—a war imposed by foreign infidels seeking to deconstruct the Islamic Revolution. Ideology was also a key driver shaping Iran's military strategy and tactics, as witnessed by its decision to continue hostilities in 1982, after Iraqi forces had been repelled from Iranian territory, and by the repeated use of the "human wave" tactic, whereby masses of poorly armed and trained conscripts were sent to the front against the superior Iraqi military, basically as cannon fodder. Iran's ruling elites gradually moved toward a more pragmatic position in the latter half of the war, however, as years of a bloody and violent stalemate increasingly took its toll on the Iranian economy and on domestic public opinion of the regime. Ultimately, US attacks on Iranian oil platforms during the tanker war of the late 1980s and the downing of an Iranian aircraft by the *USS Vincennes*, killing 290 civilians, convinced Khomeini to accept a cease-fire with Iraq.

Both countries suffered economically, as their oil exports were adversely affected by the war. The war, experts noted, significantly diminished the global and regional production of oil. As major producing countries and members of OPEC, Iran and Iraq failed to reach prewar production levels. Oil prices spiked dramatically. Saudi

Arabia's oil industry and export corridors, situated very close to the war front, were affected by the war, just as oil production was impacted throughout the Persian Gulf area. After 1987, the so-called "tanker war" expanded to include all tankers exporting oil from the region. This was mainly an Iranian attempt to stop the Arab Gulf states from supporting Iraq. Instead, it led to the first vast US military deployment in the area to protect Gulf tankers from Iranian attacks.[10] The upshot was that Iran's revolutionary mantra alienated—with the exception of Syria, which remained Iran's sole Arab ally—most of its neighboring Arab countries.[11]

Israel's Invasion of Lebanon in 1982

Having signed a peace treaty with Egypt in 1978, Israeli leaders turned their attention to the Palestinian guerrillas operating out of Lebanon, where many had reorganized themselves after being expelled from Jordan. The Palestinians, led by Yasser Arafat and his PLO, began attacking Israel from Lebanon. On June 6, 1982, Israeli Prime Minister Menachem Begin launched Operation Peace for Galilee, invading Lebanon and seeking to force the PLO out of the country, thereby drawing the Israelis into an occupation of the southern portion of Lebanon that lasted for eighteen years until 2000.

The struggle against the Israeli occupation led to the birth, with considerable Iranian assistance, of Hezbollah, a resistance movement among Lebanon's downtrodden Shi'a. Hezbollah initially concentrated its efforts on fighting the Israeli occupation in cooperation with other Lebanese and Palestinian groups. By the 1990s, however, it had emerged as the key force in the resistance. Today, Hezbollah claims to have become a national liberation movement, and is still supported militarily and financially by Iran and Syria. Increasingly, however, Hezbollah has achieved a degree of independence in its policies and strategies from Iran and Syria by becoming as much a social welfare and political organization as an armed resistance militia.[12] Moreover, as the nation's largest community, with forty percent of the population, and having seen their Shi'a co-religionists in Iraq succeed in local elections there, Lebanon's Shi'a increasingly aspired to assume a fair share of power and resources in Lebanon.[13]

Through a relentless stream of casualties inflicted on Israeli troops, Hezbollah eventually forced their withdrawal in 2000, allowing it to gain a reputation as a tenacious and durable resistance force. The then prime minister of Israel, Ehud Barak, ordered the withdrawal, as nearly seventy percent of Israelis said that they could no longer see any compelling reason for sending their sons and daughters to die in Lebanon in the vain pursuit of security for Israel's northernmost towns.[14] The failure of Arab nationalism, Sunni fundamentalism, and secular nationalism in the Middle East gave the Islamic Republic a great ideological and strategic boost, allowing it to occupy an ideational vacuum with its message of resistance.[15] Indeed, one of Iran's highest priorities was—and continues to be—to export its soft power of Islamism and anti-colonialism throughout the region. Tehran has become adept at breaking down sectarian divides between Sunni and Shi'a by emphasizing common enemies, namely Israel and the United States, arguing that the spectacular rise of Hezbollah in Lebanon is due to its opposition to Israel.[16]

It is worth noting that the relations between Iran and Hezbollah are not of a patron—client type; they are much more complex. Although there exists a natural affinity between the two—Shi'ism, and, more specifically, a shared militant interpretation—Iran also considers Hezbollah a strategic asset against Israel. Hezbollah in turn balances its local and regional interests and maneuverability vis-à-vis Iran and Syria. Since Syria's withdrawal from Lebanon in 2005, Iran's influence has noticeably surged in Lebanon.

Some experts in the Middle East argue that Hezbollah should be seen not as a marginal pro-Iranian group but rather as a key player that holds considerable sway over Lebanon's domestic and foreign policy.[17] Hezbollah's deepening involvement in the Syrian civil war has provoked acute reactions from many observers in the Sunni Arab countries that are against the Bashar Assad regime, giving rise to fears of a sectarian conflict within Lebanon as well as in the rest of the region more generally. Hezbollah's leader, Hassan Nasrallah, has said that "no one can force them to leave Syria." This simply means that Hezbollah is intending to take root in Syria and subsequently apply its power and assets in certain Syrian districts the same way it has established its monopoly of power over southern Lebanon.[18]

The Rushdie Controversy

The publication of *The Satanic Verses* by Salman Rushdie in 1988 caused grim responses throughout the Muslim world because of its pejorative characterization of the Prophet Muhammad. Many Muslims saw the book "as being in the Western tradition of defamation of Islam and as part of the West's Crusade against basic Islamic values of community responsibility and obedience to God."[19] Rushdie's multiculturalism was also seen by some critics as a grotesque representation of the world, as his postcolonial stance appeared to have assumed the deconstructed style of postmodernism.[20] For some Muslims, as Homi Bhabha has noted, the transposition of sacred names (Muhammad) into profane spaces (Mahound and the prostitutes named after the wives of the Prophet) was considered destructive of the very fabric of their community. "To violate the system of naming," Bhabha argued, "is to make contingent and indeterminate... the shared standpoint of the community, its traditions of belief and enquiry."[21]

As a result, the book was banned in India, South Africa, Pakistan, Saudi Arabia, Egypt, Somalia, Bangladesh, Sudan, Malaysia, Indonesia, and Qatar. Moreover, after it won Britain's Whitbread Prize in 1988, Muslims burned the novel ceremonially in Bradford, England. Violent protests against the book flared throughout the Muslim world. In February 1989, for example, five people were killed by police gunfire during a protest in Islamabad, Pakistan. Throughout this controversy, Muslim states sought to use Islam to advance their own political objectives. Iran, in particular, sought to manipulate the controversy to gain the religious high ground and assert its leadership in the Muslim world.

It is in this context that on February 14, 1989, Khomeini infuriated the West by issuing a *fatwa* (religious edict) calling on Muslims to execute Rushdie for insulting Islam in his novel. The call was phrased in no uncertain terms: "Anyone who has access to the author of the book, but does not possess the power to execute him, should refer him to the people so that he may be punished for his actions."[22]

Because of this *fatwa*, the Rushdie controversy was thrust onto the world stage, reigniting the rhetorical confrontation between the West and the Muslim world. Khomeini argued that because Rushdie was born a Muslim and that under Islamic law he had committed apostasy by renouncing his religion and insulting the most sacred beliefs of Islam, he was subject to execution. Muslim responses to Khomeini's *fatwa* varied. The mufti of Sokoto in Nigeria also called for Rushdie's death, while other Muslim scholars and clerics, such as Sudan's Hassan Turabi, rejected the hard-line view of apostasy that called for Rushdie's death.[23] Similarly, religious scholars at Cairo's al-Azhar University stated that according to *Shari'a*, Rushdie must first have a trial and must be given an opportunity to repent. Egyptian Nobel laureate Naguib Mahfouz, who publicly supported Egypt's ban, found the call for Rushdie's execution untenable. Nevertheless, Mahfouz stated that "different cultures have different attitudes toward freedom of speech. What might be endured in Western cultures might not be acceptable in Muslim countries."[24]

On February 24, 1989, the Islamic Republic offered a three-million-dollar bounty for the death of Rushdie, which forced the author to live for a time under British government security. The resulting deterioration in relations between Iran and the United Kingdom and other Western European countries lasted for a brief period. During the 1990s, Iranian officials frequently said that their government had no plans to track down Rushdie and carry out the execution. In 1998, Iran's foreign minister, Kamal Kharrazi, announced the lifting of the death decree against Rushdie.

Although the *fatwa* technically remains in force to this day and may not change for some time to come, it has no official backing. In his visit to the United Nations in 1998, Mohammad Khatami, the then President of Iran, distanced himself from the *fatwa*. Internationally, Khatami's decision was seen by many as part of his emphasis on civilizational dialogue to bring Iran back into the international fold. Internally, however, this position was not shared by conservative factions, revealing the jockeying for power among different factions. While many hard-liners continued to insist that the death sentence against Rushdie be carried out, Khatami, who sought to improve ties with the West, appeared determined to lay the *fatwa* to rest.

Today, very few European countries consider the Rushdie issue an obstacle in their relations with Iran. Pragmatism in EU—Iran ties has seen the issue be brushed under the carpet. Most Iranian ruling elites have chosen to minimize the significance of the issue, even as it pertains to the internal political dynamics of Iran. Similarly, this realization has led to greater realism from both Washington and Tehran, and the issue no longer presents a major obstacle to repairing US–Iran relations. Nevertheless, the incident remains a classic affront to the supreme Western value of freedom of expression, just as it was equally offensive to the paramount Muslim value of respect for religion.[25] The change in Iran's position on the Rushdie issue demonstrates yet again that while the *fatwa* was initially an example of ideology influencing foreign policy, pragmatism gradually took over. As a result of this evolution, in practice the *fatwa* against Rushdie is no longer part of Iran's foreign policy.

The Post-Khomeini Era

Khomeini's death and the rise of President Ali Akbar Hashemi Rafsanjani (1989–97) diminished the populist fervor of the early years of the Islamic Revolution. A national referendum abolished the post of prime minister and replaced it with a popularly elected president as head of the government. Although the *Majles* (parliament) was important in promoting popular sovereignty in the post-Khomeini era, it failed to provide genuinely broad political participation. Parliamentary elections were manipulated by oversight committees that controlled access to the *Majles*. Interfactional disputes continued to present problems for the executive branch. The radicals in the legislature advocated for the nationalization of foreign trade and major industries, and sought land reform and progressive taxation.

The victory of the pragmatists demonstrated that Iran's devastated economy and practical needs had replaced vague political and ideological slogans. Rafsanjani's liberalization initiatives encountered many setbacks, including insufficient levels of private investment, low growth rates, budget bottlenecks, and mounting foreign debt. Corruption and mismanagement of resources also complicated these programs. His foreign policy, however, was successful in the containment of Iraq and reconciliation with the GCC member states. For Rafsanjani, the most crucial part of this reconciliation was the rapprochement with Saudi Arabia.[26]

Rafsanjani was invited to Riyadh, and Iran and Saudi Arabia exchanged ambassadors after several years of diplomatic break. Foreign Minister Ali Akbar Velayati, who is currently the top foreign policy adviser to Supreme Leader Ayatollah Ali Khamenei, led the process of reconciliation between the two countries by coordinating an oil price policy. For the first time since the bloody clashes between Iranians and Saudi security forces in Mecca in 1987, the Saudis granted permits for 110,000 pilgrims from Iran to participate in the *hajj*. At home, Rafsanjani's policy of bringing about détente with the Saudis met with much resistance from hard-liners, who criticized him for prioritizing diplomatic normalcy and economic growth over the challenging of status quo powers.[27]

The late 1990s "reform" era, characterized by the landslide victory of Mohammad Khatami in the 1997 presidential elections, ushered in the expansion of civil society, the rule of law, women's rights, and media freedom. Khatami's notable victory was also a firm rebuke to hard-line clerics who had dominated Iranian politics since the 1979 Revolution that had toppled the pro-US Pahlavi regime. Khatami's supporters—mainly youth, women, intellectuals, and ethnic minorities—demanded greater social and political freedom and increased political pluralism. Khatami contributed significantly to the growth of civil society in Iran by opening up the political climate, by espousing the formation of different political parties by civil groups, and by supporting the rule of law.

Once in office, Khatami found himself faced with the onset of a global recession and a sharp decline in oil prices. He also faced persistent inflation, unemployment, and mismanagement. Khatami's economic policies were often based on small-scale initiatives that yielded no major results.[28] Although Khatami and his reform movement were credited with some initial steps toward enacting economic reforms, they failed to build and sustain broader public support in the long term. Their political tribulations persuaded much of the Iranian public that political reforms ranked higher in priority than job creation. This strategic and gross miscalculation left the reformist camp vulnerable to a populist challenge, as the surprise election of Mahmoud Ahmadinejad in 2005 demonstrated.[29]

In foreign policy, Khatami followed his predecessor's regional détente and pursuit of normalization of ties with the West. To break

Iran's regional and global isolation, Khatami made significant strides toward revamping some of Iran's strained relations with other Middle Eastern countries, especially with the conservative states of the Persian Gulf. Iran's relations with the European Union were also noticeably improved. Some initiatives were also taken to repair relations with the United States, although in the end neither Washington nor Tehran was willing to take the major steps necessary to normalize relations.[30]

The Post-9/11 Era

The tragic 9/11 attacks on the United States in 2001—orchestrated by Al-Qaeda terrorist groups operating out of Afghanistan—prepared the ground for unprecedented US–Iran cooperation. Iran's assistance in overthrowing the Taliban regime in Afghanistan proved vital, and its attempt to stabilize the region after the subsequent US invasion of Iraq led to a palpable improvement in relations between the two countries. During the war in Afghanistan, Iran provided US forces with much needed ground intelligence through third parties such as the Northern Alliance. The post-Taliban era saw tangible shifts in Iran's foreign policy. In the UN-sponsored talks in Bonn, Germany (December 4, 2001), which focused on creating a broad-based government in Afghanistan, the Iranian representatives fully cooperated in establishing an interim government.

President George W. Bush's State of the Union address, which lumped together Iran, Iraq, and North Korea in an "Axis of Evil," substantially weakened the democratic movement in Iran, while strengthening the hands of the hard-liners representing the conservative establishment. Israeli pressure on the Bush administration to contain Iran's drive for the atomic bomb overestimated Iran's capabilities. Iran's outrage at "the Axis of Evil" label further widened the gap between the United States and the Iranian diplomatic community. Such rhetorical posturing reinforced the myth that while Islam in Bosnia represented a tolerant and "modern" Islam, the countries of Iran, Iraq, and Syria represented a militant, exclusivist, and intolerant Islam.[31] It proved disconcerting that Iran, facing nascent liberalization and democratization struggles domestically, was receiving no consideration or rhetorical peace from the Bush administration. This was perhaps the best example of the potential extremist backlash a country in a fragile ideological battle domestically could face.

The most visible aspect of US foreign policy toward Iran was its erratic shift. The Bush administration, which at one point considered Iran's role in defeating the Taliban government "constructive," accused Iran of trying to undermine the interim Afghan government of Hamid Karzai. The Bush administration subsequently dropped the charge that Iran was intent on destabilizing Afghanistan. Instead, it charged that the Islamic Republic was shielding Al-Qaeda terrorists. The Bush administration failed to recognize Iran's legitimate interests in the region and the positive role it could have played in the region's overall stability.

The US Invasion of Iraq

The 2003 US invasion of Iraq provoked feelings of opposition and resistance among both Shi'a and Sunni Muslims. For Iran and its allies, such as Hezbollah, the war provided an opportunity to disseminate the view that Islam was under attack.[32] Moreover, the war and its aftermath positioned Iraq's Shi'a majority to dominate the country's politics. This has since placed Iran in a unique situation to spread its ideological and geopolitical influence in Iraq and throughout the Middle East.

Some experts, such as Ray Takeyh, have argued that the emergence of the Shia Crescent—a tacit political alliance of Shia majority Middle East nations spearheaded by Iran—is understandable given these nations estrangement from the larger Arab world, and given the neighboring Sunni regimes' unease with their empowerment. Clearly, the Sunni monarchs of Saudi Arabia and Jordan, as well as the presidential dictatorship of Egypt, were extremely nervous at the time about the emergence of a new Shia Crescent.[33] Indeed, Iraq's new Shi'a parties, conservative or moderate, were initially drawn to Iran, as they sought natural allies in the region. "It is unlikely that this will change," Takeyh continued, "because the political alignments of the Middle East are increasingly being defined by sectarian identities."[34]

The Shi'a revival, Vali Nasr argued, depends on three pillars: "the newly empowered Shi'i majority in Iraq, the current rise of Iran as regional leader, and the empowerment of Shi'is across Lebanon, Saudi Arabia, Kuwait, the UAE, and Pakistan."[35] These three pillars are interconnected, and each reinforces the other. Together they assure a greater Shi'a voice in Middle Eastern politics, one likely to push for a new power distribution in the region.[36] The Shi'a have become increasingly cognizant of the fact that only the US occupation stood between them and the ultimate attainment of political power so long denied.[37] They had much to gain if the democratic process succeeded in Iraq.

Other commentators, however, viewed with skepticism the idea that a broad Shi'a revival was spreading throughout the Middle East, arguing that Shi'a populations were primarily influenced by local, social, political, and economic conditions, and not by transnational Shi'a solidarity. Nationalism, according to this view, outweighed Shi'ism. Moreover, the pursuit of national interests severely restrained the emergence of transnational movements based on shared meanings and belief systems, such as a Shi'a revival. As such, Shi'ism was a flexible identity constructed by the particular circumstances and contexts in which adherents live.[38] It is important to bear in mind that proponents of this view noted that the key motivations behind the Shi'a Crescent concerned the nagging geopolitical considerations in the region over nearly three decades. The sectarian argument served and continues to serve as a method of conferring legitimacy on Sunni rulers' policies.[39]

In response, proponents of the first view—that the Shi'a were rising—pointed out that the Shi'a–Sunni rift in Iraq was typical.[40] This conflict, Vali Nasr asserts, had been built around two factors: a struggle between competing theologies and conceptions of the sacred history of Islam, and a manifestation of tribal wars of ethnicities and identities—wars with both historical and contemporary roots that were emblematic of clashes of identities. Theological and historical disputes intensified this conflict, but so do today's claims to power and concerns with subjugation, freedom, social justice, and equality—not to mention regional conflicts and foreign plots. In short, faith and identity converged in this paradoxical conflict.[41]

Coming back to Iran's foreign policy, others argue that although ideology is an extremely salient factor, the role it plays in this context serves more pragmatic and strategic purposes.[42] Iran's relations with the populist, Shi'a Sadrist faction in post-Saddam Iraq, for example, are primarily tactical. Although Iran's ideological and pragmatic approaches to its foreign policy tend to converge in the new Iraq, the fact remains that Iran's complicated geopolitics will ultimately compel Iran to act pragmatically.[43] In contrast to the first decade of the Islamic Republic, when Iran's foreign policy was primarily influenced and shaped by ideological precepts, today Iran's actions are dictated more by security concerns than by expansionist ideological designs.[44]

Before explaining the role that the Iranian Revolution played in the Shi'a revival in the broader Middle East, it is helpful to put the case of the Iraqi Shi'a in perspective. Unlike Iraq's Sunni Arabs and Kurds, which denote a particular ethnic or cultural identity, the Shi'a in Iraq do not correspond to either a sociological, political, or cultural classification.[45] Instead, the Iraqi Shi'a are identified as holders of particular Islamic beliefs that distinguish them from other Muslim believers—especially the Sunni. The sheer size of their population today renders them a potent constituency. In addition to constituting the majority in Iran, Iraq, Bahrain and Azerbaijan, and a plurality in Lebanon, the Shi'a also represent significant minorities in other Arab countries such as Kuwait and Saudi Arabia. In total, about ninety percent of Iranians are Shi'a, as are nearly seventy percent of the people living in the Persian Gulf region, and some fifty percent of those in the arc from Lebanon to Pakistan—approximately 140 million people in all.[46]

The word "Shi'a" refers to "partisans," or to the party that supported Ali, the Prophet Muhammad's son-in-law, who became Islam's fourth caliph. The party coalesced during a civil war from 656–61, in which several battles were fought between Shi'a and Sunni forces over the issue of succession to the Prophet. Shi'ism suffered defeats at the hands of the Sunni, and today the Shi'a commemorate those occasions. Furthermore, several Shi'a Imams, including Ali and Hussein, are buried in the Iraqi holy cities of Najaf, Karbala, Kazmiya and Samarra. One of the key origins of the Sunni–Shi'a divide—or perhaps a major doctrinal difference between the two—stems from the fact that the Sunni reject the Shi'a contention that the Prophet Muhammad selected Ali to be the first imam of the Islamic state, and thus reject the Shi'a institution of the Imamate, which recognizes the divine right of Ali and his descendants to lead the *ummah*.[47]

Although the idea of a clerical state is not widely shared among the Shi'a, Iran has successfully forged ties with Shi'a forces across the Iraqi spectrum. Iran's powerful allies, such as the Islamic Supreme Council of Iraq and elements of the Mahdi Army, have fortified Shi'a control over Iraq by raising the costs to the United States of maintaining its presence in Iraq.[48] Iranian leaders have redefined the traditional characterization of Iraq as a counterweight to Iran and have shifted the region's putative balance of power into a new policy based on "balance of interests."[49]

There can be no doubt that Iran has benefitted from its increased influence in Iraq. The two governments have increased cooperation on a number of matters relating to security, trade, and tourism. Iran played an important role in mediating Iraq's political crisis following the 2010 elections and went on to establish ties with key Iraqi political and security forces. This was demonstrated in the case of the ensuing civil war in Syria, Iran's most important Arab ally. Iraq made it possible for Iran to funnel "personnel and tens of tons of weapons" through Iraqi airspace into Syria. In fact, Iraq served as a conduit through which Iranian weapons, supplies, and fighters were passed on to the embattled Syrian regime.[50]

In the wake of the US withdrawal from Iraq, considerable attention has turned to Iran's foreign policy toward Iraq. Many experts note that the real test for the Iraq war's impact on US foreign policy will come with Iran, as the US post-Iraq fatigue and its focus on internal problems may end up providing new opportunities for Iran to further advance its influence in Iraq.[51] By the same token, it can be argued that Iraq's stability is also a critical test for Iran. Iranian policymakers consider Iraq's stability to be in their interests—both in the short term and in the long term.[52] The post-US withdrawal period, however, could evoke mixed reactions from Iran. On the one hand, Iranians see an unstable and insecure Iraq as posing numerous challenges to their country's security. On the other hand, if US pressure to isolate Iran ratchets up—particularly through economic sanctions and coercive diplomacy—Iran could become a destabilizing factor in Iraq.

Iran's Reaction to the Arab Spring Uprisings

When turmoil swept across the Middle East in 2011, ruling elites in the region were wary of the possible domino effect, and many of them began to implement counterrevolutionary tactics and strategies. Iranian officials and state-run media were not an exception in viewing these developments with both hope and apprehension, and in perceiving their consequences as creating both opportunities and risks. Typically, the Islamic Republic's initial reactions to the protest movements in early 2011 were influenced significantly by its ideological leanings. The regime, in particular, vocally and confidently depicted the anti-government uprisings in Tunisia, Egypt, and Libya as an "Islamic Awakening" modeled after Iran's own revolution in 1979, and as a rejection of secular and corrupt pro-American regimes.

Domestically, both the leaders of the Iranian government and of the opposition praised the uprisings in Egypt, albeit for different reasons. The leadership of Iran's Green Movement, working under virtual house arrest, and dismissed by government officials as powerless "leaders of sedition," welcomed the Egyptian uprising, even calling for demonstrations in Iran on February 14, 2011, to express "solidarity with the public movement in the region, especially the freedom-seeking uprising of the peoples of Tunisia and Egypt against tyrannical governments."[53] Meanwhile, Iranian officials embraced the popular protests bursting across the Arab world as epitomizing the popular revolt that ushered in the Islamic Republic nearly three decades previously.[54] Some Iranians politicians, such as *Majles* Speaker Ali Larijani, declared Iran's support for the popular uprisings in Tunisia and Egypt, as well as for the rest of the Arab world, describing them as a spark for similar movements throughout the Middle East.[55]

It certainly was the case that for the Islamic Republic, any changes emerging from these upheavals would likely be preferable to the status quo, which it viewed as tilted in favor of Washington. There were two grounds for this view. In Tehran's assessment, any democratically elected government in North Africa was likely to challenge US foreign policy in the region—and although the emerging regimes were unlikely to follow Iran's theocratic model, they might have looked for ways to engage Iran, if for no other reason than to gain access to Iran's lucrative energy and trade contracts.

That said, as events hesitantly muddled along throughout 2011, it became clear that the Arab Awakening would not, in the longer term, necessarily benefit the Islamic Republic. The turmoil in Syria (Iran's sole ally among Arab states) forced this recognition onto the Islamic Republic. Iran's position toward the Arab Spring uprisings came to be described by Arab commentators as duplicitous, for publicly supporting rights of Bahraini citizens against their own government while simultaneously propping up the brutal regime of Bashar Assad in Syria.

While the Saudis rushed to the defense of Bahrain, Iran was preoccupied with preserving its main Arab ally: Syria. For Iran, as Anoushiravan Ehteshami notes, the collapse of the Bashar Assad regime was a strategic blow in terms of its access to its power base in Lebanese Hezbollah, as well as its execution of its forward defense strategy with regard to Israel.[56] For Saudi Arabia, the success of the revolt in Bahrain would not just undermine the GCC, but would also bring revived Shi'a power to the eastern shores of the Arabian Peninsula. Bahrain, in this regard, wrote Ehteshami, was "an existential matter for the Kingdom and its control of the GCC realm."[57]

This divergence from its declared position toward the so-called new "Islamic awakening" in the Arab world undermined Iran's legitimacy in the region, further deepening the rift between Iran and the rest of the Arab region.[58] While the anti-American position of the Islamists appealed to Iran politically, they were unlikely to become partners ideologically.[59] This reckoning only intensified as developments elsewhere in the region took a turn seemingly unfavorable to Iran. As this more realistic assessment gradually became accepted in Tehran, the country's foreign policy took its usual turn toward greater pragmatism.

In particular, it was not unreasonable to assume that the new government in Egypt would, in the longer term, be closer to Washington than Tehran. This was for several reasons. First, the Barack Obama administration and its Western allies facilitated the Egyptian revolution by compelling President Hosni Mubarak to step down. Second, the Egyptian military, which remains resolutely secular, would vehemently oppose any efforts to create a religious political order. Third,

Egyptian civil society was developed and complex, and had within it a persistent liberal strain.[60] While the Muslim Brotherhood's politics was resolutely Islamic, the organization had to strike a balance in its relations with the military in shaping the future politics of Egypt.

Were the Muslim Brotherhood to play a significant role in Egypt's political life, the new system would have possibly followed the Turkish model, blending a secular constitution with a pronounced socio-political Islamic identity.[61] In terms of foreign policy, Turkey pursued new relationships with its immediate neighbors (and beyond) based on a regional détente. The post-conflict or post-revolutionary governments of North Africa could very well follow that path. One interesting issue to examine, in this context, is the Iran-Turkey relationship: Will the two countries continue to build their ties, as they have done in recent years, or alternatively engage in competition for influence in the reshaped region, as Iran and Saudi Arabia are most likely to do? The latter is more likely, given that both Turkey and Iran are increasingly positioning themselves as competing models for the region's political development—Turkey's blending of Islam, modernity and democracy, as opposed to Iran's theocratic, rejectionist model.

On September 11, 2012, a cartoonish video on YouTube (dubbed *Innocence of Muslims*), which painted the Prophet Muhammad as a pedophile and a fraud, set off violent demonstrations across the Muslim world. These protests led to an assault on the US diplomatic facility in Benghazi, Libya, in which J. Christopher Stevens, the US ambassador to Libya, and three other Americans died. Whether this attack was premeditated and orchestrated by terrorists or spontaneous and caused by anti-US sentiment remained unclear, but one question loomed: Can Libyan leaders in the post-Qaddafi era rein in militant groups?[62]

In Egypt, an angry crowd breached the US Embassy walls and tore down the American flag, replacing it with an Islamic banner. Subsequently, in Iran, Javad Shamaghdari, from the government-controlled cinema agency, said that Iran should "avoid" the Hollywood festival of the Academy Awards by boycotting the 2013 Oscars in the wake of the anti-Islam film *Innocence of Muslims*. Following the blocking of Gmail and Google, Iran's Communications Minister Reza

Taghipour noted that the Internet was an "unsafe network," and that local software would be used to create a national grid.[63]

The Shifting Security Paradigm

The Persian Gulf region continues to face multiple and formidable challenges, ranging from the diverse effects of declining oil prices, the escalation of tensions between Iran and Saudi Arabia, the evolving threat perception emanating from civil war in Yemen, to the spread of the COVID-19 pandemic. No less significant, however, is the gradual downsizing of the US military footprint in the region and its implications for the balance of political and military power and the emergence of new alliances.[64] These new challenges may signal the end of a zero-sum game in which Iran's political, diplomatic, and economic gains have been equated with losses by its Arab neighbors in the Persian Gulf region. This mentality, which has long prevailed among the GCC member states, may be subject to enduring seismic shifts in the regional political landscape in the coming years.

For all intents and purposes, the continuation of the dual containment of Iran and Iraq (since 1994–2003), spearheaded by the United States, as well as the exclusion of these two critical countries from the Persian Gulf security architecture, has become untenable. It has brought to the region neither peace nor political stability. Ironically, as one expert notes, despite the US policy to contain and weaken Iran, the US invasion and occupation of Iraq (2003–present) increased Iran's strategic significance, as well as that of the region's other non-Arab states including Turkey and Israel. This increase in Iran's strategic influence continued unabated far beyond the eruption of the 2011 Arab Spring uprisings, even as the Arab Gulf states sought to assert their own leadership role in the region.[65]

Equally significant is the diminished saliency of the old paradigm of hostile rivalry between Iran and Saudi Arabia—one which has dominated the region's security structure since the 1979 Islamic Revolution. This obsession with the Iran–Saudi Arabia rivalry—actual or perceived—has proven to be counterproductive to the region's stability and security. As the region wrestles with the possibility of the post-petroleum era and the gradual US downsizing of its forces in the Persian Gulf region, the GCC governments are coming under massive pressure to redefine a fresh security outlook while also developing appropriate macroeconomic policies to ensure that oil wealth is managed effectively. Mindful of the impact of the US shale and renewable energy revolution as the new source of competition and the mounting public pressure on political leaders to divest from fossil fuels in the face of a growing environmental crisis, the Gulf leaders are hard pressed to see the writing on the wall. With varying levels of urgency, they are attempting to diversify their economies and prepare for the post-petroleum era.

Declining oil prices are likely to curtail government spending, enforce higher levels of taxation and fees on citizens, and reduce subsidies, as some Arab Gulf regimes recognize that they have little option but to scale back their handouts, subsidies, and social welfare policies. Some governments have already done so.[66] This has far-reaching implications for the GCC welfare states. The old social contract between the rulers and the ruled is no more, and the new one is not yet defined. In the face of their lagging political legitimacy (albeit with variations), the near-future holds the promise of a deepening economic and political crisis that will test the ability of political leadership in GCC countries to navigate the ship of their respective states effectively amidst the turbulent social storms that lay ahead.

The Downsizing of the US Military Presence

The consequences of the US military downsizing and the US aversion to becoming entangled in costly wars with unintended consequences deserves particular attention. This shift is widely seen in the context of the Trump administration's decision to gradually retreat from the region, leaving US allies and Gulf partners concerned over US security guarantees to the region. A concatenation of several factors, including capricious decisions regarding US troop commitments in Syria and the lack of a strong response to the Iranian downing of a US drone in June 2019, led to foreign policy adjustments for the United Arab Emirates (UAE), as demonstrated by its outreach to the Islamic Republic.

More crucially, on August 1, 2019, Iran and the UAE signed a memorandum of understanding (MoU) to enhance maritime border security cooperation. The document was signed by the commander of Iran's border police, Brigadier General Qassem Rezaie, and Emirati Coastguard Commander Brigadier General Mohammad Ali Mosleh al-Ahbabi during a meeting in Tehran. The officials from both countries met for the first time in six years in Tehran to discuss ways of bolstering maritime security and military cooperation. This MoU was also aimed at increasing border interaction, facilitating dispute resolution for businesspeople and fishermen, and preventing attempts to disrupt maritime security. General al-Ahbabi described the MoU as a "positive step" that can serve the two countries' interests in the region, fortify border security and border control, and facilitate crossings.[67]

The September 14, 2019 strikes on Saudi facilities in Abqaiq and Khurais, which provoked no US military reaction, further contributed to the prevalent view in the region that Washington was no longer as committed to defending its Arab allies as in the past. Similarly, recent developments in Yemen point to the shift in regional politics, where the UAE, bent on cutting its losses, drew down its forces from supporting the Southern Transitional Council in south Yemen, leaving Saudi Arabia to find its way out of the quagmire of its own making. At the end of the day, neither Obama's political outreach toward the Islamic Republic that culminated in the 2015 nuclear agreement, nor Trump's refusal to take on the Iranian government militarily despite the administration's policy of maximum pressure, are comforting signs for such GCC anti-Iran hawks as Saudi Arabia and Bahrain. Coming to grips with these new realities will occupy the GCC member states' imagination in the coming years. The crucial question is this: Will the GCC states take a hostile posture toward Iran or will they reinvent themselves by re-imagining and recalibrating their relations with Tehran?

The 2019 US National Security Strategy, which enjoys bipartisan support in Congress and among think tanks in Washington, identified China and Russia as major threats to US global primacy. It exhorted the White House to focus on great power competition and rivalry. It remains to be seen if this fundamental shift in US foreign policy calculus will culminate in changing the balance of power in favor of Iran—the most populous and militarily potent power in the region. It is worth noting that Iran views itself, as Mehran Kamrava rightly maintains, as a "global middle power with regional great power aspirations."[68]

In the meantime, the powerful presence of Israeli, Saudi, and UAE lobbies in the US Congress continue to intensify the lingering hostilities between the United States and Iran, no matter who resides in the White House. Hence, expanding Chinese economic influence and increasing Russian political and military assertiveness in the region, often in direct divergence from Tehran's policy preference (for example, their bilateral relations with Israel and Saudi Arabia), may become new challenges to Iran's regional ambitions.

The Cold War between Riyadh and Tehran

Saudi Arabia's frustrating and catastrophic entanglements in Yemen have spilled over into Lebanon, where the Saudi prince Mohamed Bin Salman seems fixated on encouraging the Israeli invasion of Lebanon to eradicate Hezbollah's influence in that country and more broadly the region. This troubling situation was a direct consequence of the Trump administration's encouragement. In the context of the tense political climate in the region, two basic questions arise. First, does Washington's downsizing signal a US return to an offshore balancing strategy, in which the United States provides the necessary military wherewithal to its allies in the region to counter Iran? Second, is the new leadership in Saudi Arabia emboldened by such a strategy?

The sudden abdication of Lebanese Prime Minister Saad Hariri, who had become a pawn in Saudi efforts to isolate their regional rival, Iran, and its ally, Hezbollah, illustrates one way in which Riyadh intends to undercut Iranian influence in the region.[69] Hariri's resignation under pressure from Riyadh was also a direct result of giving the Saudis the go-ahead to reclaim and redirect the power structure of the Middle East. This development demonstrated a partnership of sorts among Saudi Arabia, Israel, and the United States, aimed at rolling back increasing Iranian influence in Lebanon, Syria, and Iraq. Yet this partnership contained its own limits and perils. A fundamental question is whether a new war between Israel and Hezbollah would serve the region's order and stability, and to what extent.

History is full of instructive examples. Israeli attacks on South Lebanon (1985–2000) and the 2006 Lebanon War in response to the abduction of two Israeli reserve soldiers by Hezbollah have shown that Hezbollah cannot easily be defeated or dismantled. If Israel decides to attack Hezbollah, however, the new war would be an invitation to a risky and uncertain venture that should concern most Israelis, even as Israel's military superiority is not in question. Knowing that Hezbollah has 120,000 rockets and missiles would most certainly factor into Israel's decision to go to war. Hezbollah now possesses, an Israeli spokesperson noted, "more missiles below ground in Lebanon than the European NATO allies have above ground."[70] Any attacks against Hezbollah would likely become a wider confrontation involving Iran. It is unlikely that Washington's ongoing strategic interests in the Middle East (stability in Iraq and Afghanistan, defeating the Islamic State of Iraq and Syria (ISIS) and radical Islamic movements, and stable oil prices and markets) would be best served as a result.

How did the crisis and rivalry between Iran and Saudi Arabia reach this critical point? The rise of Prince Mohammed bin Salman to power has introduced a new element into Saudi strategy for coping with the challenges of domestic politics and regional chaos. Thus far, Saudi involvement—both directly and indirectly—in Syria, Yemen, Iraq, and Lebanon has failed to pay political dividends. Furthermore, it appears now that the young Saudi prince seeks to shift attention away from his domestic troubles and challenges (reform, purges, young demographics, unemployment, declining oil prices, and the COVID-19 pandemic) to more nationalistic and foreign policy-oriented contexts so as to further consolidate his power at home.

The Divisions Within the GCC

The ongoing tensions within the GCC are not new—nor are the divisions in that organization likely to take a backseat to the broader geopolitical interests of the member states. The lack of common interests among the member states is often reflected in their competing and at times conflicting foreign policy orientations. Saudi Arabia's longstanding efforts to deepen its existing security relationship with its GCC partners, under the rubric of "Gulf Union," have repeatedly met resistance in some smaller GCC member states—especially in those with a potent skepticism of Saudi motives. While Kuwaiti officials have referred to the deep-seated political differences between the Gulf elites, some commentators in the UAE and Oman have pointed to the existence of differences among the six GCC member countries over sovereignty and independence.[71]

What has gradually emerged from the ongoing divisions among the GCC member states is the outline of an alternative approach to foreign policy. Since June 2017, when Saudi Arabia, the UAE, and Bahrain upended diplomatic relations with Qatar and placed it under a complete economic and cultural embargo, such rifts within the organization deepened. This embargo was widely regarded as the most serious internal rift since the GCC's establishment in 1981, as it cast a huge cloud of uncertainty over the future viability of an organization that was once regarded as essential to regional stability.

On January 30, 2018, the then US Defense Secretary James N. Mattis and the then Secretary of State Rex W. Tillerson, alongside their Qatari counterparts, spoke in favor of further cooperation between Washington and Doha at the opening session of the inaugural US–Qatar Strategic Dialogue at the State Department. This event raised a question: Was embarking on a new strategic talk between the two countries aimed at repairing the rift within the GCC? Or was this new foreign policy directed at rolling back the resurgent regional powers of Iran and Turkey given the current conflict in Syria?

Looking at the bigger picture, it is worth noting that since the fractures within the GCC have concrete geopolitical and economic—and to a lesser extent, ideological—roots, it is highly unlikely that such divisions will be resolved permanently. The fact remains that the United States is neither willing nor capable of reconciling differences between or among the GCC states. The US–Qatar Strategic Dialogue, therefore, had one central goal: to contain the regional influence of Iran and Turkey.

The dispute between Saudi Arabia and Qatar intensified divisions within the GCC, and it also benefited countries such as Turkey and Iran, whose economic ties with Qatar dramatically deepened. The dispute placed Qatar in a much stronger position to outlast the political ambitions of the three other Persian Gulf states (the United Arab Emirates, Kuwait, and Bahrain) that followed the Saudis' lead to punish Qatar for its unorthodox support for the Arab Spring uprisings and their pragmatic economic and political relationship with Iran. Similarly, Qatar's moves in the region to protect migrant workers' rights by abolishing the *kafala* system of guardianship, as well as serving as a mediator in some key regional conflicts (Lebanon, Afghanistan, and Palestine, to mention only a few), clearly out-staged Riyadh's status-quo and counterrevolutionary proclivities. Meanwhile, the Al Udeid Air Base in Doha, the region's largest US air base and home to 11,000 US personnel, gives Qatar a clear advantage in its bargaining position vis-à-vis the other GCC member states. Several factors may account for the US attempts at establishing an annual strategic dialogue with Qatar.

First and foremost, Iran's burgeoning status as a regional power has been strengthened by the widening divisions within the GCC. The embargo against Qatar pushed Doha further toward economic and pragmatic cooperation with Tehran. Doha's increased commercial and political ties with Tehran enhanced Iranian stature and influence, both domestically and regionally. The Qatar crisis helped Tehran put to rest the narrative that Iran's foreign policy is sectarian. The Islamic Republic's foreign policy focused on improving relations with Sunni actors in the Middle East, including Turkey and Hamas, in addition to Qatar, despite differing views on regional crises such as Syria. Closer Iran–Qatar relations, as one observer notes, could help enhance a Sunni–Shi'ite dialogue in the region, especially given that both Doha and Tehran continue to maintain relations with a host of non-state actors whose cooperation is needed to resolve certain regional conflicts.[72]

Second, Turkey has benefited even more from the GCC rift and its deepening ties with Qatar. This has occurred within the context of Turkey's expansive military role in Syria, the latest example of which, Operation Olive Branch, has witnessed the unleashing of Turkish military might against the Kurdish People's Protection Units (YPG). The YPG is a Syrian offshoot of the Kurdistan Workers' Party (PKK), a faction that has long been at war with Ankara over its demands for Kurdish self-rule. This may help explain why Turkey has always prioritized fighting against the Kurds above defeating ISIS.

The recent Turkish military intervention in Afrin, northern Syria, ostensibly as part of an agreement reached with Russia, has opened a new front in Syria's lingering civil war, and has further intensified existing tensions between Ankara and Washington. Turkey's President Erdogan is keenly aware that a tough stance in Syria, and strong support for Qatar, is likely to bolster his standing at home.

Finally, Qatar's cooperation with the United States and other regional states to combat terrorist operations carried out by ISIS and Al-Qaeda agents continues to be crucial to present and future counterterrorism programs by the United States and its allies. Qatar's pivotal role in containing such threats has increasingly gained traction in Washington and throughout Europe. Without denying the importance of the anti-terrorism campaign, it must be remembered that the US–Qatar Strategic Dialogue is essentially designed to ratchet up US pressure on Doha to align its foreign policy with that of Washington, while also keeping both Tehran and Ankara at bay.

The Biden administration's policy of finding a path to return to the Joint Comprehensive Plan of Action (JCPOA) has arguably influenced the Saudi decision to lift the embargo they imposed on Qatar in mid-2017. Resolving the tensions between the two Gulf countries appears to have been a reaction to a potential US reengagement with Iran. The breakthrough in the Gulf crisis may arguably be a reaction to Doha's efforts to forge closer links with Iran and Turkey. Crucially, Qatar's relations with Turkey could still present the main impediment to the resumption of negotiations to end the embargo. Both the UAE and Saudi Arabia have expressed real concerns about Turkey's role in regional affairs. Turkey has adopted a conciliatory approach toward repairing its relations with Saudi Arabia.

Tensions with Ankara, however, have been most apparent in Libya, where the UAE and Turkey have continued to support opposing proxies in the ongoing civil war.[73] The current conflict between the internationally organized, Tripoli-based Government of National Accord (GNA) and the runaway General Khalifa Haftar, supported by Egypt, the UAE, France, and Russia, has placed Abu Dhabi and Ankara on opposing sides of the turmoil in Libya. Turkey's military involvement in Libya is a bid to be an influential actor in the Eastern Mediterranean power game aimed at protecting its national security of hydrocarbon exploitation in Libya. An emerging alliance composed of seven countries—Greece, Greek Cypriot Administration (GCA),

Egypt, Israel, Jordan, Palestine, and Italy—appears intent on excluding and sidelining Turkey from Eastern Mediterranean geopolitical and geo-economic projects.[74]

Turkey's Blue Homeland doctrine, which aims to establish Turkish naval supremacy in the Eastern Mediterranean, has been formulated to support its geopolitical interests in the region.[75] The UAE's ideological commitment to protecting Haftar's rule has clearly overshadowed any potential economic gains that the former might have. This policy appears directed toward cutting Turkey off from North Africa and depriving it of a key gateway into Sub-Saharan Africa.[76] Abu Dhabi's counterrevolutionary and counter-Islamist agenda is clearly aimed at a broader geopolitical goal of competing with Turkey, while preventing the spread of democratic movements that may ultimately endanger its own regime.[77] If the UAE's zero-sum game in Libya fails to pay any dividends, it will pave the way for the rival camp—Turkey and Qatar—to exert greater influence, both geopolitically and from a geo-economic standpoint, in Libya and further afield.[78]

The Abraham Accords

In anticipation of a piecemeal US withdrawal from the Persian Gulf region, some Arab Gulf states wasted no time in normalizing relations with Israel. This move is likely to isolate Iran, but its immediate impact has much to do with expanding ties with Israel, be they trade, technological, or scientific. On September 15, 2020, Israel, the UAE, and Bahrain signed the so-called "Abraham Accords," which are aimed at fostering closer cooperation and normalizing diplomatic relations. These accords mark the first time Gulf countries have established full diplomatic relations with Israel since Israel's declaration of independence in 1948. It should be noted, however, that Israel has long been actively engaged with these countries. Nevertheless, in some way normalization formalizes and elevates cooperation to a much higher level than has existed before.

The announcement that Israel, the UAE, and Bahrain would be embarking on normalization of relations reflected shared and overlapping concerns regarding the growing regional influence of Iran, the rise of Islamic extremists in the region, and burgeoning uncertainties about future US strategy and engagement in the Middle East.[79] Several factors led to the Abraham Accords, the most important of which was timing. With the election prospects of former Vice President Joe Biden looking formidable in late 2020, the Arab Gulf states presumed that Biden might adopt a different position regarding human rights and regional arms transfers, as well as a softer approach toward Iran. The possibility of a US military drawdown in the region, a policy advocated by the two previous US administrations, was a factor in shaping the foreign policy of some Gulf Arab states.

Increasing concerns regarding Iran's aggressive regional actions, along with swirling questions over the ambitions of Turkey and its presence in the Persian Gulf region in the aftermath of the Saudi-led boycott against Qatar, forced the Emiratis to seriously consider a new relationship with Israel.[80] Other Gulf Arab countries, such as Kuwait and Qatar, have refused to join these accords, objecting to any hint of unilateral Israeli annexation of territory in the West Bank, which they have long deemed contrary to both the Palestinian cause and international law. Both countries have explicitly excluded the possibility of normalizing relations with Israel without a resolution to the Palestinian issue.[81]

There is still uncertainty over whether Jerusalem will withdraw its opposition to the US sale of F-35s to Abu Dhabi. For the UAE, the purchasing US multirole combat aircrafts, such as F-35s, and other advanced weaponry was a major incentive to normalize relations with Israel. Whether or not the region will undergo a profound rebalancing of power remains to be seen. Equally relevant is the extent to which these agreements may result in decoupling the Israeli-Palestinian conflict from normalization pacts. It seems impossible to foretell what the outcome of these agreements would be. What is clear, however, is that if Palestinian aspirations for state sovereignty and independence are reduced to a mere slogan, this will have negative consequences for sustainable relations between Israel and the rest of the Arab states.

For now at least, Israel–UAE normalization is likely to facilitate intelligence sharing between the two countries. This is likely to remove Iran's natural buffer with Israel, exposing it to Israel's 2018 theft of top-secret Iranian nuclear documents from a Tehran warehouse and to the assassination of Mohsen Fakhrizadeh in late 2020.[82] The Israeli–UAE normalization agreement also entails joint work in building an intelligence base on the island of Socotra in the Arabian Sea, adjacent to the Bab el-Mandeb Strait, which provides the southern entrance to the Red Sea. This agreement will make it possible to monitor and inspect vessels suspected of carrying Iranian weapons to Houthi rebels in Yemen and to Bedouins in Egypt's Sinai Peninsula, who then smuggle the arms to Hamas fighters inside the Gaza Strip.[83]

Washington views this new geopolitical agreement between Israel and the Gulf Arab states as an effective method of neutralizing Iran's influence in the region. It is still too early to gauge its effectiveness in this regard, or just how far this agreement will go in changing the region's geopolitical landscape for decades to come. Given the absence of Saudi Arabia—the key actor in the Arabian Peninsula—from normalizing relations with Israel, and given the fact that Shi'ites constitute a majority in Bahrain, it is unclear how the public will react to this new development. The fact remains that while the United States and Israel recognize Jerusalem as its capital, the international community has yet to do so. The vast majority of UN member states continue to recognize East Jerusalem as the capital of a future Palestinian state, even as the Abraham Accords could seriously undermine any prospects of a two-state solution for Palestinian statehood.[84]

Conclusion

Since the 1979 Revolution, the Islamic Republic of Iran has shown an unrelenting commitment to advancing its ideology throughout the region and beyond, while at the same time pursuing a pragmatic foreign policy when necessary. When pragmatism has receded, ideology has moved in to fill the vacuum. Iran's foreign policy also reflects the way in which the country is ruled by multiple power centers. The major differences among the ruling elite have centered around the methods by which such a goal might be achieved. In this context, both Shi'ism and Islamic ideology have assumed an important albeit fluctuating role in Iran's foreign policy. Since Shi'ism is political in nature and tends to attach much importance to gaining and maintaining power, it has been a critical part of Iran's foreign policy.

On a broader level, however, promoting Islamism in the region has assumed a much larger role than advancing Shi'ism, given that the Shi'a constitute a minority in the Middle East and the Muslim world. Iran's commitment to both the Lebanese Hezbollah, a Shi'a movement, and Hamas, a Palestinian *Sunni*-Islamic militant movement in the Gaza Strip, is emblematic of such an approach. Strategic and political issues also continue to affect the nature and intensity of Iran's cultural and ideological relations. This is especially true in the case of the Iran–Hezbollah relationship, in which both ideological and geostrategic considerations figure prominently. The same can be said of the relationship between Iran and Syria. Their alliance hinges more on the two sides' common perceptions of the threat posed by the United States and Israel than the Shi'a origins of their ruling elites.[85]

Whether one agrees with or opposes Iran's foreign policies, as Dina Esfandiari notes, it is clear that the Iranian ruling elite follow a rationale grounded in their interests and their internal political context. The common view in the region, however, is that Iran is "an expansionist, ideology driven country, bent on spreading its revolution."[86] Unlike the decade that followed the revolution, today's Islamic Republic is an opportunistic country with strategically calculated actions. Contrary to popular belief, Iran's geopolitical and pragmatic goals play a far more decisive role in shaping its foreign policy than its ideology does.[87]

Nowhere is the pursuit of geopolitical goals more apparent than in the country's regional energy policy. The competition over energy security and pipeline politics has placed Iran and Turkey on opposite sides of an intense regional rivalry. Iran's foreign policy behavior is evidently driven by geopolitical and strategic calculations. Armenia, Azerbaijan, and Georgia—the three countries that make up the South Caucasus—have emerged as key areas of competition between Iran and Turkey as the two countries seek to expand their spheres of influence. The region will continue to be the arena of intense rivalry between and among United States, the European Union, Russia, and some key regional actors, such as Iran and Turkey. These regional rivalries involving so many players that they have come to be known as the "New Great Game."

In managing the many complexities that Iran's foreign policy faces, perhaps the perennial challenge for Tehran has been its anti-US and anti-Israeli propaganda. In both cases, Iran's ideological positions and activities in the region have strengthened the hands of conservative hawks in the United States and right-wing hard-liners in Israel by providing the pretext for aggression, and inviting militarized responses based primarily on heated rhetoric. The Islamic Republic's hostile ideological position vis-à-vis the United States and Israel has painted a monolithic picture of these two countries, overlooking the diversity of views and perceived threats emanating from Iran. This has presented a key paradox for Iran's foreign policy—one that has rendered diplomatic rapprochement with Washington unsustainable, if not impossible. Nor has the ongoing rhetoric of destroying Israel coming from some ultra-conservative factions within Iran gained much traction in the region and beyond, especially as no actual destruction seems planned or has ever been attempted.

The purpose of why or how this rhetoric benefits Tehran is then perceived to be persuasive to the core IRGC base or to the revolutionary gerontocracy, but will arguably, as time passes, have less and less impact on persuading the rest of the population—especially the younger generation. The latter may, arguably, have some negative feelings about Israel, but will not puppet the concerns of the revolutionary generation in perpetuity. The Green Movement, for example, showed that younger Iranians seem to question how Iran's support for the Houthis can ameliorate the humanitarian crisis in Yemen. The movement appears to take greater issue with domestic economic uncertainties and the resounding failure of Iran's response to the COVID-19 pandemic than with Saudi Arabia and its regional policies. Hence, the appeal of anti-US, anti-Israel, and anti-Saudi rhetoric may ring hollow in the future. In the next chapter, I will expound on Iran's renewed geopolitical interest in the South Caucasus and the other parts of the Middle East region.

5

REGIONAL CONFLICTS

SYRIA, SOUTH CAUCASUS, AND YEMEN

By virtue of its size, influence, history, and ambitions, Iran has been drawn into several regional conflicts. This is bound to bring it into conflict or reconciliation with other regional actors. As a result, Iran's foreign policy has almost always involved a careful balancing act. In recent years, Iran has broadened its influence and leverage beyond its immediate neighbors of Afghanistan and Iraq. Tehran's efforts to stamp its imprint across these often-volatile political situations, especially in a region already befuddled by several wars, the remnants of the Arab Spring uprisings, and an intensifying Sunni–Shi'ite divide, raise a key question: How far can Tehran widen its reach?[1]

Iran's proxy efforts across the Middle East had been led by General Qassem Soleimani, who was killed by US drone strikes in Iraq on January 3, 2020. His death will probably increase rather than decrease the likelihood of Iran's network of proxy forces expanding their operations linked to paramilitary groups from Syria to Yemen. Iranian weapons and technology continue to be transferred to its regional allies, including Yemeni Houthi fighters. But more importantly, pro-Iranian militias have proven to be critical assets in stemming the expansion of the Islamic State of Iraq and Syria (ISIS) in the region. The presence of the militias has afforded Iran additional and unique influence over Iraq's political landscape.[2]

The Islamic Republic of Iran's ruling elites view Iran's presence in Syria as a crucial element of its counterterrorism strategy, which involves fighting terrorists outside its national borders rather than on its own territory. Although Iran's fights against Al-Qaeda and ISIS broadly align with the interests and alliances of the international community, Tehran's support for the Assad regime collides with US, European, and Gulf Arab interests.[3] The hefty cost of Iranian involvement in the region has become particularly unpopular domestically, as some political elites have begun to question why precious Iranian resources are being squandered outside of the country.[4] Similarly, Iran's presence in southern Iraq has fueled resentment, as Iraqi Shi'a, who share a faith with Iran, appear less than willing to blindly follow Tehran's dictates. In fact, they tend to hold tenaciously to their ethnic and national identities as Arabs and Iraqis.[5]

Similarly, the growing regional activities of Turkey since the 2011 Arab Spring uprisings have raised real concerns on the part of Saudi Arabia and the United Arab Emirates (UAE), who have themselves adopted a more interventionist foreign policy. The two countries opposed and continue to oppose Turkey's support for the Muslim Brotherhood's assumption of power in Egypt and Tunisia, viewing Ankara's moves as a bid to expand its influence, given the Islamist roots of the ruling Justice and Development Party (AKP). These two Gulf states, by contrast, regard the Muslim Brotherhood as a regional and ideological threat to their political stability. Turkey's support for Qatar in the aftermath of the 2017 Saudi-led boycott was also viewed as another form of intervention in regional affairs.

Riyadh and Abu Dhabi see both Turkey and Iran in the same light, essentially "as non-Arab interlopers that seek to mobilize transnational and sectarian ideologies and identities and work via non-state actors to exploit the Arab state system."[6] They see themselves, by contrast, as committed to preserving current state structures and regional security architecture, while prioritizing economic development over political change.[7]

This chapter examines Iran's expanding reach in the region through its proxy networks in regional conflicts, using both ideology and geopolitics—symbiotically as well as independently—to expand its power. Iran has been successful in maintaining its strategic depth through establishing direct connections that link its interests to conflict-stricken countries that may or may not share its ideology. To demonstrate this, I will explore Iran's role in regional tensions in the examples of Iraq, Syria, South Caucasus, and Yemen.

Iraq: Beyond the US Invasion

The first weeks of the US invasion and occupation of Iraq in the name of the War on Terror led to chaos and looting. US occupation forces, as many observers have pointed out, failed to discover any evidence of close cooperation between the regime of Saddam Hussein and Al-Qaeda. Furthermore, US troops did not receive a cordial welcome in much of the country. US troops waged a low-intensity war against local Iraqi insurgency in the coming years. The transfer of sovereignty to an Iraqi government in June 2004 and the commitment to hold elections for a national assembly by the end of January 2015 were mapped out, in part, to send a positive message to the US electorate prior to the November 2004 elections.[8] Meanwhile, many human rights organizations, domestic and foreign, reported that human rights abuses by the Iraqi government, Coalition forces, paramilitary militia, and terrorist groups were pervasive in Iraq throughout the occupation and transition period. More specifically, these reports pointed to the prevalence of summary executions, extrajudicial killings, arbitrary detentions, torture, killings of civilians, and politically motivated kidnappings and assassinations.[9]

Although the democratic transformation of the Middle East became the latest vindication for US foreign policy under the George W. Bush administration toward this region, it was not clear whether this rationale would place democratization high on the US foreign policy agenda over the long term. On balance, predictions regarding the remaking of the Middle East were notoriously unreliable given the region's cultural alienation, political volatility, and ethnic and religious complexities. This unreliability emanated from the fact that competing US interests (security vs. democracy promotion) were likely to eclipse the region's democratic considerations, and also because there has always been a widespread commitment to a strong state throughout the Arab world.[10]

Perhaps most crucially, the US invasion of Iraq profoundly altered the strategic dimensions of Middle East politics, giving Iran access through its western portal to the Arab world and expanding its reach to the Shi'a heartlands in Iraq.[11] The fall of Baghdad gave a real impetus to Arab Shi'a aspirations for a stronger political voice in the Arab world. The end of centuries-old Sunni rule over Mesopotamia and control of key Shi'a sites—such as Najaf and Karbala—in Iraq posed an existential threat to Sunni neighbors, who had long feared the emergence of Shi'a-dominated states in their midst. These regimes were wary not only of a different interpretation of Islam gaining traction, but also of the political empowerment of their own Shi'a minorities.[12]

The 2011 Arab Spring uprisings led to revolts against the governments in Egypt, Tunisia, Bahrain, Libya, Syria, and Yemen, threatening the region's monarchies and republics alike and deepening sectarian divisions. Increasingly, Iraq became a bridge between Iran and Syria, giving Iran more strategic depth through greater access to Hezbollah, its core ally in Lebanon. The rise of ISIS consolidated Iran's hold on Iraqi national politics as never before, in part due to the fact that the genesis of this common threat rendered a closer military and political cooperation between the two countries imperative. Even Washington and Tehran found it prudent to cooperate on several occasions in Iraq in defeating ISIS.

With a gradual drawdown of US troops in 2011, Washington's long-term commitment to promoting democracy and stability in Iraq, and to doing so consistently, came under question. The US–Iran rivalry intensified, especially as it became abundantly clear that Tehran considered Shi'a ascendancy critical to its geopolitical goals. Iran's most pressing ambition, according to one analyst, was "to exploit the chaos of the region to project influence across Iraq and beyond."[13] Iran sought to establish a corridor on the ground through militias that, under its control, transported weapons and supplies to its proxies in Syria and Lebanon. While US officials focused on the battle against ISIS, returning more than 5,000 troops to the country and assisting Iraqis to force the militants out of Mosul (Iraq's second-largest city), Iran never lost sight of its larger mission "to dominate its neighbor so thoroughly that Iraq could never again endanger it militarily and to use the country to effectively control a corridor from Tehran to the Mediterranean."[14]

Iran and the United States seemingly pursued two very different goals in Iraq. Washington appeared keen on installing a pro-US government in Baghdad. Iran, by contrast, sought to ensure that "Baghdad politicians do not turn against Tehran and that a Shi'a government leads Iraq."[15] In 2018, Iran made it difficult for Iraqi Prime Minister Haider al-Abadi, who adopted a pro-American position, to run for re-election. Iran chose to work with local Popular Mobilization Units (PMUs), including the Hashd al-Shaabi spearheaded by Hadi al-Amiri, to defeat ISIS forces. Agents of Iran's Islamic Revolutionary Guards Corps (IRGC) recruited fighters in the Shi'a-majority cities of southern Iraq to fight ISIS. Members of the PMUs also mobilized an army of disaffected young Shi'a Iraqi men to fight anti-Assad forces on its behalf in Syria.[16] In the ensuing parliamentary elections, Iran mediated a cease-fire between rival Shi'a factions to facilitate a major victory for PMU political parties.[17]

Iran's wide-ranging networks in Iraq, both formal and informal, have solidified its influence there. In 2019, when anti-poverty protests assumed an anti-Iranian posture, the PMUs contained the crisis with the assistance of the IRGC. Since then, nearly two million Iranian pilgrims have traveled to Iraq annually to visit the holy shrines of Shi'a in Iraq. Iraqis have also continued to invest in Iranian industries, financial and banking operations, and real-estate markets. Moreover, Tehran has maintained a working relationship with the Kurdistan Regional Government (KRG) led by President Nechirvan Barzani.[18]

Iraq's recent prime minister, Mustafa al-Kadhimi, has ensured Tehran that his foreign policy is not in sync with the Trump administration's maximum pressure campaign. Kadhimi, in his visit with Iran's Foreign Minister Mohammad Javad Zarif on July 19, 2020, assured Tehran of adopting a balanced approach between Iran and the United States. Speaking to the US ambassador after being sworn in, Kadhimi asserted that "Iraq will not be a ground for settling accounts and launching attacks on any neighboring or friendly country"—a reference to the US assassinations of Quds Force commander Soleimani and Abu Mahdi al-Muhandis, deputy leader of Iraq's PMU, on Iraqi soil on January 3, 2020. Kadhimi's position resonated with

Tehran's concerns, which rejected the US use of Iraqi territory as a proxy theater to deploy its maximum pressure campaign against Iran. Among other assurances to Tehran, Kadhimi insisted: "Iraq would not allow any threat to Iran coming from its territory."[19]

Syria in the Middle of Violent Uprisings

The political unrest and civil war in Syria in the aftermath of the Arab Spring uprisings have posed daunting challenges not just to the region but to the world. The emergence of ISIS (locally known as *Daesh*), with its brutal tactics of spreading violence, has complicated legitimate internal opposition to the Assad regime. The civil war has become a catalyst for authoritarian restructuring, giving members of the political elite—including the military, Ba'ath Party leaders, high-ranking state functionaries, and members of the business oligarchy—a vested interest in supporting the Assad regime. State actors remained loyal to the survival of the state as control over parts of the decentralized system gave them much impetus for its preservation. Defection from the state slowed and a civil war ensued.[20]

The civil war was also largely facilitated by foreign intervention in the aftermath of the Arab Spring uprisings. Saudi Arabia and Qatar supported the overthrow of the Assad regime, pouring money and hardware into the conflict in support of violent extremist groups who deployed terrorist tactics to topple the Syrian government. Russia and Iran, by contrast, threw their support behind the Assad regime. Turkey took an anti-Assad posture, while making sure that it remained a relevant, albeit inconsistent, player in the Syrian crisis. Syria has since become a dangerous and deadly front line.[21]

Genocidal state conduct under Syria's Bashar al-Assad has long called for international action to protect Syrian citizens caught in the middle of violent uprisings. However, for a variety of geopolitical reasons—not least that the military intervention in Syria would be unpredictable and complicated—the case for such action was unappealing. A combination of internal and external factors accounted for a lack of geopolitical consensus favoring military intervention. Internally, the disjointed Syrian opposition movement was hampered by a lack of organization and effectiveness, largely because rebel groups were made up of different factions with diverse agendas and loose organizational affiliations. Unlike Tunisia and Egypt, where labor movements and trade organizations played an important role in toppling the regimes in power, no such trade unions independent of Syria's official trade union federation existed.[22]

Many experts argued that a military intervention was bound to make things worse for Syrian civilians, while plunging Syria and its neighboring countries into a sectarian conflagration and the West and the region into a protracted proxy war with no visible endgame in sight. Thus, no international actor was willing to face the risk of an unstable or fragmented Syria such as might follow the collapse of the regime. The fear of sectarian and ethnic tensions spilling over into neighboring countries, as well as a takeover by the Syrian Muslim Brotherhood, pitted geopolitical realities against the ethical call for military intervention.[23] This dilemma was best captured by Richard Falk: "Just as doing nothing is unacceptable, mounting a military intervention is unrealistic, and hence, impossible."[24]

Under such circumstances, as Richard Falk argued, determining what was the proper course of action appeared far from easy. "The clarity of condemnation," Falk insisted, "should not be confused with devising a prescription for action."[25] To begin with, military intervention would do more harm than good, leading to more questions than answers. Falk emphatically rejected such acts, arguing that "military intervention rarely succeeds, violates the right of self-determination, and often expands the scope and severity of violence, especially if carried out from the air."[26]

Who Are the Opposition?

A myriad of questions still surrounds the Syrian opposition. Who are they? Are they organized or disjointed? Are they affiliated with radical Islamist groups such as Al-Qaeda? Can they be trusted? Without clarity on the identity of rebel groups, there is no international consensus on how to work with the opposition or how to mobilize and legitimize a military intervention. It is widely agreed that the opposition to the Assad regime continues to suffer from two major weaknesses: its diversity and its loose structure.[27] These problems have raised some doubts among Western supporters concerning the efficacy of a military intervention. The Syrian National Council, for example, which represents a key opposition group, is utterly fragmented. It is neither broad-based nor organized. In Egypt and Libya, all the major and regional powers—either explicitly or tacitly—supported intervention. In Syria, however, there is no such consensus.

The fact remains that we know little about the opposition in Syria, or to what extent its governance of the country would be based on the rule of law and human rights. There are increasing reports about rebel atrocities as well as the role that Al-Qaeda operatives play in leading some of the rebel forces.[28] Much of the confusion surrounds US foreign policy and the role of regional actors in supporting rebel groups with arms and supplies. Considerable doubt has been raised about whether the White House's strategy of minimal and indirect intervention in the Syrian conflict is aiding a democratic-minded opposition or whether the opposition groups on the receiving end of the lethal aid are Islamic extremists. This confusion is reinforced by mounting frustration over the fact that "there is no central clearinghouse for the shipments, and no effective way of vetting the groups that ultimately receive them."[29]

The reports that Arab countries of the Persian Gulf, such as Qatar and Saudi Arabia, provide money and weapons to the anti-Assad uprising have raised serious questions about the endgame. Most of the arms shipped at the behest of Saudi Arabia and Qatar to supply Syrian rebels are going to hard-line Islamic jihadists and not the more secular opposition groups that the West wants to bolster. Thus far, the various rebel groups have failed to assemble a clear military plan, have lacked a coherent strategy for governing Syria afterward if the Assad government fell, and have too often quarreled among themselves, undermining their military and political effectiveness.[30] Meanwhile, international law experts have reminded us of the other side of these concerns: "Every government has the right to fight against its internal enemies, especially if heavily assisted by hostile external forces, although that right must be exercised within the framework of constraints imposed by international humanitarian law."[31]

Whether uprisings in Syria will morph into a revolutionary change remains the subject of much speculation. While Assad's regime seeks gradual and negotiated reforms, the protesters are interested in regime change. There is a growing power vacuum in the embattled streets, as the sorely divided exiled opposition fails to connect with the domestic protest movement.[32] That said, economic sanctions seem to be a credible option to undermine Assad's regime. The hope is that economic hardship may eventually turn more of the Syrian people, including its soldiers, against Assad.[33] Other diplomatic tools have failed to produce results. In December 2011, Syria agreed to allow 165 observers from the Arab League to monitor a deal, including ending the violence, releasing prisoners, and pulling the military out of the cities. That deal, however, failed to achieve a diplomatic solution when further violence erupted and many protesters were killed.

The Syrian government and United Nations officials have struck several deals covering how observers would operate and the responsibilities of the Syrian government. Yet the cease-fire has been repeatedly marred by lingering violence since March 15, 2011. A decade of civil war in Syria, according to one source, has left more than 380,000 people dead including over 115,000 civilians. These casualties include around 22,000 children and more than 13,000 women.[34]

Pro-Assad Actors

Iran and Russia have developed strong ties to the Assad regime. Any military intervention could turn the situation into a proxy war, and subsequently a protracted civil war with a huge number of civilian casualties, reminiscent of the decades-long civil war in Lebanon (1975–91) that resulted in over 150,000 deaths and one million displaced people.[35] Arming the Free Syrian Army or declaring safe zones increased the possibility of the civil war in a country where a strong army stood behind the Bashar Assad regime. Many Syrians felt caught in the middle, grudgingly supporting the current regime.

Since the 1979 Islamic Revolution, but more specifically during the Iran—Iraq War (1980–88), Iran and Syria have forged a new alliance that has been—and continues to be—based on geostrategic considerations rather than religion. Syria was the only Arab country that sided with Iran during that war. Iran, in turn, became a reliable supplier of energy to Syria, while the Arab countries of the Persian Gulf offered various economic incentives to Syria to bring it back into the fold. For Iran, the Syrian connection bolsters its regional status and power. Likewise, the current alliance with Iran puts Syria in a position to enhance the "price it can demand from the West in exchange for making peace with Israel or ensuring quiet in Lebanon."[36] This alliance with Iran has subsequently become known as an "Axis of Resistance," along with Hezbollah and Hamas, since the 1980s. The US invasion of Iraq in March 2003 reinvigorated that alliance.

Since the March 2011 uprisings in Syria, however, maintaining this alliance has become costly for Iran, both politically and financially, as it has led to further isolation of Iran, while jeopardizing its most important Arab ally. Some experts have reminded us that Iran has paid a prohibitive price to stay in Syria. It has paid over $16 billion to support the Syrian army and an additional $7 billion in credit lines and humanitarian assistance. Nevertheless, Tehran has taken advantage of economic opportunities in Syria to dodge sanctions and supply petroleum to the Syrian Baniyas port on the Mediterranean, while also benefiting from the expansion of a pipeline and railroad through Iraq to the port.[37] Furthermore, Iran has broadened commercial and naval operations near the port of Latakia in an effort to link it to Iran's ports in the Persian Gulf.[38]

Iranians also insisted that the Syrian opposition was by no means a popular force, as the Sunni majority feared a Salafi minority. Iran was also highly critical of the offer made by then UN General Secretary Kofi Annan (March 10, 2012) that revolved around a six-point plan:

> (1) commit to work with the Envoy in an inclusive Syrian-led political process to address the legitimate aspirations and concerns of the Syrian people; (2) commit to stop the fighting and achieve urgently an effective UN supervised cessation of armed violence in all its forms by all parties to protect civilians and stabilize the country; (3) ensure timely provision of humanitarian assistance to all areas affected by the fighting; (4) intensify the pace and scale of release of arbitrarily detained persons, including especially vulnerable categories of persons, and persons involved in peaceful political activities, provide without delay through appropriate channels a list of all places in which such persons are being detained; (5) ensure freedom of movement throughout the country for journalists and a non-discriminatory visa

policy for them; (6) respect freedom of association and the right to demonstrate peacefully as legally guaranteed.[39]

Iranians criticized Annan's plan: "It never clarified in what way the crisis in Syria is supposed to hit its end. It was also silent on the future power structure in the country and specifications of the transition period."[40] Iranian officials noted that the United States and other regional players were bent on turning the Arab Spring into a conflict between Shi'as and Sunnis. To Iranians, the Syrian government and army maintain a firm grip over the country. Thus, Iranians noted that it was unlikely that Russia and China would reach an agreement with the West over Syria. Iranians saw forging a reliable anti-Western front consisting of Russia and China as a strategic goal.[41]

Russia and China, on several occasions (albeit for different reasons), have blocked Western-backed UN Security Council (UNSC) resolutions on Syria that aimed at placing more pressure on Syrian President Bashar al-Assad to step down. China's relations with the Middle East were undergoing a major shift, in large part due to its "Energy First" policy focus. China's diplomacy was transforming from reactive to more proactive. Chinese officials seemed to pursue three objectives: First, China as a net importer of oil had to secure strong, stable ties with oil-exporting countries. Second, China had problems in Xinjiang, where the local population is of Turkic origin and of Muslim religion. Thus, China had to make sure that Islamic countries of the Middle East did not become safe havens for anti-Chinese groups operating in the region. Finally, as Washington played the Taiwan card to put the pressure on Beijing, Beijing was tempted to play the Syrian card in return to secure concessions from Washington.[42]

Adopting a position of neutrality, Chinese Foreign Minister Yang Jiechi noted that China favored a period of political transition in Syria, while expressing Beijing's opposition to forceful military intervention. Jiechi's remarks struck a cautionary note: "any solution should come from the people of Syria and reflect their wishes. It should not be imposed from outside."[43] Like Russia, China was wary of calls for change escalating into foreign intervention. In 2011, China joined Russia in approving a UNSC resolution on intervening in Libya to prevent further bloodshed and attacks on civilians, but later suggested NATO powers had exceeded the UN mandate by expanding a bombing campaign that proved decisive in toppling Libyan leader Muammar Qaddafi.[44]

Russia's interests in Syria, by contrast, were (and are) deeply commercial and strategic. Russia's naval facility at the Syrian port of Tartus—Russia's sole remaining naval base on the Mediterranean—is of enormous military-strategic significance. Its loss would have negative consequences, including the loss of political influence in the region. Commercially speaking, present and future contracts to sell arms to Damascus, one expert notes, amount to a total of $5 billion. Russia's defense industry, having lost $13 billion due to international sanctions on Iran and $4.5 billion in canceled contracts to Libya, was facing financial difficulties. In addition to arms exports, Russian companies had major investments in Syria's infrastructure, energy, and tourism sectors, worth $19.4 billion in 2009.[45]

From a strategic standpoint, other experts remind us that the real reason why Russia resisted strong international action against the Assad regime was that it feared the spread of Islamic militancy and the diminution of its great-power status in a world where Western nations were increasingly undertaking unilateral military interventions. Many Russian observers believed that the 2011 Arab uprisings had completely destabilized the region, while paving the way for the Islamists' ascendancy to power. In Moscow, they argued, secular authoritarian governments, such as Syria, were on balance viewed as the sole realistic alternative to Islamic dominance.[46] The active support from Saudi Arabia, Qatar, and Turkey's Islamist government for rebels in Syria, they concluded, further heightened Russian suspicions concerning the Islamist-led revolutions in Syria and in other uprisings throughout the Middle East.[47]

No Good Options in Syria

The bloody uprising in Syria thrust the Obama administration into an increasingly tough and complicated position as the conflict proceeded. The then US Secretary of State Hillary Clinton frequently accused Russia of sending attack helicopters to Syria in order to defeat anti-Assad rebels. Meanwhile, opposition forces received more powerful anti-tank missiles from Turkey, with the financial support of Saudi

Arabia and Qatar. The shipment of these heavier weapons to both sides plunged Syria into a bloody civil war.[48]

Turkey and the United States adopted a similar position vis-à-vis Syria, condemning Bashar al-Assad and the spread of violence against civilians in the ongoing Syrian conflict. The Turkish government sought to establish itself as a regional power—an eventuality that Washington welcomed. Since 9/11 and the US wars in Afghanistan and Iraq, the United States viewed Turkey as a counterbalance to Iran, Lebanese Hezbollah, Hamas in Gaza, Saudi-supported Salafists, and Al-Qaeda and Islamic Jihad. Both the United States and the Arab countries of the Persian Gulf, along with the rest of the Middle East, recognized and welcomed Turkey's role as counterbalance to Iran.

This perspective, however, did not entirely gloss over the fact that external intervention and support for rebels—both inside and outside the country—raised fears that the unrest in Syria would most likely broaden into a regional war. Ultimately, seeking a solution to the crisis in Syria required Iran's active participation for any conceivable regional agreement. Iran's regional policies mattered—possibly more so than in the past—insofar as they supported a regional consensus with Egypt and Turkey that a NATO-initiated international military intervention had to be avoided.

From Tehran's perspective, the potential collapse of Assad's regime would have profound implications for the regional as well as trans-regional balance of power to the detriment of Iran's position, leaving it virtually alone among an array of bitter rivals, such as Saudi Arabia and Israel, not to mention competitors such as Turkey and Egypt. Iranians feared that any major change in Syria would likely undermine Iran's connections with its "resistance proxies" such as Hezbollah in Lebanon and Hamas in Palestine.[49] In the meantime, the fear of a Sunni Islamist takeover after the collapse of Assad's regime in Syria loomed large. As noted above, a military attack on Syria by NATO—à la the military intervention in Libya—was risky and unlikely.

Several possible scenarios, according to the region's experts, were visualized. One scenario was that leftist and secular groups would spearhead a revolutionary mass movement. The other was that Islamist groups would take over the movement. This possibility could divert the movement toward a religious civil war. Shortly after the revolt broke out, a small group of Syrian people began chanting: "The Alawites to their grave, the Christians to Beirut."[50] Yet another scenario was a military coup that would replace political leadership with one unburdened by an alliance with Iran and Hezbollah.[51]

This last scenario continued to appeal to the fragile anti-Assad coalition. Indeed, shortly after the initial round of violence, an unconfirmed video of Syrian protests posted on the Internet showed Syrian protesters chanting, "la Hezbollah, la Iran," meaning "no Hezbollah, no Iran."[52] Yet violence continued, despite several UN-brokered cease-fires. On June 27, 2012, Annan announced the creation of an "action group," composed of the UNSC's five permanent members, representatives of the European Union, the Arab League, Qatar, Kuwait, Turkey, and Iraq. Conspicuously absent from the list of the nations invited were Iran, the staunch regional ally of President Basher al-Assad of Syria, and Saudi Arabia, a prominent supporter of Assad's opponents. The aim of this group was to "identity the steps and measures to secure full implementation of Mr. Annan's six-point plan" and to bring "an immediate cessation of violence in all forms."[53]

Many observers, including Mr. Annan, warned that the turmoil, which began as a peaceful Arab Spring opposition movement against President Assad in March 2011, could potentially plunge Syria and its neighboring countries into a sectarian conflagration. The outcome of this new initiative would depend, among other things, on whether the United States and Russia could bridge their differences over Syria. While the United States insisted that President Assad step down, Russia, the main military supplier to Assad's government, disapproved of any solution in which political change in Syria was to be imposed by outside powers.[54]

Some experts argued that, despite the fact that a decision to intervene in Syria was complex and daunting, the escalating atrocities, the continued stalemate, the remote likelihood for a negotiated settlement in the current state of the conflict, and the strategic benefits provided sufficient grounds for the United States and its allies to act.[55] Yet other observers, while warning against foreign military intervention in Syria, noted that the Syrians themselves should win this struggle. The international community was unlikely to act as it did in the case of Libya. Military intervention was immensely difficult in

Syria. Moreover, the political will in the West to do so was conspicuously lacking.[56]

Cooperation in Syria

Russia has found a useful ally in Iran for supporting Syria's Assad regime. For Iran, cooperation with Russia during the Syrian civil war has been rationalized on pragmatic and geostrategic grounds. Both countries have cooperated to prevent yet another regime change in their spheres of influence. While Russia's presence in Syria was motivated by its interest in containing the US presence in that part of the Mediterranean, Iran seeks to consolidate its access to Lebanon and Syria and undermine the influence of its Arab rivals and Israel. The question remains whether this short-term cooperation—marked by strategic dependence between Moscow and Tehran—would last in post-conflict Syria.

Both Russia and Iran intend to expand their footprints across the region. Iran's support for the Assad regime is motivated by its access to Lebanon, while Russia's interests revolve around its access to the Mediterranean region. Russia's evolving and improving ties with Iran's key regional rivals—Saudi Arabia and Israel—are likely to pose a serious challenge to its relations with Iran. However, the divergent and overlapping interests of these states are not new to either country. Today, Tehran and Moscow appear set to promote economic ties even further in the post-nuclear-deal era. One major question in the context of Iran–Russia relations is whether some modicum of the rapprochement between Iran and the West will adversely affect Tehran's relations with Moscow.

It is worth noting that the Iran nuclear deal offered numerous economic and political challenges as well as potential advantages to Russia. With sanctions removed and expanding Iranian oil production added to a market in which prices are near a decade-long low, Moscow is likely to suffer significant losses in revenue due to increased oil production and lower prices. Russia did stand to gain, however, from additional arms sales, expanding economic investments—including in the lucrative broader alternative energy sector—and an internationally approved partnership in the nuclear enrichment plant in Bushehr.

Another notable area of expanding economic ties between the two countries is investment in infrastructure, where Iran needed major overhauls to accommodate a new economic opening after sanctions relief. Building rail lines and reactors are the main goals of such cooperation. There are also multiple, additional regional opportunities for cooperation on infrastructure development involving Iran's projected growth of commodity and manufactured product exports to markets in the region and beyond. These opportunities also pave the way for a mutual investment to build and expand links to some of Iran's Middle Eastern neighbors and to Central Asia—a transaction that could significantly bolster Russia's chance to develop a sphere of influence in that region.

Beyond economic ties, Iranian and Russian cooperation in defeating ISIS and the Levant Conquest Front (formerly known as the al-Nusra Front) and bolstering the Assad regime ushered in a convergence of interests between the two nations. With the cultivation of a closer partnership with Iran as a result of the lifting of sanctions, Russia aimed for a stronger role in the Middle East while attempting to curb Western influence in the region. In this context, Moscow found the Iranian and Syrian regimes, and their regional proxies (such as Hezbollah), keys to its strategy of securing a counter-US camp that could play a role in expanding its influence in the region.

Given Russia's strained relations with the United States and its allies over its annexation of Crimea and interference in eastern Ukraine, and the subsequent imposition of Western economic sanctions since mid-2014, this strategy gained even greater traction. In fact, it is not far-fetched to argue that since the 2014 imposition of Western sanctions on Russia, Moscow has forged its own version of an Eastern Strategy, seeking closer alliances with countries such as China, India, and Iran. Russia's commitment to China-initiated cooperation among Brazil, Russia, India, China, and South Africa (generally known as BRICS) in 2015, and the enlistment of these countries in the Asian Infrastructure Investment Bank—regarded by many as an alternative to the World Bank—were also indicative of Moscow's embrace of this new policy orientation.

The emergence of ISIS transformed the nature of Iran–Russia relations from a bilateral connection to a regional or multilateral one.

That is to say, the crisis spurred by ISIS intensified the competition among Saudi Arabia, Iran, and Turkey on the one hand, and Russia and the West on the other, over influence in Syria, Iraq, and the larger Middle East. The ISIS terrorist attacks in Paris on November 13, 2015, by gunmen and suicide bombers hit a concert hall, a major stadium, restaurants, and bars all at the same time, leaving 130 people dead and hundreds wounded. The attacks invariably influenced these connections. If nothing else, they crystallized the flaw in US-EU-GCC-Turkey policy that stipulated that the most effective way to fight ISIS was to topple the Assad regime. In the aftermath of the Paris attacks, the United States and its allies changed their position from prioritizing the removal of the Assad regime to retaining Assad in order to preserve the Syrian state system. The fight against ISIS became the top priority of countering the breakup of the state system in the Middle East and North Africa (MENA) region. The nature of any future government in Syria, and whether Assad would have a role in it, was to be decided later through negotiations.

Reportedly, there was some coordination between Iranian and Hezbollah ground troops in Syria and the Russian air force on the battlefield as Russia assumed a more pro-active role in the Syrian civil war since October 2015. It was likely that Russia, after the downing of its passenger jet by ISIS over Egypt's Sinai desert and the attack on Paris, would be looking to bolster Iran–Russia military cooperation in Syria. President Putin's trip to Tehran and his meeting with Khamenei and Rouhani in November 2015 were designed to achieve these goals.

Thus, Iran–Russia ties were not going to be drastically affected by Tehran's anticipated rapprochement with the West, in large part because Iran's cooperation with Russia had already solidified in the wake of the rising threat from extremists and terrorist groups in the region such as ISIS and the Levant Conquest Front. In 2015, deaths of Iranian and Hezbollah troops in Syria spiked. Experts estimated that Hezbollah lost between 1,000 and 2,500 members of its militia, while Iran lost 300 fighters battling ISIS, forty of whom have died since September 30, 2015. Several top commanders of Iran's Revolutionary Guards also died in the Syrian civil war.

Similarly, Iran's cooperation with Russia in the South Caucasus has long endured many uncertainties, as the latter's foreign policy toward the South Caucasus has proven remarkably durable. Both Tehran and Moscow shared a concern over the emergence of the independent state of Azerbaijan and the possibility of separatist tendencies among Iranian Azaris. They both also displayed an increasing desire to control the development of petroleum resources in the Caspian Basin while seeking to restrain Turkish influence over pipeline routes. The subsequent fallout between Moscow and Ankara over Turkey's downing of a Russian fighter jet in Syria also accentuated the Russian desire for closer relations with Iran.

More recently, Iran's regional and strategic goals in the context of its relations with Russia revolved not only around the traditional form of ties between the two countries, which has entailed the development of civil nuclear projects and broader cooperation in South Caucasus, but also the transfer to Iran of sophisticated weapons systems, items that the West has refrained from selling to Tehran. Consider, for example, Russia's sale of the S-300PMU-2 long-range surface-to-air missile (SAM) batteries. These systems have reinforced the air defense of the Islamic Republic of Iran,[57] while Washington considered this deal destabilizing to the region.

Russia, as experts remind us, has intimately cooperated with Iran in Syria by creating an electronic payment system that facilitates direct financial transfers between Iran and Russia. Yet Moscow has refused to give Iran its S-400 air-defense systems. During 2019, Russia, China, and Iran held naval exercises in the Indian Ocean and the Gulf of Oman, indicating a way in which Iran enhances its regional standing. Tehran views these joint exercises as a sign that "China and Russia are able to challenge the hegemonic power of the United States."[58]

Ironically (but understandably), Russia has a great deal to lose if Iran regains its political and economic role in the region and beyond once previous restrictive measures rooted in the sanctions are no longer in place. If not managed skillfully, the Iranian-Russian marriage of convenience is likely to end once the two countries start competing over European and Asian energy markets. Should Iran pour millions of additional barrels of oil into the market, it would likely exert much greater downward pressure on the price of oil in the short term. However, this is only one part of the equation determining the future course of Iran–Russia relations. Much is contingent on the policies of Western powers, led by the United States, toward Iran, as well as the opportunities and obstacles that arise in Tehran's relations with the other pillar of its Eastern Strategy—China.

Iran's Strategy in the South Caucasus

The South Caucasus region, comprising Armenia, Azerbaijan, and Georgia, is an immensely important area known for its geopolitical location, largely as a crossing point between the Middle East, Europe, and Asia. It is also known for its vast oil deposits. The region continues to hold pivotal geopolitical significance, situated where many countries' interests—including the United States, the European Union, Russia, and some key regional actors, such as Iran and Turkey—intersect.[59] The competition between and among regional actors—Russia, Iran, and Turkey—has become an enduring feature of the South Caucasus region.

The motives and policies of regional and external actors in South Caucasus are frequently at odds, adding to the complexity, volatility, and political instability of the region. While each of these actors are driven by different motives, as Marzieh Kouhi-Esfahani notes, they all seem to be acutely aware of the power struggle over the control of energy resources and transport routes that has created a post-Soviet "Great Game" with varied actors and greater gains.[60] A combination of concerns over the region's stability and investment in its energy supplies has drawn Western corporates to the South Caucasus, creating an unprecedented amount of foreign trade with these countries. With a population of approximately eighteen million, this small market serves as an important transit route for Europe and for Eastern countries such as China through its transport systems, while simultaneously providing trade opportunities for both sides. The prospect of full integration into the "Belt and Road initiative" through advanced transport and technological resources is likely to appreciate the region's market value.[61]

Increasingly, the rivalry between Iran and Turkey to get access to South Caucasus energy routes has become nearly impossible to avoid. Following the collapse of the Soviet Union and the independence of the newly emerged states since the early 1990s, the conflict between

Armenia and Azerbaijan has intensified. Consequently, we have witnessed major tradeoffs in the foreign policy strategy of the Islamic Republic, as Iran has chosen to support Armenia in this conflict. The adoption of this foreign policy position by Iran has demonstrated that economic and political considerations—not religious factors—have dominated this mutually beneficial relationship.

This suggests that when geopolitical interests conflict with commitments of Islamic ideology, beliefs, and solidarity, too often Tehran prioritizes the country's security and economic considerations above all others.[62] While Iran's border with both Azerbaijan and Armenia has afforded Tehran a great advantage, its close relations with Armenia has taken a hefty geopolitical toll. This includes the intensification of pan-Turkish sentiments in neighboring Azerbaijan.[63]

In short, Iran's policy in the Caucasus has been (and continues to be) based largely on geopolitical concerns. Domestic factors, such as the presence of a significant Azerbaijani minority in Iran, also influence Iran's policies toward the region. More importantly, however, regional competition with Russia and Turkey, as well as a rivalry with the US presence and interests, broadly shapes Iran's foreign policy. Officially, Iran declares itself neutral in the conflict between Armenia and Azerbaijan. However, Tehran lacks any desire to see the tensions between Azerbaijan and Armenia escalate and create waves of refugees and other potentially destabilizing developments on its northwest border. Tehran adopts anti-Armenian rhetoric, however, only when the results of the conflict between these two countries pose a direct threat to Iranian state interests or when pressured by the political activities of Iranian Azerbaijanis.[64]

Iran's relations with Azerbaijan could deteriorate rapidly if there is any Azerbaijani involvement in supporting nationalist and secessionist feelings among ethnic Azeris in Iran, who make up nearly sixteen percent of the population.[65] The rise of secessionist and nationalistic sentiments has limited Iran's ability to play a constructive role in the Caucasus region. Increased Azerbaijan–Armenia hostility has historically provoked nationalist attitudes on both sides, arousing narrowly based parochial sentiments that Iran seeks to avoid.[66]

Baku's irredentist idea of a "united Azerbaijan" and the notion of "southern Azerbaijan" have generated counterclaims from Iranian

Azerbaijanis, whose strong Iranian identity tends to overshadow their religious identity as Shi'a Muslims. Although authorities from the Republic of Azerbaijan have denied taking any apparent anti-Iranian ethno-nationalistic positions, the activities of irredentist elements such as the World Azerbaijanis Congress (WAC) or The Southern Azerbaijan National Awakening Movement (SANAM—also known as GAMOH), a Baku-based opposition movement, have rendered Iranian nationalist circles—particularly Iranian Azeris—skeptical about Baku's intentions.[67]

Interestingly enough, despite Azerbaijan and Armenia's three-decades-long hostilities over the region of Nagorno-Karabakh, their reactions to the US drone strike on January 3, 2020, that killed General Qassem Soleimani, head of the Islamic Revolutionary Guard Corps (IRGC) Quds Force, was almost identical: Both conveyed condolences to Tehran and called for US–Iran de-escalation. Were a conflict to break out between Iran and the US, it would have had serious consequences by spreading far beyond the Middle East, including—due to its geographical and strategic importance—the South Caucasus. A resulting refugee crisis could overwhelm the small states of Azerbaijan, Armenia, and Georgia, and would most likely disrupt the oil and gas flow to the region if attacks targeted regional pipelines.[68] Undoubtedly, as experts remind us, "security challenges faced by Iran can affect the security and stability of this small region."[69]

Iran's leverage in the South Caucasus is greatly limited by two major factors. First, the ongoing US–Iran hostility and Washington's policies to isolate Iran in both the MENA region and the South Caucasus have contained Iran's influence in its northern neighborhood. US sanctions have effectively limited Iran's ability to exploit its vast potential economic and political opportunities in the South Caucasus. Even in the aftermath of the Joint Comprehensive Plan of Action (JCPOA), and following the removal of nuclear-related sanctions, continuous US sanctions have substantially hampered Iran's investments in the region. Given the risks associated with investing in and doing business with Iran, the countries of the South Caucasus have refrained from forging extensive and closer relations with Iran.

Second, these economic and political burdens have contributed greatly to the development of Iran's Russo-centric policy, compelling

Iran to avoid alienating Russia by aligning its interests with those of Moscow as much as possible. Both Russia and Iran, however, sought to contain Western influence as well as limit the expansion of Turkey's growing role in Azerbaijan. For Iran, cooperation with Russia also meant securing Moscow's support for avoiding the ongoing tensions between Tehran and the West over its nuclear program.[70] Consequently, Iran's more proactive policies and increased outreach in the region have been significantly compromised.[71]

Conflict in Armenia

Landlocked between Turkey, Azerbaijan, and Georgia, Armenia has relied on Russia and Iran to break from its enclave. Armenia has no confirmed oil or gas reserves and currently imports nearly all of its gas from Russia. At times, this increasing dependence on Russia has proven problematic. Although it is believed that strong ties with Russia are crucial for Armenia over the long term, the so-called "strategic partnership" with Moscow has frequently become one-sided, marked by Russian control over key sectors of the Armenian economy, including much of the energy sector and the rail network, as well as an expanding hold over the mining, construction, and telecommunications sectors.[72]

Natural gas represents a large portion of total energy consumption in Armenia and is the primary means of winter heating in the country. Gazprom Armenia (owned by the Russian gas giant Gazprom) owns the natural gas pipeline network within Armenia and holds a monopoly over the import and distribution of natural gas to consumers and businesses. Armenia's thermal power stations (which supply approximately twenty-four percent of Armenia's electricity needs) run on natural gas, making Armenia (at the present time) dependent on imported Russian gas.

The Iran–Armenia gas pipeline (constructed in 2007) is operative with a capacity of 22.2 million cubic feet of gas per day.[73] The Iranian section runs from Tabriz to the Iran–Armenia border. The Armenian section runs from the Meghri region to Sardarian. Isolated either by drastic sanctions, as is the case for Iran, or surrounded by hostile countries such as Turkey and Azerbaijan, as is the case for Armenia, both countries face many rivals in their immediate region. Both countries pursue the politics of survival while also desperately seeking regional allies. The symbiotic relationship between the two is rooted in the exigencies that their national interests demand.[74] Any US efforts to reduce cross-border trade in electricity and hydrocarbon is bound to encounter substantial opposition in Yerevan.[75]

Armenia has maintained and continued to preserve its security relationship with Moscow, in large part because Russia has offered a security umbrella for Armenia, given Armenia's tacit state of war with Azerbaijan over Nagorno-Karabakh. Today, Armenia is the only country in the region to host a Russian military base.[76] It has repeatedly ruled out any aspirations for full NATO membership, reinforcing its commitment to the Russian strategic relationship.[77]

In 2019, Iran proposed an Iran–Armenia gas transit to Georgia, which would most likely reduce the Caucasus's reliance on Russia—but would likely provoke reactions from both Moscow and Washington. "If implemented," according to one source, "the plan would introduce some competition into the Georgian gas market. Georgia is currently supplied entirely from Azerbaijan."[78] Iran regards Armenia as key to accessing South Caucasus and thus, European countries. Azerbaijanis resent Iran's ties with Armenia, viewing the closer relationship between these two countries as deleterious to their interests.[79] Since the end of the first Nagorno-Karabakh war (1994), diplomatic ties between Iran and Azerbaijan have been difficult to say the least. While economic and energy relations have resumed, with Iran being the only natural gas supplier to the Azerbaijani exclave of Nakhchivan, diplomatic relations between the two countries have remained fraught if not frozen. Tehran continues to be wary of Baku issuing ongoing irredentist calls in Iran's ethnic Azeri regions and displays of pan-Turkic sentiments.[80]

The recent conflict over the disputed Nagorno-Karabakh region ended through a Moscow-brokered truce that resulted in the deployment of some 2,000 Russian peacekeepers and significant Armenian territorial concessions. Armenian officials insisted that Azerbaijan fired the first shots. Azerbaijani officials maintained that they launched a "counter-offensive" in response to Armenian aggression. Under the trilateral truce agreement facilitated by Russia, Yerevan will return territories it has held since the 1990s. Clearly, the current "ceasefire agreement" will undermine Iran's economic interests. Before this agreement, Iranian territory provided the only land connections between Azerbaijan and its exclave of Nakhichevan. The new route, experts remind us, will significantly diminish Iran's regional transit, and hence its leverage over Nakhchivan.

From the Iranian point of view, the elongation of the war would have a spillover impact and afford Western powers the ability to use the "Azeri card" to destabilize Northern Iran. Tehran is equally concerned about increasing military cooperation between Azerbaijan and Israel following the signing of a $1.6 billion arms deal in 2012. Israeli defense officials agreed to sell drones as well as anti-aircraft and missile defense systems to Azerbaijan, bringing sophisticated Israeli military technology to the doorstep of a key adversary in the region—that is, Iran.[81] It should be noted in the 1990s Israel built electronic intelligence-gathering stations along the Azerbaijani border with Iran. The Rouhani administration has long realized that the deterioration of ties with Azerbaijan could handicap Iran's position in the South Caucasus, thus reinforcing the rationale behind building closer ties with Baku.[82] Some experts have warned, however, against the speculation that Iran may be shifting away from its policy of neutrality to a more explicit support of Azerbaijan.[83]

Yemen's Civil War

Yemen has experienced internal divisions and civil conflicts for decades. As the region's poorest country, it has battled violence, instability, water scarcity, and food insecurity. The roots of recent troubles, however, lie in the 2011 Arab Spring uprisings that evolved into a brutal civil war agitated by foreign intervention. Pro-democracy protesters took to the streets in order to end the thirty-three-year rule of the then president, Ali Abdullah Saleh. Growing tensions on the streets of Sana'a resulted in police violence against protesters. Yemenis experienced a brief moment of optimism after the Arab Spring uprisings toppled Saleh, but those hopes evaporated into civil war. Following an internationally brokered deal, there was a transfer of power to the vice president, Abd Rabbu Mansour Hadi—widely regarded as a puppet ruler. The real powers in the areas he seemingly controlled—the country's south and east—were an unruly collection of armed groups and jihadists, including Al-Qaeda. Most of these groups were sponsored by Saudi Arabia or the UAE.[84]

In the ensuing elections in February 2012, Hadi became the only candidate to lead a transitional government. His rule and attempts at constitutional and economic reforms were resisted by Houthi rebels from the north. The Houthis, who center their belief system on the Zaydi branch of Islam linked to Shi'ism, captured the capital in 2014, demanding a new government. Following botched negotiations, the rebels seized the presidential palace in January 2015, forcing President Hadi to flee to Saudi Arabia. Subsequently, Saudi Arabia intervened in Yemen's civil war to back President Hadi and to facilitate his return to Yemen. To that end, Saudi Arabia led a Sunni Arab coalition to fight the Houthis in lockstep with pursuing a regional strategy aimed at toppling the Assad regime in Syria. In the meantime, Houthis consolidated their control over most population centers in the northwest, including Sana'a.

In March 2015, Saudi Arabia and the UAE spearheaded a military intervention against the Houthis. The Houthis responded by launching missile and drone strikes against the Saudis. The subsequent Saudi air strikes of Yemen led to one of the region's greatest humanitarian disasters. Iranian support for the Houthis prompted fear of a sectarian war. While the Houthis have benefited from the Iranian support, the notion that they are an Iranian proxy is exaggerated. Tehran's support for the Houthis is negligible, and its influence in Yemen, insignificant.[85] Iran, however, views its military alliance with the Houthis as a low-cost, effective way to retaliate against Saudi Arabia.[86]

As the war has dragged on, Iranian influences have also grown. The prospect of the Houthi–Iran relationship evolving into a Hezbollahlike proxy network, however, remains unlikely. Iran prefers to invest more resources in Iraqi proxies than in Houthis. In all likelihood, as one expert points out, Yemen's future will remain inextricably linked to the future of its neighbors in the Arabian Peninsula more than to Iran.[87] There is little or no evidence that Iran controls the Houthis' movement or strategy. Apparently, the Houthis disregarded Iranian advice not to take over Sana'a in 2014. While the Arab coalition spends anywhere from $5–6 billion on the war every month, Iran's financial support for the Houthis has never exceeded several million dollars annually.[88] Framing the conflict as a sectarian war by proxy overlooks the complexity of the warring factions' strategies and alliances. After taking control of the capital, the Houthi movement drew considerable support from a wide but complex array of local groups, tribes, and military officers, who begrudged their exclusion at the hands of the central government.[89]

Similarly, viewing this conflict from a sectarian perspective also misses the extent to which regional players have historically used the crisis for their own political gain. Since the early 1980s, the Saudi leadership, alarmed by the Iranian Revolution, was suspicious of the Zaydis' tendency to gravitate toward Shi'ite Islam as practiced in Iran. The Saudis began a campaign to intrusively advance their own hardline Sunni religious ideas across the border in a bid to curb Tehran's influence. This included the creation of a Salafist school in the city of Dammaj, where several Al-Qaeda figures became indoctrinated. This strategy, alongside previous Saudi efforts to control Yemen's politics via regular payments to tribal sheikhs, military officers, and other political elites, enabled the Saudis to regularly manipulate the country's politics.

The Saudis, as Robert F. Worth notes, "exported a toxic cocktail of sectarianism and corruption to Yemen."[90] Similarly, the UAE promoted its interventionist strategy in Yemen in order to develop its own economic and geopolitical interests, while taking advantage of its presence in southern Yemen and its patronage of local actors, including local Salafis and southern secessionist forces. This strategy allowed the UAE effective control of energy infrastructure, oil fields, and commercial ports, all of which link to broader Emirati objectives in the region.[91]

On September 14, 2019, the attacks on oil production facilities at Abqaiq and Khurais in Saudi Arabia drew renewed focus to Yemen's Houthi movement, which claimed responsibility for the strikes. There was, however, no evidence that these attacks had been launched by the Houthis. UN investigators underlined the fact that they doubted that the drones and land attack cruise missiles used in these attacks "have a sufficient range to have been launched from Yemeni territory under the control of the Houthis."[92]

With the war in Yemen stalemated, the UAE pulled back its troops from a military base in Khokha, some 80 miles south of the Red Sea city of Hodeidah, handing over control to Saudi Arabia and Yemeni forces. UAE officials insisted that the decision to redeploy was a result of the diplomatic breakthrough made by the UN in the strategically important Hodeidah. Emirati officials denied the notion that the drawdown reflected a growing disagreement between Abu Dhabi and Riyadh. Yet this move clearly exposed the reality that their military and political leaders held different views and strategies, regarding not only the bloody impasse in Yemen, but also how to deal with the threat posed by Iran to Arab Gulf states and interests.[93]

Conclusion

Many factors shape Iran's foreign policy and the sustainability of its power. Iran's most crucial ambition is to capitalize on regional conflicts and the chaos they generate so as to extend its influence. To that end, Iran has pursued different strategies to promote its interests in the face of regional conflicts. In some cases, such as Iraq's political instability following the US invasion of that country, Iran doubled down on Shi'ite ascendancy as a geopolitical goal. In other conflict-ridden areas, such as Syria, Yemen, and South Caucasus, its ideational pursuits have played a lesser role in advancing its goals.

The outbreak of civil war in Iraq in the aftermath of the US invasion, for example, opened up a unique opportunity for Iran both to influence Iraqi politics and to sponsor a militia that could establish a corridor to ship weapons and men to proxy forces in Syria and Lebanon. The Syrian civil war, which erupted in the wake of the 2011 Arab Spring uprisings, became a litmus test for Iran's regional policy and its commitment to protect its sole ally in the Arab world. Iran's support for the Assad regime was motivated by the campaign against ISIS and Jabhat al-Nusra more generally. The preservation of the Assad regime also had less to do with the connection between Syria's Alawites, who are the ruling minority in that country, and Iranian Shi'ites, and much to do with the fact that Syria is a major conduit for the transfer of arms to Lebanese Hezbollah.

Iran's reaction to the recent war between Azerbaijan and Armenia over the Nagorno-Karabakh dispute illustrated Tehran's rational, calculated, and pragmatic approach. While reassuring the conflicting parties of its neutral position, Iran made clear that it recognized Azerbaijan's territorial integrity. Tehran's decision to be neutral in this conflict was in fact intended to avoid antagonizing the two key regional actors involved in it, namely Russia and Turkey. Furthermore, this conflict presented a security dilemma of sorts to Iran, as it fueled Azerbaijani ethnic nationalism inside the country. This explained Iran's preference to end the conflict swiftly. Understandably, Iran counted on Russia's mediation, knowing that it was unlikely that Moscow would allow the entire territory of Nagorno-Karabakh to fall into Azeri hands and thus allow the regional balance of power to shift in favor of Baku.[94]

Iran's support for the Houthis in Yemen has been limited, and less driven by ideological factors than by geopolitical competition with Saudi Arabia. Given that the current tensions in Yemen predate the 2011 Arab Spring uprisings, it is safe to argue, as some experts do, that "Houthis are neither a proxy nor a pawn of Tehran."[95] Iran's influence in Yemen is marginal. So too is its ability to project power in the country. While ideology and faith served Iran's interests in Iraq, Iran's foreign policy toward the Caucasus and Central Asia in the aftermath of the dissolution of the Soviet Union pointed to the needs of practical action. Another illustrative case is the Nagorno-Karabakh conflict over an enclave of majority ethnic Armenians in Azerbaijan in which Iran chose to support Armenia. Iran's mediating efforts, which ran counter to its Islamic ideology and which resulted in its support for Christian Armenia in its conflict with Shi'a Azerbaijan, are primarily driven by pragmatic motivations, such as becoming a transit route for Caspian Sea oil resources to the Persian Gulf and preventing any spillover of the conflict across its borders.[96]

PART III

INTERNATIONAL CONTEXT

6

THE IRAN NUCLEAR PROGRAM

Iran's nuclear program, once bolstered by US technical assistance, became the subject of intense international diplomacy and sanctions with the 1979 Iranian Revolution, prompting an ongoing dispute with the West, especially in the first two decades of the twenty-first century. In recent decades, as Iran's capacity to produce highly enriched uranium and an extensive nuclear fuel cycle has dramatically increased in recent decades, concerns about the future development of nuclear weapons have also sparked an intense debate in the West. At the regional level, two issues have been at the forefront of such concerns. First, in Israel, the pervasive perception is that an Iran with nuclear weapons poses "an existential threat" to their survival.[1]

The second issue is the ramifications for the Arab world, as a nuclear Iran and a nuclear Israel would most likely put pressure on Arab states to seek nuclear weapons for their own security, a trend that is likely to result in a new nuclear arms race.[2] Despite these concerns, there has emerged a larger consensus both in the West and in the region that any military assault on Iran can only temporarily discontinue—not end—Iran's attempts to acquire nuclear weapons.[3]

The prospects of a military confrontation with Iran and the placing of further sanctions on the country receded with the United States' release of the National Intelligence Estimate (NIE) report in December 2007. The report, composed by sixteen US intelligence agencies, emphatically concluded that Iran had ended the military component of its nuclear program in 2003. This revelation exposed the extent to which the Iranian threat had been exaggerated. It has since become evident that US diplomatic attempts to isolate Iran have also failed. The EU, Russia, and China resumed trade and commercial ties with Iran, up until at least 2015. Russia, for example, continued its efforts to help construct the Bushehr nuclear facility. Since the NIE report on Iran, US policymakers found it difficult to convince all regional players that Iran constituted a present and clear nuclear threat. The NIE revelations weakened the rationale for the US containment policy toward Iran, as the political situation appeared to have never been more propitious for a diplomatic breakthrough of sorts between the two countries.

The Obama administration put aside talk of "regime change" and doubled down on sanctions policy vis-à-vis Iran, while at the same time sending a clear signal to the Rouhani administration that it was serious about pursuing direct negotiations with Iran to resolve the nuclear situation. After several years of covert negotiations, all parties concerned—including the United States, the EU, China, and Russia—came to the negotiating table, ultimately generating a historic nuclear deal. Notwithstanding vigorous opposition from certain groups in both Tehran and Washington, this agreement was largely enforced in the ensuing months and years.

In a deliberately outrageous breach of the 2015 nuclear accord, the Trump administration pushed, however unsuccessfully, for tearing up the agreement, opening the door to the unconstrained resumption of Iran's nuclear program. This set in motion uncertain escalatory pressures in an already volatile Middle East. Trump's move, as Suzanne Maloney put it, represented a relinquishment of American leadership on the international scene that was unparalleled in recent history.[4] This chapter provides a nuanced understanding of the history, dynamics, and broader implications of the US–Iran relationship in this context, underscoring the importance of the role that diplomacy played in producing the 2015 nuclear deal.

A Historical Overview

Iran's nuclear program was launched in 1957—approximately four years after the CIA and MI6 helped restore the Shah to power—when the United States and Iran signed a civil nuclear cooperation accord as part of the US Atoms for Peace Program. This was part of President Eisenhower's high-profile initiative crafted to share US mastery of peaceful nuclear energy with developing countries.[5] In the ensuing administrations of Johnson and Nixon, Washington considered nuclear energy "critical to Iran's economic development and stood ready to do all it could to help the Shah obtain it."[6]

In 1960, Iran established a 5-megawatt (MW) research center at Tehran University. In his visit to the United States in 1964, the Shah laid out Iran's ambitious plan for nuclear power. Tehran's Nuclear Research Center became operational in 1967, when the United States supplied a limited amount of enriched uranium to Iran for fuel in a research reactor. Iran signed the global nuclear Non-Proliferation Treaty (NPT) and ratified it in 1970.[7]

In 1974, Iran signed several agreements to purchase two 1,200-MW pressurized water reactors from the German firm Kraftwerk Union (to be installed at Bushehr) and two 900-MW reactors from Framatome of France (to be installed at Bandar-e Abbas). At the same time, the United States, under President Gerald Ford, pledged to assist Iran in operating a US-built reprocessing facility for extracting plutonium from nuclear reactor fuel, a process that entailed a complete nuclear fuel cycle. Under such conditions, Iran benefitted from the competition between US and European nuclear energy companies—especially German and French firms—to assist it in launching its nuclear program.[8]

After the 1979 Islamic Revolution, Iran and the International Atomic Energy Agency (IAEA) agreed to cooperate in the fields of nuclear reactor technology and fuel cycle technology. The IAEA, however, under US pressure, was forced to terminate the program. It is worth noting that prior to the revolution, Iran had contracts with Germany, France, and the United States for a total of six nuclear power reactors, along with agreements to receive low-enriched uranium and nuclear training. After the revolution, Western countries canceled these nuclear agreements. The Bushehr reactors, which were not fully operative, were damaged by several Iraqi air strikes during the 1980s war with Iraq. When the war ended, Iran turned to Russia to finish up the Bushehr projects. In 1995, Iran and Russia signed a contract to that end. Similarly, US sanctions on Iran failed to prevent China from providing Tehran with a conversion plan and materials needed to test the uranium enrichment process.[9]

By 2000, Iranian officials revealed the existence of two nuclear sites under construction in Natanz and Arak. Under the IAEA rules, Iran had no obligation to report the existence of these sites while they were still under construction. Iran's nuclear facilities are located in Anarak, Arak, Ardekan, Bushehr, Chalus, Darkhovin, Esfahan, Karaj/Karai/ Hashtgerd, Kolahdouz, Lashkar Abad, Lavizan, Meysami, Natanz, Parchin, Sagend, Qatran, Tabas, and Tehran.[10] While Iranian leaders had expressed principled objections to nuclear weapons, they could not have afforded to be oblivious to the region's political realities.

Throughout the 1990s, as experts remind us, US intelligence agencies warned of Saddam Hussein's attempts to obtain a nuclear bomb. In 1998, India and Pakistan both successfully tested nuclear weapons. Surrounded by:

> a nuclear Israel to its west, a nuclear Russia to its north, and a nuclear (and highly volatile) Pakistan to its east, as well as an Iraqi neighbor that nursed megalomaniac tendencies and had a history of using chemical weapons—not to mention the enduring antipathy of the United States—Iranians understood that they were in no position to be overly relaxed about their security needs.[11]

This helps explain why in the post-Khomeini era, Presidents Rafsanjani and Khatami, as well as the Supreme Leader Khamenei, all felt it would be utterly imprudent not to at least explore the viability of a full-scale nuclear program.[12]

In late 2003, the IAEA reported that it had found no evidence that Iran had engaged in any diversion of fissile material to military use. The IAEA deferred a final decision on this situation pending further European diplomatic negotiations with Iran. With the Iranians insisting on their right to enrich uranium, and the Europeans convinced that Iran should forgo this process, diplomatic contacts produced no mutually agreed results. With the failure of the EU-3 (Great Britain, Germany, and France) diplomatic initiatives, the United Nations Security Council demanded Iran suspend its enrichment and reprocessing activities.

Having secured no concessions from Iran, the UN threatened to put further sanctions on the country. Two rounds of UN sanctions were subsequently imposed on Iran during 2006–07, with increasing unwillingness on the part of China, Russia, and the EU to push Iran beyond these sanctions by imposing more intrusive ones. Russia's reluctance to impose further sanctions on Iran served to underline Moscow's independence from the United States. Meanwhile, the then head of the IAEA, Mohammed ElBaradei, stated on numerous occasions that he had seen "no evidence" of Iran attempting to develop nuclear weapons.

Iran's Nuclear Program

In late 2003, Iran and the EU3, comprising France, Germany, and the United Kingdom, reached an agreement known as the Tehran Declaration, which placed restrictions on Iran's nuclear program. In exchange for Iran's provisional rollback, the EU3 agreed to recognize "the right of Iran to enjoy peaceful use of nuclear energy in accordance with the NPT" and to collaborate with Iran on "regional security."[13] Iran's deferment of enrichment and reprocessing activities was viewed as "voluntary" and not a "legal obligation." In the meantime, the United States and the member states of the European Union (EU) offered several gestures to Iran—supporting Iran's entry into the World Trade Organization (WTO), supplying Iran with aircraft spare parts, and agreeing that Iran could develop the capacity to enrich limited amount of uranium—to alter their policies on Iran's nuclear program.[14]

In November 2004, in the so-called Paris Agreement, Iran and the EU3 agreed to suspend its uranium enrichment activities. In August 2005, however, Iran rejected the EU3 proposal to render the temporary suspensions of its nuclear program into a long-term agreement. In January 2006, Iran resumed its nuclear activities at the Natanz plant in the face of ongoing sanctions. Iran's new six-point proposal with regard to its nuclear program was dismissed by the EU3. Subsequently, the Ahmadinejad administration decided to end its two-year implementation of the Additional Protocol. In February 2006, the IAEA referred Iran to the UN Security Council (UNSC). In the ensuring years, the UNSC adopted several resolutions calling for the immediate suspension of Iran's uranium enrichment activities, imposing sanctions on Iran for failing to stop its uranium enrichment program, and implementing a conventional arms embargo on Iran while expanding the sanctions already in place.[15]

Iran's nuclear program, however, presented a deeper challenge. Unlike Khatami, Ahmadinejad was part of a system that had a complete monopoly over all levers of power, including the executive, judicial, and legislative branches that were all but controlled by the hard-liners. Ahmadinejad and his aides failed to convince the West that Iran's nuclear program was peaceful, and the Iranian case was referred to the UNSC, pitting Iran against an international consensus hard to ignore or defeat. The resultant UN resolutions led to harsh economic sanctions against Iran, with grave diplomatic costs to follow. With conservative forces in control of the Iranian parliament (*Majles*) and presidency, Iran's leaders seemed to have equated the country's nuclear program with its security. During the Ahmadinejad era (2005–13), Iran went from possessing a few hundred centrifuges to more than 1,300 centrifuges, stockpiling enough fissile material to make several bombs.[16]

The Iranian government claimed that it had suspended its activities on a voluntary basis and that it had a legal right to develop its nuclear program for peaceful purposes, according to Article 4 of the NPT.[17] This article stipulates that member states pledge not to seek a weapons capability and are entitled to acquire the means of generating nuclear power for civilian purposes. It should be noted, however, that the NPT contains ambiguous language. For example, it does not guarantee signatories the "right" to enrich uranium. It only supports "the benefit of nuclear technology" for peaceful purposes.

Beyond legal justification, Iranian officials pointed to pure and simple economics, arguing that while Iran's GDP is likely to grow by six percent in the near future, its young population's demand for power consumption was projected to grow by seven percent annually. Iran's capacity, experts note, must nearly triple over the next fifteen years to meet projected demand.[18] At the same time, Iran's daily consumption of 1.5 million barrels of oil per day meant the country loses $75 million every day.[19] Moreover, Iran has argued that with diminishing water resources, the use of hydroelectric as a means to generate power has become less viable. Nuclear energy, Iranian officials have insisted, seems to be the most economically viable method of energy production, leading to Iran's plan to generate 7,000 MW of nuclear power by 2020 through the construction of twenty nuclear power plants.[20]

According to the 2007 National Intelligence Estimate report,[21] Iran had halted its program to develop a nuclear weapon in 2003 and was far from manufacturing the key ingredient for a nuclear weapon.[22] The threat of Iran's nuclear program was exaggerated. In fact, Robert Baer, an ex-CIA operative, argued that Iran's highest priority, as agreed upon by all of its multiple power centers, was not to become a nuclear player in the region. Instead, he argued, Iran's most important ambition was to take control of the Persian Gulf region (a region he allegedly claimed was running out of oil)[23] and then to export its soft power of Islamism and anti-colonialism throughout the region.[24]

Some observers have offered a different perspective, arguing that an Iranian bomb would not be good news, but it would not be cataclysmic either, especially when compared to Pakistan's sixty nuclear weapons, and the possibility that Al-Qaeda sympathizers might gain access to those weapons. Compounding the picture is the fact that the IAEA, the so-called "UN Watchdog," was caught in the middle of this controversy, unable to issue Tehran a clean bill of health or to confirm the suspicions of the United States and the EU.[25]

The US invasion and subsequent occupation of Iraq in 2003 and its policy blunders also emboldened Iranian intransigence. The Bush administration's central message that it would not tolerate Iran's growing ability to develop a nuclear weapon fell by the wayside, in large part owing to the fact that Washington's hands were tied in Iraq and Afghanistan. Yet US and Israeli claims that Iran was assembling an atomic bomb were unproven.[26] For its part, Iran had signed an Additional Protocol on December 18, 2003, which had given IAEA inspectors access to suspected nuclear research sites. Still, much remained subject to negotiations and it was too soon to call the diplomatic track a failure.

The End of 'Coercive Diplomacy'

The wars in Iraq and Afghanistan ushered "cowboy diplomacy" to the forefront of US foreign policy toward the Middle East, and their consequences brought the flaws of such a policy into the limelight. There were some doubts regarding the notion that US global primacy was absolute and that its military might could effectively put an end to regional tensions in the Middle East. The inability of the Bush administration to achieve its foreign policy goals in Iraq, advance the larger campaign against terrorism, or push for more comprehensive and multilateral sanctions against Iran suggested the need for the skillful deployment of the diplomatic means and resources at the United States' disposal.[27]

The Iraqi debacle demonstrated that it was time to move away from the US hegemonic role by focusing on dialogue and cooperation with key regional players, such as Iran.[28] Equally ominous was the lesson that the US invasions of Afghanistan and Iraq had diverted attention away from waging an effective campaign against terrorist operations in Afghanistan and adjacent, federally administered tribal areas in Pakistan and Iraq.[29] Since the end of the Iran—Iraq War, successive US administrations have predicated their Iran policy upon the condition that Iran forgo sponsoring terrorism, cease supporting movements opposed to Israel and the US-sponsored "peace process," and relinquish its pursuit of strategic weapons. The US approach to Iran was influenced equally by geostrategic considerations, residual animosity from the 1979–81 hostage crisis, and pressure from neo-conservatives dominating the Bush administration and pro-Israel lobbies. On the Iranian side, however, only the conservative clerical hierarchy and the military high command, including the Revolutionary Guards, could negotiate over these demands.[30]

A wide political spectrum in the United States and the European Union, as well as in Israel, cautioned against the potential repercussions of the air campaign against Iran's nuclear facilities, arguing that the military actions would at best delay Iran's nuclear program, perhaps only for months. If, during the Ahmadinejad presidency (2005–13), Iran remained undecided about whether to weaponize its nuclear efforts, an attack could only precipitate the rationale to proceed with weapons development.[31]

There were many reasons to hold talks with Iran. To begin with, a dialogue with Iran would have shored up a multilateral diplomacy initiative already in place known as P5+1. This initiative consisted of senior officials from the five veto-wielding powers of the UNSC plus Germany who sought to negotiate a long-term solution to Iran's nuclear program.

For Iran, there were many incentives to continue working toward establishing a dialogue with the United States. Iranians could have played a constructive role in rebuilding Afghanistan and Iraq. They might have been able to convince the United States of their overlapping long-term interests in maintaining regional stability if they could have demonstrated transparency in their nuclear program.[32] The mutual security interests of the United States and Iran in restoring stability to Iraq and Afghanistan could have merged. Moreover, there was a growing consensus in Iran—in spite of its polarized politics—that dialogue with the United States could lay to rest the talk of "regime change" in Iran.

On November 18, 2008, Ayatollah Mahmoud Hashemi Shahroudi, the head of Iran's judiciary at the time, supported the negotiated Status of Forces Agreement between the United States and Iraq, an accord that guaranteed the presence of US troops in Iraq until 2011. Shahroudi's positive reaction to the security pact, however, was also followed by critical remarks by Ali Larijani, the then Speaker of the House (*Majles*), urging the Iraqi National Assembly to reject the agreement.

Larijani's opposition to this security pact illustrated an ambiguity in Iranian policy. By sending mixed messages to Washington, Tehran intended to show the Obama administration that it was willing to collaborate, but would push for its own interests when necessary as well. This rhetorical posturing aside, Tehran took a fresh and softer attitude toward the US troop presence in Iraq, which paved the way for future negotiations on other issues.[33] Increasingly, the need for stabilizing conditions in the post-military interventions in Afghanistan and Iraq made it very difficult to ignore Iran's role in this endeavor, given Iran considerable leverage in both countries. Furthermore, any rapprochement between Iran and the United States could have had a moderating impact on Saudi Arabia's foreign policy toward Iran. The tense competition between Iran and Saudi Arabia has proven to be destabilizing. It bears mentioning that the ideological rivalry between Iran and Saudi Arabia in Afghanistan, both during and after the Soviet invasion of that country, led to the rise of the Taliban, Al-Qaeda, and consequently the 9/11 terrorist attacks in the United States.

Arguably, the best way to deal with Iran was to engage it in a regional security framework and structure that gives the Iranians a stake in protecting such a structure. The old method of offshore balancing of power has led to unintended consequences and policy ramifications that have in fact undermined US power to influence the shape of things to come in the region. Exaggerating the threat of an Iranian bomb had failed to contribute to a solution. The US policy of containment and deterrence protected its Western European allies for four decades during the Cold War. That lesson has not been lost on the part of Iranian ruling elites. Instead, the focus needed to be shifted to treating Iran as a partner in a regional security structure. That could have significantly curtailed Iranian leaders' fears and provided a basis for them to reframe their legitimate regional interests in ways consonant with those of their neighbors.

Domestically, however, Iran's growing economic problems were bound to undermine its dysfunctional theocracy. The possibility of reform from within was likely to increase even further if the ruling clerical regime could no longer use the excuse of the threat of US military intervention. This was not a far-fetched perspective, given the increasing discontent of the youth and women—once among the major supporters of reform—who had lost hope in reform and who openly questioned Ahmadinejad's economic and foreign policies. They represented human capital crucial to the struggle for democratic reform in Iran.

Nuclear Dispute and Framework Agreement

Just as Europeans expressed skepticism about the value of military force—as well as other policies that Washington favors, including isolation and regime change—China and Russia insisted that pushing for a diplomatic solution would bear a more fruitful outcome given the uncertainties surrounding the use of coercive diplomacy and force. The art of brinkmanship, combined with the right personalities on the stage in 2015, produced a promising framework agreement that speaks volumes about the fruits of diplomacy and engagement. Experts and policymakers kept reminding us that while there is no perfect arrangement, from a non-proliferation standpoint, the P5+1 agreement (permanent members of the UNSC: China, France, Great Britain, Russia, and the United States, plus Germany) was a good deal.

The surprisingly detailed and thorough terms set out in the Joint Comprehensive Plan of Action (JCPOA) issued after the April 2, 2015, negotiations at the nuclear talks in Switzerland were a clear illustration. Experts have underlined the fact that no state has ever voluntarily negotiated special restrictions on its own ongoing nuclear program as severe as the ones Iran has accepted, and no state has ever previously negotiated inspection methods on its own installations as intrusive and extensive as the ones that Iran accepted.[34]

Within the nuclear deal framework, Iran's enrichment program continued, but was to be capped at much lower—3.67 percent—for the next fifteen years. This cut Iran's capacity to enrich uranium by about two-thirds. Monitoring and verification methods were installed to prevent—and block—any covert pathways. The breakout period of two to three months was increased to twelve months, and robust and intrusive inspections were enforced to ensure that the process of enrichment remained focused on the generation of nuclear energy for civilian purposes. The Fordow facility was converted into a research center focusing on medical isotopes that had no military utility. Iran's heavy water reactor at Arak stopped producing weapons-grade plutonium. All nuclear facilities were open to inspection by the IAEA, demonstrating maximum transparency and openness on Iran's part. In exchange, Iran was promised relief from some of the sanctions that have crippled its economy in recent years. In the case of any violations of the terms of agreement, "snapback" provisions were put in place to immediately activate to reimpose the sanctions.

The roots of this rapprochement must not be exclusively sought in the crippling sanctions and the threat of war against Iran, but rather in three major developments that facilitated this reconciliation: the tragic events of 9/11, the failure of military interventions in Afghanistan and Iraq, and the rise of radical Sunni Islamism in the region (mostly manifested in the genesis of the Islamic State of Iraq and Syria—ISIS). It is evident that the growing menace of ISIS in Iraq rendered the country largely dependent on Iran's military assistance and involvement to curb its spread. Paradoxically, but understandably, several countries in the region that opposed the regime in Damascus, including Turkey, Qatar, and Saudi Arabia, were culprits in supporting ISIS, in hopes of toppling Syria's Assad regime.

These three developments—9/11, failed military interventions in Afghanistan and Iraq, and the rise of radical Sunni Islamism—changed the political dynamics not only in the region but also in Washington and Tehran. In Iran, the threat of Islamic radicalism in the region helped moderates and pragmatists rise to power. The nuclear deal considerably improved President Rouhani's clout, giving moderates a noticeable boost. The dynamics of the youth bulge and the educated populace in Iran, coupled with the reformists winning a majority in the 2016 parliamentary elections, surely favored this power transition in Iran.

Were the consequences of the nuclear deal positive for the region's geopolitical stability? This deal, were it to be sustained, could potentially lead to a broader reordering of a region roiling in deep disarray. If the United States decides to withdraw from parts of the Middle East region—at least on the ground, while still maintaining control of the skies and sea lanes—in order to manage its other strategic interests in Asia (a policy that has come to be known as "pivot to Asia") then seeking some political reconciliation with Iran made perfect sense.

Regional Politics After the Nuclear Deal

President Obama's trip to Saudi Arabia in April 2016 was an ardent attempt to reassure the Saudis that the United States sought to support their efforts to maintain regional and domestic stability. However, partly because of his stated personal convictions that the Saudis have acted as "free riders" in the region under the US security umbrella, and partly because of the pressure from the US Congress to divulge the Saudis' alleged involvement (in terms of funding and ideological support) in the 9/11 attacks on the United States, the nature of this visit and Obama's message sharply contrasted with the cordial nature of his previous meetings.

Furthermore, the tentative rapprochement with Iran and the US recognition of the fact that Iran could play a much more constructive role in the region, especially if it was fairly engaged, fueled speculation—better yet, suspicion—on the part of the Saudis that Riyadh's geopolitical salience had dramatically declined in the eyes of US policymakers. More significantly, the nuclear agreement with Iran was widely seen within Saudi Arabia as emblematic of a shift in strategic fortunes regarding the longstanding alliance with the United States—a shift to the detriment of Saudi interests. The Saudis' views on several trouble spots in the region, including Libya, Yemen, and Syria, failed to completely overlap with those of the United States. The fight against terrorist groups such as ISIS also became a point of contention between the Americans and the Saudis. The Obama administration saw Iran as a more reliable partner in the struggle against ISIS than the Saudis, even though the United States continued to consider some of Iran's activities in the region—including its involvement in Syria's civil war and its alleged engagement in cyberattacks—destabilizing.

Furthermore, President Obama's insistence that the Saudis should accept greater cooperation with Iran in the region were seen by many in Riyadh as a major shift in US foreign policy toward the Arabian Peninsula. In an interview with *The Atlantic*, Obama said that Saudi Arabia should share control of the region with Iran:

> The competition between the Saudis and the Iranians, which has helped to feed proxy wars and chaos in Syria and Iraq and Yemen, requires us to say to our friends, as well as to the Iranians, that they need to find an effective way to share the neighborhood and institute some sort of cold peace. [35]

Obama then went on to say:

> An approach that said to our friends "You are right, Iran is the source of all problems, and we will support you in dealing with Iran" would essentially mean that as these sectarian conflicts continue to rage and our Gulf partners, our traditional friends, do not have the ability to put out the flames on their own or decisively win on their own, and would mean that we have to start coming in and using our military power to settle scores. And that would be in the interest neither of the United States nor of the Middle East. [36]

In hindsight, it is clear that some expectations regarding the implications of the nuclear deal were dashed. While Obama was far more discreet in his rhetoric, limiting his expectation only to one element of the threat posed by Iran, some US officials within his administration were hoping that this deal could conceivably lead to other avenues of cooperation with Iran. That expectation never came to fruition as Tehran continued and in some cases even intensified its regional activities. Fine-tuning the JCPOA could not have fundamentally altered the fact that it represented a transactional—not a transformational—deal.[37]

The Nuclear Dispute

Although there is a consensus in the West about finding a way to deal with Iran's nuclear dossier, Europeans have expressed skepticism about the value of policies that Washington favors, including military force, isolation, and regime change. Absent evidence that Iran is building nuclear weapons, it would be difficult to line up Europeans behind such militaristic policies.[38] The imposition of dual containment on Iran and Iraq has been costly for both countries, but it has also pushed Iran toward Asian markets and interactions.

Although the threat of military attack against Iran by the United States, Israel, or both has subsided for the time being, sanctioning of Iran has continued. In fact, unilateral US sanctions, as well as UN multilateral sanctions, have intensified in recent years. It is, however, unclear whether this pain was (or is) sufficient for Iran to abandon its rights to "develop research, production and use of nuclear energy for peaceful purposes without discrimination," as guaranteed under Article 4 of the NPT.[39] According to Article 4, Iran is well within its rights as a member of the NPT to demand nuclear technology and utilize that technology to produce nuclear energy. Similarly, China and Russia have been against such a containment policy. They have frequently insisted that pushing for a diplomatic solution rather than pursuing the use of force would bear a fruitful outcome.

Surrounded by US forces on two of its borders, it is likely that Iranians would be inclined to develop a nuclear deterrent.[40] However, the threats posed by a nuclear-armed Iran are exaggerated at best. Today, as one expert points out, after more than two decades, Iran has a single nuclear power plant, which is still not functioning, and a uranium enrichment program involving some 6,000 low-capacity centrifuges under regular monitoring and inspection by the International Atomic Energy Agency.[41] The excessive hype about the so-called Iranian threat overlooks the fact that Iran has no capability to project military power beyond its own borders and that Iran is not immune to classic policies of deterrence.[42] Furthermore, Iranian possession of a nuclear weapon is unlikely to alter the balance of power in the region.

Still, Iran's neighbors are nagged by the question: Would nuclear weapons necessarily lead to regional hegemony? Opinions differ. Some experts warn that once Iran has a nuclear deterrent, it may feel emboldened to step up subversion efforts across the region. Tehran would also have the potential to provide nuclear materials or even a crude fission device to one of the terrorist organizations it supports.[43]

Others argue that a nuclear-armed Iran would not fundamentally disturb the regional balance of power, or radically alter the political dynamics of the Persian Gulf region, for several reasons. To begin with, the idea that nuclear weapons automatically deliver regional influence has little to no historical precedent. "No nuclear power," Samir Tata writes, "has been able to use nuclear weapons to 'blackmail' an adversary. There is no basis to assume that the situation would be different in the case of Iran."[44] Second, nuclear Iran might be even more cautious about regional meddling, given the possibility of nuclear conflict with Israel. Third, and more importantly, a nuclear Iran would not be able to dictate terms to its neighbors—nor would it necessarily be more aggressive in regional politics.[45]

Equally debatable is the notion that Iran could give nuclear weapons to terrorist groups or could use them to blackmail others. In both cases, the reactions against Iran will be unbearably costly. Given that all of Iran's neighbors rely on an American deterrent threat, such potential pressures from Iran are overstated at best. Thus, it follows that a nuclear-armed Iran would be extremely circumspect about initiating hostilities of the sort that could lead to its own destruction. There is reason, as one observer notes, to believe that we could readily manage a nuclear Iran by relying on containment and deterrence.[46] But beyond that, some observers, such as Ambassador Thomas Pickering and Hillary Mann Leverett, have endorsed a plan to establish a multinational uranium enrichment facility on Iranian soil as a feasible solution to the nuclear dispute.[47]

Regime Change or Sanctions

The talk of regime change via the military option was seen as counterproductive in Tehran, even though a genuine political settlement was not in sight. In the first place, the threat of regime change was not practical given the country's vast terrain and Iranians' nationalistic sentiments. An Osiraq-style attack, like the one that took place in 1981 against Iraq, stood little chance of success in a huge country like Iran that had dispersed its nuclear power plants across the country. If utilized, this option would have undermined any confidence-building measures in the process of securing an eventual compromise. The fact remained that national policy regarding the nuclear program rested with Iran's supreme leader, whose decision reflected a view shared by many different players—military and otherwise. Ironically, the US presence in the region had heightened Iran's sense of urgency for acquiring some form of strategic deterrence.

Second, Iran became the target of the US mainstream media, which refused to provide compelling reasons as to why Iran posed a real threat. The Bush administration supported a media propaganda campaign aimed at vilifying Iran under the assumption that Iran was trying to become a nuclear power. The option of imposing economic sanctions on Iran was also risky, partly because not everyone was willing to participate in enforcing them, and partly because they would have deprived international markets of nearly four million barrels of oil per day. Moreover, sanctions, some experts rightly observed, would only hold back a nuclear assembly line in the short run should Iran's clerical rulers decide to proceed. Iranian officials had raised the question all along concerning why other nuclear-equipped countries are not subject to such sanction threats. They have said that they would withdraw from the NPT if faced with military and economic threats.

Withdrawal from the NPT was, however, unlikely, and it would prove to be too costly for a country where industrial infrastructure is heavily dependent on production machinery and spare parts from EU countries. Sanctions would hurt Iran's booming trade with the United Arab Emirates (UAE), which totals $8 billion a year. There were nearly 4,500 Iranian companies that had invested in the UAE. The possibility of trade sanctions was arguably a strong deterrent—an unreasonable risk for the Iranian government to take.

Iran's Future Policy Choices

In 2015, when almost thirty percent of the Iranian population lived below the poverty line, the inflation rate exceeded sixteen percent, and more than seven million were unemployed, Iran needed trade and development more than ever before. Mishandling this challenge held colossal risks and potential consequences. Some Iranians embraced the notion that nuclear weapons would have afforded Iran a modicum of security cover in a neighborhood where it was hard to predict political games. Yet signing the Additional Protocol to the NPT was a prudent policy because it led to international assurance that Iran's nuclear programs was peaceful.

The failure to reach an agreement with the Europeans would have placed Iran's European allies in a very awkward position, making it extremely difficult for them to support Iran's security and economic needs. Absent a nuclear deal, the proliferation of nuclear arms in the region would have widened and deepened US involvement there as a step toward efforts to contain the further spread of such weapons. Europeans would have certainly regarded this development as a scary forecast. France, for example, has made it abundantly clear to Iranian officials that it would not stand against the United States were Iran–US disagreements to reach a confrontational stage.

While the Europeans had reassured Iran that sanctions on technical assistance on matters relating to Iran's peaceful nuclear program would be lifted in due course, the Bush administration faced a fundamental dilemma: how to deal with a country that it has labeled as part of an "Axis of Evil"—and driven by domestic concerns that see it as the major threat to Israel—and how to justify allowing Iran's civilian nuclear programs and subsequently finding a way to open a dialogue with Iran. The EU diplomatic proposals did not resolve the extant squabble between Iran and the United States, but they defused the tension between the two for a while. Meanwhile, the Europeans continued to argue that trade deals and technical assistance could have a positive influence on Iran. The hope was that economic necessities and pressures for rebuilding the country would eventually compel Iran to engage with the West rather than pursuing confrontation. Multilateral diplomacy and dialogue were thought to be among the most reasonable ways of resolving such tensions.

The US military fiasco in Iraq at the same time had awakened some policymakers in the Bush administration to the fact that a military approach toward Iran would have been questionable at best and perilous at worst, especially at a time when the United States was largely preoccupied with reconstructing Iraq and Afghanistan. The assassination of Pakistani politician Benazir Bhutto in late December of 2007 fueled speculation that further instability awaited the region. Pakistan—a nuclear-equipped power with an army that had close ties with the Taliban regime in Afghanistan—took the front line. Hence the prevailing assumption that the US military would become involved in Pakistan could not be entirely ruled out in the coming years.

Under such circumstances, Iran's interest in playing a positive role in stabilizing US efforts in war-torn Iraq, Afghanistan, and Pakistan had dramatically increased. If Iran's true intentions were to attain energy security for the long term, then the previous standoff with the United States and the EU would be subject to negotiations. Iran was likely to reach a mutual accommodation that would allow it to develop nuclear energy locally in a way that satisfied all parties. If, however, Iranian ambitions were truly military in nature as well, the nuclear dispute would have boded ill for a reasonable accommodation with the West over the long haul.

In the meantime, a contrarian view holds that a nuclear Iran would render Iran and the Middle East more secure, and that nuclear balancing would mean stability. Unlike many US and Israeli officials and analysts, who have portrayed and continue to depict Iran as irrational and argue that the logic of nuclear deterrence does not apply to the Islamic Republic, Kenneth N. Waltz claims that although it is impossible to precisely know Iranian intentions, it is highly likely that if Iran seeks nuclear weapons, it is for defensive purposes and not to improve its offensive capabilities (or destroy itself). A nuclear-armed Iran would not be the worst possible outcome. Quite the contrary, it would probably be the best possible result. Since power begs to be balanced, the so-called power parity—not preponderance—is likely to restore stability in the Middle East. The Iranian regime, Waltz goes on to argue, would be less likely to initiate a nuclear conflict, given that such a move would certainly provoke a swift and devastating American response.[48]

The Nuclear Agreement

Whereas President George W. Bush's "Axis of Evil" characterization of Iran prevented any meaningful diplomatic opening with Iran, President Obama's crisis-avoidance mindset paid dividends with engaging Iran, eventually culminating in a set of negotiations that resulted in a diplomatic resolution to the nuclear stalemate—the JCPOA.[49] This agreement called for a significant reduction in the number and types of Iranian centrifuges for a fifteen-year period. Iran agreed to dismantle nearly two-thirds of its installed centrifuges and one-third of its operating centrifuges.[50]

Similarly, the ceiling for the maximum level of enrichment was put at 3.67 percent for a period of fifteen years. Iran also agreed to limit its stockpile of five-percent-enriched uranium to 300 kilograms. Iran agreed that for a period of fifteen years uranium testing would only take place at the Natanz Pilot Fuel Enrichment Plant and mechanical testing at the Tehran Research Center.[51] The JCPOA also imposed a thorough and intrusive inspection regime on Iran's nuclear program. The agreement also called upon Iran "not to undertake any activity related to ballistic missiles designed to be capable of delivering nuclear weapons, including launches using ballistic missile technology."[52]

The agreement also outlined the details of the commitments and obligations of the P5+1 parties to the agreement. The European countries were obligated to dismantle their sanctions regime on Iran, thus allowing the normalization of commercial relations with Iran, except the embargo on sales to Iran of arms, missile technology, and other proliferation-sensitive items. The United States, by contrast, agreed to lift only secondary sanctions—that is, those that had been imposed to deter non-US entities from doing business with Iran under the threat of facing punitive measures—as opposed to primary sanctions intended to ban US companies or persons from doing business with Iran.[53]

For its part, the United States made several commitments under the JCPOA, including but not limited to: suspending its efforts to curb Iran's crude oil sales, lifting sanctions with respect to financial transactions between non-US persons or entities and Iranian entities (such as the Iranian Central Bank, the National Iranian Oil Company,

National Iranian Tanker Company, and Naftiran Intertrade Company), lifting sanctions on Iran's automotive sector, removing sanctions on the provision of underwriting services and insurance, removing certain individuals and groups from its sanctions list, refraining from reimposing the sanctions lifted pursuant to the JCPOA, and removing all existing restrictions on Iran's civilian nuclear program after a fifteen-year period.[54]

The JCPOA also set up a dispute resolution mechanism to deal with potential disputes that might arise during the implementation phase of the accord. The UNSC allows any party to bring a complaint of non-compliance directly to the Council. Following the dispute-settlement procedure, the snapback mechanism can be triggered simply by the assertion of "significant non-compliance" on the part of a participating state. The unilateral use of the snapback procedure, however, can be rescinded if the Security Council votes within thirty days of the claim to repel the snapback and to retain the termination of previous sanctions. The Council president should put forward a draft resolution proposing to counter a snapback within ten days of any complaint if no member state does so. It should be noted, however, that any one of the Permanent Members can then block the adoption of such a resolution through a veto, thus allowing for broad UN sanctions to resume.[55]

The JCPOA's sunset clause provides for the removal of all existing sanctions on Iran's civilian nuclear program after a fifteen-year period. This has caused some concern among some of Iran's neighboring countries and Israel. A possible means, according to Robert Goldston, to address the "sunset clause" would be for the United States to work with its European allies and other like-minded states to assist the IAEA in moving toward executing enhanced monitoring at uranium enrichment plants worldwide. Rapid detection of misuse serves as a strong deterrent to transgression at an enrichment plant. Israel's concern that in the future, Iran could process the fuel for nuclear weapons, before detection, would be resolved. A global commitment to improving enrichment plant safeguards is likely to profoundly alter the international regime to which Iran is scheduled to acquiesce in 2031, rendering this accession acceptable.[56]

It is also important to bear in mind that other key clauses in the JCPOA extend past 2031, facilitating oversight of centrifuge production and uranium mining. There are also several clauses that never expire, such as the "Additional Protocol" and modified Code 3.1 to Iran's safeguards agreement with the IAEA, which are essential for allowing conclusive inspections. Iran's commitment not to perform nuclear-weapons-related R&D does not terminate either. Additionally, the JCPOA provides a context within which to negotiate on future Iranian activities, including any limits on levels of enrichment, stockpiles of enriched uranium, and on the use of multilateral cooperation for uranium enrichment. To summarize, the JCPOA provides a basis for guaranteeing that any nuclear program in Iran "after sunset" will be surely peaceful. It would be imprudent to abandon it.[57]

Trump and the Nuclear Deal

As a populist outsider promising to reshape US foreign policy toward the Middle East, Trump rebuked the US invasion of Iraq, arguing that it made the region less secure and more chaotic than ever before. Taking a tough stance toward Tehran, Trump saw Iran as the key enemy in the region and viewed the nuclear deal as deeply flawed because it incited Iranian expansionism.[58]

The Trump administration referred to Iran's ballistic missile tests as a violation of the JCPOA and a UN resolution. In the meantime, Iran test-fired two ballistic missiles on March 9, 2016, according to the country's semi-official Fars News Agency. The missiles, capable of reaching Israel, were marked with a statement in Hebrew reading "Israel must be wiped off the Earth."[59] These tests took place as part of a large-scale military drill, which marked the first time Tehran had fired ballistic missiles since signing on to the nuclear deal in July 2015. Washington indicated that the first tests did not violate the JCPOA, but were certainly in breach of a UN resolution calling on Iran not to undertake ballistic missile activity.[60] Most non-proliferation experts concurred that the test did not technically violate the nuclear deal, but certainly defied the spirit of the UN resolution because it contained no prohibition against such testing in the previous resolution.

Additionally, Iran noted that its missile tests did not violate the Security Council resolutions because there were no nuclear warheads involved and that Iran's management of conventional defenses is within its national prerogative. Iranian officials have also added that they have never agreed to missile restrictions in the JCPOA and claimed that their missiles are not designed to carry nuclear warheads.[61] Yet, for all the drama and bluster of US President Donald Trump's tough new stand on the nuclear deal with Iran, nothing fundamentally changed, other than Trump pulling out of the nuclear deal. Over the growing dissension within his administration and his party, President Trump withdrew from the JCPOA on May 8, 2018, while overriding advice from his close aides, such as the then Secretary of State Rex Tillerson, the then Secretary of Defense James Mattis, and the then White House Chief of Staff John Kelly, all of whom objected to his decision to withdraw from the Iran agreement.

This unilateral decision, however, was espoused through influence-peddling and lobbying on the part of Israeli, Saudi, and UAE diplomats in the United States. Some reports noted that Saudi Arabia has gone on a hiring spree for lobbyists as the then President-elect Joe Biden, who had signaled that he would take a tougher stance on the nation, was preparing to take office. With the potential for a more tempestuous relationship with the United States, the Saudis inched closer toward hiring some lobbyists with ties to Republican congressional leaders.[62]

The implications of President Trump's decision were profound, given that Iran remained in full compliance based on ongoing IAEA reports at the time and in light of the fact that the Western world's unified position, so arduously formed under the Obama administration, eventually collapsed, seriously undermining the US reputation as a trusted ally. The European allies of the United States strongly rejected the far-fetched notion that Trump can somehow conjure up a better deal. Legally, the United States—not Iran—was in violation of the accord. Other foreign policy implications flowing from this move were equally destabilizing. North Korea, for instance, turned out to be just as perplexed as to the value of negotiating a deal with the United States. One result of subjecting Iran to more punitive sanctions has been that it has strengthened hard-liners in Iran and dramatically undercut the Rouhani government and its moderate allies.

In the meantime, conflicting messages from the White House to Tehran filled the air as some in the Trump administration noted that their endgame was not regime change but negotiation with Iran. But at the same time, as experts maintained, the regional allies of the United States—namely, Israel and Saudi Arabia—doubled down on their efforts to steer the Trump administration toward "confrontation rather than reconciliation with Iran, thus underscoring the need for the administration to insulate its Iran policy from third-party influences and make the necessary adjustments in that policy based on the national interests of the United States."[63]

Several developments triggered an extremely tense political climate between Tehran and Washington. On January 3, 2020, General Qassem Soleimani, who led the powerful Quds Force of the Islamic Revolutionary Guards Corps, was killed by an American drone, as were several Iraqi militia members. Soleimani was the architect of many significant operations conducted by Iranian intelligence and military forces, and his death dealt a substantial blow to Iran at a time of growing regional tensions. The tension between the United States and Iran reached a new height on June 20, 2019, when Iran's Islamic Revolutionary Guard Corps (IRGC) shot down a United States surveillance drone with a surface-to-air missile over the Strait of Hormuz. President Trump then ordered a retaliatory military strike against IRGC radar and missile sites, before rescinding the decision.

The assassination of Mohsen Fakhrizadeh, a renowned Iranian nuclear scientist, on November 27, 2020, in Iran—allegedly by Israeli agents within the country—added yet a new twist to US–Iran relations, as the incoming Biden administration was sending signals that his national security team would be willing to return to the JCPOA provided that Iranians lived up to their end of the bargain. Coming after a covert meeting in the Red Sea city of Neom between Prime Minister Benjamin Netanyahu and Crown Prince Mohammad bin Salman on November 22, 2020, the first such meeting between Israeli and Saudi leaders, it was undoubtedly aimed at sabotaging US de-escalation with Iran during the Biden administration.[64] Secretary of State Mike Pompeo's presence at the meeting showed that the US supported closer ties between Riyadh and Tel Aviv.[65]

On August 20, the Trump administration submitted a letter to the president of the UNSC indicating that the efforts of the EU states participating in the Iran nuclear deal to bring Iran back into full compliance had failed. Hence, Washington claimed that "significant non-compliance" had occurred, warranting the reimposition of sanctions. Thirteen of the fifteen members of the Security Council (except the United States and the Dominican Republic) rejected the attempted use of the snapback provision on the grounds that the United States had withdrawn from the JCPOA. No consensus forged on the matter within the council and thus no action was taken. Thirty days after the United States invoked the snapback, Secretary of State Michael Pompeo claimed that UN sanctions had now been automatically reinstalled.

Germany, France, and the United Kingdom issued a joint statement indicating formally that "the US ceased to be a participant to the JCPOA following their withdrawal from the deal on 8 May 2018. Consequently, the purported notification under paragraph eleven of UNSCR 2231 (2015) … is incapable of having legal effect."[66] Ironically, according to one legal expert, Washington could have simply succeeded in terminating the Iranian deal altogether had it remained a participant and appealed to the snapback mechanism from within. The Trump administration's insistence that universal UN sanctions should have been deployed against Iran had little effect, undermining the credibility of both the United States and the UNSC. The fact remains that the United States cannot opt out of formal multilateral cooperation and act alone, while still reaping the benefits of concerted multilateral action, such as universal sanctions. The division created among the Security Council as a result of this action by the Trump administration further isolated Washington rather than Tehran. Yet the urgent need to bring Iran back into compliance persisted.[67]

Raisi and the Future of the JCPOA

The fate of the 2015 nuclear deal hangs in balance. Raisi took office at a time when indirect talks in Vienna have yet to generate any agreement. The ongoing disagreement over how to return to the JCPOA's original framework has intensified. Washington insists on an explicit Iranian pledge to engage in follow-on negotiations toward a "stronger and longer" deal that would likely include Iran's regional activities and policies. Tehran, having experienced the shock of the Trump administration, seeks assurances that Washington would not pull out of the JCPOA incessantly and undermine it by imposing new sanctions. The compliance-for-compliance proposal still remains a viable option.[68] It is not clear, however, how Iran can achieve these goals without any progress made in the JCPOA negotiations.

In the meantime, Raisi appears focused on improving Iran's ties with its neighbors, especially through a comprehensive regional dialogue. The Raisi government is likely to pursue security and economic engagement with Iran's Arab neighbors in the Persian Gulf, broaden strategic ties with Russia and China, and jettison residual notions of rapprochement with the United States and Europe.[69] Raisi's choice of Hossein Amirabdollahian as foreign minister goes to show that he affords great importance to regional issues in his foreign policy and that Amirabdollahian will be an integral part of his foreign policy, with a regional focus. Amirabdollahian was a former ambassador to Bahrain, who was also deputy foreign minister for Arab and African Affairs between 2011 and 2016 and served as deputy chief of mission at Iran's embassy in Baghdad from 1997 until 2001. Amirabdollahian is a hard-line diplomat expected to adopt a very tough stance in the nuclear talks. He is known to have close ties with Iran's revolutionary guards, with Lebanese Hezbollah, and with other Iranian proxies in the region.[70]

As noted above, a key sticking point is Tehran's demand that Washington guarantee that future administrations will fully abide by the deal. "There is no such thing as a guarantee," Robert Malley, lead US negotiator in Vienna, has made clear, as future administrations will have the freedom to make their own choices. The US has noted that if the agreement is sufficiently compelling, future administrations will most likely stick to it.[71] There are, however, other options available to strengthen such executive deals.

On a broader level, some observers have pointed out that the Iran deal can be directly linked to United Nations Security Council (UNSC) Resolution 2231, which represents the nuclear agreement. The Trump sanctions, which are currently not seen as a violation of that resolution, must be rectified so that any party that abandons the agreement without noncompliance by the other parties finds itself in violation of the UNSC resolution. This would allow for the possibility of further political and financial costs for the withdrawing party. Similarly, these observers add, the best way to guarantee the US' long-term commitment to the Iran deal is through a broader agreement (with give-and-take) between the two countries on several trade fronts in return for the lifting of US primary sanctions on Iran.[72]

On the positive side, some experts, such as Vali Nasr, have noted that Raisi could prove to be the West's best hope for a deal with Iran—in part because hard-liners would never approve of an agreement signed by a moderate, but would if it came from one of their own. Now that all levers of powers, including parliament, judiciary, and presidency, are controlled by the hard-liners, the blame game becomes useless. A unified position—dominated by hard-liners in control of all levers of power—is likely to facilitate the reaching of an agreement with the United States.[73]

Conclusion

Iran's road to develop nuclear energy since the 1970s was paved by the Shah, who leaned on the nation's US and European allies to accomplish this goal. Iran successfully launched an extensive nuclear program under the Shah. Despite notable advances, the 1979 Iranian Revolution disrupted much of the progress that had been achieved up to that point. During the 1990s, Iran is also believed to have received uranium enrichment technology through black market networks run by Pakistani scientist A. Q. Khan. By the late 1990s and the early 2000s, it was clear that Iran was continuing to produce enriched uranium.

In 2003, however, an assessment conducted by the US intelligence agencies, based on an estimate that represents the consensus view of all sixteen American spy agencies, stated that Tehran had stopped building a nuclear weapon. The new estimate declared with "high confidence" that a military-run Iranian program intended to transform raw material into a nuclear weapon had been discontinued in 2003, and also added with considerable confidence that the halt "was directed primarily in response to increasing international scrutiny and pressure."[74]

While not directly involved in supervising nuclear negotiations with the P5+1 talks, Ahmadinejad's combative and inflammatory remarks, including repeatedly denying the Holocaust, rendered it impossible for his administration to pursue a sustainable foreign policy.[75] Although Iran claimed that its nuclear program was for peaceful purposes, it still raised real security concerns, both regionally and globally. These alarmist concerns led to the IAEA monitoring Iran's nuclear projects, followed by the United States and its European allies imposing severe economic sanctions on the country. These sanctions had a devastating impact on Iran's economy. Aware of the impacts of these economic sanctions, and reluctant to resort to any military options against Iran, the Obama administration pulled Iran into a series of covert diplomatic talks in Oman. When the Rouhani administration assumed the presidency, expressing its willingness to pursue a diplomatic route in the face of Iran's nuclear conundrum, the diplomatic alternative became real.

On July 14, 2015, the P5+1 nuclear deal with Iran was signed to limit Iran's nuclear production in exchange for lifting the sanctions. Iran lived up to its commitments, as did the other parties to the deal. The most important part of the JCPOA was that it noticeably reduced Iran's ability to weaponize its nuclear program. Iran's commitment was systematically monitored by an intrusive set of inspections by UN authorities. The result was that Iran's ability to achieve a nuclear capability increased to one year, giving Western intelligence agencies ample time to respond. While Iran's regional activities and its ballistic missiles were left out of the JCPOA, the agreement was beneficial to all sides. The Trump administration, however, withdrew from the nuclear accord in 2018, on the grounds that it was a flawed accord, hoping to pressure Iran into an entirely new agreement. This move was met with a great deal of resistance by other members of the JCPOA and understandably a major pushback from Iran, who argued that the United States had no reasonable grounds to pull out of the agreement, given a total lack of violations on the part of Iran.

The Biden administration has sought a path to resurrect the deal by persuading Iran into full compliance. Two questions remain. First, can things return to where they were before Trump took office in 2016? Second, will Raisi follow Rouhani's path to revive the Iran nuclear deal? The Trump administration was hard at work to bring Iran to the negotiating table. However, Trump's policy comprehensively failed to do so. In the following chapters, I compare and contrast the policies of the Trump and Biden administrations to demonstrate that the former's approach toward Iran proved to be a strategic mistake, as it risked provoking Tehran not to comply with the 2015 nuclear agreement.

7

TRUMP'S WITHDRAWAL FROM THE JCPOA

SOME IMPLICATIONS

The diplomatic agreement of the Iran nuclear deal, as noted in the previous chapter, had given Obama hope that this could lead to a fundamental reset of US–Iran relations—and could conceivably form part of his broader vision for peace in the Middle East. Yet the steadfast Israeli opposition to the deal slowed the trajectory of this anticipation, turning the Joint Comprehensive Plan of Action (JCPOA) into such a burdensome pressure on the White House that it became impossible to consider any kind of larger improvement in relations with Iran.[1] The lack of substantial sanctions relief, however, rendered Iran's economy more debilitated than before. Iran became even more isolated from the West than it had been in the early 2000s.[2]

Still, the then Secretary of State John Kerry and Iran's Foreign Minister Javad Zarif had developed a genuine trust over the years of nuclear talks that allowed them to keep the lines of communication open. In January 2016, following several months of behind-the-scenes talks between the two men, Iran released four Americans from judicial custody in exchange for Washington dropping charges against seven Iranians who had been convicted of sanction violations. At around the same time, when ten US sailors inadvertently wandered into Iranian waters and were apprehended by the Revolutionary

Guards, Kerry called Zarif and quickly secured their release. Such diplomatic ties and interactions represented remarkable progress. This stood in stark contrast to what had happened nearly thirty-six years earlier, when the hostage crisis in Iran dragged on for fourteen months before the US Embassy hostages were released.[3]

Those new and cordial diplomatic relations came to an abrupt end when newly elected President Donald Trump took office and stated that the United States would no longer uphold its end of the nuclear deal. The relationship between Iran and Washington retrogressed, in the words of John Ghazvinian, "into the state of poorly managed cycles of provocation and counter-provocation, accusation and counter-accusation that characterized their interactions for years."[4] The implications of President Trump's decision to withdraw from the JCPOA were profound, and it is hard to see how US national security interests have been effectively served given that Iran remained in full compliance based on ongoing International Atomic Energy Agency (IAEA) reports between 2015 and 2018. The United States had no option but to kill the agreement. What did this mean for US credibility? And if Washington insisted on renegotiating the deal and Tehran refused to comply and was thus forced to withdraw from the deal, would the Trump administration eventually turn to an unprovoked military action against Iran?

The Trump administration's subsequent imposition of maximum pressure-based sanctions on Iran constituted a form of economic warfare. In response to these sanctions, Iran initiated a series of actions to demonstrate its ability to disrupt traffic in and near the Strait of Hormuz, sending a signal to the United States and its regional allies that they would also pay a price. The policy of maximum pressure led to no diplomatic breakthrough or change in Iranian foreign policy behavior. Instead, it gave rise to further uncertainty and insecurity in the region.

The imposition of a Muslim travel ban was yet another Trump foreign policy decision that carried negative implications. On January 27, 2017, the Trump administration issued an executive order temporarily banning citizens from Iran and several other Muslim countries from entering the United States. Many of those impacted by the ban were family members who wanted to reunite with one another, and some were students, scholars, and researchers who had been in the United States for some time but were now prevented from returning.

Other foreign policy implications flowing from this move were equally destabilizing. Iran was compelled to gravitate toward maintaining stronger economic and military ties with China, a development commonly known as Asianization. To many countries in the region, China has become a more and more reliable economic and diplomatic partner. This trend would add another layer of complexity to the ongoing conflicts and tensions in the Middle East. Was the Trump administration slowly moving in the direction of confronting Iran—reminiscent of the way the US administrations, especially that of George W. Bush, paved the way for the war with Iraq? Clearly, economic sanctions imposed on Iraq during 1990–2003 were the most sweeping and destructive of any established in the name of international governance. These sanctions, along with the bombing campaign of 1991, brought about the near disintegration of Iraq's infrastructure and severely compromised basic living conditions in the country.[5]

Similarly, US unilateral sanctions, as well as UN multilateral sanctions, intensified pressure on Iran under the Trump administration. It is unclear whether this pain was sufficient for Iran to abandon its rights to "develop research, production, and use of nuclear energy for peaceful purposes without discrimination," as guaranteed under Article 4 of the Nuclear Non-Proliferation Treaty (NPT).[6] According to Article 4, Iran, as a member of the NPT, is well within its rights to demand nuclear technology and utilize it to produce nuclear energy. China and Russia have opposed the new US containment policy and have frequently advocated for a diplomatic solution rather than a coercive one.[7]

In this chapter, I critically assess Trump's Iran policy within the larger context of the Middle East with an eye toward gauging the net results of this policy and its wide-ranging implications. The key issue raised in this chapter is whether or not the application of the maximum pressure policy yielded the outcome favored by the Trump administration. I argue against this contention, demonstrating how the Trump administration's disjointed and dangerous policy of maximum pressure pushed Iran further into the arms of Russia and China and revealing other detrimental regional implications of this failed policy. The 2021 Iran–China strategic long-term cooperation agreement, which covers multiple security measures, including joint naval exercise and a variety of economic activity—from oil and mining to upgrading industrial activity in Iran, as well as telecommunication, transportation, and agricultural collaboration—will have a significant impact, not just on Iran but also on the rest of the region. Subjecting Iran to more punitive sanctions also strengthened hardliners in Iran and dramatically undercut the Rouhani government and its moderate allies.

Trump's Iran Policy

The then US Secretary of State Mike Pompeo used the first speech in his new position at the Heritage Foundation in Washington, DC, on May 21, 2018, to send a message directly to the Iranian leadership and its people with a twelve-point plan—or, more accurately, an ultimatum of twelve conditions requiring Iran to:

- Declare to the International Atomic Energy Agency (IAEA) a full account of the prior military dimensions of its nuclear program and permanently and verifiably abandon such work in perpetuity.
- Stop enrichment and never pursue plutonium reprocessing, including closing its heavy water reactor.
- Provide the IAEA with unqualified access to all sites throughout the entire country.
- End its proliferation of ballistic missiles and halt further launching or development of nuclear-capable missile systems.
- Release all US citizens as well as citizens of US partners and allies.
- End support to Middle East "terrorist" groups, including Hezbollah, Hamas and Islamic Jihad.
- Respect the sovereignty of the Iraqi government and permit the disarming, demobilization and reintegration of Shia militias.
- End its military support for the Houthi rebels and work toward a peaceful, political settlement in Yemen.
- Withdraw all forces under Iran's command throughout the entirety of Syria.
- End support for the Taliban and other "terrorists" in Afghanistan and the region and cease harboring senior Al-Qaeda leaders.

- End the Islamic Revolutionary Guard corps-linked Quds Force's support for "terrorists" and "militant" partners around the world.
- End its threatening behavior against its neighbors, many of whom are US allies, including its threats to destroy Israel and its firing of missiles at Saudi Arabia and the United Arab Emirates, and threats to international shipping and destructive cyberattacks.[8]

Secretary Pompeo noted that all these goals were broadly shared by European allies of the United States. It is not clear if that was the case. In response to this new policy, the then British Foreign Secretary Boris Johnson noted that packaging all of Iran's worrisome conduct into one agreement would be a daunting challenge at best and very difficult at worst.[9] Similarly, the then European Union foreign policy chief Federica Mogherini pointed out that this new US policy fell well short of showing how these conditions could be fulfilled outside the nuclear deal.

> Secretary Pompeo's speech has not demonstrated how walking away from the JCPOA has made or will make the region safer from the threat of nuclear proliferation or how it puts us in a better position to influence Iran's conduct in areas outside the scope of the JCPOA. There is no alternative to the JCPOA.[10]

Perhaps the most legitimate criticism leveled against Pompeo's speech was the conditions he laid out failed to add up to a clear strategy, and simply included a number of delusional demands that were completely divorced from reality. If nothing else, they pointed to provoking a revolution from within, or regime change from without. Neither of these possibilities could have been facilitated by such a policy. It was unclear if longstanding US allies would completely agree with these points or would prefer to salvage the nuclear deal.

Furthermore, the extra-territorial stance of the sanctions raised serious concerns about penalizing foreign businesses that traded with or invested in Iran. The US sanctions on Iran not only blocked American firms from doing business in Tehran, but also prohibited foreign firms that did business there from accessing the larger US banking and financial system. Renewing sanctions made it immensely difficult for Iran to sell its oil abroad or use the international banking system. In fact, this policy deprived the international oil markets of roughly four million barrels of Iranian crude oil per day—nearly four percent of global supply at the time, two-thirds of which was regularly exported to China, India, Japan, and South Korea.

More crucially, the sanctions on Iran's oil industry exposed an apparent vulnerability of Iran's economy. Some experts, such as Anoushiravan Ehteshami, have long warned that excessive reliance on oil revenues has rendered the country much more vulnerable to systemic change. The Islamic Republic has shown that the more it relied on hydrocarbons to finance its development projects and promote its foreign policy, the more it became susceptible to pressures outside its control—and ultimately, the more economic imperatives have come to shape its foreign policy. The most discernible consequence of an inordinate reliance on hydrocarbons, Ehteshami cautions, was "Iran's vulnerability to US-orchestrated economic sanctions aimed at its oil and financial sectors."[11]

Meanwhile, the Trump administration's policy of maximum pressure further pushed Tehran more firmly to the east, where China and Russia are likely to become its major trading partners as a result. This policy, which also pushed states to choose between banking in US dollars and with US firms operating under a different financial system, could not have come at a worse time, as the United States engaged in an increasingly fruitless trade war with the Chinese. Could these points and similar policies ironically expedite the move toward a potential post-American world where recalibration of financial interests would be forthcoming?

The Muslim Ban

On January 28, 2017, President Trump placed a travel ban on nine countries, seven of which—Iran, Iraq, Libya, Somalia, Sudan, Syria, and Yemen—were Muslim-majority countries. The other two countries included in the travel ban were North Korea and Venezuela. The travel ban halted the flow of all regular people and refugees into the United States. Trump's decision to put seven majority-Muslim countries on the blacklist had religious connotations. Moreover, the ban had a clause suggesting that members of "minority religions" in the banned nations be allowed entry. This enabled Christians and Jews from the seven blacklisted nations to immigrate, while Muslims were barred from doing so.[12] Instead of searching for ways to work with Iran, Trump chose to validate Iranians' fears that the United States was their enemy. Although the rationale behind this ban centered on fighting terrorism, the evidence thereof was woefully inadequate. In fact, the grand total of deaths caused by terrorists from these seven Muslim-majority countries between 1975 and 2018 was zero.[13] This policy dealt a serious blow to US prestige and values across the world.

A 2017 petition signed by more than 7,000 academics, including thirty-seven Nobel laureates, condemned the entry ban based on religion and national origin as unfair and deleterious to US interests. The petition argued that the action by President Trump undermined the nation's position of leadership in higher education and research and laid an "undue burden" on certain international students and scholars. It also added that this measure was noticeably disruptive to the lives of these immigrants, their families, and their communities, and that it was inhumane, futile, and un-American.[14] One observer specifically criticized the ban on the Iranians from a knowledge-based standpoint, arguing that there were many ongoing scientific partnerships between US and Iranian scientists. Banning Iranians from entering the United States would not only inhibit the free exchange of ideas, but also could do tremendous harm to scientific progress in both countries and could have a negative global effect on science.[15]

The Trump administration's subsequent immigration policy of separating children from their parents and arraigning immigrants fleeing from brutal repression and violence in Central America was followed by the US Supreme Court's June 26, 2018, ruling (5 to 4) in favor of the ban on Muslims traveling to the United States. These policies reflected a pernicious populist mood reminiscent of the 1940s. Repeating the tragic mistakes of the past under the same, old familiar logic underlying the Korematsu decision that upheld FDR's executive order to forcibly remove American citizens of Japanese ancestry from the West Coast and intern them in camps during World War II, Trump's travel ban followed in the footsteps of that misguided and exclusionary policy and also had painful consequences in human terms, dashing the hopes of many migrants for a better life.

What message did this decision send? The message, which ran counter to the principle of religious neutrality in the First Amendment of the US Constitution, was that Muslims were regarded as "nefarious outsiders" and should not be given an equal opportunity to enter into the country or be treated as equal citizens with the same rights and obligations granted to non-Muslims.[16] This discriminatory policy was justified under the pretext of protecting national security. Yet many Muslims saw it as just another sign of animus toward their faith.

It is not clear what credible national security threat lingered against the United States given that no one from any of the countries included in the ban was involved in any deadly terrorist attacks in the United States over the past two decades. The 9/11 attacks of 2001 were directed by citizens of other countries, most notably Saudi Arabia, Egypt, Lebanon, and Pakistan, which were not on this list. Most terrorist attacks inside US cities were conducted by those already residing in the United States. Blocking the arrival of new immigrants— who potentially provide useful additions to the labor force and contributions to the US economy—was to play on the fears of the public and risk deepening the mistrust between the US government and its Muslim population.

The economic and market rationale was also an important part of the national security assessment. National security was not necessarily gauged entirely in terms of threat. It could have been seen in terms of opportunity as well. What did the "absolute and complete shutdown of Muslims" entering the United States mean at a time when the vast majority of Muslims living in the United States were positively integrated into local economies and assimilated into local social milieus and the fabric of US society? Research done by Pew, James Zogby, and Shibley Telhami indicated that the overwhelming majority of American Muslims have adapted to or adopted US democratic values and identity as their own.[17] Would initiating such a discriminatory and divisive policy that treats Muslims as unwelcome "others" contribute to national security? Rather than confrontation, the policy of accommodation and integration was more likely to prevent radicalization among Muslim youths and contribute to political assimilation and coexistence. It is worth noting that the Biden administration immediately issued an executive order ending the Muslim ban effective November 8, 2021.

Trump's Anti-Iranian Gambit

The Trump administration embarked on forging an informal coalition with Saudi Arabia, Israel, the United Arab Emirates (UAE), and other Sunni Gulf Cooperation Council (GCC) countries, with a view toward reversing Iran's influence in the region. Trump's first trip abroad to Saudi Arabia and Israel was marked by the ratcheting up of his anti-Iranian rhetoric and a huge arms sale ($110 billion) to Saudi Arabia.[18] Trump's approach toward Saudi Arabia stood in stark contrast to that of Obama, who suggested that Saudi Arabia had to find an effective way to share the neighborhood with Iran and institute some sort of cold peace with its major rival in the region.[19]

Meanwhile, the massive infusion of military hardware and technology into the region raised many questions—not least what the Saudis planned to do once they acquired such military might.[20] Historically, the Saudis have never contributed any substantial number of ground troops to regional wars. In recent years, they have relied on air power. But even then, they have had limited success or effectiveness, as was evident in the case of their military involvement in Yemen. The steady and brutal punishment of Houthis in Yemen failed to yield a desirable outcome for them. Air power alone has never determined the outcome of a war on the ground.

On June 5, 2017, Saudi Arabia and some of its GCC allies, including the UAE and Bahrain, severed diplomatic ties with Qatar, accusing Doha of backing the Muslim Brotherhood and pursuing friendly relations with Iran. Egypt, Libya, Yemen, and the Maldives also joined this diplomatic spat, suspending air, land, and sea travel to and from the country.[21] These developments were indicative of new divisions and discord among the GCC member states. It is worth remembering that since its inception in 1981, the GCC and its member states have never been united on all fronts, often lacking a unified foreign policy approach. The GCC, a regional multilateral organization, has suffered from an identity crisis of sorts, leaving unanswered the question of whether it is a security structure, a political or monetary union, or some combination of all of these.

However, with Trump's visit to Saudi Arabia on May 21, 2017, the Saudis felt emboldened to talk about spearheading a new order—

one ruled and heavily influenced by the royal family in Riyadh. It seemed as though the Trump administration had given the Saudis the green light to organize and influence this new order as they wish. Clearly, Qatar and its young leader, Sheikh Tamim, stood in the way of this so-called "new order," as their free media (particularly *Al Jazeera*) and their sympathetic approach toward the Arab Spring uprisings unnerved the Saudis with regard to policies in the region. In this sense, Qatar posed a major threat to the advocates of the status quo, particularly Saudi Arabia and the UAE.

Except for opposing the Bashar al-Assad regime in Syria and fighting the Islamic State of Iraq and Syria (ISIS), not much common ground existed among the GCC member states. Qatar—a country that acted pragmatically and was at peace with its neighbors—presented a tantalizing example of prosperity and political stability in a region surrounded by turbulence and rising tensions. The political rifts between the Saudis and Qataris were not new, nor was their competition over political influence as they jostled for power and autonomy throughout the region. It was an open secret that Qatar's rulers have pursued pragmatic and relatively open-door policies toward Iran—an approach that the Saudis strongly resented and have described as the foremost cause of discord and division among the dynastic monarchies in the Persian Gulf.

The timing of these diplomatic breakups invited a wide variety of reactions. One view held that the Emiratis appeared keen on destabilizing Qatar, thus compelling the United States to move its military airbase from Doha to Abu Dhabi. It should be noted that there were some 11,000 US troops at Al Udeid Air Base in Qatar, where the air war against ISIS was conducted and carried out. Given that the air base was the largest US military base in the Middle East, this move could potentially embolden the Emirati rulers to settle their accounts with Iran over the disputed islands of Abu Musa and the Greater and Lesser Tunbs near the Strait of Hormuz.[22]

How could this confrontational scenario have played out? Had a conflict with Iran over these islands intensified, it was not unreasonable to assume that the Trump administration would have sided with the conservative Arab regimes vis-à-vis Iran. The question of how these pieces all fitted together to encourage or inhibit US intervention in favor of the UAE in the dispute between Tehran and Abu Dhabi remained, at best, unanswered, and hard to predict at this point. There was a questionable simplicity to the Emirati narrative—that they would have US backing against Qatar—in part because such a scenario was fraught with risks and unpredictable turns and twists.

The consequences of the June 7, 2017, ISIS attacks on Iran, in which the Iranian parliament and Ayatollah Khomeini's mausoleum were attacked, seventeen people were killed, and more than fifty were injured, should not be understated. Tehran blamed Riyadh for these attacks. The two sides were likely to further stoke the kind of sectarian tensions that emboldened ISIS, who would exploit them to spread its terrorist message in the region. The rise of sectarian identity politics, experts noted, created a great deal of tension among communities across the region. Sectarianism bolstered the rhetoric of state and non-state actors who advanced their own agendas, while "claiming to be defenders of supposedly threatened identities and communities."[23] In short, sectarian identity politics was not just a government invention but the result of the varying ruling elites—in the political, religious, social, and economic realms—who often used sectarianism to enhance their personal aims.[24]

The GCC appeared to be in crisis and could unravel if its most significant actors decided to write the script for other members on how to conduct their foreign policies or manage their domestic politics. In some ways, Tehran was the major beneficiary of this rift among GCC members, especially given that other member states, such as Kuwait, failed to mediate this tension. As noted above, GCC unity suffered a substantial setback as a result of the rift between Saudi Arabia and Qatar, with the latter opting to move closer to Iran and Turkey regarding the Saudi-led embargo. Kuwait also maintained good relations with Iran, while seeking to avoid alienating Iran by adhering to the Saudi propaganda that characterized Iran as a key source of threat to regional security.[25]

Likewise, Oman, which played a significant role in hosting secret US–Iran negotiations on the nuclear deal, has historically had healthy and balanced relations with both Iran and Saudi Arabia. Oman and Iran have long planned a gas pipeline that would benefit them both economically. The UAE has maintained economic ties with Iran without irritating Washington. Bahrain was the only GCC member state that approved of the Saudi stance against Iran, leaving any clear road-map for future relations with Iran ambiguous.[26]

The larger issue that confronted US policymakers was the likelihood of this political cleavage to undermine the anti-Iran coalition that the Trump administration had so painstakingly sought to put together in its initial months in office. It soon became apparent that this was very likely, especially if the Saudis and its Persian Gulf allies had continued to isolate Qatar at a time when they needed to be unified in their attempts to defeat and dismantle ISIS. Because the Saudis proved unable to maintain sufficient leverage in shaping outcomes in Yemen, Syria, and Iraq, they most likely preferred to drag the United States into a regional military conflict with Iran—an eventuality that would have resulted in devastating consequences for the entire region and further afield. The transactional nature of arms sales to the Saudis notwithstanding, the danger lay in a slow drift into a military confrontation with Iran. The old, simplistic cliché rang true: US allies need not necessarily pass the test of democratic governance if they help Washington in its fight against terrorism.

It became evident that the Trump administration's plans to isolate Iran proved more difficult than initially envisioned, in large part because America's European allies—as well as Russia and China—had decided to abide by the 2015 Iran nuclear deal, and ironically, outside their rhetorical flourishes, so too had the Trump administration. The rest of the world had accepted the legitimacy of the nuclear deal, and Iran has indicated that it will fulfill its obligations in accordance with the agreement. Perhaps the most disturbing aspect of such inflammatory anti-Iranian rhetoric was that President Trump kept turning a blind eye to Iran's internal political dynamics, ignoring opportunities for a less confrontational relationship from within Iran.

Domestically, Iran was undergoing a massive transformation caused by technology, evolving civic culture, and a growing determination on the part of the youth to control their destiny. The mood changed in Iran and the public was in favor of integrating into the world economy and breaking from years of strategic isolation. Two groups—youth and women—overwhelmingly supported President Hassan Rouhani in his 2017 re-election bid. These groups were hopeful that he would ease some domestic social restrictions and normalize ties with the West. Demographics became destiny in Iran, as population dynamics caught up with Iran's internal politics. The religious right lost its ideological and political appeal to a younger generation.

Iranian elections were yet another testament to the social power prevailing over established authority, with the power of new communication technologies and social media playing a crucial role in Rouhani's victory. Although President Rouhani faced many formidable challenges, he secured a resounding public endorsement, in part because concluding the nuclear deal constituted the apotheosis of his career. Given the ongoing tension between hard-liners and more modern pragmatists in Iran, the time was right for diplomacy, dialogue, and engagement, not only in Iran but throughout the region.

In the face of new developments in the region, most experts noted, rapprochement between Iran and the United States became not just inevitable but a preferred policy option. The Saudis, meanwhile, considered the rapprochement detrimental to the balance of power in the region. The Saudis faced a key choice as to which Iran they preferred to face: an empowered yet cooperative Iran, or a belligerent Iran bent on intensifying its ideological competition with the monarchical regime in Saudi Arabia. Acutely aware of the possible outcomes, Saudi leaders decided to remain in the game by simply cutting their losses and readjusting their policies toward Iran.

US Blunders

Shutting the doors to diplomacy and escalating tensions with Iran—while Tehran was abiding by all the provisions of the nuclear deal—reveals that the US hawks in the Trump administration, in alliance with Israel and Saudi Arabia and their powerful lobbies in Washington, were all along intent on disarming Iran and ultimately overthrowing its government. Israel, like Saudi Arabia, did what they could to scrap the Iran nuclear deal. For them, the deal was not strong enough to entirely dismantle Iran's nuclear program; rather, it only delayed and weakened the program. Both countries urged Washington not to sign the deal. Instead, they lobbied the United States to take military action to prevent Iran from enriching weapons-grade uranium. The then Israeli Prime Minister Benjamin Netanyahu even circumvented the White House and took his case directly to the US Congress. However, the Obama administration signed the deal, as it perceived nuclear proliferation in the region as an existential threat to both the United States and the Middle East. Obama's administration was surely intent on preventing a nuclear arms race in the Middle East.[27]

The emerging dynamics in the region marked by the Iran–Saudi Arabia rivalry, Iran–Israel tensions, and a new anti-Iranian bloc—Israel, Saudi Arabia, and the United States—have led to a cascade of interconnected regional crises, reinforcing the hand of the Iranian hard-liners and supporting their narrative of a deep ideological chasm between the Islamic Republic and the United States. The Islamic Republic, Iranian conservatives argue, is inherently opposed to the US-led hegemonic world order and its power projection in the Persian Gulf region. Furthermore, Iran's implacable opposition to the state of Israel—a close ally to the US—stands in the way of any form of rapprochement with Washington.[28]

There are no indications that Iran's foreign policy conduct in the region has noticeably changed. Iran's regional policies are tied to its perception of threats and opportunities. Its support for Lebanese Hezbollah is unwavering and steady. Its intervention in Syria, for example, was motivated by a perceived need to preserve a long-time ally, the Assad regime, and to defeat Sunni Muslim fundamentalist militants linked to Al-Qaeda and ISIS. Its posture in Iraq and Afghanistan remains directly linked to its broader regional role, as does its support for the Houthis in Yemen (albeit on a much smaller scale). Some sources have even indicated that Iran's support for Hamas continues unabated.[29]

To drive Iranian oil exports and revenues down to zero, the Trump administration announced that it would no longer provide any waivers allowing countries to buy oil from Iran. With declining oil revenue, Iranian leaders decided to demonstrate to the United States the costs of imposing maximum pressure by sending a message to Saudi Arabia and the UAE that if Iran was unable to sell its oil, their oil exports would also come under fire. On May 12, 2019, several commercial oil tankers were damaged by mines near the UAE port of

Fujairah. The UAE declined to publicly attribute the Fujairah attacks to Iran, but US officials suspected that proxies sympathetic to or working for Iran might have been involved in these attacks. Tehran denied any direct or indirect role in these incidents.[30]

Additionally, several events in the summer and fall of 2019 compelled some regional actors, including Saudi Arabia and the UAE, to consider either direct negotiations with Tehran or mediation by regional actors to resolve tensions with Iran in the near future. On June 13, 2019, two oil tankers were attacked near the Strait of Hormuz as they transited the Gulf of Oman, further raising regional tensions virtually a month after the similar Fujairah incident, which involved four tankers. These attacks took place on the same day that the Supreme Leader of Iran Ali Khamenei met with Japanese Prime Minister Shinzō Abe in Iran. According to some sources, Abe had sought, albeit unsuccessfully, to broker talks between President Trump and his Iranian counterpart, President Hassan Rouhani.[31]

Shortly thereafter, another alarming event again heightened the risk of conflict in the Persian Gulf. On June 20, 2019, a US drone that had penetrated Iranian airspace was shot down by the Iranians. There was no retaliation to the event by the US military present in the Persian Gulf region. As noted in chapter 4, in 2019, a memorandum of understanding (MoU) was signed between Iran and the UAE, paving the way for holding regular meetings to boost cooperation between the two countries on wide-ranging issues, including border control zones at the invitation of one another and maritime activities. What made this possible was the conciliatory tone struck by Iran articulated by the then Foreign Minister Javad Zarif who had voiced Iran's readiness to maintain diplomatic relations with Saudi Arabia, the United Arab Emirates, and their allies. While noting Iran's steady and close relations with Qatar, Kuwait, and Oman, Zarif had told reporters at the Asian Cooperation Dialogue in Doha, "We hope to have the same type of relations with Saudi Arabia, Bahrain, and the United Arab Emirates."[32]

Subsequently, when faced with attacks on Saudi oil facilities on September 14, 2019, US reluctance to engage in a military intervention in the Persian Gulf sent yet another clear signal that the Trump administration was unlikely to get embroiled in another military confrontation in the region. The attacks on two Saudi Aramco oil facilities were another harbinger of escalating tensions in the region. Both Riyadh and Washington alleged that the scale, finesse, and precision with which these strikes were conducted all suggested that Iran most likely was behind them. The strikes also demonstrated the policy failure of the Trump administration, which triggered the crisis in the first place by inflicting economic pressure on Iran, before worsening the situation through political and strategic blunders.[33]

The Trump administration's decision to withdraw US troops stationed along the border in northern Syria on October 7, 2019, paved the way for the ensuing Turkish incursion into that region to create a buffer zone inside Syria and defeat and remove the Kurdish-dominated Syrian Democratic Forces (SDF) coalition—of which the Kurdish Democratic Union Party (PYD) and its military wing, the Kurdish People's Protection Units (YPG), are key parts. This military operation, dubbed "Operation Peace Spring," sent another signal to US allies in the region that US deterrence of Iran seemed no longer to be working and that US allies had been left exposed. The ostensible abandonment of Kurdish allies who were instrumental in defeating ISIS in northern Syria fostered further recalibration and hedging options among US allies.[34]

Not surprisingly, Iran and Syria, both of which are against the establishment of an autonomous Kurdish enclave in northern Syria—much less an independent Kurdish state—widely regarded Turkey's incursion as geopolitically favorable. Tehran and Damascus have been deeply concerned about the Rojava administration of the Kurds in northern Syria that has aimed to create a model of autonomy for the rest of the Kurdish population in the region. This explains why Iran and Syria seem to have tacitly approved of Ankara's plan to overcome the region's Kurds with millions of Syrian refugees currently residing in Turkey. At least, they were reluctant to criticize Turkey's plan to impose a new demographic order on the ground.[35]

The targeted killing of Qassem Soleimani, the commander of Iran's elite Quds Force of the Islamic Revolutionary Guards Corps (IRGC), on January 3, 2020, in Baghdad again elevated regional tensions, bringing Iran and the United States to the brink of a military confrontation. There was little or no evidence that Soleimani was intent on launching an imminent attack on US' forces. A preemptive action against an imminent attack is regarded in international law as a legitimate form of self-defense. However, a preventive attack (mounted against a gathering threat rather than an impending one) is something very different. It is not in the US interest to lower the legal norm against preventive attacks lest they become much more frequent. While Soleimani was not an innocent bystander, his killing had negative consequences.[36] On November 27, 2020, Mohsen Fakhrizadeh, a renowned Iranian nuclear scientist, was assassinated in Damavand, a city near Tehran, allegedly by Israeli agents operating in Iran.

All of these developments will most likely complicate the possibility of any conceivable rapprochement between the two countries in the coming years. The return to multilateral diplomacy—involving the EU, Russia, and China—under the Biden administration could potentially pave the way for a new round of talks between the United States and Iran, spawning a newfound hope that Washington and Tehran can still engage each other diplomatically. The rewards of seeking diplomatic solutions outweigh the risks of the intractable hostility that has come to characterize Trump's dismissive approach toward Iran.

The Biden administration's preference to return to the JCPOA has arguably precipitated the Saudi decision to lift the embargo they imposed on Qatar since mid-2017. Resolving the rift between the two Gulf countries appears to have been a backlash to a potential US reengagement with Iran. Some observers have noted that the breakthrough in the Gulf crisis may be a reaction to Doha's efforts to forge closer links with Iran and Turkey. More specifically, Qatar's relations with Turkey could still present a key barrier to the resumption of negotiations to end the embargo. Both the UAE and Saudi Arabia have expressed real concerns about Turkey's role in regional affairs. For its part, Turkey has in fact tried to improve its relations with Saudi Arabia. The tensions with Ankara, however, have been most apparent in Libya, where the UAE and Turkey have continued to support rival proxies in the ongoing civil war.[37]

It is worth noting that the Abraham Accords signed between Israel, the UAE, and Bahrain on September 15, 2020, will most likely foster closer cooperation between these states, easing the path toward normalizing diplomatic relations. These accords could also have beneficial spillover impacts on the economies of these countries. Facing an increased isolation, Iran senses an urgency to forge closer ties with Russia and China. However, these accords are unlikely to fundamentally change the region's strategic context, as they fail to address the region's key problems, including sectarian tensions, civil wars, nationalistic pursuit of power and hegemony, the Palestinian quest for statehood, and ongoing political divisions.

Given these new realities on the ground and the gradual US withdrawal from the region, I argue that while negotiations between Iran and the United States are essential to reduce hostilities between the two countries, normalization of relations appears unrealistic if not inconceivable, at least for the near future. Iran should thus focus on reaching a regional détente with its neighbors—a goal far more attainable and prudent than normalization of relations with the United States.

Consequences of Withdrawal from the JCPOA

The Trump administration's unilateral withdrawal from the JCPOA and the reimposition of crippling sanctions on Iran increased tensions in the Persian Gulf and all but removed any incentives for Iran to continue to comply with the JCPOA. More importantly, it antagonized many US allies, who appeared eager to do normal business with Iran. Citing the vigorous JCPOA inspection and verification regimes imposed on Iran's nuclear program, Obama officials underscored the importance of two points. First, that Iran had unquestionably stated its non-proliferation commitments to steer clear of nuclear weapons. Second, that while some nuclear restrictions are implemented under certain deadlines, others, such as Iran's adherence to the IAEA's intrusive Additional Protocol, have no time limit and would continue to subject Iran to robust external inspections on a regular and recurring basis.[38]

The Additional Protocol significantly expands the IAEA's access to Iranian nuclear facilities under the Iran–IAEA Safeguards Agreement. While still considered a "voluntary agreement," the P5+1 group insisted on Iran's compliance with the Additional Protocol, which was initially introduced between Iran and the IAEA in 2003 and observed by Iran until 2006, when the Ahmadinejad administration, in protest against imposed sanctions, ceased its compliance with the protocol.[39] Under the JCPOA, Iran has agreed to execute and legislate the Additional Protocol, which lacks any sunset clauses and will continue permanently.

Iran has regularly provided declarations under the terms of the Additional Protocol to the IAEA, facilitating the agency's evaluation of the veracity of the information provided by Iran on its past and ongoing nuclear activities. It should be noted, however, that under the JCPOA, Iran has 24 days to comply with an IAEA request to inspect a suspected undeclared nuclear facility, including military sites suspected of enrichment or development activities. Section 74 of Annex I of the JCPOA does not permit inspections that are not implemented "in good faith." This means that the IAEA's suspicions must be predicated upon valid and verified information.[40]

If the Trump administration had legitimate concerns about these sunset provisions in the JCPOA, according to one expert, it could have improved the agreement rather than quashing it and starting again, or abandoning the project wholesale without any substantive plans for reengagement. Furthermore, the Trump team could have pressed for negotiations on a testing moratorium or regional accession to the Comprehensive Nuclear-Test-Ban Treaty (CTBT), as Egypt, Iran, and Israel are all signatories to that agreement. Either recourse would have minimized proliferation threats in the region, while also providing guarantees to Iran on potentially painful sanctions policies or its own legitimate security concerns.[41]

Moreover, there were other ways to address some faltering aspects of the nuclear deal without discarding it. The Trump administration's key criticism of the JCPOA was that it "did nothing to address Iran's continuing development of ballistic and cruise missiles, which could deliver nuclear warheads."[42] Former US Energy Secretary Ernest Moniz, one of the key negotiators in the JCPOA, responded that the nuclear deal imposed a "strong nonproliferation regime" on Iran and that "it is essentially impossible" for Iran to legitimize or hide its nuclear activities in such a short period of time as the IAEA is likely to detect even minor traces of nuclear materials.[43] That may explain why the JCPOA is referred to as "Additional Protocol plus," since it provides greater latitude for IAEA inspections than are contained in the Additional Protocol. It includes "monitoring of uranium mining and milling, centrifuge manufacturing, R & D, storage, and spent fuel."[44] However, it was never within the remit of the deal to adjudicate Iran's missile programs, unless they specifically dealt with its nuclear armament ambitions. Traditional security negotiations may have addressed this issue, but alas, the abandonment of the deal poisoned the well on any good faith talks in the short term.

While the JCPOA focused entirely on the Iranian nuclear program, UN Security Council (UNSC) Resolution 2231—which sets out an inspection process by the IAEA to closely monitor Iran's nuclear program under the JCPOA—also calls upon Iran "not to undertake any activity related to ballistic missiles designed to be capable of delivering nuclear weapons" until 2023.[45] The Trump administration could have pursued negotiations to address this and other related concerns. Two years later, it became evident that President Trump had achieved nothing, as his policy has led to increasing US isolation on the global scene and an Iranian government much closer to a nuclear capability than ever before.[46]

Meanwhile, as some observers have asserted, the IAEA's inspectors conducted 402 site visits and twenty-five snap inspections during the first year of the JCPOA. By 2018, the agency had issued thirteen reports confirming Iran's full compliance with and steadfast implementation of its commitments under the JCPOA. According to the November 2018 IAEA report, the agency maintained its regular access to relevant buildings in Iran while deploying necessary surveillance technologies to verify "the non-diversion of declared nuclear material at the facilities."[47] While the nuclear deal provided the most realistic opportunity for a major change in Iran's foreign policy, as critics have pointed out, the Trump administration ruined this chance and institutionalized enmities between Tehran and Washington for years to come, succeeding only in driving Iran further in an eastern direction.[48]

Some US allies in the West resented the fact that the Trump administration superimposed its own interpretation when it came to the nuclear deal. Lambasting Trump's anti-JCPOA decision, Volker Perthes, Executive Chairman and Director of the German Institute for International and Security Affairs in Berlin, wrote that the unilateral US withdrawal represented a stark challenge to the international community of states, and particularly to the European allies of the United States. The situation differed from the dispute over the US invasion of Iraq in 2003 that created deep divisions within the European Union, especially between the United Kingdom on the one hand and Germany and France on the other.

This time, Volker went on to argue, France, Germany, and the UK have all considered this decision a major strategic blunder. By breaking an agreement that had been negotiated together by three key EU member states, Russia, and China, Trump has undermined a credible multilateral agreement. The extraterritorial consequences of such decisions were largely unwarranted. Not only were European companies targeted by US sanctions unless they stopped doing business with Iran, an eventuality that benefited their Chinese competitors, but many European policymakers also found Trump's policies in the region utterly perilous, counterproductive, and short-sighted.[49]

Perhaps the most important implication of the Trump administration's maximum pressure was driving Iran into the China's arms. On March 27, 2021, China and Iran signed a twenty-five-year cooperation agreement in which China promised to invest a total of $400 billion to secure long-term energy supplies from Iran and help rebuild Iran's economy, which has been under crippling US sanctions. The deal consists of several projects under the "Belt and Road Initiative" covering wide-ranging cooperation on energy supplies and security and military areas, including banking, telecommunications, ports, railways, health care, information technology, oil, gas, and nuclear energy over the next twenty-five years.[50]

In his visit to Tehran on March 27, 2021, China's Foreign Minister Wang Yi spoke of a momentous shift in Beijing's relations with Tehran and the region after signing the twenty-five-year agreement worth $400 billion. In an implied reference to the United States, Wang told Iran's President Hassan Rouhani that "it is time to seriously reflect on the bad consequences inflicted on the region by external interference, and work together to explore effective ways to maintain long-term regional security and stability."[51] For Tehran, its reliance on Beijing has noticeably increased after the devastating COVID-19 pandemic. China remains Iran's biggest trading partner, a key arms supplier since the 1980s, and one of its few allies to counter the US sanctions.[52] This deal is likely to magnify China's influence in the Middle East and disrupt US efforts to keep Iran isolated. It is unclear, however, how much of the agreement can be implemented while the current US dispute with Iran over its nuclear program remains unresolved.[53] This agreement also illustrated China's growing desire to play a far more significant role in a region that has been a strategic preoccupation of the United States for decades.[54]

Trump's Muddling Through

President Trump's pivot away from the Middle East never came to fruition, largely due to the lack of a clear and advanceable strategy. On the contrary, US involvement in the Persian Gulf region dramatically surged. The Trump administration's policy of maximum pressure neither succeeded in bringing Iran to the negotiating table, nor forced the regime to change. Rather, this policy triggered, within Iran, unemployment, inflation, shortages of medicines and a drastic decline in the value of the *rial*.[55] All of these mounting pressures and their painful consequences, as Barbara Slavin rightly noted, were unfolding inhumanely during a global health emergency: the COVID-19 pandemic.

This crisis could have provided the Trump administration with a humanitarian rationale to ease sanctions on Iran as a gesture to the long-suffering Iranian people, garnering goodwill and creating a separation between the mistreated people and their incompetent governance. However, the Trump administration failed to take the required steps to alleviate Iran's quandary. Instead, the US sought to block Iran's request for an emergency $5 billion loan from the IMF and to block Iran's access to funds frozen in foreign banks.[56] This represented a further tone-deaf measure that not only set back US–Iran relations but damaged the credibility of US claims of support for human rights in the future.

In 2019, in response to large-scale economic warfare against Iran, Iranians fired missiles at Saudi oil refineries. The Gulf states sensed the impending turmoil in the region, and the Trump administration demonstrated restraint by ratcheting down its confrontational rhetoric.[57]

In his last days in office, however, in response to rocket attacks on the American Embassy in Baghdad on December 20, 2020, Trump entertained the thought of bombing Iran—a decision that his advisers dissuaded him of given its potentially dangerous repercussions. Again, the decision to attack Iran indicated a further sign of a failed and inconsistent policy of more sticks than carrots, demonstrating broad incompetence at associating actions with restrained reactions. Trump, in aligning his Middle East policy with Israel, Saudi Arabia, and other Sunni Arab states in a campaign against Shi'ite Iran, left the region even more precarious than before. His close alignment with the Saudis led him to overlook their brutal and villainous military intervention in Yemen and their ongoing domestic repression, including the murder and dismemberment of exiled journalist Jamal Khashoggi.[58]

Iran's persistent presence in Iraq, Syria, and Lebanon served as a reminder that Tehran continued its relentless pursuit of regional influence and proxy networks.[59] It is worth noting, as Robert A. Pape observes, that sanctions seldom (if ever) alter regime conduct, especially when that behavior relates to the regime's vital security interests and its broader alliance networks. Too often sanctions are counterproductive. States that impose sanctions despite the knowledge that they will fail to coerce the target state enhance the costs and risks for themselves by escalating the danger of the sanctioned ultimately resorting to force. Sanctions work when they force the target to make necessary concessions and when they are imposed as a standalone tool—not as a complement to military action.[60]

Following Trump's denouncement of the JCPOA, and given the reluctance shown by other participants in the nuclear deal to challenge the US position and continue to maintain normal economic ties with Iran, Tehran increased its uranium enrichment. This all-out assault on Iran, writes Ishaan Tharoor, compelled Iran's rulers to renew building up their cache of enriched uranium, exceeding twelve times the limit set by the 2015 nuclear deal and inching closer to creating a nuclear weapon than when Trump took office. Several intelligence assessments underscored the importance of the nuclear deal, arguing that the deal was achieving its stated goal of restricting Iran's enriched uranium supply before Trump's order to pull out.[61]

Between February and May 2019, Nuclear Threat Initiative (NTI), a non-profit NGO in Washington, DC, reported that the IAEA released compliance reports demonstrating that Iran was in good standing pursuant to its IAEA agreements relating to verification and monitoring, heavy water processing, uranium enrichment, centrifuge R & D, manufacturing and inventory, and other related transparency measures. However, in response to the US reimposition of nuclear-related sanctions, Iran has reduced its compliance with the JCPOA in five phases:

> On July 1, 2019, Iran exceeded 300 kilograms of uranium hexafluoride; on July 8, 2019, Iran enriched uranium past 3.67% up to 4.5%; and on September 8, Iran announced that its commitments for research and development under the JCPOA would be completely removed. Iran proceeded to invest in research and development of centrifuge technology that is not compliant with IAEA monitoring and safeguards, and on November 16, Iran notified the Agency that its stock of heavy water had exceeded 130 metric tons. On January 5, 2020, Iran proceeded with the planned fifth and final rollback to its commitments, forgoing all agreed-to limits on centrifuges. Iran did not declare any intent to pursue a nuclear weapon and pledged to continue cooperation with the IAEA.[62]

Throughout 2020, the reported continued, Iran has exceeded the limits on uranium enrichment levels cited in the JCPOA. However, Iran also chose not to enrich U-235 beyond five percent. Iran continued to cooperate with IAEA inspectors in verification and monitoring of sites as outlined in the JCPOA, and refused to grant the IAEA access to sites revealed from the "atomic archive" released by Israel in 2018. In June 2020, the United Kingdom, France, and Germany joined the United States in submitting a resolution to the IAEA Board of Governors asking Iran to allow IAEA inspection teams to all requested sites. The IAEA Board of Governors supported the resolution on June 19, 2020.[63]

Conclusion

Trump's disdain for international institutions and the liberal order reflected an ultranationalist and unilateralist worldview that alienated Washington from the rest of the world. Nowhere was such a perspective more evident than in dealing with the Iran nuclear deal. The Trump administration policy of imposing sanctions on Iran constituted a form of economic warfare at a time when Iran was in full compliance with the agreement. The United States fell short of citing any specific Iranian violations of the JCPOA. Washington never provided a diplomatic alternative to Tehran when it imposed these sanctions.[64] The assassination of Qassem Soleimani disrupted useful political dynamics in both Iran (where domestic anti-regime protests had been gathering momentum and intensity) and in Iraq (where anti-Iranian protests had been mounting). The consequences of this included Iran's attempts to disregard the JCPOA by choosing to shrink the window it needs to build a nuclear weapon if it so desires. This will most likely present the United States and Israel with difficult choices in the future.[65]

Similarly, the Trump administration never accepted the reality that regime change in Iran via economic and political warfare was unlikely. The days leading up to the one-year anniversary of Soleimani's assassination (January 3, 2021) were particularly stressful. Washington flew B-52 bombers to the Persian Gulf region in a show of force and the US intelligence community revealed that Iran had been moving short-range ballistic missiles into Iraq with the possibility of preparing for an attack on US personnel or assets. These developments highlighted how badly Trump's Iran strategy had progressed. The Soleimani assassination failed to weaken Iran's attacks against the United States and its regional allies. Iran-backed proxies in Iraq were allegedly behind a 2019 rocket attack that killed an American contractor and led to an assault on the US Embassy in Baghdad in December 2020. While the impact of US sanctions and the COVID-19 pandemic have affected Iran's funding for proxies, these groups have been active throughout the region and—if anything—have gained ground in the wake of the US retreat from strategic interests and the reshuffling of US forces.[66]

On balance, it is safe to argue that US foreign policy under the Trump administration lacked a consistent logic and often failed to achieve its stated goals. Iran was a cheap and easy target for Trump to buttress electoral support at home and political backing from key allies in the region: Israel and Saudi Arabia.[67] Trump's attempts to strangle Iran's economy and upend the nuclear deal made the living conditions of ordinary Iranians miserable. However, it failed to precipitate the fall of the Islamic Republic. On the contrary, his policy of maximum pressure fortified the position of Iran's hard-liners ahead of the presidential elections in 2021, complicating the prospect of a general thaw in relations between the two countries.

Although imperfect in some areas, the JCPOA managed to temporarily stabilize the Iranian nuclear problem and was perhaps the most realistic option at the time. Trump's decision to dump it without anything to immediately replace it with gave the Iranians an excuse to resume their previous programs.[68] Perhaps more significantly, the failure of Trump's unilateral approach toward Iran was evident when on December 8, 2020, the United States circulated a revised resolution that would extend a UN arms embargo on Iran indefinitely. Only one country—the Dominican Republic—voted with Washington; even worse, close allies among the fifteen-member Security Council voiced their strong opposition.[69]

The way forward is to work within the JCPOA framework to see if legal and diplomatic solutions will pay dividends. A smart strategy for Iran would be to keep its economic and commercial ties with the EU, Russia, China, India, South Korea, and Japan. History suggests that a withdrawal from legal commitments, while relying solely on saber-rattling, is usually counterproductive at best. A prudent course of action for the United States is to offer serious diplomacy as an alternative to sanctions, along with a competent and focused application of carrots and sticks to motivate behavior that the United States and its allies find palatable.

Robert Malley, the Biden administration's special envoy on Iran, writes that US unilateral sanctions ravaged Iran's economy but achieved little else. Iran's nuclear program expanded further still, increasingly unrestrained by the JCPOA. After returning to the JCPOA, the larger challenge will be to address the regional tensions and divisions created by four years of pouring gasoline onto every regional fire imaginable, as well as the possibility of wider conflict between the Sunni states and Shi'ite states in the region. If left unchecked, these polarizations will likely undermine the Iran nuclear deal and could spur war. European governments are exploring the possibility of fostering a dialogue between Iran and its Gulf neighbors in an effort to curtail regional tensions and prevent an accidental outbreak of a war with the potential to spill out of the region and onto the global stage—an effort that the Biden administration would do well to endorse.[70]

The most effective path forward in the face of the Trump administration's failed policy is a more sensible effort by the JCPOA's parties to facilitate legitimate trade and a regularization of diplomacy with Iran.[71] Similarly, Iran's interests will be best served if it continues to cooperate with the IAEA and seek the relief and benefit of the enrichment and weapons limitations it is already engaged in. At this stage, hostility and faith may be a foregone conclusion for the near future.

In the context of the COVID-19 pandemic, ongoing regional instability and tensions, and a faltering economy, a change in relations between the US and Iran has many obstacles to navigate. However, such circumstances may also signify that Iran has much to gain from a renewed partnership with the United States. If ever there was a time for a diplomatic reset, this is it, and if ever there was a moment where so much regional and international goodwill for the United States could be generated with even marginally effective diplomatic investitures, that time is now. Hopefully, four years of Trump have put to rest the notion that an immensely coercive and incoherent diplomatic effort can achieve the security and economic goals that many in the region would want to see. A prudent, sensible, and focused economic and security effort could remake the region's stability in the coming years.

8

THE BIDEN ADMINISTRATION

CHANGE IN THE GEOPOLITICAL WINDS

President Biden took office at a time when US–Iran relations had reached their nadir since the 1979 hostage crisis. Iran is one of Biden's most daunting foreign policy challenges. In the last few years, there have been several incidents that could have brought the two countries to the brink of war. If for some reason the Biden administration fails to restore diplomatic channels with Iran, US–Iran relations "will likely fall back into the same old pattern of distrust and hostility that have characterized the relationship for the last four decades."[1] Many experts have advised and continue to advise the Biden administration that lifting the sanctions and recognizing Iran's legitimate security concerns is the right place to start a new diplomatic path.[2]

Biden's promise to repair alliances through diplomacy and restore Washington's leadership position on the global stage has been viewed by Iran as a welcome gesture that starkly separates this new adminis-tration from the previous one. So has his policy toward ending the humanitarian crisis in Yemen. The Biden administration has under-lined the fact that the United States will no longer support Saudi Arabia's offensive operations in Yemen. The key challenge for the Biden administration is to map out a way to revive the Joint Comprehensive Plan of Action (JCPOA), given that some in the

Biden administration and the US Congress have insisted that any deal that results in waving or removing sanctions must include negotiated limits on two fronts: Iran's ballistic missile program, and Iran's support for proxy forces fighting in other countries such as Iraq, Syria, and Yemen.[3]

Meanwhile, the International Atomic Energy Agency (IAEA) reported that Iran has made significant—if not irreversible—advances in its nuclear program, and that it will continue to undo its implementation of the deal if it sees no economic benefits from the restored agreement. As the process for such negotiations unfolds, US politicians must be prepared to deal with a new Iran led by a hard-liner or a military man. Will this possibility complicate or facilitate the nature of negotiations between the two countries? What are the prospects for establishing a modicum of trust between the two countries after three years of mistrust following the US withdrawal from the nuclear deal?

In this chapter, I explore several alternative scenarios and their policy implications for restarting the original nuclear deal. I argue that the most likely scenario is that the United States seeks to reshape the deal, demanding more stringent reinforcement for the long term—a move that Iranian officials currently view as counterproductive, arguing that this will contribute to further diplomatic impasse. It is clear that the Trump administration's maximum pressure campaign failed to achieve its stated goals as it neither brought Iran to the negotiating table nor forced a regime change. In the future, too, there is no evidence that a containment of Iran will work. The maximum pressure campaign, in which sanctions were reimposed to isolate and punish Iran, proved ineffective and untenable. A better approach would emphasize a diplomatic course of action. After looking into Biden's foreign policy experience with Iran, I will strengthen the case for diplomacy and multilateralism, arguing that negotiations across different political and military agendas is difficult but necessary if tensions between the two countries, as well as regional tensions, are to be lessened.

'Back-Channel' Diplomacy: Looking Back and Ahead

Foreign policy experts, such as William J. Burns, former undersecretary of state for political affairs, inform us that conducting policy process through quiet diplomacy is probably the most effective way to engage one's rivals or foes. In some cases, Burns notes, it is a sobering method of managing the world's inexorable disorders and crises. It requires a deep understanding of geopolitical history and existent complexities, a long strategic view, and virtually incessant patience and restraint. Burns points out four factors that have applied to behind-the-scenes negotiations with Iran in 2013: "Tough-minded diplomacy, backed up by the economic leverage of sanctions, the political leverage of an international consensus, and the military leverage of the potential use of force."[4]

The attention to these factors (diplomacy, sanctions, multilateralism, and the threat of use of force) is a testament to how back-channel talks have worked effectively. Burns' career triumph was marked by the Iran nuclear deal, which involved a back channel to the Iranians through a contact in Oman. Unfolding in secret under the direction of President Obama, the deal involved intensive person-to-person negotiations over eight months. In a memo sent to the then Secretary of State Hillary Clinton entitled "A New Strategy Toward Iran," Burns underlined the importance of the core US purpose being to "change Iran's behavior but not its regime."[5] To do so, cooperation with China (and especially Russia) was crucial to making the P5+1 effective. The agreement that took shape (JCPOA) was facilitated by long and painstaking negotiations.[6]

President Obama had smoothed the path by initial outreach and "confidence-building measures" to reduce distrust and convey goodwill, such as using the country's true name—the Islamic Republic—in a message marking the Persian holiday of Nowruz. He also made clear, in communication with Supreme Leader Khamenei, that "it was not the policy of the United States to seek regime change in Iran, but we were absolutely determined to ensure that Iran did not acquire a nuclear weapon"[7] and that Washington "would be willing to explore whether and how a domestic enrichment program could be pursued in Iran, as part of a comprehensive settlement of the nuclear issue."[8] These agreements were departures from the approach of the previous US administration.

Burns makes a compelling case for secrecy, as he highlights the importance of keeping negotiations as back-channel talks; it gave the

Iranians "plausible deniability" in case the effort turned out to be futile. Those who opposed this agreement, such as Israeli Prime Minister Netanyahu, vehemently excoriated the so-called back-channel negotiations. The result was, according to Burns, well warranted. In return for the gradual lifting of sanctions, Iran made an enduring commitment never to develop a nuclear weapon, and agreed to significant, long-term limitations on its civilian program. Ninety-eight percent of Iran's supply of enriched uranium and approximately two-thirds of its centrifuges were removed. Iran's other potential routes to a bomb were cut off, eliminating the heavy water reactor core at Arak and the capacity to produce weapons-grade plutonium. Intrusive monitoring measures were put in place. Iran's "breakout time"—that is, the time it would likely take to enrich enough weapons-grade uranium for a bomb—was extended from two or three months to at least one year.[9]

In the first few years, according to the IAEA and the US intelligence community, Iran remained in full compliance. Iran's economy, Burns maintains, did not become an unrestrainable force due to sanctions relief. The agreement called into question the regime's argument that outside pressure—not persistent mismanagement, corruption, and misallocation of resources—was the source of the harsh economic circumstance of most Iranians. Widespread problems in the summer of 2017, which led to street protests, demonstrated that the clerical leadership was facing serious internal challenges. In fact, the deal had, as Burns asserted, exposed the regime's vulnerabilities—not eradicated them.[10]

The deal's success has been all but denied as Trump scrapped the JCPOA in May 2018. The abandoning of the deal was followed by intense economic warfare against Iran, as the nation found itself reeling under new US sanctions. Two years of an unsettled relationship between Iran and the United States entered yet another intense period after the death, by US drone, of Iran's top military official—Qassem Soleimani—and the ensuing elevated tensions between the two countries.

On February 10, 2021, Qatar's Foreign Minister Sheikh Mohammed bin Abdulrahman al-Thani announced that Qatar was ready to mediate the tensions between Iran and the United States. Doha, al-Thani notes, was working on de-escalating the US–Iran standoff through political and diplomatic channels. Alex Vatanka, Director of the Middle East Eye's Iran Program and a senior fellow with the Frontier Europe Initiative, considers Qatar to be in a prime position to do so, arguing that unlike other countries in the region, the Qataris have had covert intelligence sharing with their Iranian counterparts.[11]

Vatanka points out that if the Biden administration is seeking ways to talk to Tehran through a third-party mediator and venue, Doha might just provide such an opportunity. "Recent history," Vatanka adds, "shows that Doha has a working relationship not just with the Foreign Ministry in Tehran, but also [with] the so-called Iranian 'deep state.'" In this case, this ominous classification refers to the powerful Revolutionary Guards—a state-within-a-state in Iran. The Guards control Tehran's regional agenda and its ballistic missile program—two areas the Biden administration is keen to include in future talks with the Iranians.[12]

To Escalate or to Climb Down

Trump's choice to escalate—not to climb down—had bleak implications for Iran's economy. The devastating economic consequences of the US withdrawal from the JCPOA and the ensuing harsh sanctions on Iran were exacerbated by the spread of the COVID-19 pandemic. All of these pressures took their toll on the country's economy and public health, leading to social disorder and having a debilitating impact on the morale of large segments of the population. Lost in these tough times has been the faltering credibility of clerics and lay politicians—on both the left and the right—whose internal infighting has undermined the search for a national strategy to contain the spread of the coronavirus. Meanwhile, the country has faced a significant economic disruption under the Trump administration's maximum pressure campaign, which has left Iran riddled with political uncertainties and disrupted by periodic flare ups of nationwide protests.

Amid these national crises, the rumor that hard-liners were likely to win the next presidential election no longer appeared to be a far-fetched claim.[13] Nor could the prospect of a hard-liner victory be completely ruled out, as the administration of President Hassan Rouhani was besieged by numerous economic difficulties and widespread public discontent. Hamidreza Taraghi, a spokesman for Iranian fundamentalists, even defended the idea of military officials as presidential candidates in recent statements. "If the military can [pass the requirements] of the Guardians Council and [maintain] other required characteristics, they will have no problem participating in the presidential race."[14] Speaking to the Iranian Students' News Agency, Taraghi added:

> Current conditions in the country are far different than those of the past because of the military forces' playing a role in crises and unexpected events such as the coronavirus outbreak, and this has changed the [view] of the military in public opinion. The public sees the military as a force that confronts crises without any fear.[15]

While praising the role of the Islamic Revolutionary Guard Corps (IRGC) in confronting crises, Taraghi criticizes Rouhani's government: "The management of these incidents proved that without the Army and the IRGC, the government could have not eliminated the effects and aftermaths of these crises."[16] If the IRGC wins the presidency, the reformists and their middle-class supporters lose what little influence they have over the country's politics.

The 2020 Iranian parliamentary elections led to the increasing election of representatives from the radical conservatives (otherwise known as "fundamentalists"), an outcome made possible by the lack of participation of the middle classes in these elections. This has fueled speculation that the results of the 2021 presidential elections are also likely to be determined by the same scenario. The turnout rate of 42.5 percent in these parliamentary elections was indeed the lowest turnout in the history of the Islamic Republic, giving rise to conjecture that the new president will come from the ranks of the IRGC.

A quick glance at the current conditions on the ground sheds some light on the shifting power within Iran's domestic politics. The failure of the reformists to meet the economic demands of the middle class, along with the imposition of increased limitations on quasi-democratic bodies (including the parliament and the presidency, by revolutionary institutions such as the Guardians Council and the IRGC), dramatically weakened the reformists' stance, smoothing the path for the hard-liners to seriously consider vying for office in the next presidential election.

In the wake of the assassination of Mohsen Fakhrizadeh, an Iranian nuclear scientist, on November 27, 2020, Iran's conservative parliament expedited legislation requiring the government to expand certain nuclear activities unless key sanctions are lifted. The law's swift passage was motivated by hard-liners' political strategy to ratchet up the pressure on moderate President Hassan Rouhani, whose government had to negotiate the deal ahead of the June 2021 presidential elections. The law called for everything from ramping up uranium enrichment to installing advanced centrifuges. It also included a February 21, 2021, deadline for lifting sanctions; if this deadline was not met, the law added, Iran would limit the work of United Nations inspectors.[17]

Fakhrizadeh's killing reinforced the idea that the rise of fundamentalists and radical elements to the presidency in Iran has become increasingly possible. Brigadier General Hossein Dehghan, a former IRGC air force officer and a former minister of defense, as well as a prominent military adviser to the Iranian supreme leader, announced his candidacy for the next presidential election. Dehghan held senior government positions in the administrations of Mohammad Khatami, Mahmoud Ahmadinejad, and Hassan Rouhani. He, along with nine other individuals close to the supreme leader, were identified by the US Treasury Department as the main targets of sanctions on the grounds of committing terrorist actions against US targets in Lebanon and Argentina. What pushed his name to the forefront of Iran's national politics was the growing frustration of vast segments of the population with the performance of current politicians, who were too often preoccupied with partisan bickering. Separating himself from fundamentalists and reformists, Dehghan presented himself as the country's unifier, committed to loosening the grip of poverty on the working poor and lower middle classes amid ideological and political divisions that have long stymied Iran's domestic political progress.[18]

Remarks by Parviz Fattah, head of the Mostazafan Foundation, in a TV interview were emblematic of support for such a political campaign. As the head of a foundation that sought to enforce the rights of the poor, Fattah waged attacks against some revolutionary institutions along with leftist and rightist officials, introducing himself as the bearer of a discourse that has no fear of other powers, even the IRGC, in pursuit of enforcing the rights of the poor. The groundwork for this discourse was laid when the fundamentalists' took power in the eleventh parliament.[19]

Another candidate who eventually became president was Ebrahim Raisi, due to his close ties with Supreme Leader Ayatollah Khamenei, his ultra conservative political views and credentials, and his service as Head of the General Inspection office as well as Aston Quds Razavi. His candidacy uniquely benefited from a strong support by Iran's supreme leader, making him a credible candidate to win the presidency. Raisi's chances of becoming Iran's next president significantly increased given the low turnout in the presidential elections.

The growing disenchantment among middle-class supporters of the reformists due to the unfulfilled promises of their leaders—especially those of the Rouhani administration—helped explain why they were less likely to participate in the next presidential election. This pervasive public discontent was widely regarded as a major contributing factor to low voter turnout by the middle class, whose support often constituted the backbone of reformists' social base. This helped to account for the possibility of a military person entering the presidential arena. Iran's economic decay increasingly turned the attention of the middle class from their democratic aspirations to their immediate socioeconomic needs.[20]

Breaking with Trump's Toxic Legacy

Trump's Iran policy triggered a volatile period of US–Iran relations, provoking resistance by Iran to return to a new round of negotiations with Washington under such hostile circumstances. This resulted in a strategic conundrum that severely complicated any conceivable diplomatic efforts at the time. By any metric, the undoing of the damage done by Trump is no mean feat, and may take much longer than expected. The irreversible damage to the global standing of the US cannot be undone by Biden's presidency any time soon, in large part due to the loss of trust caused by the confusion and disorderliness of the Trump administration. Some observers assert that "it will take decades if not generations to regain the lost trust,"[21] and that "America under Trump has lost the credibility and legitimacy that were cornerstones of its influence."[22]

Lifting the travel ban on Muslims' entry into the United States, revising immigration policies, and ending the dehumanizing policies of separating children from their parents at the border appear to be manageable tasks in the short term—as does forgoing the obsession with building walls around the country's southern borders. However, there are limits to what Biden can do to unravel Trump's populist and protectionist policies, which may not be easily reversed to simply resume the level of trust and commitment that for seven decades had characterized US foreign policy as the leader of the free world. The election of Trump to the presidency in 2016 called into question the commitment of the American public to progressive global leadership.

However, it is possible—and even necessary—for the United States to do damage control by returning to the rules-based international order and repairing relations with their allies. Well before the United States was overwhelmed by the COVID-19 pandemic, it was clear that the gradual US retreat from leading the global liberal order was the hallmark of its waning global role under Trump. Confidence in the ability of the United States to take the lead in contemporary global affairs dramatically eroded under the Trump administration.

These difficulties aside, managing international relations can and should start with respecting and working within international organizations and agreements, such as the World Health Organization (WHO), the Paris agreement on climate change, and the Iran nuclear deal. There can be no doubt that US competence will likely be disputed, and its global influence questioned, in the coming years. Domestically, the appropriate place to focus is the containment of the surge of the COVID-19 pandemic. Some experts, such as Paul Wiseman, have suggested that tensions between the world's two biggest economies (China and the United States), which have intensified since Trump blamed Beijing for unleashing the "China virus," will likely linger in the post-Trump era.[23] Regardless, Biden may choose to prioritize ratchetting down the rhetoric of a trade war with China while also seeking mutually beneficial transactions over other common foreign policy issues. Rethinking relations with Beijing is likely to present a monumental challenge to the Biden administration, and one that requires a new approach.[24]

The US threat of using sanction policies against countries that don't toe the line deserves serious consideration. Four years of lost credibility and the retrenchment of international obligations under the Trump administration have undermined the US global reputation. To undo the damage inflicted, experts maintain, requires significant investment to "help build capable and willing allies, to negotiate and collectively enforce international rules and practices that restrain adversaries."[25] It follows that boosting national security must begin with the reality that not even the United States can safeguard itself or its broader interests without the help of others.[26]

On February 19, 2021, in his first foreign policy speech to allies, President Biden repeated his post-election mantra: "We are not looking backward. We are looking forward, together."[27] He went on to tell the annual Munich Security Conference: "We're prepared to re-engage in negotiations with the P5-plus-1 on Iran's nuclear program."[28] This message meant "compliance for compliance" as a way of re-engaging Iran. Iran's consent to go back to the implementation of the so-called Additional Protocol, which allows snap inspections of undeclared sites suspected of operating nuclear activity, has become imperative to the success of diplomacy.[29] Following an intensive discussion in Tehran on February 20, 2021, IAEA Director General Rafael Grossi announced that Iran's cooperation with the agency would continue for the ensuing three month, as Iran would keep the data recorded by camera monitors at nuclear sites for this period. If US sanctions are lifted, Iran will then turn over the information to the IAEA. Otherwise, Iran will erase the tapes, a possibility that could complicate any diplomatic negotiations in the future.[30]

The Case for Re-engagement with Iran

The composition of Biden's team and the presence of key negotiators of the Obama administration's nuclear deal, including Robert Malley, Wendy Sherman, Antony Blinken, Jacob Sullivan, and William J. Burns fueled speculation that the United States and Iran will return to nuclear talks. The Biden administration assumed power at a time when the prospect of the hard-liners coming to power in Iran's presidential election in June appeared more realistic than ever. This eventuality would necessitate a change in the US designation of IRGC as a Foreign Terrorist Organization—not an option if any form of détente between the two countries was to be seriously pursued in the coming years. Biden has indicated that if Tehran were to resume strict compliance with the nuclear deal, he would rejoin the accord as a departure for follow-on negotiations.[31] In an op-ed on CNN (September 13, 2020), Biden appears to be keen on taking a different—yet tougher—stance toward Iran than the reckless unilateral policies pursued by the Trump administration.

More specifically, Biden pointed to three aspects of his approach. First, he insisted that he would make an unwavering commitment to prevent Iran from acquiring a nuclear weapon. Second, he stated that he was willing to offer Tehran a credible path back to the diplomatic track. If Iran returns to full adherence to the nuclear deal, Biden added, the United States would rejoin the agreement as a point of departure for ensuing negotiations. The United States, with the support of its allies, Biden noted, would work toward strengthening and extending the nuclear deal's provisions, while also addressing other issues of concern, including Iran's human rights record and, most notably, the disastrous war in Yemen. Additionally, Biden went on to explain that he would take steps to loosen restrictions on humanitarian imports to Iran, especially regarding Iran's campaign against the COVID-19 pandemic, while working toward repealing Trump's disgraceful travel ban targeting Muslim-majority countries.[32]

Third, Biden maintained that he would continue to push back against Iran's destabilizing activities, which threatened US friends and partners in the region. Drawing on the record-setting US-Israeli security assistance agreement signed when he served as vice president during the Obama administration, Biden would also work closely with Israel to bolster and ensure its security. Biden would keep using targeted sanctions against Iran's human rights abuses, its support for terrorism, and its ballistic missile program. Within the context of multilateral and broader efforts to contain Iran's nuclear program, the Biden administration would make it a priority to set Iran policy on a clear path of carrots and sticks.[33]

On February 18, 2021, the Biden administration formally offered to restart nuclear talks with Iran, joining European nations in what came to be the first substantial diplomacy with Tehran in more than four years. This shift of approach on the part of the Biden administration was facilitated by a unified US-European statement that "reaffirmed the centrality of the transatlantic partnership" and demanded that the Rouhani administration take "no additional steps" to breach the pact. Similarly, in a subtle shift of position, the Biden administration also agreed to "engage in discussions with Iran toward that end," a rather dramatic change from its previous outright insistence that Tehran first return to full compliance before any other action is taken.[34] Subsequently, Iranian officials indicated that they were willing to hold a meeting with EU members in which the United States would participate as an observer, rather than direct formal talks with Washington as a participant.[35]

Even so, several challenges render the restoration of trust between the two countries difficult. Iran's leadership has ruled out halting its missile program or changing its regional policy, although they have frequently noted that they have no plans to increase the range of their missiles. Furthermore, Tehran has made it abundantly clear that they will negotiate only if Washington lifts sanctions.[36] The sequencing of the talks—whether Iran should take the first step to reduce its amount of enriched uranium to 3.67 percent or the United States should return to the JCPOA without any preconditions—has been resolved through an effective mediation by European representatives.

On February 21, 2021, IAEA Director General Rafael Grossi announced that he had reached a "temporary bilateral technical understanding" to retain access to Iran's nuclear sites for the next three months.[37] This has been seen as a first step toward a new and more substantial diplomatic move aimed at the restoration of nuclear talks. One question looms large: What sanctions will be lifted once the nuclear program is constrained and how quickly will this be done?

The operation against Iran's Natanz nuclear facility on April 11, 2021, which led to a power failure in a deliberately planned explosion, inserted new uncertainty into diplomatic efforts in Vienna to restore the 2015 nuclear deal that the Trump administration renounced in 2018.[38] Absent progress in these negotiations and delay in lifting sanctions imposed by the previous administration could push Iran closer to the acquisition of nuclear weapons. If progress is achieved in the Vienna talks, one analyst points out, Washington and its Western and regional allies could then turn their attention to effectively addressing Iran's ballistic missile program, human rights issues, and regional activities.[39]

The January 6, 2021 attacks on the US Congress by Trump supporters, however, distracted the Biden administration's focus on foreign policy matters, causing noticeable delay in seriously pursuing the nuclear talks. In the following months, US Secretary of State, Antony Blinken, while emphasizing "offshore balancing" as US strategy toward the Persian Gulf region, noted that Washington would support diplomacy and interaction between regional actors on the one hand and the inclusion of other actors, such as France and Israel, in regional politics on the other.[40]

France attended the Baghdad summit to facilitate Iran–Saudi Arabia talks in late August 2021, and the United States subsequently named France as its strategic partner in the region. The Biden administration, while appearing keen on pursuing the nuclear talks with Iran, has simultaneously sought a new regional order in which all key actors can participate, in order to solve their problems through diplomatic means rather than saber-rattling and proxy wars.[41] This may, in part, explain the Biden administration's support for inter-regional cooperation and dialogue.[42]

Significantly, some members of the Biden administration, such as Robert Malley—Biden's Special Envoy for Iran—argue that the nuclear talks and the negotiations on Iran's "missile program" and "regional policies" should be decoupled. The issues of Iran's missiles and regional politics are part of the complex and multidimensional structure that represents the balance of power in the region. These issues are directly linked to the fate of several countries in the region, and therefore do not constitute an issue that can be easily resolved, even in the first term of Biden's presidency. In short, Malley concluded, the resumption of the nuclear talks cannot be realistically tied to the resolution of these regional issues. It is in this context that Washington has welcomed the Iran–Saudi Arabia negotiations.[43]

Europe's Role in Salvaging the JCPOA

A far more constructive diplomatic strategy to resolve this issue would be to restore transatlantic cooperation. A joint US–Europe initiative to seek a diplomatic solution for the Iran nuclear deal could prove to be sustainable. The governments of France, Germany, and the UK (known as E3), however, have expressed concern over Iran's reported plan to install additional centrifuges at its Natanz nuclear facility, warning that such a move could compromise multilateral efforts to salvage the nuclear deal.[44] The EU foreign policy chief Josep Borrell noted that Europe "deeply regrets the worrying steps taken by Iran over the past two years," describing Tehran's initiative to enhance its uranium enrichment program up to twenty percent as "a matter of deep concern."[45] Regardless, Borrel added, the European Union "reiterates its strong commitment" to the deal and acknowledges the issues arising from Washington's unilateral withdrawal.[46]

The negotiations over Iran's missile program are likely to be complex. It is worth remembering that Iran has kept its missile range at a maximum of 2,000 kilometers to reassure European countries. Supreme Leader Khamenei has also stated that Iran voluntarily refuses to produce ballistic missiles with a range of more than 2,000 kilometers. Major General Mohammad Ali Jafari, the former commander-in-chief of the IRGC, also commented on the IRGC's missile capability to respond to threats: "Our missile range is limited to 2,000 kilometers according to the policies set by the leadership, although there is capability to increase this range."[47]

Accordingly, the range of Iran's theater ballistic missiles has been designed to include only targets located in the Middle East. Although Iranian satellite tests are considered a simulation of the construction of intercontinental ballistic missiles capable of carrying nuclear warheads, experts believe that the similarities between intercontinental ballistic missiles and satellite launchers are not so great that Iran can be accused of gaining technical experience from launching satellites that can be used in building intercontinental ballistic missiles.[48] For example, Michael Ellman, a missile defense expert at the International Institute for Strategic Studies, downplays the technical similarities between satellite launchers and intercontinental ballistic missiles.[49]

Furthermore, Iran's focus on cruise missiles means that Iran does not emphasize "missile range" in building and expanding its missile program. Although they are essentially capable of accurate targeting, radar evasion, and low-altitude flight in medium-range tactical scenarios, cruise missiles have not been designed to be used for long-range targets.[50]

Saudi Arabia, by contrast, has missiles with a range of more than 4,000 kilometers, and it also has a missile factory.[51] Likewise, Israel's formidable nuclear arsenal is an open secret in the region.[52] Meanwhile, Iranian politicians have sent out contrasting messages regarding the country's missile program. President Rouhani has made clear he was not inclined to discuss any changes to the nuclear deal or any restrictions on Iran's ballistic missile program.[53] In the past, however, some Iranian officials have stated that the missile issue can be negotiated if the weapons status in the region is applied evenly. Iran's former Foreign Minister Mohammad Javad Zarif, for example, made it clear:

> If you want to talk about a missile program, then you have to talk about the amount of weapons sold to our region. It is American weapons that are entering our region and putting our region on the brink of explosion. So if they want to talk about our missiles, they must first stop selling these weapons, including missiles.[54]

It should be noted, however, that there is no international body to verify whether missiles are defensive or not. On the subject of missiles, there are only two global treaties: the Missile Technology Control Regime and The Hague Code of Conduct against Ballistic Missile Proliferation. These treaties are voluntary sets of measures that promote transparency and confidence-building.[55] Security Council Resolution 2231, which is the basis of Western countries' opposition to Iran's missile program, falls short of specifying missile "types." In other words, Resolution 2231 prohibits Iranian missiles not on the basis of the "technical characteristics" of the missile but on the basis of their "purpose," whether they are intended to carry nuclear weapons or not.[56] The resolution "calls upon" Iran to refrain from developing missiles aimed at carrying nuclear warheads. The phrase "calls upon" makes it clear that the resolution is not legally binding and carries no legal obligations.[57]

While much of the focus has been on Iran's missile program, traditional US allies in the region are buyers of advanced US weapons and hosts of US military bases. The US military hardware that these countries possess comes nowhere close to the effectiveness and lethality of the military equipment that Iran possesses, which is largely domestically produced. This may be the reason that the Iranians feel comfortable keeping their missile range within the region's limits.

Moreover, the choice of Iran's missile range, as noted above, illustrates that Tehran's goal is to achieve a regional deterrence of sorts, indicating that Iran is unlikely to mount a nuclear warhead on these missiles. Iran claims that its missile program serves only one key goal: deterring attacks. Iran has not invaded a neighbor for more than two centuries. For the Biden administration, negotiation with Iran makes practical sense if it results in reducing regional tensions, but just as importantly, if it helps build trust and helps restore US credibility as a legitimate broker of peace across the world.

In one interview, the then Foreign Minister Zarif insisted that the Biden administration should take the first major step by returning to the negotiating table. "The administration should begin by unconditionally removing, with full effect, all sanctions imposed, reimposed, or relabeled since Trump took office. In turn, Iran would reverse all the remedial measures it has taken in the wake of Trump's withdrawal from the nuclear deal."[58] Zarif went on to note that a "return to the table will be jeopardized" if Washington and its European partners insist on linking a profile of other concerns—including Iran's ballistic missile program and ongoing support for proxy militias elsewhere in the Middle East—to the resumption of negotiations surrounding the nuclear deal.[59]

Some European experts echoed a similar sentiment, arguing that

> if Europeans want to contain the risks from Iran's expanding nuclear activities quickly, it is critical that they avoid obstructing the process by pressuring Biden to tie the nuclear talks to negotiations on regional security: this approach would almost certainly doom the nuclear discussions—and broader Western ambitions on regional issues—to collapse.[60]

Thus, making the US return to the JCPOA contingent on regional security concerns, which was likely to take years, came across as a non-starter. Some European leaders, while maintaining that they want Washington and Tehran to return to full JCPOA compliance, seek further concessions from Iran as part of the process. German Foreign Minister Heiko Maas, for instance, has called for a "broader deal," while French President Emmanuel Macron has said that parties to the JCPOA "need to include our allies in the region for a nuclear deal," leaving it unclear whether he was actually referring to a formal process.[61]

With only a narrow window of opportunity left before the June 2021 Iranian presidential elections in which hard-liners were likely to prevail, Biden did well by securing Iran's return to its responsibilities under the JCPOA before attempting to renegotiate a follow-on deal. For now, Biden might be interested in working with the Iranian team that negotiated the deal before they leave office next year.[62] This scenario is realistic given that the Rouhani administration appeared reluctant to accept a renegotiated re-entry. For now, as UN officials suggest, a compromise is possible. The United States can commit to lifting the sanctions, albeit partially, while allowing Iranians four–six weeks to return to full compliance by demonstrating that they have stopped enriching uranium above 3.67 percent and have brought the stockpile of low-enriched uranium down to 300 kg. Upon verification of Iran's full compliance, Washington can proceed with waiving statutory sanctions, thus allowing international banks to facilitate financial transactions with Iran as agreed upon under the JCPOA.[63]

In the meantime, re-entry into the JCPOA could pave the way for moving toward a prisoner swap between Tehran and Washington and reaching a tacit regional agreement between key regional actors—Saudi Arabia and Iran—to end the war in Yemen.[64] It is important to bear in mind that the Trump administration became complicit in one of the region's most horrific conflicts by sharing intelligence, refueling aircraft, selling weapons, and providing diplomatic cover for the Saudis in this war. The conflict has further destabilized the Middle East, emboldened Iran, undercut US credibility and reputation, and above all, devastated the Yemeni people, who are living through an ongoing humanitarian catastrophe. Almost six years after Saudi intervention, experts noted, the war in Yemen has been nothing short of an absolute fiasco.[65] The Trump administration used the crisis in Yemen as a way to make Saudi Arabia an even bigger purchaser of US weapons and a partner in a potential future Israeli-Palestinian peace deal while turning Yemen into a front in its maximum pressure policy against Iran.[66]

After taking office, the Biden administration has made several moves to disentangle the United States from the tragic war in Yemen. These include, among other things, reversing the Trump administration's designation of the Houthis as a terrorist organization, appointing a special envoy for Yemen, reducing support for offensive operations by the Saudi-led coalition in the conflict, espousing the UN-led peace process, and giving assurances to Saudi Arabia regarding the defense of its territorial integrity.[67] In the past, the proactive-but-quiet US diplomatic approach has paid dividends with Iran. It could very well be fruitful in the future.

Failure Is Not an Option

Following Fakhrizadeh's killing, there has been increasing debate on an emerging new constraint on the revival of the nuclear deal. The challenging task that lies ahead seems to be one of navigating this moment of disruption as effectively as possible by returning to the JCPOA. Politicians from each side face a choice, and we know where military retaliation leads: to the inevitable broadening of tensions, not just between the US and Iran but throughout the region. An Iranian military retaliation against the United States could scuttle any future reset in relations with Washington. The legality and legitimacy of killing a nuclear scientist of a sovereign state aside, it is important to ensure that the opportunities inherent in working with the Biden administration are aptly and effectively capitalized upon, even as the real purpose of this assassination may have been to prevent Biden from resuming diplomacy with Tehran.[68] In the meantime, a clear consensus among members of the Biden administration's national security team is that military strikes are unlikely to bring about a long-term diminution of Iran's nuclear program.[69]

Both the Raisi and Biden administrations, however, should pursue rational policies from which both parties can benefit—that is, to avoid military escalation while ending nuclear-related sanctions. Biden and the heads of European governments must work closely to establish a viable roadmap to revive the Iran nuclear deal, appreciative of the fact that failure to reach an agreement is not an option. Similarly, the tough economic conditions under which Iran finds itself dictate a prudent and diplomatic track. It is critically important to realize that Iran's nuclear program is a manageable—not insolvable—problem. Over the past four decades, US opportunities to negotiate with Iran have been rare—partly due to opposition by the Israelis and the Saudis—and yet whenever these opportunities have been utilized, they have contributed to the region's stability.

Trump's maximum pressure and unilateral reimposition of sanctions on Iran failed to achieve its stated goals, as it neither succeeded in bringing Iran to the negotiating table nor forced a regime change.[70] It also failed to curtail Iran's involvement in Iraq, Syria, or Lebanon. Instead, the impacts of these sanctions were largely felt by ordinary Iranians hit with rampant inflation. The other signatories to the JCPOA opposed this unilateral US policy, given that Iran had kept to its side of the bargain.

Likewise, the so-called "containment of Iran," recently called a panacea by some experts, is not a risk-free or cost-free policy. Those who suggest that the containment of Iran will work tend to argue that no matter how much military hardware the United States offers Iran's neighboring countries for their assent, regional tensions will continue.[71] It is not clear, however, how the costs and burdens of containment can be borne over the long term, or how US military interventions in the region could be drastically curtailed.

Rather than isolating and punishing Iran by imposing draconian and wide-ranging sanctions, a better approach would emphasize negotiation and a diplomatic track. Negotiations across different political and military agendas are difficult but necessary if regional tensions are to be reduced. A clear alternative for the Biden administration, as noted above, is a quick re-entry into the Iran nuclear deal. As Seyed Hossein Mousavian, a former Iranian nuclear negotiator, has observed, Washington would do well by returning to the JCPOA without any preconditions, while also suspending its primary sanctions on Iran, if further complications in the relationship between the two countries are to be avoided.[72]

Similarly, Robert Einhorn, a nuclear arms control negotiator now at the Brookings Institution, notes that the P5+1 and Iran should work toward an interim agreement in which Iran rescinds a significant part of its current nuclear buildup in exchange for partial sanctions relief—especially if this facilitates Iranian access to some of its oil revenues now frozen in overseas bank accounts. Iran would most likely embrace such an interim arrangement if it gave the economy a quick lift.[73] In the long term, however, Biden's foreign policy approach toward Iran is likely to remain predicated upon a deal that addresses Iran's missile program, regional activities, and human rights. Such a deal might even include an extension of the terms of the JCPOA. Regardless, the price of non-negotiation for both countries—and for the region—would be exorbitantly high and would most likely drive Tehran further into Beijing's widening economic orbit.

There is no guarantee that diplomacy will eventually resolve all the tensions between the two countries. However, it could surely lower the political temperature and open up opportunities to address some concerns. To resuscitate the JCPOA by convincing both sides to restore compliance, several possibilities exist. One suggestion is that the Biden administration could

> restore temporary waivers that enable Iran to sell oil while U.S. sanctions remain intact. Iran's earnings from oil sales would be accrued in escrow accounts and subject to strict oversight as per the waiver terms. Revenues would be used by Iran for sanctions-exempt trade with the country in which the funds are held. Such a step would serve to remove a key piece of tension with U.S. allies such as South Korea, Japan, and India whose energy security has been impacted by U.S. sanctions on Iran.[74]

Second, as Robert Malley (Biden's new Special Envoy for Iran) has suggested, it is feasible and prudent to grant Iran a coronavirus-related loan from the International Monetary Fund (IMF). These funds would not flow directly into Iranian government coffers. Rather, they would be used to address trade deficits. The Biden administration should grant this loan as part of its commitment to addressing the humanitarian impact of sanctions. Such a move would also be part of a wider drive to encourage the IMF to deploy its full financial capacities to address the ongoing economic crisis brought on by the pandemic.[75]

A third option could be facilitating Iran's access to its existing foreign exchange reserves. As things currently stand, Iran has free and ready access to roughly ten percent of its reserves—a situation that has placed unprecedented pressure on Iran's currency, generating high levels of inflation that harm ordinary Iranians. Iran has been engaged in frantic negotiations to gain access to frozen assets with numerous countries, which continue to look to the US Treasury Department for final approval. The Biden administration could give these countries, including US allies such as Germany and South Korea, the approval to enable both central and commercial banks to voluntarily make payments on behalf of Iranian account holders. As with the oil waivers and IMF loan, these payments could be constrained to sanctions-exempt trade, the upshot of which would be lower rates of inflation in Iran.[76]

Finally, aside from these practical possibilities, the Biden administration should recognize that any attempt to diminish Iran's conventional deterrence renders it imprudent for Iran to accept limits on its ballistic missile program or even to reconsider its regional activities. Rather, as Abdolrasool Divsallar—an expert on Iran's foreign and defense policy—notes, weakening Iran's traditional deterrence is likely to intensify its threat perception, ramping up pressure on the country's security elites to further boost the strategic logic for pursuing the nuclear option in Tehran.[77] A sustainable, long-term JCPOA will hinge upon policies that reduce any incentives for Iran to pursue nuclear weapons. This could only materialize "through a de-escalated security landscape in which Tehran sees the continued effectiveness of its conventional deterrence."[78]

Biden's decision to order retaliatory military strikes on February 25, 2021, on several buildings used by the Iran-backed militia Kataib Hezbollah and other groups in eastern Syria near the Iraqi border demonstrated that the United States would treat different tracks (Syria and Iran) differently. The strikes were a response to a rocket attack on February 15, 2021, in northern Iraq that killed one civilian contractor and wounded an American service member and several coalition troops. Following the strikes, Iran rejected a European proposal to re-enter nuclear talks with the United States.[79]

Some Iranian analysts, such as Kayhan Barzegar, have pointed to the centrality of the role that the supreme leader plays in matters relating to strategic foreign policy and national security domains. Although Iran has a complicated political system and grants some degree of autonomy to the country's president, Barzegar notes, his ability to shape foreign policy in contrast to that of other leaders in the area is inconsequential at best.[80] It is in this context that Iranian experts have attempted to analyze the Biden administration's view of Iran. One expert has described Biden's foreign policy approach in this and similar contexts as "measured confrontation." Mahmood Sariolghalam, an Iranian expert on international relations writes that Biden's foreign policy team proceeds from the assumption that Iran's nuclear policy and more generally its foreign policy are not ultimately shaped by the government, although government officials can influence its contours. Thus, from the Biden administration's standpoint, it matters little which political wing or party—moderate or hardliner—is at the negotiating table.[81]

Biden pursues a policy of simultaneous "reward and punishment" toward Iran, while contemplating a new recalibration negotiating strategy. Biden's foreign policy can be best described, Sariolghalam adds, as one of navigating a piecemeal approach toward going back to the terms of the original agreement and move toward negotiating a new version of the JCPOA (2.0) in which the Iranian nuclear program is invariably linked to its regional activities, including pressuring Iran on its human rights record.[82] It is worth pointing out, Sariolghalam goes on to argue, that the Biden administration, the US Congress, the European Union, and some regional countries, such as Saudi Arabia and Israel, insist that the 2015 nuclear deal is untenable and that the new JCPOA needs to address other ambiguities surrounding nonnuclear issues. The new deal should at least minimize (as much as possible) the ability of Iran to restore its nuclear program and activities, as in the past.[83]

In the meantime, Iran's demands for strictly observing the provisions of the nuclear deal are multiple. Tehran wants all Trump administration sanctions to be lifted along with a prompt release of blocked international loans and frozen funds. Tehran also seeks foreign investment and removal of bans on oil sales, and demands assurances that ensuing US administrations will not revoke the deal again. For its part, the Biden administration appears willing to re-enter the deal as long as it serves as a "platform" to renegotiate its sunset provisions— that is, the future dates when certain stipulations are set to expire.[84]

Aside from the technical issues, it is important that the Biden administration recognizes, as one Iran's expert notes, that a decade of economic stagnation caused by sanctions and broken international promises may undermine the role that Iran's middle class has played as a force for political moderation and globalization. As the largest social class with the most education, Iran's middle class is a strong voting bloc. In 1997, when Iran elected its first moderate and pro-rapprochement president, Mohammad Khatami, the middle class accounted for only 30.5 percent of the population and 56.1 percent of the educated population of voting age (persons older than 16 with at least a high school education). By 2011, the middle class had doubled their share of the population to nearly sixty percent, and educated voters to roughly eighty-one percent.[85]

Sanctions policy worked because the primary aim of the sanctions was not to cause regime change or to pit Iran's middle class against the country's leadership and its security forces. In fall 2018, when protests erupted following energy price hikes, the middle class in Tehran and other larger cities refrained from participating in such protests. Since 2011, however, the middle class has shrunk by about eight million people.[86] Clearly, economic hardship has dramatically altered the outlook of Iranians away from support for moderate politicians and globalization. Support for the JCPOA had declined from approximately eighty percent when it was initially signed to fifty percent as of early April 2021. Many Iranians believed that their government should wait for the Biden administration to remove sanctions before talking to Washington. Consistently, polls also showed the popularity of President Rouhani and his administration was significantly dwindling in the run up to the June 2021 elections.[87]

Regional Security Dialogue

One of the most contentious issues facing the Biden administration is how to manage US relations with countries on both sides of the

Persian Gulf. Rather than treating Iran and the Gulf Arab states as separate policy areas, Sanam Vakil—Deputy Director and Senior Research Fellow at the Middle East North Africa Program at Chatham House—maintains that the Biden administration should regard all regional issues as interrelated. To do so effectively, Washington should put the region's security in a holistic perspective that includes the JCPOA, Tehran's regional activities, its ballistic missile program, the lack of a regional security structure, and US support for the military intervention of Gulf Arab states in Yemen and Libya.[88] Without a holistic, long-term strategy based on multilateral collaboration, Vakil argues, the region is likely to further disintegrate. For such a strategy to be successful, the United States and its European allies should work toward a regional détente that advances the mutual security concerns of all parties involved, "including promoting peace and stability, nuclear non-proliferation, counterterrorism, energy and maritime security, and stemming refugee flows."[89]

It is necessary to lay the foundation of a regional security architecture by relying on focus groups trying to tackle several issue areas: arms control, nuclear security, maritime security, environmental cooperation, cultural exchanges, and communication channels. The United States and its European allies can serve as external supporters of the negotiation process while also providing incentives, such as sanctions relief for Iran and security guarantees for member states of the Gulf Cooperation Council (GCC). A new security structure will likely restrain the growing militarization of the broader region, contribute to the regional balance of power, and have a stabilizing impact on conflict zones in Yemen, Libya, and Syria.[90] A viable strategy would also take into account the surging role of Russia, China, and India in the region.[91]

Many regional experts have suggested that, alongside the nuclear talks, new regional security initiatives directed toward altering the zero-sum context that has long fueled tensions between Tehran and Washington should also be pursued. Such a regional security dialogue would help manage a process of gradual de-escalation between Iran and the United States and between Iran and other regional actors. With the declining role of the United States in the Persian Gulf region, Iran and some GCC member states have increasingly referred to a regional security process capable of generating détente in the region and beyond. What must be determined is the role the US and its European allies should play in promoting such a regional security complex.

Javad Zarif, Iran's foreign minister from 2013–21, initiated the Hormuz Peace Endeavor (HOPE)—an intra-regional cooperation on security and non-security issues. Similarly, regional initiatives for talks with Iran have gained much traction following President Biden's expressed willingness to resume diplomacy. For their part, Iranian officials, such as the then Deputy Foreign Minister Abbas Araghchi, have stated that Iran will not negotiate regional issues with world powers. Rather, Tehran is prepared to discuss Gulf security with regional countries.[92] GCC countries find themselves in a difficult situation as their economies are impaired and weakened by the ongoing COVID-19 pandemic. Their large regional development projects could lose allure if conflict breaks out with Iran.[93]

The objectives of regional initiatives, some observers have pointed out, should reflect the legitimate security interests and concerns of all parties involved. Following the guidance of international law and UN Resolution 598—which, in 1987, called for an immediate cease-fire between Iran and Iraq, the repatriation of prisoners of war, and withdrawal to the international border—parties can move toward curtailing tensions in the region, restraining their rivalries, and forging a regional security and cooperation system based on a sustainable long-term solution. This regional security and cooperation mechanism could lead to wider collective regional efforts to tackle deep-rooted challenges such as energy security, shared environmental problems, maritime safety, organized crime, drug trafficking, and regional stability.[94]

Enter the Taliban

The Taliban's swift return to power has Afghanistan's neighboring countries worried about political instability, new waves of refugees and migrants, and the prospect of Afghanistan becoming a safe haven for terrorists. New Delhi is equally concerned that Pakistan's growing control over Afghanistan could embolden the former to pose new threats to India. Understandably, India's main concerns regarding the Taliban relate to the future of the Taliban's relationship with Pakistan, whether the new government in Afghanistan would be able to curb violence, and how it would manage its ties with terrorist groups that threaten India.[95]

China, by contrast, will pursue a pragmatic and sustainable political settlement with the Taliban, seeking their cooperation for two major reasons: "a secure environment for Chinese infrastructure projects, and the isolation of Uyghur militants."[96] Chinese leaders worry that instability in Afghanistan might spill over into China. They are equally concerned about the inspiration that Islamic militancy could provide to its Muslim minority ethnic groups. Beijing will most likely urge the Taliban to deny safe haven to Uyghur fighters and other groups that could potentially destabilize Central Asia or undermine Chinese interests in the region.[97]

Likewise, Russia has legitimate concerns about the risk of instability, fighting, and the penetration of extremist groups into the Central Asian republics along Afghanistan's northern border.[98] Moscow is likely to seek pragmatic engagement with the Taliban. On July 23, 2021, Minister of Foreign Affairs Sergey Lavrov said:

> They are sane people. They clearly stated that they have no plans to create problems for Afghanistan's Central Asian neighbors, that they would uncompromisingly fight the ISIS (ISIL), and that they are ready to discuss the political structure of their nation with other Afghans because they used to be accused of wanting to create an Islamic emirate based on the *Shari'a* law.[99]

It remains to be seen if such sanguine views will hold overtime. Iran's strategic objective will revolve around curbing the flow of refugees and drugs, as well as preventing the persecution of the Hazaras, who are largely Shi'ites. The Hazaras, who are the third-largest ethnic group in mostly-Sunni Afghanistan, could face a precarious future, as they have a well-founded fear of persecution and discrimination at the hands of the Taliban.[100] In recent years, Iran has used diplomacy to try to defuse tensions in Afghanistan. After President Biden announced the withdrawal of US forces in April 2021, Iran began new diplomatic contacts with both the Taliban and the Afghan government, anticipating the possibility of the Taliban's resurgence. In July 2021, Tehran hosted peace talks with both Taliban and Afghan government representatives. In August 2021, following the Taliban's takeover of power, Iran's new president, Ebrahim Raisi, welcomed the US withdrawal as "an opportunity to restore life, security, and durable peace."[101] He encouraged different Afghan factions "to reach a national agreement."[102]

Conclusion

Whether Biden's presidency may herald a shift in US foreign policy toward Iran's nuclear program remains to be seen. Biden's admiration for international organizations and his desire to return to global agreements, however, stands in stark contrast to Trump's scornful attitude toward liberal, institutionalist traditions. Increasingly—especially in the aftermath of US withdrawal from Afghanistan—a Biden doctrine has emerged: "a foreign policy that avoids the aggressive tactics of forever wars and nation building, while uniting allies against the authoritarianism of rising powers."[103] This doctrine sees China as America's existential rival, Russia as a disrupter, Iran and North Korea as nuclear proliferators, growing cyberthreats, and terrorism spreading far beyond Afghanistan. Reluctant to use force to remake the world in America's image, Biden relies heavily on negotiations, diplomacy, and discussing options with European allies to revive the Iran nuclear deal.[104]

This may help explain why Biden was swift and assertive to recognize that diplomacy was the primary corrective for the ongoing tensions between Iran and the United States. The reinvigoration of multilateralism has given Biden new traction to challenge previous assumptions about unilateralism and the maximum pressure campaign pursued by the Trump administration. For Biden, returning to the JCPOA will offer many advantages. Much can be accomplished even with a hard-liner president in Iran. The Biden administration can subsequently pursue a more conditional return and renegotiation. A follow-on negotiation could include not only the original signatories to the deal—the United States, Iran, Russia, China, Britain, France, Germany, and the European Union—but also Iran's Arab neighbors, particularly Saudi Arabia and the United Arab Emirates (UAE).

The US re-entry will most likely be contingent upon security assurances to Israel and the Arab countries of the Persian Gulf.

Washington can also use its sway to persuade Tehran to constrain its exports of precision-guided missiles to its allies in Iraq, Lebanon, Syria, and Yemen, where they could pose a threat to Israel and several Arab states.[105] While this offers grounds for modest optimism about the potential revival of multilateralism, the domestic politics of Iran present a fresh barrier to the restoration of the pact. In Tehran, despite President Rouhani's objection, conservative lawmakers have sought to place a rigid time constraint on the Biden administration, passing legislation requiring Iran to expedite its production of enriched uranium and expel UN nuclear inspectors if sanctions on the country's oil and banking sectors are not lifted by certain dates.

Similarly, Biden's national security team also faces domestic constraints on formulating a new US foreign policy.[106] For all its limitations, the JCPOA was endorsed by the key actors on the global scene and offered perhaps the only hope for the prevention of proliferation of nuclear arms in the region. Just how far the P5+1 group is willing to go to meet the demands of the Biden administration remains to be seen. As difficult as it is to reverse the diplomatic standoff and heightened tensions caused by Trump's Iran policy, the challenge is much greater for the Biden team to return to full compliance with the JCPOA without follow-on negotiations concerning Iran's ballistic missile program and its regional activities. Biden has inherited the difficult task of where to begin, stop, or close. While difficult enough to tackle Iran's missile program and its regional activities, the obstacles to working with a new hard-liner at the helm of the Iranian government would be far more formidable. Given the complete failure of Trump's maximum pressure campaign, many Middle East analysts argue that it is high time to try something new—that is, replacing broad economic sanctions with maximum diplomacy.[107]

Clearly, each side should move back to the JCPOA on the basis of the agreement that already exists, rather than trying to pressure the other for concessions. It is important to remember that "holding a return to full JCPOA compliance subject to resolving everything runs the risk of solving nothing at all."[108] Iran experts in the West widely regard the resumption of nuclear talks as fruitful, arguing that if the United States and Iran come to terms on the JCPOA, they can certainly reconstitute a channel to negotiate about other regional issues.

This is not to suggest that the tensions surrounding regional issues will slowly vanish, but rather that Iran's regional activities will be subject to negotiation. Trump's withdrawal from the JCPOA practically ended his ability to have regular diplomatic conversations with Iran.[109]

The problem with sanctions policy is that sanctions often hurt the whole country by imposing a kind of collective punishment on large segments of the population. Sanctions are often indiscriminate attacks on a state, its military, and an entire country's economic development, resulting in the cutting off of diverse foreign investment. These policies have adversely affected Iran's poor and lower-middle classes—groups which have borne the brunt of ongoing sanctions. Absent diplomatic efforts, the vast majority of Iranians will face further economic hardship and the current standoff may simply continue. The effectiveness of targeted sanctions notwithstanding, there is ample reason to worry that relying on wide-ranging sanctions may be neither politically potent enough nor morally commendable. The Biden administration can significantly reduce tensions between Iran and the United States by making the JCPOA a lasting and sustainable agreement. The benefits of such an accord can only accrue if the Biden administration takes note of Iran's security needs—especially its legitimate defensive and deterrence capabilities.

9

BALANCING THREATS AND INCENTIVES

Pundits, scholars, world citizens, and foreign policy wonks all ask the same question: Is there a way out of a US–Iran zero-sum calculation in our strategic thinking? History provides palpable instruction in leadership, moral fortitude, and hope. A leader's moral strength and rectitude, however, are no substitute for sound strategies and tactics. Trump's Iran policy, the so-called maximum pressure campaign against Iran, clearly bore no fruit from the standpoint of coercive diplomacy and a sustainable US foreign policy toward the broader Middle East.

Despite strategic differences between the United States and Iran, engagement remains a malleable and potent tool for coping with tensions between the two countries, as well as curbing regional instability. Restrictions on Iran's economic relations with the West rooted in the US sanctions have driven Iran into the arms of China and Russia, while also intensifying Iran's trade ties with India. In the meantime, the EU–Iran trading mechanism known as the Instrument in Support of Trade Exchanges (INSTEX), designed to allow Europeans to bypass US sanctions and continue normal trade with Tehran, has had little impact so far, raising doubts about whether it is an effective workaround.

Once allies, the United States and Iran have seen the deterioration of their relations over nearly half a century since the 1979 Islamic

Revolution. Their relations in the post-war era have gone from friendly ties to intractable hostility, a dramatic change facilitated by the political dynamics of regional politics, including revolution, radicalism, the hostage crisis, terrorism, US intervention in Afghanistan and Iraq, the 2011 Arab Spring uprisings, the rise of the Islamic State of Iraq and Syria (ISIS), and the ongoing draconian sanctions on Iran. Despite all of this, however, US–Iran relations have not fractured beyond repair.

Although the 2015 nuclear deal led to a hiatus from the ongoing confrontational political atmosphere between the two countries, the Trump administration's reckless disregard for multilateral diplomacy heightened tensions between the two countries, undoing any benefits yielded from negotiation and agreement on the nuclear deal. The mutual hostility, writes Barbara Slavin, serves "hardliners on both sides—and the arms dealers that cater to their respective regional partners—but also hurts the national interest of the United States and, most especially, the Iranian people. It also hobbles Iran's ties with European and Asian democracies."[1] Antagonism between the two countries, Slavin points out, has left consecutive US administrations susceptible to Arab autocrats and an increasingly undemocratic Israel, which, in turn, has bolstered Iran's influence among Arab Shi'as and afforded China and Russia an opening to increase their burgeoning economic and strategic power in the region.[2]

If past is prologue, any prediction in this regard remains contingent on who occupies the White House and who has the supreme leader's ear. While Trump showed us how to break deals and withdraw from international accords with diminishing returns, Biden appears keen on showing us how to fix them. For the United States, the path to a smart way out of the Middle East remains unclear. In this chapter, I revisit the strategic standoff trapping both countries, as well as the extent to which sanctions have been effective in bringing Iran to the negotiating table. I also address the extent to which Iranian threats have been overblown. Straddling threats and incentives, supporting opposing proxy agents, securitizing the Iranian threat, maintaining occasional back-channel communications, and rarely (if ever) engaging in direct negotiations have all bore the hallmarks of a persistent cold war and a strategic conundrum that have long characterized

US–Iran relations. What lessons can be learned? And why is a reduction in the enmity between the two countries indispensable to regional stability?

Trapped in a Strategic Stalemate

President Obama inherited thirty years of antagonism between the United States and Iran, and yet he was willing and able to go further than any previous administration since Reagan in normalizing US–Iran relations. Despite frequent setbacks, the Obama administration continued to look for opportunities to crack the diplomatic door open by continuing to work with Britain, France, and Germany— the three key European countries that had led international diplomatic efforts with Iran in the past.[3] It was after several excruciating years of detailed negotiation that the so-called P5+1 negotiations came to fruition when the Iranian nuclear deal was agreed upon on July 14, 2015.

Sanctions relief provided in the deal promised tangible improvements in the living standards of many Iranians, while also raising the prospect of turning a corner in the vexing relationship between Iran and the Western world after three decades of isolation and anomie.[4] The Joint Comprehensive Plan of Action (JCPOA), however, changed nothing in Iran's immediate geopolitical neighborhood, as Tehran's relations with its Gulf Arab neighbors—especially Saudi Arabia—remained complicated and tendentious, given their competing and conflicting positions in Syria and other regional conflicts. Would the nuclear agreement allow reformists in Iran to gain sufficient influence to move their democratic agenda forward?[5]

The fact remains that the United States and Iran are caught in an unrelenting strategic conundrum that has to be tackled before any easing of regional tensions can occur. Neither the maximum pressure strategy of the Trump administration nor the "no war, no negotiation" strategy of Iran's Supreme Leader Ayatollah Khamenei had been likely to lead to a productive diplomatic solution. If anything, these strategies set the stage for a military confrontation—an eventuality that both countries sought to avoid. The June 20, 2019, downing of a US RQ-4A Global Hawk drone, claimed to be within Iranian airspace, provoked no immediate response from the United States. This sent a strong signal to Iran's neighbors that the United States was reluctant to entangle itself in yet another complicated regional war and that Iran, when faced with nothing to lose under the pressure of crippling and warlike sanctions, could become a more destabilizing actor in the region.[6]

With Iran's alleged attacks on Saudi oil facilities, however, the risk of military violence in the region quickly became a reality. Although Iranian military forces could not match the United States or even Saudi firepower, their asymmetric tactics and their network of regional allies and proxies could make any war with Iran complicated and difficult to contain for Washington and its regional allies. While the downing of the US drone created a unique opportunity for Iran to enter a diplomatic phase to resolve the incident—in large part because both Washington and Tehran figured out how costly any military confrontation would prove to be—the September 14, 2019 attacks on Saudi Aramco, the country's state-controlled oil company, generated countervailing forces that rendered the diplomatic status quo chaotic and dangerous.

The lingering deadlock created by the Trump administration enhanced the possibility that future negotiations might be preceded by Iran transferring responsibility for the talks from the Foreign Ministry to the Supreme National Security Council, while also appointing new negotiators to represent the Islamic Revolutionary Guard Corps (IRGC) rather than the president. This possibility is more likely if the scope of negotiations expands to include Iran's missile program and regional activities, as neither the president nor the foreign minister has the authority to make decisions in such areas on behalf of Iran's supreme leader and the top military echelon.[7]

For the Trump administration, hope lay in the assumption that its strategy of maximum pressure would force the Iranians back to the table. The sanctions policy failed to do so, as it produced no change in Iran's foreign policy behavior.[8] But neither did the "no war, no negotiation" strategy of Iran's supreme leader, which trapped both parties in a strategic impasse. It has become increasingly clear that diplomacy is the only viable solution. The likely result of a US–Iran conflict not only involves Iranian proxies (including the Hezbollah militia, or Hamas) but two others as well: Israel and Saudi Arabia, both of which, in the past, have overtly postured for an escalation with Iran.

Israel continues to express an interest in military strikes if no agreement is reached on the JCPOA. An Israeli attack on Iran's nuclear facilities, experts warn, could spur a wider regional war with significant ramifications for the Persian Gulf region, leading to a dramatic spike in oil prices and a potential conflict between Iran and the key Gulf Arab allies of the United States: Saudi Arabia and the United Arab Emirates (UAE).[9] One of the primary systemic causes of tension in the Persian Gulf, Mehran Kamrava states, is the steady exclusion of Iran thus far from the regional security structure. As Washington and its regional allies have sought to isolate and contain Iran in the region, the Islamic Republic has cultivated ties with militias and other non-state actors—as part of its proxy networks—across the Middle East. These include Hezbollah in Lebanon, the Islamic Resistance in Iraq, and even the Taliban in Afghanistan. The result has often been a zero-sum game in which the strategic rivalry between Iran and its southern Gulf neighbors has only intensified regional and international tensions and instability.[10]

Willfully dismissive of the Iranians, the Trump administration simply failed to understand the need to integrate Iran into a regional security framework. A strong case can be made for such a strategic recalibration. The mutual interests of Iran and the United States in stabilizing both Iraq and Afghanistan as well as in diminishing the influence of Al-Qaeda and ISIS in the larger region suggest that major regional conflicts cannot be settled without some level of US–Iran cooperation.[11] Furthermore, a new strategic perception has emerged in which the gradual US military disengagement from the region, along with the post-petroleum economic scenario taking on a new significance, has further weakened the rationale for the United States to maintain a massive military presence and regional hegemony in the Persian Gulf.[12]

Under such circumstances, it is safe to argue that Iran's role in regional stability and détente is likely to grow. Seeking a shift in its approach toward Iraq, the Biden administration's reaction to a strike on a US military base at the airport in Erbil, in northern Iraq, on

February 16, 2021—which some US officials blamed on an Iran-backed militia, such as Kataib Hezbollah, or Asa'ib Ahl al-Haq—was noticeably limited and measured. This attempt to avoid setting red lines with Iran stood in sharp contrast to the Trump-era campaign against the country.[13]

Understandably, creating a stable post-war order in Iraq and Syria is a formidable and complex strategic challenge that cannot be effectively managed without the military and political participation of Iran. "Iran's future position in this escalating conflict in Syria," Malici and Walker write, "will not only be a crucial factor in the fate of the country and its people. It will also crucially affect American influence and interests in the region."[14] Given the volatile and deteriorating environment in the Middle East, abandoning the campaign of mutual demonization in US–Iran relations in favor of diplomatic reconciliation would provide a way out of the current strategic conundrum these two countries face.

Meanwhile, the stakes are too high for the EU, China, and Russia to allow ongoing tensions between the United States and Iran to escalate into war. Without an exit strategy to de-escalate these tensions, regional conflicts such as these tend to evolve into wider conflagrations with unpredictable results. If Washington wishes to build trust, the Biden administration should return to the JCPOA. "It is indeed," as some experts assert, "the most comprehensive nonproliferation agreement, containing the most intrusive policies of transparency and verification in the history of the NPT."[15]

The dilemma of US–Iran relations is how to convert four decades of varying levels of hostility into normal relations. This could be achieved, as one of the most eminent Iranian foreign policy experts states, "if the two countries recognize that they have common interests in preventing the rise of Al-Qaeda in Afghanistan and Iraq, avoiding a nuclear arms race in the Middle East and securing the uninterrupted flow of Persian Gulf oil to world markets."[16]

Ultimately, there is no substitute for diplomacy if the tensions between the United States and Iran are to be overcome.[17] That may in part explain why the Obama administration worked toward a reconciliation of sorts between the two countries, rendering possible a nuclear deal that effectively imposed a multifaceted verification regimen. While the Biden administration insists that negotiations regarding the Iranian nuclear program cannot be resuscitated without the inclusion of non-nuclear issues, such as Iran's regional activities, missile program, and human rights situation, Tehran's position all along has been that non-nuclear issues are not subject to negotiation within the context of an arms control agreement such as the JCPOA. Thus, the United States and Iran have reached a strategic stalemate. Iran should take full advantage of the opportunity to break this impasse by negotiating with the United States, in large part because an agreement with Washington will render reaching a regional détente with its Arab neighbors more plausible in light of the gradual US withdrawal from the region.

Re-assessing Sanctions

Successive US administrations and Senate foreign policy committees have deployed economic sanctions to try to change Iran's foreign policy behavior. US sanctions on Iran, according to one study, are primarily "secondary sanctions,"—penalties placed on companies that conduct business with Iran not placed directly on Iranian individuals and businesses. These sanctions have negatively affected Iran's economy but have failed to fundamentally alter Iran's pursuit of its core strategic goals in the region, including the support for its proxies in Iraq, Syria, and Lebanon, as well as the development of its missile program. In one rare exception, however, Kenneth Katzman maintains, sanctions have proven effective in bringing Iran to the negotiating table, prompting its decision to enter into a 2015 agreement that put substantial restrictions on its nuclear program.[18]

Sanctions during the first two years of Trump's maximum pressure campaign, according to one source, caused Iran's economy to shrink by nearly twelve percent, and oil exports—the country's core source of foreign currency—to decline by eighty percent.[19] An independent expert appointed by the Human Rights Council expressed serious concerns over the unilateral coercive sanctions imposed by the United States on Cuba, Venezuela, and Iran, maintaining that the use of economic sanctions for political purposes clearly violates human rights and the norms of the international community. Such actions are likely to precipitate man-made humanitarian catastrophes.[20] Sanctions contribute to the further deterioration of the human rights in a target country. In rights-abusive nations, the leader of the target government may in fact heighten the repression of their opponents and others as "justifiable action" given the economic constraints caused by sanctions.[21]

The Trump administration's sanctions have harmed Iranians' right to health, as they have drastically constrained the ability of the Iranian government to finance humanitarian imports including medicines.[22] The imposition of broad restrictions on financial trans-actions, along with aggressive rhetoric from Washington, has drasti-cally restricted the ability of the Iranian government and the private sector to finance humanitarian imports, including vital medicines and medical equipment.

While the Trump administration claimed that it had built exemp-tions for humanitarian imports into its sanctions regime, Human Rights Watch found that in practice these exemptions failed to miti-gate the trepidations of US and European companies and banks to risk incurring sanctions and legal action by exporting or funding exempted humanitarian goods to Iran. It should be noted that international law applies strict prohibitions on sanctions that negatively impact the humanitarian needs and the enjoyment of the right to health of ordi-nary people in a target state.[23]

On October 25, 2019, the Trump administration announced new sanctions on Iran, as former Treasury Secretary Steven T. Mnuchin asserted that, "This administration remains committed to the unfet-tered flow of humanitarian aid to the Iranian people, who have suf-fered for forty years under the mismanagement of this corrupt regime."[24] At the same time, US officials sent a contradictory mes-sage, noting that the strategy would in fact cause enough distress for the Iranian people that they would force the government to change its foreign policy conduct—a policy that certainly infringed on the economic and health rights of ordinary Iranians. On February 14, 2019, the then US Secretary of State Mike Pompeo told CBS News: "Things are much worse for the Iranian people [with the US sanc-tions], and we are convinced that will lead the Iranian people to rise up and change the behavior of the regime."[25]

The Trump administration's erratic use of "terrorist" designations further imperiled humanitarian trade with Iran. The April 2019 designation of the IRGC, part of Iran's military force, as a Foreign Terrorist Organization (FTO) is likely to affect millions of Iranians. While these designations do not apply to medicines, they increase the potential risks for companies that may wind up delaying or avoiding transactions with such designated entities. Moreover, a September 20, 2019, decision to impose further sanctions on Iran's Central Bank fiercely constrained the country's last remaining financial institution capable of engaging in foreign exchange transactions relating to humanitarian imports, while also further disregarding the "humanitarian exemption" for sanctions.[26]

Human Rights Watch goes on to mention other complications that US economic sanctions have caused for international humanitarian activities. Consider, for example, what Jan Egeland, Secretary General of the Norwegian Refugee Council, which supports thousands of Afghan refugees in Iran, said in August 2019:

> We have now, for a full year, tried to find banks that are able and willing to transfer money from donors [for our humanitarian operations]. But we are hitting a brick wall on every side. Norwegian and other international banks are afraid of U.S. sanctions to transfer the money that governments have given for our vital aid work.[27]

Beyond threatening Iranian access to medicine and medical equipment, these sanctions have undermined civil society, given rise to informal economies that lack transparency, spawned corruption and crony capitalism, fueled combative politics, accelerated widespread poverty, and amplified the securitization of society. The maximum pressure strategy has further harmed the Iranian people by restricting their opportunities for economic growth.[28] In short, sanctions have inflicted gratuitous pain on ordinary people by politicizing Iranian society and treating it as a threat, along with the Iranian government.[29]

Is the Iranian Threat Overblown?

Following the 1979 Iranian Revolution, successive US administrations have balanced hostility with pragmatism and even periodic attempts at outreach with Iran, often disguised in the lexicon of confrontation.

Warning against more than four decades of US obsession with Iran, Daniel Benjamin and Steven Simon maintain "Iran is not an existential threat to the United States, but a serious conflict with it—at a time when Washington is threatened by great-power rivals and committed to drawing down its presence in the Middle East—would be costly and counterproductive."[30]

Iran hawks in Washington, Benjamin and Simon go on to argue, too often exaggerate the threat posed by Iran-sponsored terrorism, which is relatively moderate compared with the jihadi terrorism that has occasionally been tolerated or even funded by Washington's Sunni partners. "Iran's activities are less damaging to global stability than, say, Pakistan's support for terrorist groups that target India or Russia's annexation of Crimea, yet Washington treats Tehran as a pariah while preserving relations with Islamabad and Moscow."[31]

In Washington, it is frequently assumed that Iran's foreign policy is driven by ideology and ideology alone. This is vastly overblown, as the Islamic Republic's foreign policy is instead motivated by pragmatic considerations in most cases. Framing Iran as an ideologically driven and hostile power toward the United States and its interests in the Middle East overlooks Tehran's real motivations, which are the maximizing of its security interests in an exceedingly hostile and difficult environment. From this vantage point, it is easy to see why missiles are Iran's main strategic deterrent against Israel. Israel's ongoing conflict with the empowered Lebanese Hezbollah notwithstanding, neither Iran nor Israel has an interest in disturbing the status quo.[32] Trump's hostile approach toward Iran had a net negative impact on US–EU relations, as it risked driving a wedge between the United States and Europe. Washington's European partners have often preferred negotiation to conflict, while also regarding the JCPOA as a substantial multilateral, diplomatic achievement. Trump's misguided decision to pull out of the JCPOA struck a sour note between the United States and Europe.[33]

A comparative look at Iran and its Gulf neighbors in terms of military spending and modernization demonstrates that the Iranian threat (in terms of its military superiority) is inflated at best and greatly overblown at worst. The Gulf Arab countries, Trita Parsi and Tyler Cullis note, have acquired some of the most modern and state-of-the-art US military hardware. This includes the latest jets from Boeing and Lockheed Martin, Predator drones, Apache attack helicopters, Patriot air-defense systems, and an array of the latest missiles, bombs, and other weapon systems. The Gulf Cooperation Council (GCC) states of Bahrain, Oman, Qatar, Saudi Arabia, Kuwait, and the UAE outspend Iran on arms by a factor of about eight.[34] The balance of conventional capabilities is patently opposed to the Iranians. Despite this reality, the prevailing perception in Washington wrongly remained that a domineering Iran would overshadow its Gulf Arab rivals following the signing of JCPOA.[35]

The Gulf Arab states have outspent Iran for decades. The GCC states, according to one study, spent $95–128 billion on military forces in 2017. This was six to nine times the estimate compiled by the study's authors of Iran's $15–16 billion. The Saudi military budget, by contrast, stood at $76 billion, and that of the UAE, $30 billion.[36] The military spending and arms imports of the Gulf Arab states have allowed them to develop a major comprehensive lead in conventional weapons, hardware, and modernization over Iran. For its part, Iran has focused on exploiting domestic and national discord within the Arab world. Iran has steadily built weapon systems enabling it to pose a massive asymmetric threat—often by its proxies—relative to its conventional military prowess, its poor economy, and its exclusion from global markets.[37]

Iran has improved its land-based air defense as well as its naval-missile air capability to attack maritime forces and coastal targets. At the same time, Iran has used its acquired missile technology to build up its strategic partners—usually sub-state actors—in an attempt to expand its regional influence and establish a potential strategic shield against any kind of attacks through Iraq. On balance, however, military experts have shown that Iran's air force cannot rival those of its Gulf Arab neighbors.[38] Land-based ballistic and cruise missiles, as well as long-range artillery rockets, give Iran a significant edge.

Despite their shortcomings, these missile forces can supplement Iran's air, sea, and land power. They are likely to compensate for Iran's deficiencies in airpower and ground forces. Crucially, its missile program has become a decisive instrument of Iranian power projection, a fact that goes a long way to showing why there is little chance that Iran will ever surrender its missile capabilities in any conceivable arms control agreement.[39]

Clearly, a spiraling arms race in the Middle East and North Africa is highly unlikely to lead to further stability. There is substantial evidence to suggest that the threat of an arms race and a so-called "proliferation cascade" is a bogus excuse to thwart Iran's nuclear deal with the P5+1 group. The notion that arms races intensify regional rivalries may seem reasonable on its face, but it fails to match reality. Arguably, an arms race does not currently exist between Saudi Arabia and Iran. More accurately, the situation can be described as a one-sided arms buildup in which Saudi Arabia has out-spent Iran by colossal amounts, while Iran has worked to compete with Saudi Arabia without a corresponding increase in military spending. While it is possible in theory that improved efficiency in the procurement of arms could result in real military capability gains—often disguised by stable military expenditure—there is not ample evidence to support the idea that this is indeed the case with Iran.[40]

Essentially, the myth of the Iran-Saudi Arabia arms race has thus far been employed as a cautionary tale, but the conflicting interests of Saudi Arabia and Iran suggest that such an arms race has every reason to exist. Iran, gazing toward Saudi Arabia and its allies in the Gulf, may notice the gaping hole in military spending between itself and its neighbors, tilting the military balance firmly and decidedly in favor of Saudi Arabia. Conversely, when Saudi Arabia confronts Iran, they may be unnerved by their much larger (by population) foe, and see military technology paid for by petrodollars as the only means of compensating for the deficit. The worst-case scenario would be if both powers decided that only nuclear arms could guarantee their security.[41]

The threat from Iran, writes former Deputy Assistant Secretary of State for Iran John Limbert, has been overblown for various reasons, including the expensive sale of armaments to Iran's Arab neighbors. This has been done by those who seek to construct a frightening enemy to attract political support. Iran's military is beleaguered by aging, depleted, and commonplace equipment, a lack of spare parts, and underfunding. The weakening of the Iranian military establishment is not a mistake, as Jonathon Whooley reminds us. Rather, it is the impact of long-term underfunding by the Iranian state and the refusal of the United States, once Iran's ally, of military sanctions and co-production deals which would have left Iran capable of manufacturing its own domestic arms supply.[42]

Also rendering Iran less threatening is its poor economy—a result of international sanctions and internal mismanagement.[43] On the exaggerated threat of Iran, Representative Ruben Gallego (D-Arizona) has echoed a similar sentiment, noting that he received a classified briefing on May 17, 2019, about Iran: "What I saw was a lot of misinterpretation and wanting conflict coming from the [Trump] administration and intelligence community. Intelligence doesn't show existential threats. Even what it shows, it doesn't show threats to US interests."[44]

As noted before, Trump's unilaterally scuttling of the JCPOA while also halting Iran's ability to develop its civilian centrifuge program met with a fierce response from other members of the P5+1 group. Similarly, halting Iran's ballistic missile program as part of the Trump administration policy of bolstering Iranian containment proved counterproductive. Iran's military capabilities, writes Seyed Hossein Mousavian, an Iranian policymaker and scholar who served on Iran's nuclear diplomacy team in negotiations with the EU and International Atomic Energy Agency, are defensive in nature and were created to deter foreign attack. Mousavian adds:

> Any U.S. insistence on weakening Iran's military capabilities signals a desire to make Iran an easier target should the United States decide to attack. Consequently, Iran naturally views the preservation of its military capabilities as critical to maintaining its security, territorial integrity, and independence and will never put them up for negotiation.[45]

Iran will not allow itself to be unilaterally disarmed in a region so replete with enemies and with a powerful international adversary in the United States. A recognition of this simple fact is vital to understanding the position of the Iranians.

There is a broad consensus among experts that without major US sanctions relief, Iran is unlikely to walk back its recent progress in its nuclear program. The notion that Iran could pose a serious threat to other regional actors as the sole hegemon in the region is baseless. While Tehran enjoys significant influence in Lebanon, Syria, and Iraq, it is important to bear in mind that, as Robert Hunter posits, these countries are more or less "failed states" and not serious contenders for power in the region. The Islamic Republic's larger ambitions crumbled more than two decades ago, when it attempted, in vain, to export its revolution across the Middle East and Central Asia.[46]

Furthermore, as noted above, Iran's military capabilities, although exaggerated by some outside analysts, are too modest to justify the saturation of the Arab countries of the Persian Gulf with advanced weapons. It is unlikely that these weapons would be immensely helpful in dealing with Iran's serious challenges—notably its ability to promote "destabilization" or to engage in "terrorism." The fact remains that Iran poses no economic threat to the region. It should be noted, however, that given its relative advances in universal education, technology, entrepreneurship, and middle-class values compared to most of its Arab neighbors, regional states—certainly not Israel—do have legitimate concerns regarding Iran's potential for modernity and integration into the global economy.[47]

How to Bury the Hatchet

The benefits of diplomacy far outweigh the risks of confrontation with Iran. The US military presence in the Persian Gulf region is the clear driver behind the current enmity between the United States and Iran. With so many missed opportunities and the ceaseless mistrust between Washington and Tehran, it is difficult to escape the conclusion that the maximum pressure campaign enormously accelerated the risk of a confrontation. The JCPOA, however briefly, marked a new era in which the rewards of negotiations with the United States far outweighed the risks.[48] Some experts have suggested that Washington can use measured sanctions relief as leverage and that its prime objective should be to "contain Iran rather than try to roll back its gains or topple its regime."[49] After all, it is certainly an impractical relationship if toppling your diplomatic partner is on the table.

Washington should return to a diplomatic resolution of its tensions with Iran. Perhaps the most viable diplomatic option remains a regional détente based on a process of sustainable cooperation between Iran and its Gulf Arab neighbors. The United States should throw its diplomatic support behind three major undertakings, each of which will have profound ramifications for regional stability and security.

First, an immediate resolution of the civil war and humanitarian crisis in Yemen appears critical to the region's political stability, as well as to possible rapprochement between Tehran and Riyadh. In an effort to combat Iran's influence in Yemen, the Saudis exported a virulent mixture of sectarianism and corruption in that country, effectively turning the Zaydis—who made up about a third of Yemen's population—into a fierce religious competitor determined to fight against Saudi intrusion. In fact, the war has created the most serious humanitarian crisis in the world.[50] Since the attacks on the Saudi oil fields, Riyadh and the Houthis have retreated from the disastrous ongoing war. The United States should encourage its Saudi allies to reach a broader understanding with the Houthis to resolve this conflict and end the humanitarian crisis there.[51]

The resolution of this conflict is likely to dramatically reduce the sectarian tensions fueled by the Iran–Saudi Arabia rivalry. Some experts, such as Robert Malley—a senior adviser to the Obama and Biden administrations—argue that Washington could encourage Tehran and Riyadh to work on several intermediate measures, including maritime security, environmental protections, nuclear safety protocols, and transparent military exercises as a precursor to addressing larger regional architecture and security concerns.[52] These acts of reciprocity could pay dividends by breaching the walls of cynicism and vitriol on both sides of the Gulf.

Second, Washington, through its leverage over Iraq, should facilitate a mediation between Iran and Saudi Arabia. Iraqi Prime Ministers Adel Abdul Mahdi and Mustafa al-Kadhimi have played a constructive role in this regard, largely because Iraq is better positioned as a potential mediator. Iraq's good rapport with Iran, Saudi Arabia, and the United States renders it a unique candidate to do so. Iraq's Sunni population would most likely welcome such a move, in part because it allows Saudi Arabia to counterbalance Iranian influence in their country.[53]

Third, a Saudi-led trade embargo against Qatar, in place since June 4, 2017, should end. The embargo, which was supported by the UAE, Bahrain, and Egypt, resulted in the severing of diplomatic ties with Qatar and the imposition of travel and trade bans on that country.[54] The crisis impacted the country's food security, demonstrating the effectiveness of food security as a political weapon even among GCC member states. The embargo posed a serious challenge to Qatar, given that forty percent of its food imports enter the country across the Saudi border. In 2015, Qatar imported slightly more than $400 million worth of agricultural products from Saudi Arabia—largely dairy products and vegetables.[55]

This crisis forced Qatar to turn to Turkey, Iran, Oman, and India to fill the gaps in its food imports, as well as those in construction materials needed to build infrastructure for the FIFA World Cup to be held in Qatar in 2022. Iran's location makes it a natural supply route for Qatar since the closure of its only land border with Saudi Arabia. The sea link between Iran and Qatar is also critical for its supplies from Turkey.[56] Managing the chaos and uncertainty resulting from these conflicts in the region remains largely contingent upon regional initiatives and solutions that demand creative leadership and balanced diplomacy.

Furthermore, from Iran's perspective, the war against terrorism and extremism cannot be successfully managed without regional cooperation. Beyond cooperation in the Persian Gulf over taking ownership of regional security, all parties can engage in regular dialogue regarding non-political and relatively uncontentious issues about which they all have shared concerns, including environmental issues, water scarcity, nuclear safety and security, and narcotics trafficking. Such regular and sustained cooperation will help eliminate misperceptions about one another and is likely to foster trust-building.[57]

Fostering a Regional Détente

It is evident that Washington has been redressing balance away from the Middle East for almost a decade now. The United States, weary and wary of committing blood and treasure to a region whose problems persist and whose oil-based prominence in the global economy seems destined to recede, has clearly shifted its focus to Southeast Asia.[58] The time has come to consider new ways of moving toward a regional détente. Sectarian tensions are not new in the Middle East, but political manipulations have placed them in an explosive context and amplified the urgency to curb them with nuance and sensitivity. Sectarianism and identity politics are contagious and destabilizing in a region where political rivalries in the post-Arab Spring region have manifested themselves in an excessive attachment to a particular sect or party.

One regional expert has warned against this trajectory: "As long as Tehran's blind spot to the sectarian consequences of its own actions persists, social strife in Iraq and Iran's own tensions with Saudi Arabia are also likely to continue."[59] Regional cooperation must pave the way for the creation of new security structures before sectarian strife calcifies into something more ominous, violent, and destabilizing. If left to fester, such tensions will likely precipitate the potentially dangerous rise of religious nationalism that could threaten regional peace and stability for many years to come.[60]

In light of this, it is easy to see why a regional détente will benefit all sides of the Persian Gulf. In 2020, the United States was almost dragged into war in the Persian Gulf, rendering it all the more imperative for the Biden administration to think about what could or should be done to de-escalate tensions in the region. The most prudent approach would be to use hard-nosed diplomacy and smart statecraft to pursue de-escalation. This effort should be pursued without apology as several years of the opposite and strictly confrontational tact has only produced intransigence and fortification of existing enmities. From the standpoint of Iran's Arab neighbors, there are also good reasons to pursue détente. Iran, with its colossal economic problems at home and a disgruntled population hit hard by the COVID-19 pandemic, is not only desperate for sanctions relief, but knows it would suffer massively in a military confrontation.[61]

On Iran's side, the military escalation that took place in the region during 2019—with attacks on oil tankers in the Persian Gulf, missile strikes in Iraq, and alleged attacks on Saudi Arabia's Aramco oil refinery at Abqaiq and Khurais—was a harbinger of further attacks on Saudi and Emirati oil fields. These attacks exposed the vulnerability of both countries to possible military actions in the region, a reality that subsequently compelled the UAE to seek quiet diplomacy and détente with Iran. The Biden administration's decision to halt the sale of weapons that Saudi Arabia has been using for offensive operations in Yemen—but not the arms that it needs to defend its territory—was in lockstep with fostering a regional détente.[62] Such vulnerabilities to asymmetric attacks are precisely why diplomacy is not faint-hearted. Rather, it is required to resolve security issues and encourage reciprocity.

Even amid escalating tensions in the region, Tehran and Riyadh have engaged in fruitful dialogue over facilitating Iranian Muslim participation in the *hajj* pilgrimage.[63] Biden administration officials, along with some GCC member states, could mediate the tensions between the two countries. The onset of behind-the-scenes talks between Iran and Saudi Arabia—initially mediated by Iraqi officials—has offered hopes of defusing regional tensions. According to experts, Saudi Arabia's relations with Iran, especially following Biden's presidency, are influenced more by international factors rather than internal and regional variables.[64] The drivers that triggered the Iran–Saudi Arabia dialogue were caused by the pressure emanating from Biden coming to power in the United States and the efforts of Iran and the United States to revive the JCPOA. This approach is due to the declining importance of the Middle East and its subset, the Persian Gulf, to the United States. "The Middle East is no longer the United States' number one priority, and the United States is stepping back from the wider region, withdrawing from Iraq, Jordan, Kuwait and Saudi Arabia, while increasing its focus on China and Russia."[65]

Washington's search for a balance between the reduction of its military commitments to the Middle East and ensuring the stability of the region has created a rare opportunity for Iran and Saudi Arabia to settle their regional differences. Without negotiations between these two significant regional powers, sectarian tensions and rivalries could overwhelm the region, resulting in further political instability. Saudi Arabia's costly Yemeni quagmire and its vulnerability to Iran's drone attacks has put it in a much weaker position vis-à-vis Iran. On the other hand, Iranians know that reaching a regional détente with their Arab neighbors could dramatically improve the chances of pursuing successful negotiations with Washington over the JCPOA. Moreover, competition with Turkey and Israel at regional level has compelled Iran to seek rapprochement with Saudi Arabia, keeping the latter away from joining its two other key regional rivals.[66]

New talks between Tehran and Riyadh reflect a wide gamut of issues concerning regional problems, from the political instability in Yemen, Syria, and Lebanon to stabilization programs in Iraq. Saudi Arabia's Crown Prince Mohammed bin Salman, one of the Arab leaders most blatantly critical of Iran, opined in a major televised interview that his government sought "good relations" with the country and was "working with our partners in the region to overcome our differences with Iran."[67]

Iran, to its credit, has long sought negotiations with Arab neighbors and even the development of a much broader regional security framework. On numerous occasions, Iran's former Foreign Minister Javad Zarif expressed willingness to resolve differences in the region, frequently defending Iran's Hormuz Peace Endeavor (HOPE) as a forum to reduce regional tensions. Zarif clearly stated Iran was willing to discuss the problems of the region:

> But the peoples of the region, not outsiders, must resolve these issues. Neither the United States nor its European allies have the prerogative to lead or sponsor future talks. Rather, the Persian Gulf region needs an inclusive regional mechanism to encourage diplomacy and cooperation and to lower the risk of miscalculation and conflict.[68]

Meanwhile, Iran's frequent attacks on maritime targets as part of its maximum resistance has been driven by the desire to assert Tehran's actual right to be part of a maritime security framework in the Persian Gulf. Iran has felt excluded from this framework and sought to send a clear message that, "if it could not sell its oil because of sanctions, its neighbors would eventually not be able to sell their oil either because of Iran's disruption of maritime security."[69] The fact remains that all countries in the region have real interest in freedom of navigation and commerce. The diplomacy with Iran over the Yemen war and its ongoing humanitarian crisis is crucial now more than ever. Iran and its network of non-state actors, including Hezbollah, have been the major external supporters of the Houthis in Yemen. Saudi Arabia's entanglement in a conflict of uncertain outcome has compelled Riyadh to ease tensions with Tehran, hoping to facilitate an end to the Yemen war.[70]

Iran's new president Ebrahim Raisi has said that one of his foreign policy priorities is to improve relations with regional counties, especially the Persian Gulf Arab countries led by Saudi Arabia.[71] Raisi has made clear that his administration would be open to restoring ties with Riyadh and opening diplomatic offices. "There are no obstacles from Iran's side to reopening embassies… there are no obstacles to ties with Saudi Arabia."[72] Iraj Masjedi, Iranian ambassador to Iraq, has asserted that Tehran and Riyadh have discussed the reopening of the two countries' embassies, and that future talks in Iran or Saudi Arabia were likely to follow.[73] The Saudis have also expressed hopes of continuing talks with Iran. Likewise, the UAE, a close ally of the Saudis, has expressed similar sentiments. Leaders of the UAE congratulated Raisi on his election.[74]

As noted in the previous chapters, one of the main causes of tension in the Persian Gulf is the intentional exclusion of Iran thus far from the predominant regional security arrangement. The more the United States and its regional allies have sought to isolate and securitize Iran in the Persian Gulf and beyond, Mehran Kamrava argues, the more Tehran has cultivated ties with militias and other non-state actors across the region. An active and comprehensive integration of Iran into a regional security structure, instead, would most likely drastically reduce Arab-Iranian tensions, promote trade, and give the United States the space it needs to pivot away from a region where its resources have been spent painfully.[75] That, coupled with the reluctance of the United States to act as an external balancer via shaky and unreliable regional allies, calls for a new security framework based on learned lessons and clear thinking.[76]

China Plays Its Great Game in Iran

The reluctance of European countries to fulfill their obligations toward Iran under the nuclear deal—largely to avoid antagonizing the Trump administration—has driven Iran into the arms of China. The void left by the lack of European and North American companies to do business with Iran has been filled by a China rich with foreign reserves and desperate for new oil markets. Although the Chinese have never allowed Middle Eastern issues and conflicts to present themselves as major obstacles to their relations with Washington, they have exploited such cases in their broad geopolitical and economic calculus to adjust certain policies. In the last decade or so, in which US foreign policy toward Tehran has chiefly revolved around Iran's nuclear policy and ongoing sanctions, China has emerged as an economic beneficiary by defusing pressure on Iran while also garnering political advantages in its interactions with the United States.[77]

In early July 2020, Iran announced that it was in the process of negotiating a twenty-five-year strategic agreement with China known as the "Comprehensive Plan for Cooperation between Iran and China." Worth approximately $400 billion, the agreement aims to ramp up cooperation between the two countries economically and militarily in the coming years and decades.[78] This all-encompassing deal includes the development of airports and high-speed railways and subways, and has the potential to affect the lives of millions of Iranians. China will commit to building the infrastructure for a 5G telecommunications network, offering access to the new Chinese Global Positioning System (Beidou), and helping Iranian authorities assert greater control over what flows in cyberspace.[79]

It should be noted that Beijing sees Iran as a key state and a potentially valuable ally and asset in Western Asia. It is a country with abundant natural resources, vast human capital, and a massive and relatively untapped market.[80] China is in fact Iran's largest trading partner. As Iran continues to be treated as a political outlier on the global scene, it has the potential to become a Chinese client state of sorts.[81] The broader vision for Iran–China cooperation was outlined during President Xi's January 2016 state visit to Tehran. The two countries

> agreed to expand trade to $600 billion over a 10-year period while also building stronger cooperation as part of a 25-year plan. In addition to trade, China is a leading investor in the Iranian market. About 100 major Chinese companies invest in Iran's key economic sectors, especially energy and transportation. For example, the China National Nuclear Corporation is redesigning Iran's Arak IR-40 heavy water reactor to address nonproliferation requirements as part of the 2015 Iran nuclear deal.[82]

Consider, for example, the way Iran has dealt with the COVID-19 pandemic. Historically, Iranian religious authorities have almost always accused foreign agents and enemies of being the source of the plague, buttressing a widely held perception that foreigners are spreading such diseases to nefarious ends. But this time around, Iranian leadership refrained from blaming foreigners, namely China, as the place from which the virus originated, in large part owing to Iran's ongoing political and economic ties with that country. A close relationship between Chinese Muslims and the city of Qom—considered the largest center for Shi'a scholarship in the world, as well as a significant pilgrimage destination—rendered that city vulnerable to a highly infectious coronavirus. Similarly, Iran's silence about the way in which China has treated its own Muslim minority (Uyghurs) has been deafening. Yet the Islamic Republic deliberately chose to avoid blaming China publicly.

Trump's policy of maximum pressure has driven Iran away from its traditional policy of negotiating its interests and balancing the East vs. the West, while also seeking an alternative pathway to its political and economic survival. Unless the United States and its European allies develop effective diplomatic initiatives to countervail Chinese efforts to commit Iran to a long-term pact, and if Iran's international isolation resumes, we may be witnessing the passing of the era of an opening to bilateral and multilateral trade ties with the West.[83] Iran will not remain isolated as long as interested parties like the Chinese look for ways to exploit frayed US–Iran ties.

Some Important Lessons

Since the 1950s, Philip H. Gordon, who is now special assistant to President Biden and deputy national security adviser to US Vice President Kamala Harris, argues that the United States has set out to replace governments and transform political systems in Iran, Afghanistan (twice), Iraq, Egypt, Libya, and Syria. The rationale behind US interventions in the Middle East has often been motivated by geopolitical concerns, that is, fighting terrorism, advancing humanitarian causes, promoting democracy, and rarely—if ever—driven by human rights considerations. Common to all operations, however, has been that they all failed to achieve their stated goals and generated unintended and unproductive consequences with significant financial and human costs.[84]

Although the United States has successfully ousted hostile regimes in places such as Afghanistan and Iraq, it has found itself coping with an ensuing long-term conflict, thousands of lost lives, and trillions of dollars of spending to manage their aftermath. All these events have demonstrated that US staying power is limited and necessarily curtailed by the weariness of its public and the strain on its coffers.[85] Over time, with escalating violence as well as US casualties, public disapproval of keeping troops in costly conflicts weakens the administration's goals and restricts its policy options.[86] The truth is that economic sanctions and isolation have an imperfect track record of generating political change and revolution; neither have they ever pressed leaders to give up power voluntarily.[87]

Looking back over forty-two years of US–Iran relations and contemplating how best to approach that relationship in the future, several key lessons emerge. One clear lesson from more than four decades of tense relations between the two countries is that although the US overthrow of the Iranian government in 1953 might have succeeded in precluding a potential Iranian pivot into the Soviet orbit, it also terminated Iran's democratic development and stymied the role of legitimate dissent in Iran. It helped create an autocratic regime lasting for twenty-six years, only to be overthrown by another repressive regime, fueling an ongoing hostility toward Washington.[88]

It is worth noting that Iran has been under sanctions for the last forty-two years and the regime has survived. In fact, these sanctions have fortified the place of the Islamic Revolutionary Guard Corps in the economy. The spread of Iranian influence in the region is not strictly determined by its financial assets. If that were the decisive factor, Saudi Arabia, which marshals much more significant economic resources, would be the preeminent regional political power. The expansion of Iran's regional influence is primarily due to two factors. The first is a Shi'ite awakening and movement for empowerment among hitherto suppressed communities in countries such as Iraq and Lebanon, in part inspired by the example of the 1979 Iranian Revolution.

The second factor is the US toppling of Iran's regional foes, in Afghanistan in 2001 and Iraq in 2003. Iran's regional policies are tied to its perception of threats and opportunities, not to its bank account. Iran's intervention in Syria, for example, was motivated by a perceived need to preserve a long-time ally—the Assad regime—and to defeat Sunni Muslim fundamentalist militants linked to Al-Qaeda, and later ISIS. Another reason why the Trump administration's demands were unrealistic was that they failed to consider Iranian nationalism. However much they may dislike the Islamic regime, Iranians do not welcome foreigners deciding the type of government they should have or want.

Bitter memories of the 1953 CIA coup that overthrew popularly elected Iranian Prime Minister Mohammad Mossadegh and restored an absolute monarch still linger. The death and destruction in Afghanistan and Iraq since 2001 and 2003, respectively, under the guise of exporting democracy, have erased any illusions in Iran about the outcome of US military intervention and regime change. What government should rule in Iran is the prerogative of the Iranian people, not right-wing US politicians obsessed with Iranophobia. What is more, the main victims of restored US sanctions will be the very same Iranian public that the Trump administration purported to want to save. Shutting the doors to diplomacy and escalating tensions with Iran while it was abiding by all the provisions of the nuclear deal revealed that these US hawks—in alliance with Israel and Saudi Arabia and their powerful lobbies in Washington—were all along intent on disarming Iran and, ultimately, overthrowing its government.[89]

Fearful of the impact of secondary US sanctions and the expulsion from the larger US market, many European companies terminated their operations in Iran. This compelled Iran to expand trade ties with China, Russia, and India. The Iranian government will find other ways to work around the sanctions. This suggests that the real casualty of Trump's Iran policy will be US credibility, access, and leverage. US military interventions in Afghanistan and Iraq, however, revealed that the power to destroy is different from the power to control or subdue. Iran is a much larger country, with a population of eighty-five million, and many more capabilities to deter foreign intervention.

The advocates of regime change in Iran should look closely at the lessons of Iraq and Afghanistan and the high human, financial, and political costs of choosing the wrong political course of action. The Taliban's return to power in Afghanistan after two decades of US nation-building attempts there serves as a grim reminder of misguided foreign policies. The lessons of history loom large here and should be properly heeded lest the possibilities for conflict are realized and the door to de-escalation is firmly closed. At the time of writing, in late 2021, much debate surrounded the future of the JCPOA.[90]

A growing consensus holds that hardheaded and clear-eyed diplomacy rather than regime change is the most effective way to promote US interests in the Middle East and mitigate the risk of potentially bloody confrontation. The confrontational maximum pressure campaign has given Iran an incentive to resist US pressure to come to the negotiating table. Despite ratcheting up pressure, Trump, ironically, has encouraged Iran to increase its investment in its nuclear program. "The lesson Tehran has learned," Vali Nasr observers, "is that a nuclear deal will only be successful if Iran has enough leverage to force the United States to lift more sanctions and then remain committed to a deal."[91]

But the larger lesson, Nasr goes on to argue, is that

> in the deal Iran gave up tangible physical assets that it had built over time and at great cost, whereas the United States merely agreed to rescind laws that could one day come back into force. Thus, while one side wielded massive pain and power, the other was left to merely seek whatever assistance the world stage had to offer. There was no meaningful cost to lifting sanctions nor to reimposing them, as it rarely affected the United States. It is to change that calculus that Iran has resisted sanctions pressure, and recently demanded that the U.S. government pay compensation for abandoning the deal and inflicting economic pain on Iran.[92]

Given the ongoing sanctions and lack of trust between the two countries, the road to any future nuclear agreement will be immensely difficult—but worth whatever effort is necessary. It is difficult to avoid the conclusion that these missteps chiefly hold lessons for US non-proliferation policy, as continued US pressure with underlying support for regime change over the past four years has actually enhanced Iran's incentives to acquire nuclear weapons.[93] The long and tumultuous history of exchanging threats and incentives that has characterized US–Iran relations since the 1979 Revolution suggests that temptations to resort to military action have thus far been strongly resisted. This leaves the door wide open for diplomacy.

10

CONCLUSION

THE PATH FORWARD

US–Iran relations have never normalized following the 1979 Revolution except for two short-lived encounters. There was a brief diplomatic initiative between the two countries under President George W. Bush in the aftermath of the US invasion of Afghanistan, and then a relatively longer period of engagement during Barack Obama's second term. While the latter led to the watershed 2015 nuclear deal, the former brought about a short period of cooperation between the two nations as Iran assisted the United States in many aspects of post-invasion reconstruction. Tehran's close ties with Shi'a political parties in Iraq, however, was seen by Washington as thwarting its strategic objective of forming an inclusive government in Baghdad.[1]

In the aftermath of the wars in Afghanistan and Iraq, it became evident that without the cooperation of central regional players like Iran, the United States was likely to fail to contain and defeat terrorism. The longstanding distrust between the two countries has stood in the way of close cooperation much less sustainable diplomatic ties. For a significant part of the last four decades, however, pragmatism has taken a back seat to cynicism, as the two sides have continued to act on their deep-rooted suspicion of each other. The Islamic Republic has plausibly interpreted US policy in the Persian Gulf as directed at eventual regime change in Iran, either by military attacks or covert actions.[2]

This external threat, however, has almost always helped spark national unity and populism inside the country. In the US, the continued hawkish policy toward Iran has had an adverse impact on Iran, hindering the possibility of genuine reform within the country and preventing any prospect of sustainable political openings in the intractable, ongoing impasse in US–Iran relations. The momentum that Iranian reformists won after concluding the Joint Comprehensive Plan of Action (JCPOA) has given way to a strengthening of the hand of hard-line populist leaders who continue to nurse deep skepticism about the value of diplomatic plugging toward the United States in the aftermath of their experience with the Trump administration.[3] Using harsh sanctions as well as covert means to overthrow the Islamic Republic have proven counterproductive.

Furthermore, the Islamic Republic has frequently viewed the US–Israel strategic alliance as an existential threat to Iran's national security. To counter this threat, Iran has continued to arm Hezbollah in Lebanon, assist Hamas in Palestine, bolster its proxy operations in Syria and Yemen, and maximize its political influence in Iraq. Meanwhile, Israel's reliance on Washington to prevent Iran from challenging the Israeli nuclear monopoly in the Middle East has contributed to—among other things—a broadened US presence in the region. With Washington seemingly bent on reducing the costs of its security responsibility in the Persian Gulf through burden-sharing, while also contemplating gradual withdrawal from the region, Tehran is poised to welcome and take advantage of such a reduced US role.[4] This may provide a unique geopolitical opportunity to salvage the nuclear deal.

The Taliban's return to power in Afghanistan is likely to present new opportunities and constraints to the United States and Iran. Short of extending official recognition to a Taliban-led Afghan government, Washington may consider opportunities to engage such a government. The Taliban are not a US-designated Foreign Terrorist Organization (FTO), despite the fact that many of the group's members have been designated as Specially Designated Global Terrorists (SDGTs) under Executive Order 13224.[5] Al-Qaeda is believed to have a presence in Afghanistan and its long-held ties with the Taliban seem to have been sustained over the years. The Islamic State affiliate in Afghanistan (known as the Islamic State of Khorasan Province—ISKP) views the Taliban's nationalistic agenda as opposed to their own universalist vision of a global caliphate.[6] On August 23, 2021, CIA Director William J. Burns held a secret meeting with deputy Taliban leader Abdul Ghani Baradar. A close aide of the Taliban's founding supreme leader, Mohammad Omar, Baradar is said to hold significant influence over Taliban soldiers. He fought Soviet forces during their occupation of Afghanistan (1980–88) and served as the governor of several provinces in the late 1990s when the Taliban last ruled the country.[7] The governments of Pakistan, China, Iran, and the Central Asian Republics appear concerned, to varying degrees, about the possibility of terrorist threats emanating from Afghanistan. These governments are likely to cooperate with Washington to deter such threats. All this may offer additional incentive for the Taliban to contain Al-Qaeda and other terrorist groups operating in Afghanistan.[8]

Similarly, Iran faces new challenges and opportunities in Afghanistan under the Taliban. As in the past, Iran and Afghanistan can become important trading partners—with Afghanistan's needs for Iran's oil and gas and Iran's attempts to seek new markets. However, many challenges lie ahead. Iran's worry about new refugee influx across its border and the possible return of Al-Qaeda to Afghanistan cannot be underestimated. The presence of terrorist groups such as ISKP continues to be a major concern for Iran. After two decades of US military presence on Iran's eastern border, Tehran is poised to take full advantage of US withdrawal from Afghanistan.

Iran shares a 572-mile border with Afghanistan and is host to millions of Afghan refugees. It has a substantial cultural imprint in Afghanistan. Dari, with various dialects of the Persian language, is spoken by seventy-eight percent of the population and is the favored language of governance in Kabul. Herat province, on Iran's eastern border, is a historic portal to Iran, and was a pivotal cultural and religious hub of the Persian Empire. Afghanistan is ninety percent Muslim, with Sunni Muslims constituting nearly eighty-three percent of the population, and Shi'a Muslims seventeen percent of the population.[9]

Furthermore, the Taliban's rise to power and their anti-Western sentiments will dovetail nicely with the resurgence of Islamic populism in Iran. Tehran will find a way to engage with the Taliban on several issues, including counterterrorism, political stability, non-intervention, and counter-narcotics. The Iranian government has characterized the departure of US troops from Afghanistan as a positive development, calling for national unity government in Afghanistan. Iranian Foreign Ministry spokesperson Saeed Khatibzadeh underlined the need for dialogue and the peaceful resolution of conflict in Afghanistan: "Iran is in constant contact and dialogue with all parties and groups in Afghanistan."[10] Iran will only recognize the Taliban's rule, Khatibzadeh went on to assert, if they form an all-inclusive government committed to safeguarding the rights of all Afghan ethnoreligious groups. Iran will also welcome the opportunity to cooperate with Pakistan in order to facilitate peaceful transition of power in Afghanistan.

One Western journalist has underlined this narrative, arguing that the Sunni–Shi'ite divide between Iran and the Taliban is not an issue, given their growing ties over the past two decades: "Tehran's Shiite regime has strategic, economic, ideological, and ecological reasons for backing Sunni extremists."[11]

Had it not been for the repudiation of the JCPOA by the Trump administration, Dina Esfandiary points out, the nuclear deal could have created a broader framework for negotiating other critical issues relating to Iran's missile program and regional activities. If the nuclear deal collapses, however, there can be no doubt that the United States' leverage over Iran will significantly diminish. Under such circumstances, Washington would likely face a daunting task to rebuild trust in order to forge a new diplomatic path. For the time being, the United States must restore the nuclear deal to engage Iran even as there are multiple constraints on the cooperation between the two nations on all levels. "To this end," Esfandiary warns, "the United States' first step must be to accept that, while Iran is a problematic actor, Washington has only a limited capacity to control its behavior."[12]

Equally important is the realization that the harsh sanctions imposed on Iran by the Trump administration's maximum pressure campaign have failed to exact satisfactory alterations in Iran's foreign policy behavior. While authoritarian governments will often find ways to bypass sanctions, ordinary people will suffer disproportion-ately—from both the pandemic and poor economic conditions—

whether due to the sanctions or to mismanagement, failed government policies, and falls in oil prices. Although there are humanitarian exceptions to sanctions for the procurement of food and medical supplies, the widespread use of sanctions against Iranian banks has complicated such attempts. Iran has encountered serious difficulties in paying for coronavirus vaccine because its foreign currency has been frozen in banks overseas. The current situation poses serious threats not only to Iran but also to the rest of the region.[13]

Moreover, it bears remembering that sanctions can delay or even truncate Iran's nuclear program but not terminate it. A broad consensus holds that engaging Iran in diplomacy is indeed the most effective way to leverage its foreign policy conduct. Former Deputy Secretary of State and CIA Director William J. Burns, who was also the lead US negotiator for the 2015 Iran nuclear deal, underlines the rational impulses of the Islamic Republic, arguing that although Iran is far from being the easiest negotiating partner, the Iranian regime, overall, is amenable to diplomatic overtures.[14]

Similarly, on another level, as noted in the preceding chapters, attempts to isolate and exclude Iran from the prevailing regional security architecture are likely to fail. The United States and its regional allies should seek ways to integrate Iran into present and future security frameworks if Arab-Iranian tensions are to be mitigated. Some experts have suggested that a "Persian Gulf Security and Cooperation Organization", comprising the six states of the Gulf Cooperation Council (GCC) plus Iran and Iraq, could be established in accordance with Paragraph 8 of UN Security Council (UNSC) Resolution 598. Such a common security arrangement could work toward the creation of a framework of a collective security system aimed at fighting terrorism, extremism, sectarianism, organized crime, counter-narcotics, and other common security concerns.[15] Whether or not there is a consensus within the larger US foreign policy establishment to lessen US military commitment to and presence in the Persian Gulf, the task of this final chapter is to demonstrate that a more stable security order is untenable in the absence of an effective deployment of diplomacy and dialogue involving all key players in the region. Mehran Kamrava underlines this point aptly insofar as he identifies several dynamics that have generated long-term unpredictability and lingering tensions within the region, especially the exclusion of Iran and Iraq from any conceivable regional security architecture.[16]

Prospects for Normalization

The nagging question persists—how can the colossal wall of mistrust between Iran and the United States be dismantled? Analysts have chronicled the history of failed opportunities and political blunders that defines the tragic tale of US–Iran relations since World War II.[17] Ever since the establishment of the Islamic Republic in 1979, Middle East experts have told us that the normalization of relations between the United States and Iran requires constant "thinking outside the box." The result has been counterproductive, as this way of thinking has failed to generate the most helpful way of approaching an effective policy. The normalization of relations with the United States runs counter to the interests of the core of Iran's political and military elite. Such a normalization, Mahmood Sariolghalam maintains, is likely to upset two balances: "The revolutionary-reformist duality in domestic politics in favor of the latter, and relations between the society and the state in favor of the former."[18] It is unlikely that the security elites within the military field will tolerate this.

The zero-sum nature of Iranian domestic politics also restricts consensus-building processes, while stifling creativity and pragmatic innovation in favor of groupthink. Furthermore, normalizing relations with the United States is regarded as compromising the Iranian elite's leverage in shaping economic, security, and cultural policies at home. Washington sees Tehran as a revolutionary state bent on pursuing goals contradictory to those of its political and military interests in the region. In Tehran, by contrast, fear persists that a diplomatic or economic normalization would mean that Tehran and Washington would have to share power and decision-making across the region.[19]

These fears will linger for as long as both countries continue to hold fundamental security concerns about the other's intentions. Further complicating this narrative is the fact that those who play crucial roles in shaping Iran's foreign policy toward the United States appear to be solely interested in conflict management—not conflict resolution. Sariolghalam correctly points out that without a profound shift in their perceptions of each other, Washington and Tehran are unlikely to create a workable roadmap geared toward constructing a long-term, stable, and mutually respectful relationship.[20]

In a leaked interview released by the Iran International news channel on April 25, 2021, Javad Zarif, the then Iranian foreign minister, revealed that tensions within the Islamic Republic between the security and diplomatic camps have influenced the direction of Iran's foreign policy. Decisions made in the military field have dramatically impacted and, perhaps more accurately, overruled governmental policies and advice on the diplomatic side. The nation's Revolutionary Guard have set policy beyond the reach of official governmental authorities: "The general structure of our foreign ministry," Zarif stressed, "is security-based."[21] The conservative camp, which was and continues to be wary of any engagement with the West, has incessantly undermined decisions made by Zarif on matters involving diplomacy and foreign policy.[22]

Furthermore, according to Zarif, any such normalization of relations between Iran and the West is viewed by Russia as contrary to its interests. From this standpoint, Moscow strategized to secure its influence over Iran by ensuring that the nuclear agreement had little chance of succeeding and thus put all of its weight behind creating impediments to an effective détente. To this end, Zarif noted, General Soleimani traveled to Russia to undermine the nuclear deal. Zarif also criticized Soleimani for allowing Russian warplanes to fly over Iran to bomb the rebels against the Assad regime, for transferring military equipment and personnel to Syria on the state-owned Iran Air airline without the approval of the government, and for deploying Iranian ground forces to Syria. It is clear, Zarif went on to conclude, that Iran's elected officials are not fully in charge and are unlikely to call the final shots.[23]

In effect, this is a soft or quiet coup of Iran's official governmental organ by the well-armed, enriched, and politically influential Islamic Revolutionary Guards Corps (IRGC). That the military now appears to be setting policy above and beyond the reach of civilian authority is a troubling possibility that the world is only now beginning to effectively take account of. This also goes a long way to explain why the need for reconciliation with the West is simultaneously complicated and simple.[24]

It is worth noting, as Shireen T. Hunter points out, that Iran's definition of reconciliation and the West's are utterly different. While Iran expects reciprocity in its dealings with the United States and the West, the latter insists upon concessions that Iran often finds unacceptable. Hence, a substantial improvement in US–Iran relations is improbable if not impossible in the short term.[25] That may help explain why direct negotiations between the two nations over Iran's nuclear program, however narrow in scope, may be a good place to start, given that a paradigm shift in their perceptions of each other is implausible in the short term.

Thinking Inside the Box

The time has come for Washington and Tehran to resort to familiar thinking—one within a traditional diplomatic context. Given that both countries must wrestle with stubborn domestic and foreign policy constraints, thinking outside the box has become virtually impossible. While the foreign policies of both countries during the nuclear deal negotiations were clear-cut, their domestic politics were anything but. Clearly, both Saudi and Israeli lobbyists in Washington played a crucial role in opposing the deal, albeit for different reasons. Saudis worry that a US rapprochement with Iran would most likely undermine the Saudi regime's power in the region, giving a major boost to Iran's resurgent regional powers. Israelis, however, appear to be concerned about a core challenge to their hegemonic powers in the region.

Saudi Arabia orchestrated an effective lobbying and public relations move to dismantle the nuclear deal. The Saudis' arguments apparently influenced Trump's decision to withdraw from a laboriously crafted agreement that even some of his own military leaders had supported. The Saudi lobby's attempt began well before the JCPOA was formally signed on July 14, 2015. In fact, Saudi lobbyists had worked hard behind the scenes to ensure that their concerns were incorporated into any possible deal to which Washington would agree. In 2015, according to one source, Saudi Arabia spent $11 million on the Foreign Agents Registration Act (FARA), with much of it linked to Iran.[26]

Two key pro-Israel lobby groups, the American Israel Public Affairs Committee (AIPAC) and J Street, appeared divided in their reactions to the Iran nuclear deal. AIPAC members, who advocated for stricter terms, indicated that they were "deeply concerned" that the agreement failed to meet the "five requirements" the group said were necessary for a good deal. Those included:

> unimpeded access to inspect Iran nuclear sites; a full explanation by Iran on all of its prior nuclear work; gradual sanctions relief only after Iran meets its obligations under the agreement; long-term prevention of Iran nuclear weapons; and requirements that Iran dismantle its nuclear infrastructure and give up its uranium.[27]

Subsequently, AIPAC went on to launch a new advocacy group—Citizens for a Nuclear Free Iran—to oppose the Iran nuclear deal.

However, J Street, which had lobbied in support of the deal, welcomed the agreement, noting that it appeared to have met the parameters outlined in the original framework. The members of J Street also noted that the deal has met the critical criteria around which a consensus of US and international non-proliferation experts has formed. The deal, as J Street members concluded, has verifiably prevented each of Iran's pathways to a nuclear weapon.[28] Jeremy Ben-Ami, the president of J Street, has consistently underscored the importance of an urgent return to the nuclear deal. The vast majority of Jewish Americans opposed Trump's withdrawal from the deal.[29]

Given these domestic pressures, the United States should be realistic, some experts suggest, about what it can and cannot accomplish concerning Iran. "On the immediate horizon, there are no grand bargains or sweeping negotiated deals with Tehran that can address all major US or regional partners' concerns."[30] Thus, solutions should be sought in traditional, quiet, and back-channel diplomacy. Washington should pursue tested pathways, such as private diplomatic routes, that have been proven effective in the past.

Clearly, the law of diminishing returns has set in insofar as sanctions policy is concerned. As noted in the preceding chapters, the track record of economic sanctions and economic hardship leading to regime change is notoriously unreliable. The fact remains, as Philip H. Gordon maintains, that economic sanctions and isolation have a dismal track record of producing revolution and are unlikely to convince leaders to willingly surrender power. This is the case largely because the gains of sanctions relief are unlikely to outweigh the costs of yielding power.[31] US foreign policy in the Middle East and North Africa (MENA) region and Iran's interests are much better served by pursuing a post-interventionist logic of action, informed by offshore balancing and inclusionary security policies designed to de-escalate tensions and allow the pursuit of a peaceful and stable regional context.[32]

Thinking inside the box should begin by noting that weakening Iran's traditional deterrence is likely to exacerbate its threat perception, ratcheting up pressure on the country's officials to further embolden the strategic logic behind pursuing the nuclear option in Tehran. A sustainable, long-term nuclear deal will depend upon a set of policies that reduce any incentives for Iran to pursue nuclear weapons. This will only be possible if Tehran sees the ongoing effectiveness of its conventional deterrence.[33] A total lack of regard for Iran's deterrence capability and the fact that Iran is justified in maximizing its security interests in a deeply hostile environment runs counter to finding a path to enduring success in future diplomatic endeavors.[34]

The Trump administration's refusal to consider even temporary sanctions relief in the wake of the COVID-19 pandemic made the Iranian public less receptive to his wrong-headed and populist messages expressing a desire to coerce Iran back to the international fold by forcing public discontent. The Iranians' popular response to the ongoing harsh economic sanctions fell short of what Trump thought would be the case—that is, external pressure that would either cause regime change or a return to the negotiating table. The fact remains, as John Ghazvinian, Director of the Middle East Center at the University of Pennsylvania, notes, "However much the Iranian people might resent their politicians, they resent foreign interference in their affairs even more."[35] As the United States seeks to weaken theocratic power and promote democratic interests, it must not play into the hands of the hard-liners on both sides.

Trump's reimposition of devastating sanctions on Iran fueled much uncertainty and mistrust in an already fragile relationship desperate for the restoration of diplomatic ties. Iranian hard-liners, who have consistently opposed any rapprochement with the United States, felt vindicated in their mistrust of Washington. Some would argue that these hard-liners gleefully pilloried the moderates for their trust and extension of goodwill. Having gained an unprecedented momentum to sideline pragmatic reformists even further, they pushed for terminating Iran's compliance with the JCPOA. Trump's overall unilateralist approach, in addition to looming as the biggest threat to any possible future negotiations between Iran and the United States, posed a serious challenge to the rule-based international order. Among other things, it alienated European allies and deepened the rift with its global rivals including China and Russia. For the United States to reset relations, their relationship with Iran must be the cornerstone of this new approach.

With the disruptions in US–Iran diplomatic relations caused by the Trump administration, finding a way to restore some channels of communication between the two countries has never been more important. Whether the Biden administration can return to the original nuclear deal or pursue follow-on negotiations, the need to restore traditional or back-channel diplomacy is undeniable. To deal with each other, both Tehran and Washington need to find practical diplomatic methods in the face of massive uncertainties and unbending domestic and foreign policy constraints. Creating a safety cushion of multilateral negotiations has become even more vital, as mutuality and group pressure forces states to work together even when personal or national grievances seem to dominate.

Conceiving of a future without enmity is at times difficult to visualize. Iran has taken its place in the minds of many in Washington and in the region as a deceitful actor violating agreements and encouraging instability. Considering two points can help to unwind this issue. First, it is important for the United States to take the Iranian leadership at its word when it refers to the United States as a semi-demonic force bent on Iran's destruction. The United States is correct that it has been stigmatized as a perpetually distrusted actor. It is also reasonable for Iran to feel sanctioned, isolated, and demonized by Washington and some of its Arab neighbors.

Second, reducing sanctions keeps the lights on, goods flowing, the broaching of agreements, and a general reduction of tensions. All of this presents the best path forward for a more peaceful region. Securitization is the issue that Iran must fight against most should it seek engagement with the United States. If it turns out that Iran is not a manifest threat to US interests and its allies, then a drawing down of tensions will disprove the lie that Iran is an ongoing and continuous threat.

When the United States sees this drawdown, that is the time to act, but it requires clear thinking and pragmatism—not old ideas and prejudices. If Biden is true to his word and believes in a diplomatic path, then this fresh thinking and the disposing of old enmities is as simple as passing the torch to new diplomacy and removing the stain of a 40-year-old set of outdated, self-defeating, and now-defunct grievances. While negotiations between Iran and the United States are essential to reducing hostilities between the two countries, normalization of relations appears unrealistic if not inconceivable as long as the United States continues to look for excuses to treat Iran as a pariah, and as long as the Iranian regime continues to be motivated by its anti-American ideology. Real problems can be solved if both parties equally drop the confrontational stance and conceive of a future unbounded by mutual mistrust and enmity. This requires that both states clear their heads and practically consider their options.

With regard to the restoration of JCPOA talks, the Raisi administration, which has supported returning to the nuclear talks, has insisted that the United States should make a commitment that it will never pull out of the deal. The Biden administration is not prepared to do so as long as the JCPOA remains an executive decision. Raisi has made it clear that regional issues and Iran's missile program are not the subject of negotiations, while also questioning why Iran should negotiate with the United States on a wide range of issues when Washington has failed to fulfill its obligations under the nuclear deal. US policymakers have repeatedly raised concerns about Iran's ballistic missile activities—an issue not covered by the nuclear deal. The Biden administration, however, insists that if the nuclear deal is reinstituted, the United States will have additional tools to tackle issues outside of the nuclear deal, including Iran's ballistic missiles. [36]

Although both parties deserve praise for moving toward negotiating to reduce tensions surrounding Iran's nuclear program, this is far from evidence of a new phase in US–Iran relations. It is worth noting that US–Iran relations, as one observer rightly notes, will be transactional and revolve around regional security concerns. The tempting promise of a broader rapprochement appears unlikely to find a fruitful venue in Tehran. The window of opportunity for an eclectic compromise and bargain between the countries has closed—at least for now.[37] That said, Tehran should also view negotiations with Washington as a way of reaching a regional détente with its Gulf Arab neighbors. Similarly, Iran's northern neighbors in the South Caucasus (Armenia, Azerbaijan, and Georgia), which have fairly good working relations with Tehran, appear hesitant to commit to further economic ties until US–Iran tensions subside, and until the displeasure of Washington can be somehow avoided when cooperating with Tehran.[38] The key takeaway here is that until the current impasse between Iran and the United States is resolved, Iran's leverage in the South Caucasus remains halted.

It is important, however, to realize that while the success of nuclear talks will have positive consequences for regional cooperation between Iran and its Arab neighbors, this outcome is also likely to gain much traction in light of the US military drawdown from the region. The most viable option to de-escalating regional tensions is to pursue diplomatic channels while simultaneously fostering more cooperation between Iran and its Arab neighbors. These tracks are connected and mutually reinforcing—that is, rehabilitating nuclear talks while simultaneously probing the possibilities of a regional détente.

There are increasing signs, according to Trita Parsi, that the United States is determined about shifting its focus away from the Middle East. Iraqi Prime Minister Mustafa al-Kadhimi has been facilitating secret meetings between Iranian diplomats and their Saudi counterparts since January 2021. The Biden administration has shown that it is determined to promote its agenda of reducing its role in the region by pulling out US troops from Afghanistan, cutting off aid to Saudi Arabia for its war in Yemen, and rejoining the Iran nuclear deal. To that end, Washington strongly advocates regional diplomacy for its security partners in the Middle East. That may in part explain why the Saudis' Mohammed bin Salman has supported secret talks with Iran.[39]

In his first press conference since winning the presidential election, Iranian President Ebrahim Raisi prioritized his foreign policy by noting that Iran's relations with its neighbors will top the list of his agenda. With regard to Saudi Arabia, Raise pointed out:

> We have announced that our relations with all countries of the world and interaction with everyone, especially relations with our neighbors, are important to us. Our priority will be improving our ties with our neighbors, and no major impediments stand in the way of reopening of embassies in both countries. This policy has already been announced, and I reiterate that relations and dialogue with Saudi Arabia and all countries in the region present no obstacles for the Islamic Republic.[40]

While welcoming these comments, Saudi Foreign Minister Prince Faisal bin Farhan Al Saud, retorted by saying: "Saudi Arabia will judge Iranian President-elect Ebrahim Raisi's words and government by the reality on the ground."[41]

For all regional players, one expert notes, normalization is much more cost effective and secure than an outlandish arms race. While détente with Iran is one of the only affordable ways to contribute to their own security, it is also in the US interest because it dramatically reduces the burden on Washington to secure its Arab partners.[42] Several possibilities can be envisioned to strengthen such a regional cooperation. These include—but are not limited to—signing a pact of mutual non-aggression, co-developing a strategy to counter the potential for a resurgence of the Islamic State of Iraq and Syria (ISIS), establishing a forum for dialogue to address regional flare-ups before they develop into full-blown conflicts, people-to-people contacts, and incentivizing détente between Iran and the Gulf Arab states by helping to monitor compliance.[43]

Explaining US–Iran Relations through Different Eyes

Over the past four decades, any time that tensions between Tehran and Washington have noticeably subsided, Iran's contentious stance toward regional politics has also correspondingly receded, and cooperation between GCC member states and Iran has tangibly increased. During the Rafsanjani and Khatami presidencies, the policy of détente with the West and regional countries led to cooperation between Iran and its neighbors to the south. While Rafsanjani voiced support for Prince Abdullah's peace initiative, Khatami's détente policy was intended to generate confidence among Iran's Arab neighbors in the Persian Gulf concerning his commitment to reducing regional tensions.

The US withdrawal from the JCPOA ended a mutual understanding between Tehran and Washington just as much as it undermined any possibility of achieving regional détente. The maximum pressure campaign from Washington failed to coerce Iran into directions favored by the United States and became an unwinnable proposition, while fueling further mistrust between the two nations. The resultant hostility between Iran and the United States spread to other parts of the region. For those experts who have raised the question of whether any US administration can simultaneously reach out to the Iranians and mitigate the anxieties of US allies,[44] the answer is that in the past, US–Iran negotiations have positively correlated with regional stability.

These past instances offer a precedent and a potential path forward for détente and goodwill, both regionally and between Iran and the United States. It is also important to understand that the history of hostility between Iran and the US has not been completely unceasing, as both countries have closely cooperated on a number of overlapping interests, notwithstanding festering tensions on issues of regional political divergence. Consider, for example, the cooperation on releasing US hostages from Lebanon, working toward the formation of a new government in Afghanistan after the 2001 US invasion of that country in order to defeat the Taliban, coordinating their actions in Iraq in the post-Saddam era to prevent the country's partition, and working in tandem in Syria on counterterrorism projects in order to contain and defeat Al-Qaeda and ISIS.

Thus, the question persists: How can we properly contextualize US–Iran relations? Clearly, no important question of international relations today, regionally and globally, can be fully answered using only one theoretical perspective. Let's unpack this. From a realist point of view, the Iranian interest in becoming a nuclear power is clearly defensible if not preferable (a Waltzian perspective).[45] Simple neorealism, however, with its emphasis on military power, power-balancing alliances, and arms races, fails to sufficiently account for the moves toward negotiation and deal-making between the United States and Iran.

By focusing solely on foreign policy, power differentials, and the security dilemma regionally and globally, realists and neorealists tend to underestimate the relevance of domestic factors and dynamics at play. As noted in the previous chapters, the Trump administration's persistence in labeling Iran's elite as monolithic reinforced a self-fulfilling prophecy that drove Iranian politics in a more extreme direction. The relentless and punitive US sanctions policy deepened Iran's internal political divide, while also prompting a broad consensus among Iran's elites that the only way to protect the country's national security interests was to protect the regime. These new dynamics allowed the IRGC to present themselves as the bulwark of Iranian nationalism.[46]

It is worth noting that realism accurately explains Iran's foreign policy conduct in some cases. Iran has previously used its observer status in the Shanghai Cooperation Organization (SCO) to counterbalance the threats of US sanctions. With Iran becoming a full member of the SCO (on September 17, 2021), the dominant thinking among Iranian officials continues to revolve around the narrative that membership in the SCO will elevate the country's maneuverability vis-à-vis the West and will increase its resistance to unilateral US sanctions, as well as its ability to play a constructive role in conflict resolution in Central Asia and the Caucasus region.

Another example that merits particular attention is the loss of control over Nakhchivan in the aftermath of the Azerbaijan–Armenia war (2020). This transit route connecting Iran to the Republic of Azerbaijan now provides a direct corridor connecting Turkey to the Republic of Azerbaijan. This development will significantly reduce Tehran's bargaining leverage vis-à-vis other regional players—a reality that will most likely compel Iran to seriously consider another alternative such as entering the Eurasia Economic Union (EAEU), which consists of Armenia, Belarus, Kazakhstan, Kyrgyzstan, and Russia.[47] As an international economic union and free trade zone comprising countries in central and northern Asia and Eastern Europe, the EAEU is home to nearly 200 million people with $5 trillion in combined GDP.[48] Analysts warn that Iran's bid to join the EAEU will only facilitate Russian access to the Iranian market and will increase Russia's influence over Iran.[49]

CONCLUSION

As far as liberal and neoliberal theoretical assumptions about achieving international cooperation are concerned, the successful conclusion of the 2015 Iran nuclear deal gave a strong boost to their analytical posture. The nuclear deal underscored the importance of diplomacy in mitigating the ongoing tensions between Iran and the United States. This desirable narrative notwithstanding, liberal institutionalists would have preferred a move toward achieving a nuclear-free zone in the Middle East.[50] While liberal international theory attempts to disentangle domestic political processes from the foreign policy of states, it also fails to fully account for the level of distrust and biased judgment active during the Trump and early Biden administrations.

Constructivists, who have been successful in accounting for the nexus between domestic politics and foreign policies, have nevertheless failed to take account of the situations in which pragmatism has prevailed over ideology, bias, and brute force—both kinetic and sanctions-based. Iran's actions in multilateral institutions can be viewed from this perspective. Iran's conduct in the United Nations by lobbying Russia, China, and non-permanent members is emblematic of its ideational drive. On several occasions, Russia and China have used their veto powers, countervailing US efforts to take actions against Iran. In February 2018, Russia vetoed unilateral US actions against Iran when the UNSC castigated Tehran for sending weapons to Yemen's Houthi group. China, Russia, and some EU member states have advocated an easing of sanctions against Iran and North Korea. China and Russia have also questioned the extension of Iran's arms embargo in the aftermath of the 2015 Iran nuclear deal.

The English School, also known as International Society School, offers us a useful, holistic, and integrated approach that focuses on international history, structures, institutions, values, and ideas. While International Society theorists acknowledge that we live in an anarchical society, they argue that it is still based on rules, norms, and institutions. This approach argues that ideas, rather than just material capabilities, shape the direction of international relations. The English School has greater synthetic potential and is committed to ethical and identity-based factors.

Although the English School constitutes a valuable tool to challenge all-too-familiar approaches to the study of international relations (namely realism and liberalism), it fails to fully explain the circumstances under which the Islamic Republic's foreign policy conduct assumes greater geostrategic salience. Additionally, both liberalism and the English School tend to argue that not all states are presently part of the liberal order or the international society. Those not obligated or constrained by mutual ties of democracy, economic interdependence, and international institutions have fragile basis for cooperation. Where democratic linkages are still frail, the security dilemma may persist (perhaps with Iran and North Korea). Yet even with such isolated states, more stable relationships may be developed over time, perhaps with some degree of difficulty, as in the early days of US–China relations.[51]

Demystifying the complexity of Iran's foreign policy conduct is a new middle-level theory (as opposed to the mainstream, grand theories of international relations) called strategic hedging. This approach suggests that Tehran has engaged in a strategy based on nuclear hedging. Three elements, according to this strategy, have been part of Iran's nuclear stance. First, Tehran's failure in the past to fully comply with international obligations. Second, the nature and the speed with which it has made technical advances, and third, its diplomatic efforts to delay actions and blur the issues at stake. This implies that Iran has possessed many or all of technologies, expertise, resources, and other capabilities necessary for the development of nuclear weapons, without attempting full operational weaponization. "Having invested so much in nuclear nationalism," Wyn Bowen and Matthew Moran point out, "the regime cannot afford to be seen to capitulate to international pressure."[52]

This approach has allowed Tehran to accommodate restraint with an attempt to forge a domestic consensus on its nuclear program. Needless to say, international exposure of Iran's undeclared nuclear activities has had a massive impact on the direction of its nuclear program, placing considerable constraints on its nuclear advancement. Any solution to the Iranian nuclear challenge, Bowen and Moran maintain, must be predicated upon realistic goals. The international community should focus on restricting Iranian nuclear progress rather than rollback, with an eye toward constraining hedging to a low level of latency.[53]

Securitization, adopted from the Copenhagen School, represents a new and important insight into US–Iran relations, helping us to better grasp the complexities involved. To the extent that the securitization school problematizes and challenges assumptions underlying existing literature, it certainly contributes to a better contextualization and understanding of US–Iran relations. Following the US withdrawal from the JCPOA, Iran has been frequently and effectively securitized as a pariah and a deceitful actor. Iran is widely regarded as a security threat to the United States and its allies whether a real threat exists or not. Securitization school theorists have clearly differentiated security from that which is merely political.[54] President Trump repeatedly mentioned security threats posed by Iran in his speeches, seeking to transform a merely complex negotiating process into an existential security threat.

Undeniably, the Trump administration's maximum pressure strategy forced the so-called Iranian moderates to act defensively, providing further impetus to the resurgence of hard-liners and the securocrats linked to the paramilitary IRGC who advocate for a confrontational response of maximum resistance.[55] It should be noted, however, that the IRGC is also known to have engaged in transactional dealings with the United States in Iraq and Afghanistan, likely with the supreme leader's approval.[56] At the same time, Iran's Islamic populism has sustained itself politically in the face of external threat emanating largely from the ongoing US sanction policies and the threat of military intervention.[57] Finally, as to which perspective offers the best approach or answer to the complexities and contradictions that Iran's foreign policy entails, and which theoretical framework has stood the test of time, it must be noted that, on balance, a combination of these theories seems the most useful tool to analyze US–Iran relations. What best explains the intricacies of US–Iran relations continues to be the subject of considerable debate among scholars and policymakers and will be for many years to come.

The Path Forward

Ending a longstanding and turbulent history of US–Iran relations since the 1979 Revolution requires that Washington and Tehran recognize that it is in their long-term interests to marginalize skeptics by marching forward with the restoration of the nuclear deal. Lack of direct diplomatic communications for most of the past four decades has trapped Iran and the United States between past and present, presenting a major barrier to dismantling the wall of distrust between the two countries. Engagement and the weakening of the impression of Iran as a securitized threat is the way forward. A cursory glance at US–Iran relations over the past forty years demonstrates that the political management of tensions through diplomacy has proven to be the only viable path and tested bridge.

On the Iran nuclear portfolio, the core question is why Iranians regard the nuclear program as imperative to their future economic and national security, rather than how the United States or the European Union can stop it. Although we should view the Biden administration's return to the diplomatic path as a great opportunity to secure the nuclear deal, this move need not be equated with appeasement, thus antagonizing Iran's Arab neighbors that suspect that such negotiations could result in propping up Tehran's hegemonic ambitions and plans in the region. To mitigate such suspicion, experts suggest that Washington could propose a broader regional security dialogue in parallel with prospective nuclear talks with Iran.[58] It remains unclear, however, what tangible security reassurances Washington can offer to its partners in the Middle East.

Former Navy Admiral and White House Director for Defense Policy Joe Sestak summarizes a prudent pathway toward reaching an agreement on Iran's nuclear program, while also warning about the grave repercussions of a military confrontation: "Diplomacy fixed this problem before, and realistic diplomacy can do it again, so we can focus on America's urgent business, beginning in the Western Pacific."[59] If future opportunities to engage Iran are missed, however, the outcome could be costly and rife with unintended consequences, including the emergence of a new cold war era between Washington and Tehran in the coming years.

There is plenty of room to navigate traditional routes while still thinking inside the box. A new opportunity to build trust between the two countries, according to some experts, may only present itself when "there are leaders on both sides who are committed to empathizing with the security concerns of the other."[60] This means that both sides should also take their competing and irreconcilable interests into account. As discussed in the previous chapters, the Iranian "look to the East" strategy aimed at strengthening Iran's strategic cooperation with Russia and China is emblematic of a deepening mistrust toward the United States. Similarly, Washington's attempt to keep sanctions on Iran is likely to fuel further skepticism regarding the possible improvement of relations with Iran.

Criticizing the Biden administration's withdrawal policy toward the Middle East's messy politics, Kim Ghattas, a nonresident senior fellow at the Carnegie Endowment for International Peace, points out that under sanctions and disconnected from much of the global economy, Iran and Syria are likely to see Beijing as a mainstay of loans and investments, a market for their petroleum, and more. Thus, Iran and Syria refrain from criticizing Beijing on issues related to Hong Kong, Xinjiang, and Taiwan, while seeing China as a counterforce to the United States. But Iran and Syria, like many others, exaggerate China's appetite or capacity for an encounter with the United States.[61]

These ongoing doubts and this cynicism notwithstanding, diplomacy is till the cornerstone of the foreign policy attempt to mitigate this stalemate in the Middle East. Diplomacy may not settle all contentious issues between the two countries, but it bears mentioning that even imperfect deals lead to conflict less often. Without a negotiated compromise, as some experts have correctly warned, the current tensions between Tehran and Washington could easily escalate into a catastrophic war of a magnitude unseen in the region.[62]

Over time, by engaging directly with Iran and reducing tensions through negotiations, one might hope that Washington can help rejuvenate the aspirations of Iranians—not by imposing punitive sanctions that indiscriminately punish all Iranians, but rather by ensuring that US diplomacy is aimed at broadening the space for Iranian people themselves to protect and promote their rights.

Iran's Reactions to the Russian Invasion of Ukraine

The Raisi administration's reaction to the Russian invasion of Ukraine has been very calculated and noticeably cautious, avoiding criticism of Russia while also calling for a ceasefire and immediate negotiations for the political resolution of this crisis. Iranian Foreign Minister Hossein Amir-Abdollahian, for example, has referred to the Russian invasion of Ukraine without condemning it or even describing it as an unprovoked aggression, by noting that "The Ukraine crisis is rooted in NATO provocations."[63] Iran's abstention during the UN General Assembly vote condemning Russia on March 2, 2022, illustrated Tehran's hesitancy to support Moscow's challenge to Ukraine's territorial integrity. The reasons for Iran's apparent cautious response to the invasion of Ukraine can be traced to Tehran's relations with Moscow over the past few decades, especially Tehran's deteriorating relations with the Washington under the Trump administration.

It is worth mentioning that, although Iran has refrained from denouncing Russia's foreign aggression, it has never recognized the territories forcibly controlled by Moscow. Consider, for example, the annexation of Crimea to Russia, which was never recognized by Iran. Even today, Tehran refuses to openly support Russian military campaigns for fear that such an act may in the future be used against Iran itself in some of its border provinces where there are separatist sentiments.[64]

Meanwhile, the ongoing sanctioning of Russia may provide the impetus for Moscow and Tehran to pursue more cooperation on seeking an alternative to the dollar as a way of bypassing sanctions.[65] This crisis, however, could improve Iran's bargaining position in the ongoing nuclear talks, as Washington and its Western allies might be looking for ways to facilitate Iran's export of its oil and gas to global markets. Arguably, fears of oil supply disruptions could prompt further progress toward signing an additional nuclear accord with Iran. The overlapping interests of Iran and the United State, according to one view, might appear much stronger than before.[66]

Although there is a case to be made that the Ukraine war could open up opportunities for Iran to export natural gas to Europe, it should be noted that Iran's gas export capacity, the world's second-largest, is almost zero due to high domestic consumption. This is due to the lack of investment and the lack of advanced technology and knowledge to produce liquefied natural gas (LNG), convert gas to liquefied gas, and strengthen the crude oil conversion industry.

For Iran to be able to increase its export capacity, foreign investment in its energy industry will take several years and is unlikely to help supply European gas at this time.[67]

Furthermore, Russia has tried to link the final approval of the revived Iran nuclear deal to lifting sanctions on its economic cooperation with Iran.[68] With growing sanctions on its hydrocarbon industry, Moscow fears that Iran's oil entry into global energy markets will offset the absence of its oil exports. Although many in Iran's foreign ministry have spoken in favor of de-linking these issues within the context of JCPOA negotiations, the Raisi administration has prioritized good relations with Russia over returning to normal economic ties with the West. This is consistent with Iran's overall foreign policy dubbed "look to the East." The implications of such a foreign policy approach for Iran, in terms of the complications that it could present to the normalization of ties with the West more generally and the United States in particular, deserve careful attention.

NOTES

1. INTRODUCTION: CHECKERED US–IRAN RELATIONS

1. Barbara Slavin, "34 Years of Getting to No With Iran," *Politico Magazine*, November 19, 2013, available at <https://www.politico.com/magazine/story/2013/11/a-failure-to-communicate-100052>. Accessed on October 15, 2019.

2. Seyed Hossein Mousavian with Shahir ShahidSaless, *Iran and the United States: An Insider's View on the Failed Past and the Road to Peace*, New York: Bloomsbury, 2017, p. 265.

3. Daniel Benjamin and Steven Simon, "America's Great Satan: The 40-Year Obsession With Iran," *Foreign Affairs*, Vol. 98, No. 6, November/December 2019, pp. 56–66; see especially, p. 63.

4. Shireen T. Hunter, "Is Iran at Risk of Becoming a Chinese Colony?" *Lobelog*, September 12, 2019, available at <https://lobelog.com/is-iran-at-risk-of-becoming-a-chinese-colony/>. Accessed on October 1, 2019.

5. Abbas Amanat, *Iran: A Modern History*, New Haven, CT: Yale University Press, 2017, p. 367.

6. Ibid., pp. 399 and 462.

7. Stephen Kinzer, *All the Shah's Men: American Coup and the Roots of Middle East Terror*, Hoboken, New Jersey: John Wiley & Sons, 2003.

8. Ervand Abrahamian, *A History of Modern Iran: Revised and Updated*, New York: Cambridge University Press, 2018, p. 203.

9. Ibid.

10. Suzanne Maloney, "America and Iran: From Containment to Coexistence," *Brookings*, August 15, 2001, available <https://www.brookings.edu/research/america-and-iran-from-containment-to-coexistence/>. Accessed on January 5, 2021.

11. Mohsen M. Milani, "Tehran's Take: Understanding Iran's US Policy," *Foreign Affairs*, Vol. 88, No. 4, July/August 2009, pp. 46–62.

12. *CATO Institute*, "US-Iran Policy," December 4, 2019, available at <https://www.cato.org/publications/publications/us-iran-policy>. Accessed on January 5, 2021.

13. Ervand Abrahamian, op. cit., pp. 203–04.

14. Nikki R. Keddie, *Modern Iran: Roots and Results of Revolution*, New Haven, CT: Yale University Press, 2003, p. 199.

15. Gary Sick, "The Carter Administration," in Robin Wright, ed., *The Iran Primer: Power, Politics, and US Policy*, Washington, DC: United States Institute of Peace Press, 2010, pp. 129–32.

16. Nikki R. Keddie, op. cit., p. 258.

17. Charles Hauss, *Comparative Politics: Domestic Responses to Global Challenges*, Fifth Edition, Belmont, CA: Thomson Wadsworth, 2006, p. 395.

18. Rouhollah Ramazani, *Revolutionary Iran: Challenge and Response in the Middle East*, Baltimore: The Johns Hopkins University Press, 1986, p. 126.

19. Melvin Friedlander, *Conviction and Credence: U.S. Policymaking in the Middle East*, Boulder, CO: Lynne Rienner Publishers, 1991, p. 79.

20. John L. Esposito, *The Islamic Threat: Myth or Reality?* Third Edition, New York: Oxford University Press, 1999, p. 124.

21. Geoffrey Kemp, "The Reagan Administration," in Robin Wright, ed., *The Iran Primer: Power, Politics, and US Policy*, Washington, DC: United States Institute of Peace Press, 2010, pp. 133–35.

22. Michael Axworthy, *Iran: What Everyone Needs to Know*, New York: Oxford University Press, 2017, p. 106

23. Ali M. Ansari, *Confronting Iran: The Failure of American Foreign Policy and the Next Great Conflict in the Middle East*, New York: Basic Books, 2006, p. 144.

24. David E. Sanger, "US Ending a Few of the Sanctions Imposed on Iran," *The New York Times*, March 18, 2000, available at <https://www.nytimes.com/2000/03/18/world/us-ending-a-few-of-the-sanctions-imposed-on-iran.html>. Accessed on December 27, 2020.

25. Shahram Chubin, *Iran's Nuclear Ambitions*, Washington, DC: Carnegie Endowment for International Peace, 2006.

26. Kayhan Barzegar and Abdolrasol Divsallar, "Political Rationality in Iranian Foreign Policy," *The Washington Quarterly*, Vol. 40, No. 1, Spring 2017, pp. 39–53; see p. 40.

27. William Joseph Burns, *The Back Channel: A Memoir of American Diplomacy and the Case for Its Renewal*, New York: Random House, 2019, p. 364.

28. Ibid., p. 361.

29. Kian Tajbakhsh, "Who Wants What from Iran Now? The Post-Nuclear Deal U.S. Policy Debate," *The Washington Quarterly*, Vol. 41, No. 3, Fall 2018, pp. 41–61; see p. 50.

30. Negar Mortazavi, "US Sanctions on Iran are 'Limiting Import of Life-Saving Medicine,'" *Independent*, October 29, 2019, available at <https://www.independent.co.uk/news/world/americas/iran-sanctions-us-medicine-imports-hospital-disease-a9178246.html>. Accessed on October 30, 2019.

31. Vali Nasr, "Trump's 'Maximum-Pressure' Strategy is Destined to Fail," *The Atlantic*, October 3, 2019, available at <https://www.theatlantic.com/international/archive/2018/10/trump-iran-north-korea-nuclear-sanctions/572080/>. Accessed on October 16, 2019.

32. Kian Tajbakhsh, op. cit., p. 54.

33. Nasser Karimi and Jon Gambrell, "Iran Shoots Down US Surveillance Drone, Heightening Tensions," *Associated Press*, June 20, 2019, available at <https://apnews.com/article/e4316eb989d5499c9828350de8524963>. Accessed on December 27, 2020.

34. David E. Sanger, "Iran Sanctions Led to Protests, but Not U.S. Goals," *The New York Times*, December 3, 2019, p. 6.

35. Kenneth N. Waltz, *Theory of International Politics*, New York: McGraw Hill Higher Education, 1979.

36. Fareed *Zakaria, From Wealth to Power: The Unusual Origins of America's World Role*, Princeton, New Jersey: Princeton University Press, 1999.

37. Mahdi Mohammad Nia, "Understanding Iran's Foreign Policy: An Application of Holistic Constructivism," *World Affairs*, Vol. 15, No. 2, Summer 2011, pp. 196–138.

38. Rouhollah K. Ramazani, "Ideology and Pragmatism in Iran's Foreign Policy, *Middle East Journal*, Vol. 58, No. 4, Autumn 2004, pp. 549–59; see especially p. 559.

39. Robert O. Keohane, *After Hegemony: Cooperation and Discord in the World Political Economy*, Princeton, New Jersey: Princeton University Press, 1984.

40. Barry Buzan, Ole Wæver, and Jaap de Wilde, *Security: A New Framework for Analysis*, Boulder, CO: Lynne Rienner Publishers, 1998; see also Lene Hansen, "Reconstructing desecuritization: The normative-political in the Copenhagen School and directions for how to apply it," *Review of International Studies* Vol. 38, 2012, pp. 525–46.

41. Martin Beck, "An International Relations Perspective on the Iran Nuclear Deal," *E-International Relations*, August 8, 2018, pp. 1–5; see especially pp. 2–3; available at <https://www.e-ir.info/pdf/75169. Accessed on January 12, 2021.

42. Rusty Treviño, "Is Iran an Offensive Realist or a Defensive Realist? A Theoretical Reflection on Iranian Motives for Creating Instability," *Journal of Strategic Security*, Vol. 6, No. 3, Fall 2013, pp. 382–92.

43. Liam Hunt, "The Anchor of the System: The Iran Deal and the Decline of Realism in US Foreign Policy," *International Journal*, Vol. 72, No. 3, August 24, 2017, pp. 318–37; see especially p. 336.

44. Tim Dunne, "The English School," in Tim Dunne, Milja Kurki, and Steve Smith, *International Relations Theories: Discipline and Diversity*, Fifth Edition, New York: Oxford University Press, 2021, pp. 108–128; see also Christian Reus-Smit and Tim Dunne, *The Globalization of International Society*, Oxford: Oxford University Press, 2016.

45. Djavad Salehi-Isfahani, "Iran's Middle Class and the Nuclear Deal," *Brookings*, April 8, 2021, available at <https://www.brookings.edu/blog/future-development/

2021/04/08/irans-middle-class-and-the-nuclear-deal/>. Accessed on April 9, 2021.

46. Tim Dunne, "The English School," p. 112.

47. Mahmood Monshipouri and Manochehr Dorraj, "The Resilience of Populism in Iranian Politics: A Closer Look at the Nexus between Internal and External Factors," *Middle East Journal*, Vol. 75, No. 2, Summer 2021, pp. 201–20.

48. David P. Forsythe, *Advanced Introduction to the Politics of International Human Rights*, Cheltenham, UK: Edward Elgar Publishing, 2021, p. 52.

49. Shahram Akbarzadeh, "Iran Under a Conservative President Still Needs the JCPOA," *Al Jazeera*, June 22, 2021, available at <https://www.aljazeera.com/opinions/2021/6/22/iran-under-a-conservative-president-still-needs-the-jcpoa>. Accessed on August 19, 2021.

2. REVOLUTION AND ITS AFTERMATH: THE STRUGGLE FOR POWER

1. Mehran Kamrava, *The Modern Middle East: A Political History Since the First World War*, Third Edition, Berkeley, CA: University of California Press, 2013, pp. 140–41.

2. William L. Cleveland and Martin Bunton, *A History of the Modern Middle East*, Sixth Edition, New York: Routledge, 2018, p. 355.

3. Ali Ansari and Kasra Aarabi, "Ideology and Iran's Revolution: How 1979 Changed the World," Tony Blair Institute for Global Change, February 11, 2019, available at <https://institute.global/policy/ideology-and-irans-revolution-how-1979-changed-wor>. Accessed on December 21, 2020.

4. Ibid.

5. Mehrzad Boroujerdi, "Iran," in Ellen Lust, ed., *The Middle East*, Fourteenth Edition, Los Angeles: Sage, 2017, pp. 455–86; see p. 459.

6. Mahmood Monshipouri, *Middle East Politics: Changing Dynamics*, New York: Routledge, 2019, p. 270.

7. Ibid.

8. Mehran Kamrava, *The Modern Middle East: A Political History Since the First World War*, Berkeley, CA: University of California Press, 2013, p. 145.

9. Mohsen M. Milani, *The Making of Iran's Islamic Revolution: From Monarchy to Islamic Republic*, Boulder, CO: Westview Press, 1988, p. 127.

10. Mahmood Monshipouri, op. cit., p. 270.

11. For an illustrative book on this subject, see Mehran Kamrava, *Troubled Waters: Insecurity in the Persian Gulf*, Ithaca, NY: Cornell University Press, 2018, pp. 1–9.

12. Abbas Amanat, *Iran: A Modern History*, New Haven, CT: Yale University Press, 2017, pp. 447–48.

13. Mark Gasiorowski, "The Islamic Republic of Iran," in Mark Gasiorowski and Sean L. Yom, eds., *The Government and Politics of the Middle East and North Africa*, Eighth Edition, Boulder, CO: Westview Press, 2017, pp. 271–306; see especially p. 273.

14. Stephen Kinzer, *Overthrow: America's Century of Regime Change from Hawaii to Iraq*, New York: Times Books, 2006, p. 118.

15. Ibid., p. 201

16. James A. Bill, *The Eagle and the Lion: The Tragedy of American-Iranian Relations*, New Haven, CT, Yale University Press, 1988, p. 172.

17. Mahmood Monshipouri, *Islamism, Secularism, and Human Rights in the Middle East*, Boulder, CO: Lynne Rienner Publishers, 1998, p. 172.

18. Ibid.

19. Mehrzad Boroujerdi, *Iranian Intellectuals and the West: The Tormented Triumph of Nativism*, Syracuse, NY: Syracuse University Press, 1996, p. 31.

20. Mahmood Monshipouri, *Middle East Politics: Changing Dynamics*, New York: Routledge, 2019, pp. 269–71.

21. Manochehr Dorraj, *From Zarathustra to Khomeini: Populism and Dissent in Iran*, Boulder, CO: Lynne Rienner Publishers, 1990, p. 162.

22. Manochehr Dorraj, "Iranian Populism: Its Vicissitudes and Political Impact," in Dwayne Woods and Barbara Wejnert, eds., *Many Faces of Populism: Current Perspectives*, UK: Emerald Group, 2014, pp. 127–42.

23. For more on that, see Mahmood Monshipouri, ed., *Inside the Islamic Republic: Social Change in Post-Khomeini Iran*, New York: Oxford University Press, 2016.

24. Kazem Alamdari, "The Power Structure of the Islamic Republic of Iran: Transition from Populism to Clientelism, and Militarization of the Government," *Third World Quarterly*, Vol. 26, Issue 8, January 2005, pp. 1285–1301; see especially p. 1286.

25. Evaleila Pesaran, *Iran's Struggle for Economic Independence: Reform and Counter-reform in the Post-revolutionary Era*, New York: Routledge, 2011, pp. 63–96; see p. 95.

26. Sanam Vakil, "Rafsanjani, Ali Akbar Hashemi," in Mehran Kamrava and Manochehr Dorraj, eds., *Iran Today: An Encyclopedia of Life in the Islamic Republic*, Vol. II, Westport, CT: Greenwood Press, 2008, pp. 417–22; see p. 420.

27. Mahmood Monshipouri, "Iran's Search for the New Pragmatism," *Middle East Policy*, Vol. VI, No. 2, October 1998, pp. 95–112; see especially pp. 105–06.

28. Ibid., p. 105.

29. Donette Murray, *US Foreign Policy and Iran: American-Iranian Relations Since the Islamic Revolution*, Oxon, UK: Routledge, 2010, pp. 23–24; see also pp. 147–48.

30. Sasan Fayazmanesh, *The United States and Iran: Sanctions, Wars and the Policy of Dual Containment*, New York: Routledge, 2008, p. 229.

31. Ibid., pp. 230–31.

32. Ervand Abrahamian, "The Making of the Modern Iranian State," in Mark Kesselman Joel Krieger, and William A. Joseph, eds., *Introduction to Comparative Politics*, Third Edition, New York: Houghton Mifflin Company, 2004, pp. 571–618.

33. Mahmood Monshipouri, *Islamism, Secularism, and Human Rights in the Middle East*, Boulder, CO: Lynne Rienner Publishers, 1998.

34. Haleh Esfandiari, "The Politics of the 'Women's Question' in the Islamic Republic, 1979–1999," in John L. Esposito and R. K. Ramazani, eds., *Iran at the Crossroads*, New York: Palgrave, 2001, pp. 75–92.

35. Jane Mary Howard, *Inside Iran: Women's Lives*, Washington, DC: Mage Publishers, 2002.

36. Said Amir Arjomand, *After Khomeini: Iran under His Successors*, New York: Oxford University Press, 2009, p. 93.

37. David Menashri, *Post-Revolutionary Politics in Iran: Religion, Society, and Power*, London: Frank Cass Publishers, 2001.

38. Mahmood Monshipouri, "The Politics of Culture and Human Rights in Iran: Globalizing and Localizing Dynamics," in Mahmood Monshipouri, Neil Englehart, Andrew J. Nathan, and Kavita Philip, eds., *Constructing Human Rights in the Age of Globalization*, Armonk, NY: M. E. Sharpe, 2003, pp. 113–44.

39. Mehran Kamrava, "Iran and Its Persian Gulf Neighbors," in Thomas Juneau and Sam Razavi, eds., *Iranian Foreign Policy Since 2001: Alone in the World*, New York: Routledge, 2013, pp. 104–19.

40. Jack Straw, *The English Job: Understanding Iran and Why It Disturbs Britain*, London: Biteback Publishing, 2019, pp. 238–47.

41. Mahmood Monshipouri and Manochehr Dorraj, "The Resilience of Populism in Iranian Politics: A Closer Look at the Nexus between Internal and External Factors," *Middle East Journal*, Vol. 75, No. 2, Summer 2021, pp. 201–21; see especially p. 220.

42. Donette Murray, op. cit., pp. 28–9.

43. Mehran Kamrava, "Iran and Its Persian Gulf Neighbors," op. cit., p. 59.

44. Ibid., p. 60.

45. Saïd Amir Arjomand, *After Khomeini: Iran Under His Successors*, New York: Oxford University Press, 2009.

46. Abbas Milani, "Pious Populist," *Boston Review*, November–December 2007, pp. 7–14.

47. This section is based on Mahmood Monshipouri and Ali Assareh, "The Islamic Republic and the 'Green Movement': Coming Full Circle," *Middle East Policy*, Vol. XVI, No. 4, Winter 2009, pp. 27–46.

48. Nikki R. Keddie, "Secularism and Its Discontents," *Daedalus*, Vol. 132, No. 3, Summer 2003, pp. 14–30; see especially p. 25.

49. Christian Caryl, "The Great Backlash: 1979," *Foreign Policy*, No. 173, July/August 2009, pp. 50–56; see especially p. 52. Here Caryl refers to movements by Ayatollah Khomeini, Margaret Thatcher, Pope John Paul II, and Deng Xiaoping as part of the counterrevolutionaries of 1979, p. 56.

50. Mathew Krain, *Repression and Accommodation in Post-Revolutionary States*, New York: St. Martin's Press, 2000.

51. For an illuminating account of the history of uprisings in Iran see Stephen Zunes, "Iran's History of Civil Insurrections," *The Huffington Post*, August, 4, 2009, available at <http://www.huffingtonpost.com/stephen-zunes/irans-history-of-civil-in_b_217998.html>. Last accessed on August 6, 2009.

52. Michael Dodson and Manochehr Dorraj, "Populism and Foreign Policy in Venezuela and Iran," *The Whitehead Journal of Diplomacy and International Relations*, Winter/Spring 2008, pp. 71–87; see especially pp. 82–3.

53. Fareed Zakaria, "On Iran, Do Nothing. Yet," *Newsweek*, August 3, 2009, p. 26.

54. Roger Cohen, "Iran: The Tragedy and the Future," *The New York Review of Books*, Vol. LVI, No. 13, August 13, 2009, pp. 7–10; see especially p. 8.

55. Ibid., p. 8.

56. *United Nations Security Council*, "Security Council Toughens Sanctions Against Iran, Adds Arms Embargo, with Unanimous Adoption of Resolution 1747 (2007)," March 24, 2007, available at <https://www.un.org/press/en/2007/sc8980.doc.htm>. Accessed January 3, 2021.

57. Kaveh Ehsani and Chris Toensing, "Neo-Conservatives, Hardline Clerics and the Bomb," *Middle East Report*, No. 233, Vol. 34, No. 4, Winter 2004:10–15; see especially p. 10

58. Nader Entessar, "Iran's Nuclear Program and Foreign Policy," in Thomas Juneau and Sam Razavi, eds., *Iranian Foreign Policy Since 2001: Alone in the World*, New York: Routledge, 2013, pp. 70–86; see especially p. 75; see also Anthony H. Cordesman, *Iran's Developing Military Capabilities*, Washington, DC: Center for Strategic and International Studies, 2006.

59. Sasan Fayazmanesh, *The United States and Iran: Sanctions, Wars, and the Policy of Dual Containment*, New York: Routledge, 2008, pp. 205–28; see especially p. 228.

60. Ali M. Ansari, *Confronting Iran: The Failure of American Foreign Policy and the Next Great Crisis in the Middle East*, New York: Basic Books, 2006.

61. Shahram Chubin *Iran's Nuclear Ambitions*, Washington, DC: Carnegie Endowment for International Peace, 2006.

62. Stephen Kinzer, "Diplomacy Is the Best Option for American-Iranian Relations," in Julia Bauder, ed., *Is Iran a Threat to Global Security*, New York: Greenhaven Press, 2006, pp. 46–57.

63. Sasan Fayazmanesh *Containing Iran: Obama's Policy of Tough Diplomacy*, Cambridge, UK: Cambridge Scholarly Publishing, 2013.

64. Nader Entessar, "Permanent War, Elusive Peace: The Evaluation of America's Compellence Policy Towards Iran," *Journal of South Asian and Middle Eastern Studies*, Vol. 44, No. 31, Spring 2021, pp. 95–111; see especially p. 104.

65. Ibid., p. 104.

66. Ibid., p. 107.

67. This section is based on Mahmood Monshipouri and Shirin Jafarinasab Kermani, "US–Iran Relations: Competing and Overlapping Interests in a Turbulent Region," *The Maghreb Review*, Vol. 42, No. 2, 2007, pp. 164–77.

68. Mahmood Monshipouri, "Rouhani's Election: Promise of Change or More of the Same?" *Insight Turkey*, Vol. 15, No. 3, Summer 2013, pp. 45–50.

69. Mahmood Monshipouri and Manochehr Dorraj, "Iran's Foreign Policy: A Shifting Strategic Landscape," *Middle East Policy*, Vol. XX, No. 4, Winter 2013, pp. 133–47.

70. Robert A. Pape, "Why Economic Sanctions Still Do Not Work," *International Security*, Vol. 22, No. 2, Fall 1997, pp. 90–136.

71. Matthew Kroenig, *A Time to Attack: The Looming Iranian Nuclear Threat*, New York: St. Martin's Press, 2014.

72. Thomas R. Mattair, *Global Security Watch—Iran: A Reference Handbook*, Westport, CT: Praeger, 2008.

73. Mohammad Hossein Hafezian, "Relations with the Arab World," in Mehran Kamrava and Manochehr Dorraj, eds., *Iran Today: An Encyclopedia of Life in the Islamic Republic*, Vol. II, Westport, CT: Greenwood Press, 2008, pp. 435–41.

74. Mohsen Milani, "Is US-Iran Détente Possible," *Current History*, Vol. 12, Issue 758, December 2013, pp. 345–48; see especially pp. 334–38.

75. Nader Entessar, "Iran's Nuclear Program and Foreign Policy," in Thomas Juneau and Sam Razavi, eds., *Iranian Foreign Policy Since 2001: Alone in the World*, New York: Routledge, 2013, pp. 70–86; see especially p. 83.

76. Trita Parsi, "Why Did Iran Diplomacy Work this Time Around?" *Insight Turkey*, Vol. 16, No. 3, Summer 2014, pp. 47–54; see especially p. 54.

77. Mahmood Monshipouri and Manochehr Dorraj, "The Resilience of Populism in Iranian Politics: A Closer Look at the Nexus between Internal and External Factors," *Middle East Journal*, Vol. 75, No. 2, Summer 2021, pp. 201–20; see p. 218.

78. Mohammad Ayatollahi Tabaar, "Iran's War Within: Ebrahim Raisi and the Triumph of the Hardliners," *Foreign Affairs*, September/October 2021, available at <https://www.foreignaffairs.com/articles/iran/2021–08–05/irans-war-within-ebrahim-raisi>. Accessed on August 18, 2021.

79. Ibid.

80. Golnaz Esfandiari, "What Iranian Foreign Policy Could Look Like Under President Raisi," *Radio Free Europe: Radio Liberty*, June 17, 2021, available at <https://www.rferl.org/a/iran-presidential-election-raisi-foreign-policy/31313258.html>. Accessed on August 18, 2021.

81. "MP: The Taliban is one of the authentic movements in the region," *Ensafnews*, December 7, 2020, available at <http://www.ensafnews.com/270713>. Accessed on August 20, 2021.

82. Farzin Nadimi, "Iran Sets Its Eyes on Afghanistan," The Washington Institute for Near East Policy, July 19, 2021, available at <https://www.washingtoninstitute.org/policy-analysis/iran-sets-its-eyes-afghanistan>. Accessed on August 18, 2021.

83. "The US withdrawal from Afghanistan must become an opportunity to restore peace in the country," *Fars News Agency*, August 16, 2021, available at <https://www.farsnews.ir/news/14000525000423>. Accessed on August 20, 2021.

84. "Ayatollah Raisi: Iran adheres to neighborly relations with Afghanistan by closely monitoring developments," *Tasnim News Agency*, August 16, 2021, available at <https://www.tasnimnews.com/fa/news/1400/05/25/2555460>. Accessed on August 20, 2021.

85. "The US withdrawal from Afghanistan must become an opportunity to restore peace in the country," *Fars News Agency*, August 16, 2021, available at <https://www.farsnews.ir/news/14000525000423>. Accessed on August 20, 2021.

86. Mahmood Monshipouri, "The Unwinnable War in Afghanistan: What is Left to Learn?" *Tehran Times*, August 17, 2021, available at <https://www.tehrantimes.com/news/464109/The-unwinnable-war-in-Afghanistan-What-is-left-to-learn>. Accessed on August 18, 2021.

87. Kazem Alamdari, "Regarding Democracy and Development in Iran," 15 interviews conducted between 2006 and 2016, Tavaana Publishers, Tehran: Iran, 2016; available at <https://tavaana.org/fa/Democracy_Development_Iran>. Accessed on February 20, 2021.

88. Mehran Kamrava, *Troubled Waters: Insecurity in the Persian Gulf*, Ithaca, NY: Cornell University Press, 2018, pp. 8–9.

89. Mehran Kamrava, "Sources of (In)Security in the Persian Gulf," *International Studies Journal*, Vol. 17, No. 1 (65), Summer 2020, pp. 27–47.

90. Mehran Kamrava, *Troubled Waters*, op. cit., pp. 150–52.

91. Maziar Motamed, "Iran's Parliament Approves President Raisi's Conservative Cabinet," *Al Jazeera*, August 25, 2021, available at <Iran's parliament approves President Raisi's conservative cabinet | Government News | Al Jazeera>. Accessed on August 27, 2021.

3. REFORM AND THE HUMAN RIGHTS CAMPAIGN

1. Kenneth Katzman, "Iran: Internal Politics and US Policy and Options," *Congressional Research Service Report*, December 9, 2020, pp. 1–40; see especially p. 19; available at <https://www.everycrsreport.com/files/2020–12–09_RL32048_01903402 cc5ffc26d472b19977551249dbcb381d.pdf>. Accessed on January 19, 2021.

2. David P. Forsythe, "US Foreign Policy and Human Rights," *Journal of Human Rights*, Vol. 1, No. 4, December 2002, pp. 501–21; see especially pp. 518–19.

3. Ibid.

4. Todd Landman, *Protecting Human Rights: A Comparative Study*, Washington, DC: Georgetown University Press, 2005, p. 160.

5. Jack Donnelly and Daniel J. Whelan, *International Human Rights*, Fifth Edition, Boulder, CO: Westview Press, 2018, p. 130.

6. Council on Foreign Relations, "Human Rights in Iran," June 4, 2013, available at <https://www.cfr.org/backgrounder/human-rights-iran>. Accessed on December 29, 2020.

7. Ervand Abrahamian, "The Making of the Modern Iranian State," in Mark Kesselman, Joel Krieger and William A. Joseph, eds., *Introduction to Comparative Politics*, Third Edition, New York: Houghton Mifflin, 2004.

8. For further information on this, see Mahmood Monshipouri, "Reza Afshari and Cultural Relativism," *Human Rights Quarterly*, Vol. 41, No. 1, February 2019, pp. 204–08.

9. Asef Bayat, "The Fire that Fueled the Iran Protests," *The Atlantic*, January 27, 2018, available at <https://www.theatlantic.com/international/archive/2018/01/iran-protest-mashaad-green-class-labor-economy/551690/>. Accessed on August 29, 2021.

10. For further information on this, see Mahmood Monshipouri, "Human Rights," in Mehran Kamrava and Manochehr Dorraj, eds., *Iran Today: An Encyclopedia of Life in the Islamic Republic*, Vol. 1, Westport, CT: Greenwood Press, 2008, pp. 221–28.

11. Ann Elizabeth Mayer, *Islam and Human Rights: Tradition and Politics*, Boulder, CO: Westview Press, 1991.

12. Mahmood Monshipouri, *Islamism, Secularism, and Human Rights in the Middle East*, Boulder, CO: Lynne Rienner Publishers, 1998; see especially p. 175.

13. Ervand Abrahamian, *Tortured Confessions: Prisons and Public Recantations in Modern Iran*, Berkeley: University of California Press, 1999; Reza Afshari, *Human Rights in Iran: The Abuse of Cultural Relativism*, Philadelphia: University of Pennsylvania Press, 2001.

14. Mahmood Monshipouri, *Islamism, Secularism, and Human Rights in the Middle East*, op. cit., p. 187.

15. See Mahmood Monshipouri, "Iran From 1979," in David P. Forsythe, ed., *Encyclopedia of Human Rights*, Vol. 3, New York: Oxford University Press, 2009, pp. 195–206.

16. *Agence France Presse*, November 10, 2000; see also *International Iran Times*, November 17, 2000, pp. 1 and 10.

17. *Amnesty International: Report 1999*, London: Amnesty International Publications, 1999, pp. 198–202.

18. Mahmood Monshipouri, "Iran from 1979," in David P. Forsythe, ed., *Encyclopedia of Human Rights*, Vol. 3, New York: Oxford University Press, 2009, pp. 195–206; see p. 198.

19. Vali, Nasr, "Iran," in Jeffrey Kopstein and Mark Lichback, eds., *Comparative Politics: Interests, Identities, and Institutions in a Changing Global Order*, Second Edition, New York: Cambridge University Press, 2005, pp. 394–430; see p. 423.

20. The journalist Akbar Ganji, who was accused of harming Iranian security interests by participating in the Berlin Conference, has said that he had been tortured throughout his detention, placed in solitary confinement and not allowed basic rights. For further information, see *The New York Times*, November 10, 2000, p. 7.

21. Mahmood Monshipouri, "The Politics of Culture and Human Rights in Iran: Globalizing and Localizing Dynamics," in Mahmood Monshipouri, Neil Englehart, Andrew J. Nathan, and Kavita Philip, eds., *Constructing Human Rights in the Age of Globalization*, New York: M.E. Sharpe, 2003, pp. 113–44; see especially, pp. 137–39.

22. Derick L. Hulme, Jr., *The Domestic Politics of Terrorism: Lessons from the Clinton Administration*, Lanham, MD: Lexington Books, 2020, p. 98.

23. Malcolm Byrne, "Secret US Overtures to Iran in 1999 Broke Down over Terrorism Allegations," *The National Security Archive*, May 30, 2010, available at <https://nsarchive2.gwu.edu/NSAEBB/NSAEBB318/>. Accessed on January 21, 2021.

24. Josh Levs, "Fact Check: Was Obama 'Silent' on Iran 2009," *CNN Politics*, October 9, 2012, available at <https://www.cnn.com/2012/10/08/politics/fact-check-romney-iran/index.html>. Accessed on January 20, 2021.

25. Ibid.

26. For a counterargument, see Barbara Ann Rieffer-Flanagan, "Addressing Religious Intolerance in an Increasingly Illiberal World," in Mahmood Monshipouri, ed., *Why*

Human Rights Still Matter in Contemporary Global Affairs, New York: Routledge, 2020, pp. 285–302; see especially pp. 288–90.

27. Misagh Parsa, *Democracy in Iran: Why It Failed and How It Might Succeed*, Cambridge, MA: Harvard University Press, 2016, p. 4.

28. Mahmood Monshipouri, "Diplomacy with Iran: A 'Win-Win' Situation," *The Berkeley Blog*, November 18, 2014, available at <http://blogs.berkeley.edu/2014/11/18/diplomacy-with-iran-a-win-win-situation/>. Accessed on December 12, 2014.

29. Mahmood Monshipouri and Manochehr Dorraj, "Iran's Foreign Policy: Shifting Strategic Landscape," *Middle East Policy*, Vol. XX, No. 4, Winter 2013, pp. 133–47.

30. Nayereh Tohidi, "Women's Rights and Feminist Movements in Iran," *International Journal on Human Rights*, Issue 24, December 2016, available at <https://sur.conectas.org/en/womens-rights-feminist-movements-iran/>. Accessed on February 28, 2021.

31. Azadeh Kian-Thiebaut, "Women and the Making of Civil Society in Post-Islamist Iran," in Eric Hooglund, ed., *Twenty Years of Islamic Revolution: Political and Social Transition in Iran Since 1979*, Syracuse, NY: Syracuse University Press, 2002, pp. 56–73; see p. 67.

32. Ibid.

33. Hoda Mahmoudi, "Freedom and the Iranian Women's Movement," *Contexts*, Vol. 18, Issue 3, Summer 2019, pp. 14–19; see especially p. 16.

34. Ziba Mir-Hosseini, "Religious Modernists and the 'Woman Question'," in Eric Hooglund, ed., *Twenty Years of Islamic Revolution: Political and Social Transition in Iran Since 1979*, Syracuse, NY: Syracuse University Press, 2002, pp. 74–95; see p. 95.

35. Elaheh Koolaee is quoted in Rebecca Barlow and Shahram Akbarzadeh, "Prospects for Feminism in the Islamic Republic of Iran," *Human Rights Quarterly*, Vol. 30, No. 1, February 2008, pp. 21–40; see especially p. 27.

36. Valentine M. Moghadam, *Modernizing Women: Gender and Social Change in the Middle East*, Second Edition, Boulder, CO: Lynne Rienner Publishers, 2003, p. 219.

37. Nikki R. Keddie, *Modern Iran: Roots and Results of Revolution*, New Haven, CT: Yale University Press, 2003, p. 293.

38. This section is based on Mahmood Monshipouri and Mehdi Zakerian, "The State of Human Rights in Iran," in Mahmood Monshipouri, ed., *Inside the Islamic Republic: Social Change in Post-Khomeini Iran*, New York: Oxford University Press, 2016, pp. 151–75; see especially pp. 161–62.

39. Quoted in Azadeh Kian-Thiebaut, "Women and the Making of Civil Society in Post-Islamist Iran," in Eric Hooglund, ed., *Twenty Years of Islamic Revolution: Political and Social Transition in Iran Since 1979*, Syracuse, NY: Syracuse University Press, 2002, pp. 56–73; see p. 62.

40. Ibid., p. 62.

41. Ziba Mir-Hosseini, "Why Do We Need 'Islamic Feminism,'"? *Al Raida Journal*, Vol. 44, Issue 2, 2020, pp. 85–91; see especially pp. 87–89.

42. Valentine M. Moghadam, "Islamic Feminism and Its Discontents: Toward a Resolution of the Debate," *Journal of Women in Culture and Society*, Vol. 27, No. 41, Summer 2002, pp. 1135–71; see especially p. 1165.

43. Ibid., p. 1166.

44. Nayereh Tohidi, "The Women's Movement and Feminism in Iran: Revisiting A Global Perspective," in Amrita Basu, ed., *Women's Movements in the Global Era*, Boulder, CO: Westview Press, 2010, pp. 375–414.

45. Shirin Ebadi, *Until We are Free: My Fight for Human Rights in Iran*, New York: Random House, 2016, p. 68.

46. Ibid., p. 68.

47. Council on Foreign Relations, "Human Rights in Iran," June 4, 2013, available at <https://www.cfr.org/backgrounder/human-rights-iran>. Accessed on December 29, 2020.

48. Azadeh Moaveni and Ali Vaez, "US Maximum Pressure on Iran Hurts the Women It Claims to Help," International Crisis Group, March 6, 2020, available at <https://www.crisisgroup.org/middle-east-north-africa/gulf-and-arabian-peninsula/iran/us-maximum-pressure-iran-hurts-women-it-claims-help>. Accessed on March 26, 2021.

49. Ibid.

50. Micheline R. Ishay, *The Levant Express: The Arab Uprisings, Human Rights, and The Future of the Middle East*, New Haven, CT: Yale University Press, 2019, p. 211.

51. Shadi Mokhtari and Neda Nazmi, "The Politics of Human Rights in Iran Since the Green Movement," in Anthony Tirado Chase, ed., *Routledge Handbook on Human Rights and the Middle East and North Africa*, New York: Routledge, 2017, pp. 116–28; see especially p. 122.

52. Arzoo Osanloo, "Women and Criminal Law in Post-Khomeini Iran," in Mahmood Monshipouri, ed., *Inside the Islamic Republic: Social Change in Post-Khomeini Iran*, New York: Oxford University Press, 2016, pp. 91–112; see especially pp. 101 and 110.

53. Farzaneh Milani, "A Revolution Within Two Revolutions: Women and Literature in Contemporary Iran," in Mahmood Monshipouri, ed., *Inside the Islamic Republic: Social Change in Post-Khomeini Iran*, New York: Oxford University Press, 2016, pp. 113–31; see especially, p. 129.

54. Djavad Salehi-Isfahani, "The Iranian Family in Transition," in Mahmood Monshipouri, ed., *Inside the Islamic Republic: Social Change in Post-Khomeini Iran*, New York: Oxford University Press, 2016, pp. 133–50; see especially p. 133.

55. Ibid., pp. 133–4.

56. Ibid., p. 149.

57. "Remarriage Conditions for Men," *Tasnim News Agency*, May 24, 2017, available at <https://www.tasnimnews.com/fa/news/1396/03/03/1418308>. Accessed on March 27, 2021.

58. Office of International Religious Freedom: US Department of State, "2019 Report on International Religious Freedom: Iran," available at <https://www.state.gov/reports/2019-report-on-international-religious-freedom/iran/>. Accessed on February 21, 2021.

59. Ibid.

60. Ibid.

61. Michel Rosenfeld, "Can Human Rights Bridge the Gap Between Universalism and Cultural Relativism? A Pluralist Assessment Based on the Rights of Minorities," *Columbia Human Rights Law Review*, Vol. 20, No. 2, Spring 1999, pp. 249–84; see especially p. 282.

62. Jelena Pejic, "Minority Rights in International Law," *Human Rights Quarterly*, Vol. 19, No. 3, August 1997, pp. 666–85; see pp. 667 and 667.

63. Ibid., p. 669.

64. Ibid., p. 684.

65. Eliz Sanasarian, *Religious Minorities in Iran*, Cambridge: Cambridge University Press, 2000, p. 33.

66. Ibid., p. 154.

67. Ibid., p. 156.

68. Nazila Ghanea, *Human Rights, the UN and the Baha'is in Iran*, The Hague: Kluwer Law International, 2002, pp. 221–4.

69. *The New York Times*, November 15, 2019.

70. Djavad Salehi-Isfahani, "Iran's Middle Class and the Nuclear Deal," *Brookings Institution*, April 8, 2021, available at <https://www.brookings.edu/blog/future-development/2021/04/08/irans-middle-class-and-the-nuclear-deal/>. Accessed on April 9, 2021.

71. Hadi Ghaemi, "Raisi: Record on Crackdown and Human Rights," *The Iran Primer*, United States Institute of Peace, July 20, 2021, available at <https://iranprimer.usip.org/blog/2021/jul/20/raisi-record-crackdown-human-rights>. Accessed on August 18, 2021.

72. Parisa Hafezi, "Winner of Iran Presidency is Hardline Judge Who is Under U.S. Sanctions," *Reuters*, June 20, 2021, available at <https://www.reuters.com/world/middle-east/front-runner-iran-presidency-is-hardline-judge-sanctioned-by-us-2021–06–15/>. Accessed on August 18, 2021.

73. Hadi Ghaemi, "Raisi: Record on Crackdown and Human Rights," op. cit.

74. Ibid.

75. NIAC Action, "Iran's New President has a Dismal Human Rights Record," June 23, 2021, available at <https://www.niacouncil.org/human_rights_tracker/irans-new-president-has-a-dismal-human-rights-record/?locale=en>. Accessed on August 18, 2021.

76. David P. Forsythe, *Advanced Introduction to The Politics of International Human Rights*, Northampton, MA: Edward Elgar Publishing, 2021, p. 52.

77. Ibid., p. 49.

78. Karen Kramer, "Iran Isn't Just a Nuclear File," *Foreign Affairs*, February 2, 2021, available at <https://www.foreignaffairs.com/articles/united-states/2021-02-02/iran-isnt-just-nuclear-file>. Accessed on March 19, 2021.

79. Ibid.

80. Abbas Amanat, *Iran: A Modern History*, New Haven, CT: Yale University Press, 2017, p. 879.

81. Ibid.

82. Bhikhu Parekh, "Non-ethnocentric Universalism," in Tim Dunn & Nicholas J. Wheeler, eds., *Human Rights in Global Politics*, New York: Cambridge University Press, 1999, pp. 128–40.

4. IRAN'S FOREIGN POLICY: NAVIGATING IDEOLOGICAL AND GEOPOLITICAL SPHERES

1. For further information on this, see Mahmood Monshipouri, "Iran's Foreign Policy and Islamic Ideology," in Thomas Juneau and Sam Razavi, eds., *Iranian Foreign Policy Since 2001: Alone in the World*, New York: Routledge, 2013, pp. 56–69.

2. Ali Ansari and Kasra Aarabi, "Ideology and Iran's Revolution: How 1979 Changed the World," Tony Blair Institute for Global Change, February 11, 2019, available at <https://institute.global/policy/ideology-and-irans-revolution-how-1979-changed-wor>. Accessed on December 21, 2020.

3. Ibid.

4. Manochehr Dorraj, "Iran's Regional Foreign Policy," in David S. Sorenson, ed., *Interpreting the Middle East*, Boulder, CO: Westview Press, 2010, pp. 363–381; see especially p. 379.

5. Ali Ansari and Kasra Aarabi, op. cit.

6. For an illuminating book on this topic, see Shireen T. Hunter, *Iran and the World: Continuity in a Revolutionary Decade*, Bloomington, IN: Indiana University Press, 1990.

7. David Lesch, "The Iranian Revolution," in Karl Yambert, ed., *The Contemporary Middle East*, Boulder, CO: Westview Press, 2006, pp. 131–42; see especially p. 133.

8. Arshin Adib-Moghaddam, "Iran-Iraq War," in Mehran Kamrava and Manochehr Dorraj, eds., *Iran Today: An Encyclopedia of Life in the Islamic Republic*, Vol. 1, Westport, CT: Greenwood Press, 2008, pp. 250–58; see especially p. 252.

9. Kayhan Barzegar, "Iran and the Shiite Crescent: Myths and Realities," *The Brown Journal of World Affairs*, Vol. XV, No. 1, Fall/Winter 2008, pp. 87–99; see especially p. 89.

10. Ronen Zeidel, "Implications of the Iran-Iraq War," *E-International Relations*, October 7, 2013, available at <https://www.e-ir.info/2013/10/07/implications-of-the-iran-iraq-war/>. Accessed on January 23, 2021.

11. Ibid.

12. William O. Beeman, "Examining Iran's Ties to Hezbollah," *In These Times*, August 15, 2006, available at <http://www.inthesetimes.com/article/2790/>. Last accessed on July 1, 2010.

13. Ibid.

14. More information is available on <http://www.palestinefacts.org/pf_1991to_now_lebanon_withdraw_2000.php>. Last accessed on June 30, 2010.

15. Ibid., p. 182

16. Ibid., p. 176.

17. Ali Hajizade, "Place and Role of Hezbollah in Syrian War," *Al-Arabia.net*, October 18, 2018, available at <https://english.alarabiya.net/en/views/news/middle-east/2018/10/18/Place-and-role-of-Hezbollah-in-Syrian-war>. Accessed on January 23, 2021.

18. Ibid.

19. John O. Voll, "For Scholars of Islam, Interpretation Need Not Be Advocacy," *Chronicle of Higher Education*, March 22, 1989, p. 2.

20. Alessandro Monti, "Salman Rushdie (1947–)," in Alba Amoia and Bettina L. Knapp, eds., *Multicultural Writers since 1945*, Westport, CT: Greenwood Press, 2004, p. 435.

21. Quoted in Peter Mandaville (2004), *Transnational Muslim Politics: Reimagining the Ummah*, New York: Routledge, 2004, p. 103.

22. Mehdi Mozaffari, "Rushdie Affair," in John L. Esposito, ed., *The Oxford Encyclopedia of the Modern Islamic World*, New York: Oxford University Press, 1995, pp. 443–5; see especially, p. 443.

23. Graham E. Fuller, *The Future of Political Islam*, New York: Palgrave Macmillan, 2003, p. 111.

24. John L. Esposito, *The Islamic Threat: Myth or Reality?* Third Edition, New York: Oxford University Press, 1999, p. 250.

25. Graham E. Fuller, "Repairing US–Iranian Relations," *Middle East Policy*, Vol. VI, No. 2, October, 1998, pp. 140–4; see especially p. 142.

26. R. K. Ramazani, "Iran's Foreign Policy: Both North and South," *Middle East Journal*, Vol. 46, No. 3, Summer 1992, pp. 393–412.

27. Alex Vatanka, "The Saudis and Iran's Moderates," Middle East Institute, September 21, 2015, available at <https://www.mei.edu/publications/saudis-and-irans-moderates>. Accessed on December 23, 2020.

28. Suzanne Maloney, "The Revolutionary Economy," *The Iran Primer*, US Institute of Peace, available at <http://iranprimer.usip.org/resource/revolutionary-economy>. Accessed on November 16, 2014.

29. Ibid.

30. Mehran Kamrava, "Seyed Mohammad Khatami," in Mehran Kamrava and Manochehr Dorraj, eds., *Iran Today: An Encyclopedia of Life in the Islamic Republic*, Vol. 1, Westport, CT: Greenwood Press, 2008, pp. 279–81.

31. For an interesting analysis of this subject, see Nizar Messari, "Identity and Foreign Policy: The Case of Islam in U.S. Foreign Policy," in Vendulka Kubalkova, ed., *Foreign Policy in a Constructed World*, Armonk, NY: M. E. Sharpe, 2001, pp. 227–46; see pp. 242–3.

32. Walid Phares, *The Confrontation: Winning the War Against Future Jihad*, New York: Palgrave Macmillan, 2008, p. 36.

33. Ray Takeyh, *Hidden Iran: Paradox and Power in the Islamic Republic*, New York: Times Books, 2006, p. 181.

34. Ibid., p. 181.

35. Nasr, *The Shi'a Revival*, op. cit., p. 184.

36. Ibid., p. 184.

37. Graham E. Fuller, op. cit., p. 3.

38. Maximilian Terhalle, "Are the Shi'a Rising?" *Middle East Policy*, Vol. XIV, No. 2, Summer 2007, pp. 69–83; see pp. 74–9.

39. Ibid., p. 80.

40. The divide between Shi'ism and Sunnism can be traced back to their major differences over the succession to Prophet Mohammad, Qur'anic interpretation, the Prophet's *Hadith* (Sayings), Islamic jurisprudence, liturgical prayers, religious tradition, and clerical establishment, among other things. Despite a number of similarities, such as believing in the indivisibility of God and the story of creation, Islam's foundational principles, Islamic law, sanctity of life, Jihad, and the Messianic Savior, the two sects parted ways early in Muslim history, each viewing itself as the original orthodoxy. For more information on this subject, see Mir Zohair Husain, *Islam and the Muslim World*, Dubuque, IA: McGraw Hill/Contemporary Learning Series, 2006, pp. 17–21.

41. Vali Nasr, *The Shi'a Revival: How Conflict Within Islam Will Shape the Future*, New York: W. W. Norton & Company, 2006.

42. Kayhan Barzegar, "Iran's Foreign Policy in Post-Invasion Iraq," *Middle East Policy*, Vol. XV, No. 4, Winter 2008, pp. 47–58; see especially p. 53.

43. Ibid., p. 53.

44. Ibid., p. 53.

45. Liam Anderson and Gareth Stansfield, *The Future of Iraq: Dictatorship, Democracy, or Division?* New York: Palgrave, 2004, p. 119.

46. Vali Nasr, "When the Shiites Rise," *Foreign Affairs*, Vol. 85, No. 4, July/August 2006, pp. 58–74; see pp. 58–9.

47. Mir Zohair Husain, *Islam and the Muslim World*, Dubuque, IA: McGraw Hill Contemporary Learning Series, 2006, p. 15.

48. Ibid., p. 12.

49. Kayhan Barzegar, "Iran's Foreign Policy in Post-Invasion Iraq," op.cit., p. 56.

50. Agnieszka Bryc and Bartosz Bojarczyk, "Middle East in the Transition," *The Copernicus Journal of Political Studies*, Vol. 1, No. 3, 2013, pp. 1–158; especially pp. 16–17.

51. Howard LaFranchi, "How Iraq War Will Change America," *Christian Science Monitor*, December 12, 2011, pp. 27–8.

52. For further discussion on this subject, see Mahmood Monshipouri and Shirin Jafarinasab Kermani, "US–Iran Relations: Competing and Overlapping Interests in a Turbulent Region," *The Maghreb Review*, Vol. 42, No. 2, 2017, pp. 164–77.

53. "Iranian opposition bids to hold pro-Egypt rally," *Reuters*, February 6, 2011, available at http://af.reuters.com/article/topNews/idAFJOE7150AX20110206.

54. Scott Peterson, "Iran's Khamenei Praises Egyptian Protesters, Declares 'Islamic Awakening,'" *The Christian Science Monitor*, February 4, 2011. Available at <http://

www.csmonitor.com/World/Middle-East/2011/0204/Iran-s-Khamenei-praises-Egyptian-protesters-declares-Islamic-awakening>. Last accessed on Feb. 9, 2011.

55. "Larijani: Regional Uprisings Inspired by Iran's Islamic Revolution," *Fars News Agency*, March 3, 2011, available at http://english.farsnews.com/newstext. php?nn=8912120642.

56. Anoushiravan Ehteshami, *Dynamics of Change in the Persian Gulf: Political Economy, War, and Revolution*, New York: Routledge, 2013, p. 255.

57. Ibid.

58. Anoushiravan Ehteshami, "The Foreign Policy of Iran," in Raymond Hinnebusch and Anoushiravan Ehteshami, eds., *The Foreign Policy of Middle Eastern States*, Boulder, CO: Lynne Rienner Publishers, 2014, pp. 261–88; see especially pp. 282–3.

59. Ibid., pp. 283–4.

60. Fareed Zakaria, "The Revolution," *Time*, February 14, 2011, pp. 26–33. See especially p. 33.

61. See, for example, Landon Thomas, Jr., "In Turkey's Example, Some See Map for Egypt," *The New York Times*, February 5, 2011, available at http://www.nytimes. com/2011/02/06/world/middleeast/06turkey.html. But for a discussion of differences between Turkey and Egypt, including structural differences between the Egyptian Muslim Brotherhood and the AK Party in Turkey, see Ömer Taşpınar, "Egypt and the Turkish Model," The Brookings Institution, February 7, 2011, available at http://www.brookings.edu/opinions/2011/0207_egypt_turkey_taspinar.aspx.

62. John Thorne, "After an Anti-US Upsurge," *Christian Science Monitor*, September 24, 2012, p. 18 and 20.

63. Lucian Constantin and Jeremy Kirk, "Iran Blocks Access to Gmail and Google, Internet Users Say," *Computerworld*, September 24, 2012, available at <http://www.computerworld.com/s/article/9231628/Iran_blocks_access_to_Gmail_and_Google_Internet_users_say>. Accessed on September 28, 2012.

64. Mehran Kamrava, *Troubled Waters: Insecurity in the Persian Gulf*, Ithaca, NY: Cornell University Press, p. 119.

65. Ibid., p. 17.

66. Jim Krane, *Energy Kingdoms: Oil and Political Survival in the Persian Gulf*, New York: Columbia University Press, 2019, p. 159.

67. *Pars Today*, "Iran, UAE Sign Document to Boost Maritime Security Cooperation," August 1, 2019, available at <https://parstoday.com/en/news/iran-i107775-iran_uae_sign_document_to_boost_maritime_security_cooperation>. Accessed on January 7, 2021.

68. Mehran Kamrava, op. cit., p. 128.

69. Anne Barnard, "A Missing Prime Minister is the Antihero of Beirut's Marathon," *The New York Times*, November 14, 2017, available at <https://www.nytimes. com/2017/11/14/world/middleeast/lebanon-hariri-marathon-beirut.html>. Accessed on July 7, 2020.

70. Danielle Ziri, "Israel Warns UN: Hezbollah Has 120,000 Missiles Aimed at Us", *The Jerusalem Post*, July 12, 2016; available at <https://www.jpost.com/arab-israeli-conflict/israel-warns-un-hezbollah-has-120000-missiles-aimed-at-israel-460184>. Accessed on July 7, 2020.

71. Anoushiravan Ehteshami, *Dynamics of Change in the Persian Gulf: Political Economy, War, and Revolution*, New York: Routledge, 2013, pp. 249–50.

72. Giorgio Cafiero, "Iran's Role in Qatar's New Foreign Policy," *Al-Monitor*, July 11, 2017, available at <https://www.al-monitor.com/pulse/fa/originals/2017/08/iran-role-qatar-new-foreign-policy-gcc-dispute-saudi-arabia.html>. Accessed on July 7, 2020.

73. Simeon Kerr, "Saudi Arabia and Allies to Restore Ties with Qatar," *Financial Times*, January 5, 2021, available at <https://www.ft.com/content/ad2eb477-b8f8-4dae-9e4c-a441759fc897?>. Accessed on January 8, 2021.

74. Talha Köse and Bilgenhan Öztürk, "A See Change in the MENA Region: External Interventions in Libya," *Insight Turkey*, Vol. 22, No. 4, Fall 2020, pp. 113–38; see especially, p. 122.

75. Ibid., p. 123.

76. Ibid., p. 127.

77. Ibid., pp. 127–8.

78. Ali Bakir, "The UAE's Disruptive Policy in Libya," *Insight Turkey*, Vol. 22, No. 4, Fall 2020, pp. 157–77; see especially p. 173.

79. Yoel Guzansky and Zachary A. Marshall, "The Abraham Accords: Immediate Significance and Long-term Implications," *Israel Journal of Foreign Affairs*, Vol. 14, No. 3, October 2020, pp. 379–89; see especially p. 379.

80. Ibid., pp. 382–3.

81. Ibid., pp. 382–3.

82. Jonathan Broder, "The Abraham Accords: Will They Transform the Middle East?" *CQ Press*, December 11, 2020, available at <https://library.cqpress.com/cqresearcher/document.php?id=cqresrre2020121100>. Accessed on December 23, 2020.

83. Ibid.

84. Abbie Cheeseman, "UAE Cabinet Approves Establishment of Embassy in Tel Aviv in Further Sting to Palestinians," *The Telegraph*, January 24, 2021, available at <https://www.telegraph.co.uk/authors/abbie-cheeseman/>. Accessed on January 26, 2021.

85. Barzegar, "Iran and the Shiite Crescent," op. cit., p. 93.

86. Dina Esfandiary, "No Country for Oversimplifications," The Century Foundation, January 24, 2018, available at <<https://tcf.org/content/report/no-country-oversimplifications/?gclid=Cj0KCQiA88X_BRDUARIsACVMYD_rfMZmNfaN-vWburH20vE2kh3kFtcXkJr0G4RvGSh7GXczyKQoH_rQaAs7UEALw_wcB&agreed=1>. Accessed on January 4, 2021.

87. Przemyslav Osiewicz, *Foreign Policy of the Islamic Republic of Iran: Between Ideology and Pragmatism*, New York: Routledge, 2020.

5. REGIONAL CONFLICTS: SYRIA, SOUTH CAUCASUS, AND YEMEN

1. For more on this topic, see Scott Peterson, "Mideast's New Superpower," *The Christian Science Monitor Weekly*, December 18, 2017, pp. 24–30; see p. 26.
2. Claire Parker and Rick Noack, "Iran has invested in allies and proxies across the Middle East. Here's where they stand after Soleimani's death," *The Washington Post*, January 3, 2020, available at <https://www.washingtonpost.com/world/2020/01/03/iran-has-invested-allies-proxies-across-middle-east-heres-where-they-stand-after-soleimanis-death/>. Accessed on January 25, 2021.
3. Dina Esfandiary, "No Country for Oversimplications," The Century Foundation, January 24, 2018, available at <https://tcf.org/content/report/no-country-ove rsimplifications/?gclid=Cj0KCQiA88X_BRDUARIsACVMYD_rfMZmNfaNvW-burH20vE2kh3kFtcXkJr0G4RvGSh7GXczyKQoH_rQaAs7UEALw_wcB&agreed=1>. Accessed on January 4, 2021.
4. Ibid.
5. Tim Arango, "Iran Dominates in Iraq After U.S. Opened Door," *The New York Times*, July 16, 2017, pp. 1, 10–12; see especially p. 11.
6. Graham Griffiths and George Dyson, "Gulf–Turkey Rivalry will Intensify, Shaping Conflicts, Confrontations Across Region," *Control Risks*, October 23, 2020, available at <https://www.controlrisks.com/our-thinking/insights/gulf-turkey-rivalry-will-intensify>. Accessed on January 31, 2021.
7. Ibid.
8. Mark Peceny, "Democracy Promotion and American Foreign Policy: Afghanistan, Iraq, and the Future," in David P. Forsythe, Patrice C. McMahon, and Andrew Wedeman, eds., *American Foreign Policy in a Globalized World*, New York: Routledge, 2006, pp. 215–39; see especially p. 231.
9. William V. Dunlap, "Iraq: Occupation and Transition," in David P. Forsythe, ed., *Encyclopedia of Human Rights*, Vol. 3, New York: Oxford University Press, 2009, pp. 217–24.
10. Mahmood Monshipouri, "The Bush Doctrine and Democracy Promotion in the Middle East," in David P. Forsythe, Patrice C. McMahon, and Andrew Wedeman, eds., *American Foreign Policy in a Globalized World*, New York: Routledge, 2006, pp. 313–34; see especially p. 329.
11. Anoushiravan Ehteshami, *Dynamics of Change in the Persian Gulf: Political Economy, War, and Revolution*, New York: Routledge, 2013, p. 216.
12. Ibid., p. 217.
13. Tim Arango, "Iran Dominates in Iraq After U.S. Opened Door," *The New York Times*, July 16, 2017, pp. 1, 10–12; see especially p. 10.
14. Ibid., pp. 1, 10–12.
15. Banafsheh Keynoush, "Iran's Regional Dynamics: A Piecemeal Approach," *Middle East Policy*, Vol. XXVII, No. 2, Summer 2020, pp. 94–107; see especially p. 102.
16. Tim Arango, op. cit., p. 11.
17. Banafsheh Keynoush, op. cit., p. 102.

18. Banafsheh Keynoush, op. cit., p. 102.

19. Hassan Ahmadian, "Why Did Iran Back Mustafa al-Kadhimi as Iraqi Prime Minister?" *Atlantic Council*, July 24, 2021, available at <https://www.atlanticcouncil.org/blogs/iransource/why-did-iran-back-mustafa-al-kadhimi-as-iraqi-prime-minister/>. Accessed on January 25, 2021.

20. Mehran Kamrava, *Inside the Arab State*, New York: Oxford University Press, 2018, pp. 58–9 and 68.

21. Ibid., p. 68.

22. James L. Gelvin, *The Arab Uprisings: What Everyone Needs to Know*, New York: Oxford University Press, 2012, p. 114.

23. Ibid., p. 115.

24. Richard Falk, "Syria: The Tragic Space between the Unacceptable and the Impossible," *Al Jazeera*, May 31, 2012, available at <http://www.aljazeera.com/indepth/opinion/2012/05/20125318233126386.html>. Accessed on October 14, 2012.

25. Richard Falk, "A Brief Further Comment on Syria," available at <http://richard-falk.wordpress.com/2012/07/25/a-brief-further-comment-on-syria/>. Accessed on October 14, 2012.

26. Ibid.

27. James L. Gelvin, op. cit., p. 112.

28. Richard Falk, "A Brief Further Comment on Syria."

29. David E. Sanger, "Rebel Arms Flow Is Said to Benefit Jihadists in Sryia," *The New York Times*, October 14, 2012, available at <http://www.nytimes.com/2012/10/15/world/middleeast/jihadists-receiving-most-arms-sent-to-syrian-rebels.html?nl=todaysheadlines&emc=edit_th_20121015>. Accessed on April 15, 2021.

30. Ibid.

31. Richard Falk, "A Brief Further Comment on Syria."

32. Anthony Shadid, "Fear of Civil War Mounts in Syria as Crisis Deepens," *The New York Times*, January 14, 2012, available at <http://www.nytimes.com/2012/01/15/world/middleeast/syria-in-deep-crisis-may-be-slipping-out-of-control.html?pagewanted=all>. Accessed on January 18, 2012.

33. Kyle Almond, "Why the World Isn't Intervening in Syria," *CNN.com*, February 23, 2012, available at <http://www.cnn.com/2012/02/23/world/syria-intervention/index.html>. Accessed on October 15, 2012.

34. *France 24*, "Syria Death Toll Tops 380,000 in Almost Nine-Year War: Monitor," April 1, 2020, available at <https://www.france24.com/en/20200104-syria-death-toll-tops-380-000-in-almost-nine-year-war-monitor>. Accessed on December 25, 2020.

35. Fareed Zakaria, "The Case Against Intervention in Syria," *Time*, June 11, 2012, available at <http://www.time.com/time/magazine/article/0,9171,2116135-1,00.html>. Accessed on June 3, 2012.

36. James L. Gelvin, op. cit., p. 118.

37. Banafsheh Keynoush, "Iran's Regional Dynamics: A Piecemeal Approach," *Middle East Policy*, Vol. XXVII, No. 2, Summer 2020, pp. 94–107; see especially p. 101.

38. Ibid.

39. *Al Jazeera*, "Kofi Annan's Six-Point Plan for Syria," March 27, 2012, available <https://www.aljazeera.com/news/2012/3/27/kofi-annans-six-point-plan-for-syria>. Accessed on January 25, 2021.

40. Mahmood Monshipouri, *Democratic Uprisings in the New Middle East: Youth, Technology, Human Rights, and US Foreign Policy*, New York: Routledge, 2014, p. 159.

41. Mehdi Mohammadi, "Syria's Developments and Iran's National Security Equation," *Iran Review*, Sunday, July 22, 2012, available at http://www.iranreview.org/iranSpectrum/index.aspx. Last accessed October 7, 2012.

42. Logan Pauley, "China Stakes out a Role for Itself in Post-War Syria," *Asia Times*, October 3, 2018, available at < https://asiatimes.com/2018/10/china-stakes-out-a-role-for-itself-in-post-war-syria/>. Accessed on February 22, 2022.

43. "China Backs Transition in Syria, Opposes Intervention," *Reuter*, September 5, 2012, available at <http://news.yahoo.com/china-backs-transition-syria-opposes-intervention-055405757.html>. Accessed on October 14, 2012.

44. Ibid.

45. Daniel Treisman, "Why Russia Supports Syria's Assad," UCLAToday, published on *CNN.com*, February 2, 2012, available at <http://today.ucla.edu/portal/ut/PRN-russia-s-support-for-assad-regime-228392.aspx>. Accessed on October 14, 2012.

46. Ruslan Pukhov, "Why Russia is Backing Syria," op-ed piece in *The New York Times*, July 6, 2012, available at <http://www.nytimes.com/2012/07/07/opinion/why-russia-supports-syria.html>. Accessed on October 14, 2012.

47. Ibid.

48. Mark Landler and Neil MacFarquhar, "Heavier Weapons Push Syrian Crisis Toward Civil War," *The New York Times*, June 13, 2012, pp. A1 and A12.

49. Maysam Behravesh and Mohammad Reza Kiani, "The Syrian Crisis: What Is at Stake for Regional Players," *Iran Review*, September 4, 2011, available at <https://portal.research.lu.se/portal/files/6415885/3052893.pdf>. Accessed on April 15, 2021.

50. An interview by Hassan Khaled Chatila, "The Revolt in Syria: Its Roots and Prospects," *Links: International Journal of Socialist Renewal*, May 9, 2011, available at <http://links.org.au/node/2322>. Accessed on April 15, 2021.

51. Ibid.

52. The video can be accessed online at http://www.youtube.com/watch?v=vQ5kt dYZbbQ&feature=player_embedded. The chants targeting Iran start around the 1:40 mark.

53. Nick Cumming-Bruce and Rick Gladstone, "Syria Talks Won't Include the Saudis or Iranians," *The New York Times*, June 28, 2012, p. A10.

54. Ibid.

55. Brock Dahl, "Foreign Military Intervention in Syria?" *Christian Science Monitor*, July 23, 2012, p. 36.

56. John Hubbel Weiss, "Foreign Military Intervention in Syria?" *Christian Science Monitor*, July 23, 2012, p. 36.

57. Franz-Stefan Gady, "Russia Delivers First Missiles for Iran's New Air Defense," *The Diplomat*, July 19, 2016, available <ttps://thediplomat.com/2016/07/russia-delivers-first-missiles-for-irans-new-air-defense-system/>. Accessed on December 26, 2020.

58. Seyed Hossein Mousavian and Mohammad Reza Chitsazian, "Iran's Foreign Policy in the Middle East: A Grand Strategy," *Middle East Policy*, Vol. XXVII, No. 3, Fall 2020, pp. 99–114; see especially p. 109.

59. This section is based on Mahmood Monshipouri, "Pipeline Politics in Iran, Turkey, and the South Caucasus," in Mehran Kamrava, ed., *The Great Game in West Asia*, New York: Oxford University Press, 2017, pp. 57–81.

60. Marzieh Kouhi-Esfahani, *Iran's Foreign Policy in the South Caucasus: Relations with Azerbaijan and Armenia*, New York: Routledge, 2019, p. 24.

61. Ibid., p. 26.

62. Mahmood Monshipouri, "Pipeline Politics in Iran," op. cit., p. 60.

63. Ibid., p. 59.

64. Brenda Shaffer, "Iran's Role in the South Caucasus and Caspian Region: Diverging Views of the U.S. and Europe," in Eugene Whitlock, ed., *Iran and Its Neighbors*, Berlin, Germany: Stiftung Wissenschaft und Politik, 2003, pp. 17–22; see especially pp. 18–19; available at <https://www.belfercenter.org/sites/default/files/files/publication/shaffer.pdf>. Accessed on March 25, 2021.

65. *World Population Review*, available at <https://worldpopulationreview.com/countries/iran-population>. Accessed on March 25, 2021.

66. Mahmood Monshipouri, "Pipeline Politics in Iran," op. cit., p. 64.

67. Hamid Ahmadi, "The Clash of Nationalisms: Iranian Response to Baku's Irredentism," in Mehran Kamrava, ed., *The Great Game in West Asia*, New York: Oxford University Press, 2017, pp. 105–37; see especially, pp. 135–6.

68. Rauf Mammadov and Fuad Shahbazov, "US-Iran Escalation and Its Implications for the South Caucasus," *Middle East Institute*, January 28, 2020, available at <https://www.mei.edu/publications/us-iran-escalation-and-its-implications-south-caucasus>. Accessed on March 26, 2021.

69. Marzieh Kouhi-Esfahani, op. cit., p. 97.

70. Paul Goble, "Iran Seeks to Expand Its Position in South Caucasus on Wake of Karabakh War," *Eurasia Review*, January 31, 2021; available at <https://www.eurasiareview.com/31012021-iran-seeks-to-expand-its-position-in-south-caucasus-on-wake-of-karabakh-war-oped/>. Accessed on April 19, 2021.

71. Marzieh Kouhi-Esfahani, op. cit., p. 113.

72. Mahmood Monshipouri, "Pipeline Politics in Iran," op. cit., p. 66.

73. Global Energy Monitor, "Iran-Armenia Gas Pipeline," available at <https://www.

gem.wiki/Iran%E2%80%93Armenia_gas_pipeline>. Accessed on March 25, 2021.

74. Zeynep Kaya, "Iran and Armenia: A Symbiotic Relationship," *Review of Armenian Studies*, No. 24, 2011, pp. 153–72.

75. Anthony H. Cordesman, Bryan Gold, Robert Shelala, and Michael Gibbs, *US and Iranian Strategic Competition: Turkey and the South Caucasus*, Center for Strategic and International Studies (CSIS), June 6, 2013, pp. 1–100; see especially p. 65, available at <http://csis.org/files/publication/130612_turk_casp_chap9.pdf>. Accessed on March 26, 2021.

76. Richard Giragosian, "Armenia's Search for Independence," *Current History*, Vol. 113, No. 765, October 2014, pp. 285–89; see especially p. 285.

77. Ibid.

78. David O'Byrne, "Iran and Armenia Propose Gas Transit to Georgia," *Eurasianet*, March 1, 2019, available at <https://eurasianet.org/iran-and-armenia-propose-gas-transit-to-georgia>. Accessed on March 25, 2021.

79. Abdollah Baei Lashaki, Masoumeh Rad Goudarzi, and Davood Amraei, "The Roots of Tension in South Caucasus: The Case of Iran-Azerbaijan Relationship," *Journal of Politics and Law*, Vol. 6, No. 4, 2013, pp. 141–8; see p. 142.

80. Ibid.

81. *Haaretz*, "Israel Signs $1.6 Billion Arms Deal with Azerbaijan," February 26, 2012, available at <https://www.haaretz.com/1.5190757>. Accessed on March 24, 2021.

82. Emil Avdaliani, "Iran in the South Caucasus: Adjustment and Evolution," Rusi.org, February 26, 2021, available at <https://rusi.org/explore-our-research/publications/commentary/iran-south-caucasus-adjustment-and-evolution>. Accessed on January 20, 2022.

83. Eldar Mamedov, "Perspectives: How Iran Views the Nagorno Karabakh Truce," Eurasianet. November 13, 2020, available at <https://eurasianet.org/perspectives-how-iran-views-the-nagorno-karabakh-truce>. Accessed on January 20, 2022.

84. Robert F. Worth, "They Break US or We Break Them," *The New York Times Magazine*, November 4, 2018, pp. 48–57 and 69; see especially p. 51.

85. Thomas Juneau, "No, Yemen's Houthis Actually Aren't Iranian Puppets," *The Washington Post*, March 16, 2016, available at <https://www.washingtonpost.com/news/monkey-cage/wp/2016/05/16/contrary-to-popular-belief-houthis-arent-iranian-proxies/>. Accessed on December 24, 2020.

86. Samuel Ramani, "Iran's Post-Conflict Vision in Yemen," Carnegie Endowment for International Peace, December 11, 2019, available at <https://carnegieendowment.org/sada/80557>. Accessed on December 24, 2020.

87. Gerald M. Feierstein, "Iran's Role in Yemen and Prospects for Peace," *The Iran Primer,* United States Institute for Peace, December 5, 2018, available at <https://iranprimer.usip.org/blog/2018/dec/05/iran%E2%80%99s-role-yemen-and-prospects-peace>. Accessed on August 18, 2021.

88. Vincent Durac, "Yemen's Houthis—And Why They're Not Simply a Proxy of

Iran," *The Conversation*, September 19, 2019, available at <https://theconversation.com/yemens-houthis-and-why-theyre-not-simply-a-proxy-of-iran-123708>. Accessed on December 24, 2020.

89. Ibid.

90. Robert F. Worth, op. cit., p. 52.

91. Vincent Durac, op. cit.

92. Michelle Nichols, "Exclusive: UN Investigators Find Yemen's Houthis Did Not Carry Out Saudi Oil Attack," *Reuters*, January 8, 2020; available at <https://www.reuters.com/article/us-saudi-aramco-attacks-un-exclusive/exclusive-u-n-investigators-find-yemens-houthis-did-not-carry-out-saudi-oil-attack-idUSKBN1Z-72VX>. Accessed on December 24, 2020.

93. Patrick Wintour and Bethan McKernan, "Yemen: UAE Confirms Withdrawal from Port City of Hodeidah," *The Guardian*, July 9, 2019, available at <https://www.theguardian.com/world/2019/jul/09/yemen-uae-confirms-withdrawal-from-port-city-of-hodeidah>. Accessed on January 25, 2021.

94. Maysam Behravesh and Hamidreza Azizi, "Iran and the Nagorno-Karabakh Conflict: Preserving the Status Quo," Gulf International Forum, October 16, 2020, available at <https://gulfif.org/iran-and-the-nagorno-karabakh-conflict-preserving-the-status-quo/>. Accessed on December 22, 2020.

95. Thomas Juneau, "Iran's Policy Towards Houthis in Yemen: A Limited Return on a Modest Investment," *International Affairs*, Vol. 92, No. 3, 2016, pp. 647–63; see especially p. 663.

96. Kaweh Sadegh Zadeh, "Iran's Strategy in the South Caucasus," *Caucasian Review of International Affairs*, Vol. 2, Nol. 1, Winter 2008, pp. 1–7; see especially p. 7.

6. THE IRAN NUCLEAR PROGRAM

1. Shibley Telhami, "The Contemporary Middle East: Some Questions, Some Answers," in Karl Yambert, ed., *The Contemporary Middle East: A Westview Reader*, Second Edition, Boulder, CO: Westview Press, 2010, pp. 355–65; see especially p. 360.

2. Ibid.

3. Ibid.

4. Suzanne Maloney, "After Dumping the Nuclear Deal, Trump Has No Strategy for Iran," *Brookings*, May 9, 2018, available at <https://www.brookings.edu/blog/order-from-chaos/2018/05/09/after-dumping-the-nuclear-deal-trump-has-no-strategy-for-iran/>. Accessed on February 1, 2021.

5. John Ghazvinian, *America and Iran: A History, 1720 to the Present*," New York: Alfred A. Knopf, 2021, p. 451.

6. Ibid., p. 453.

7. This part is based on Mahmood Monshipouri, "Nuclear Program," in Mehran Kamrava and Manochehr Dorraj, eds., *Iran: Today: An Encyclopedia of Life in the Islamic Republic*, Vol. 2, Westport, CT: Greenwood Press, 2008, pp. 356–62.

8. Shahram Chubin, *Iran's Nuclear Ambitions*, Washington, DC: Carnegie Endowment for International Peace, 2006.

9. Anthony H. Cordesman, *Iran's Developing Military Capabilities*, Washington, DC: Center for Strategic and International Studies, 2006.

10. Ibid.

11. John Ghazvinian, *America and Iran*, op. cit., p. 455.

12. Ibid.

13. Nader Entessar and Kaveh L. Afrasiabi, *Iran Nuclear Accord and the Remaking of the Middle East*, Lanham, MD: Rowman & Littlefield, 2018, p. 16.

14. Ibid.

15. Ibid., pp. 16–17.

16. Nader Entessar and Kaveh Afrasiabi, *Iran Nuclear Accord*, op. cit., p. 68.

17. It should be noted that Iran's nuclear program has not been built since the 1979 Iranian Revolution; rather, it was built since the Shah's era with the assistance of the Europeans and the United States.

18. Christopher de Bellaigue, "Iran," *Foreign Policy*, No. 148, May–June 2005, pp. 18–24; see p. 19.

19. Meir Javedanfar, "Difficult Costumers," *Iranian.com* July 31, 2005.

20. Ibid.

21. *National Intelligence Estimate*, "Iran: Nuclear Intentions and Capabilities," November 2007, available at <http://www.dni.gov/press_releases/20071203_release.pdf>. Last accessed on July 31, 2009.

22. Dafna Linzer, "Iran Is Judged 19 Years From Nuclear Bomb," *The Washington Post*, August 2, 2005, p. A1.

23. Robert Baer, *The Devil We Know: Dealing With the New Iranian Superpower*, New York: Crown Publishers, 2008, p. 140.

24. Ibid., p. 168.

25. Kaveh Ehsani and Chris Toensing, "Neo-Conservatives, Hardline Clerics and the Bomb," *Middle East Report*, No. 233, Vol. 34, Winter 2004, pp. 10–15; see p. 12.

26. Ibid., p. 10.

27. For an illuminating discussion on this point, see Ali M. Ansari, *Confronting Iran: The Failure of American Foreign Policy and the Next Great Crisis in the Middle East*, New York: Basic Books, 2006.

28. Stephen Kinzer, "Diplomacy is the Best Option for American-Iranian Relations," in Julia Bauder, ed., *Is Iran a Threat to Global Security?*, New York: Greenhaven Press, 2006: 2006, pp. 46–57.

29. This part is based on Mahmood Monshipouri, "US–Iran Relations: Embracing a New Realism," The Emirates Center for Strategic Studies Research, Abu Dhabi, UAE, *The Emirates Lecture Series # 77*, March 22, 2009, pp. 1–61.

30. Kaveh Ehsani and Chris Toensing, "Neo-Conservatives, Hardline Clerics and the Bomb," *Middle East Report*, No. 233, Vol. 34, No. 4, Winter 2004, pp. 10–15.

31. Colbert C. Held and John Thomas Cummings, *Middle East Patterns: Places, Peoples, and Politics*, Boulder, CO: Westview Press, 2014, p. 665.

32. For more on this subject, see Mahmood Monshipouri and Banafsheh Keynoush, "Dealing with Iran: Confrontation and Cooperation?" *Insight Turkey*, Vol. 10, No. 4, 2008, pp. 135–57.

33. Antony T. Sullivan, "Regional Games: Iran and Russia," *Levant Monitor Update*, November 24, 2008, available at http://www.mepc.org/resources/Levant Monitor.asp. Last accessed on November 24, 2008; see also Howard LaFranchi, "Iran: Will Talks Happen under Obama?" *The Christian Science Monitor*, November 21, 2008, p. 3.

34. Paul R. Pillar, "The Importance of the Iran Agreement," The Brookings Institution, April 4, 2015, available at <https://www.brookings.edu/opinions/the-impor-tance-of-the-iran-agreement>. Accessed on September 1, 2016.

35. Jeffrey Goldberg, "The Obama Doctrine," *The Atlantic*, April 2016, available at <https://www.theatlantic.com/magazine/archive/2016/04/the-obama-doc-trine/471525/#5>. Accessed on February 1, 2021.

36. Ibid.

37. Suzanne Maloney, op. cit.

38. A European diplomatic adviser is being quoted in Seymour M. Hersh, "The Iran Plans," *The New Yorker*, April 17, 2006, pp. 30–7; see p. 36.

39. For an illuminating source on this subject, see Sasan Fayazmanesh, *The United States and Iran: Sanctions, Wars, and the Policy of Dual Containment*, New York: Routledge, 2008; see especially p. 236.

40. Noam Chomsky and Gilbert Achcar, eds., *Perilous Power: The Middle East and U.S. Foreign Policy*, Boulder, CO: Paradigm Publishers, 2007, p. 141.

41. Gary Sick, "The Republic and the Rahbar," *National Interest Online*, January 6, 2009, available at http://www.nationalinterest.org/Article.aspx?id=20482.

42. Ibid.

43. Richard N. Haass and Martin Indyk, "Beyond Iraq: A New U.S. Strategy for the Middle East," *Foreign Affairs*, Vol. 88, No. 1, January/February 2009, pp. 41–58; see p. 47.

44. Samir Tata, *Iran: The Case for Détente*, The Emirates Occasional Papers, Abu Dhabi, UAE: The Emirates Center for Strategic Studies and Research, 2008, p. 39.

45. Gregory Gause, "Nuclear Overreaction," *The National*, November 20, 2008, available at <http://www.thenational.ae/article/20081121/REVIEW/846523295/1008>. Last accessed on November 23, 2008.

46. Barry R. Posen, "We Can Live with a Nuclear Iran," *The New York Times*, February 27, 2006, p. A19.

47. Ali Hosseini, "What Pressure on Iran Will Do the Trick?" October 23, 2008, available at <http://www.niacouncil.org/index.php?option=com_content&task=v ...>. Last accessed on November 25, 2008.

48. Kenneth N. Waltz, "Why Iran Should Get a Bomb," *Foreign Affairs*, Vol. 91, No. 4, July/August 2012, pp. 2–5.

49. Nader Entessar and Kaveh L. Afrasiabi, *Iran Nuclear Accord and the Remaking of the Middle East*, Lanham, MD: Rowman & Littlefield, 2018, pp. 41–2.

50. Ibid., pp. 26–7.
51. Ibid., p. 27.
52. Ibid., p. 29.
53. Ibid., pp. 29–30.
54. Ibid., pp. 30–2.
55. Marc Wellner, "The Controversy about the Iranian Nuclear Sanctions Snapback," *American Society of International Law*, Vol. 24, No. 27, October 19, 2020, available at <https://www.asil.org/insights/volume/24/issue/27/controversy-about-iranian-nuclear-sanctions-snapback>. Accessed on December 16, 2020.
56. Robert Goldston, "Iran after Sunset," *Bulletin of The Atomic Scientists*, April 25, 2018, available at <https://thebulletin.org/2018/04/iran-after-sunset/>. Accessed on December 16, 2020.
57. Ibid.
58. Nader Entessar and Kaveh L. Afrasiabi, *Trump and Iran: From Containment to Confrontation*, Lanham, MD: Lexington Books, 2020, p. 11.
59. Tim Hume and Alireza Hajihosseini, "Iran Fires Ballistic Missiles a Day After Test: U.S. Officials Hint at Violation, "*CNN World*, March 9, 2016, available at <https://www.cnn.com/2016/03/09/middleeast/iran-missile-test/index.html>. Accessed on February 1, 2021.
60. Ibid.
61. Ibid., p. 84.
62. Brian Schwartz, "Saudi Arabia hires new crop of lobbyists with Joe Biden poised to roll back Trump-era relationship," *CNBC*, December 15, 2020, available at <https://www.cnbc.com/amp/2020/12/15/saudi-arabia-hires-new-lobbyists-ahead-of-joe-biden-administration.html>. Accessed on December 16, 2020.
63. Nader Entessar and Kaveh L. Afrasiabi, op. cit., *Trump and Iran*, p. 198.
64. Robert Mason, "US–Iran Relations Under President Biden: Back to the Status Quo Ante," *Georgetown Journal of International Affairs*, November 30, 2020, available at <https://gjia.georgetown.edu/2020/11/30/us-iran-relations-under-president-biden-back-to-the-status-quo-ante/>. Accessed on December 17, 2020.
65. Stratfor, "A secret, high-level meeting suggests Israel and Saudi Arabia are hedging their bets on Biden," *Business Insider*, November 30, 2020, available at <https://www.businessinsider.com/secret-israel-saudi-arabia-meeting-suggests-theyre-hedging-on-biden-2020–11>. Accessed on December 16, 2020.
66. Marc Wellner, op. cit.
67. Ibid.
68. International Crisis Group, "Iran: The Riddle of Raisi," August 5, 2021, available at <https://www.crisisgroup.org/middle-east-north-africa/gulf-and-arabian-peninsula/iran/224-iran-riddle-raisi>. Accessed on August 18, 2021.
69. Ibid.
70. Parisa Hafezi, "Iran's Raisi Names Anti-Western Hardliner as New Foreign Minister," *Reuters*, August 11, 2021, available at <https://www.reuters.com/

world/middle-east/irans-raisi-presents-new-ministers-parliament-state-tv-2021-08-11/>. Accessed on August 18, 2021.

71. Trita Parsi and Bijan Khajehpur, "How to Make Iran Trust a New Nuclear Deal," *Foreign Policy*, August 15, 2021, available at <https://foreignpolicy.com/2021/08/17/iran-nuclear-deal-talks-biden-raisi/>. Accessed on August 18, 2021.

72. Ibid.

73. Vali Nasr, "Why Raisi Is the West's Best Hope for a Deal with Iran," *Foreign Policy*, June 23, 2021, available at <https://foreignpolicy.com/2021/06/23/ebrahim-raisi-iran-nuclear-deal/>. Accessed on August 18, 2021.

74. Mark Mazzetti, "U.S. Reports Says Iran Halted Nuclear Weapon Program in 2003," *The New York Times*, December 3, 2007, available at <https://www.nytimes.com/2007/12/03/world/americas/03iht-cia.5.8573960.html>. Accessed on December 16, 2020.

75. Jahangir Amuzegar, "Ahmadinejad Legacy," *Middle East Policy*, Vol. XX, No. 4, Winter 2013, pp. 124–32; see especially pp. 130–1.

7. TRUMP'S WITHDRAWAL FROM THE JCPOA: SOME IMPLICATIONS

1. John Ghazvinian, *America and Iran: A History, 1720 to the Present*, New York: Alfred A. Knopf, 2021, p. 530.

2. Ibid., p. 529.

3. Ibid., p. 531.

4. Ibid., p. 534.

5. Joy Gordon, *Invisible War: The United States and the Iraq Sanctions*, Cambridge, MA: Harvard University Press, 2010.

6. Sasan Fayazmanesh, *The United States and Iran: Sanctions, Wars, and the Policy of Dual Containment*, New York: Routledge, 2008, p. 236.

7. Mahmood Monshipouri, "US–Iran Relations: Embracing a New Realism," *Emirates Lecture Series* #77, The Emirates Center for Strategic Studies and Research, 2009, pp. 10–59; p. 13.

8. *Al Jazeera*, "Mike Pompeo Speech: What Are the 12 Demands Given to Iran," May 21, 2018, available at <https://www.aljazeera.com/news/2018/5/21/mike-pompeo-speech-what-are-the-12-demands-given-to-iran>. Accessed on February 1, 2021.

9. Rabih Hamawi, "Pompeo Lays out US Demands on Tehran, Khamenei Sets Conditions for EU to Stay in Deal," *The Arab American News*, February 5, 2018, available at <https://www.arabamericannews.com/2018/05/25/pompeo-lays-out-u-s-demands-on-tehran-khamenei-sets-condition-for-eu-to-stay-in-deal/>. Accessed on February 1, 2021.

10. Quoted in Mahmood Monshipouri, *Middle East Politics: Changing Dynamics*, New York: Routledge, 2019, p. 4.

11. Anoushiravan Ehteshami, "The Foreign Policy of Iran," in Raymond Hinnebusch and Anoushiravan Ehteshami, eds., Second edition, *The Foreign Policies of Middle East*

States, Boulder, CO: Lynne Rienner Publishers, 2014, pp. 261–88; see especially p. 286.

12. Ali Seyedrazaghi, "US Sanctions Against Iran Embolden Its Hardliners," in Avery Elizabeth Hurt, ed., *US–Iran Relations*, New York: Greenhaven Publishing, 2018, pp. 104–9; see especially p. 105.

13. Ibid.

14. Elizabeth Redden, "Trump's Muslim Ban Could Have a Chilling Effect on US Scholars," in Avery Elizabeth Hurt, ed., *US–Iran Relations*, New York: Greenhaven Publishing, 2018, pp. 110–19; see especially pp. 116–17.

15. John Morgan, "Trump's Travel Ban Has the Potential to Damage Science," in Avery Elizabeth Hurt, ed., *US–Iran Relations*, New York: Greenhaven Publishing, 2018, pp. 125–9.

16. Catie Edmondson, "Sonia Sotomayor Delivers Sharp Dissent in Travel Ban Case," *The New York Times*, June 26, 2018, available at <https://www.nytimes.com/2018/06/26/us/sonia-sotomayor-dissent-travel-ban.html>. Accessed on February 2, 2021.

17. See Farid Senzai, "Engaging American Muslims: Political Trends and Attitudes," Institute for Social Policy and Understanding (ISPU), April 2012, available at <https://www.ispu.org/wp-content/uploads/2016/08/ISPU_Report_Political_Participation.pdf?x96702>. Accessed on February 2, 2021.

18. Kathryn Watson, "Trump Signs $110 Billion Arms Deal with Saudi Arabia," *CBS News*, May 20, 2017, available at <http://www.cbsnews.com/news/trump-signs-110-billion-arms-deal-with-saudi-arabia/>. Accessed on May 21, 2017.

19. James L. Gelvin, *The New Middle East: What Everyone Needs to Know*," New York: Oxford University Press, 2018, p. 125.

20. This section is based on Mahmood Monshipouri, *Middle East Politics: Changing Dynamics*, New York: Routledge, 2019, pp. 125–7.

21. Zeeshan Aleem, "Saudi Arabia's Diplomatic War with Qatar, Explained," *Vox*, June 6, 2017, available at <https://www.vox.com/world/2017/6/6/15739606/saudi-arabia-ties-qatar-trump>. Accessed on June 9, 2017.

22. Mehran Kamrava, "What Does the UAE Want?" *CIRS*, Georgetown University, Qatar, June 5, 2017, available at <https://cirs.georgetown.edu/news-events/news/what-does-uae-want>. Accessed on June 9, 2017.

23. Mehran Kamrava, *Troubled Waters: Insecurity in the Persian Gulf*, Ithaca, NY: Cornell University Press, 2018, p. 147.

24. Ibid., p. 51.

25. Nader Entessar and Kaveh L. Afrasiabi, *Trump and Iran: From Containment to Confrontation*, Lanham, MD: Lexington Books, 2020, p. 145.

26. Ibid., p. 146.

27. James L. Gelvin, *The New Middle East: What Everyone Needs to Know*," New York: Oxford University Press, 2018, p. 119.

28. Kian Tajbakhsh, op. cit., pp. 48–50.

29. Nicholas Miller, "Maximum Pressure is Failing: Fact-Checking Pompeo on Iran,"

Warontherocks.com, August 15, 2019. Available at <https://warontherocks. com/2019/08/maximum-pressure-is-failing-fact-checking-pompeo-on-iran/>. Accessed on October 16, 2019.

30. Ilan Goldenberg and Kaleigh Thomas, "Trump's Iran Policy is a Failure," *Foreign Policy*, September 25, 2019, available at <https://foreignpolicy.com/2019/09/25/ trumps-iran-policy-is-a-failure/>. Accessed on February 2, 2021.

31. Patrick Wintour and Julian Borger, "Two Oil Tankers Attacked in Gulf of Oman," *The Guardian*, June 13, 2019, available at <https://www.theguardian.com/ world/2019/jun/13/oil-tankers-blasts-reports-gulf-of-oman-us-navy>. Accessed on January 18, 2021.

32. Tasnim News Agency, "Iran, UAE Sign MoU on Border Security," August 1, 2019, available at <https://www.tasnimnews.com/en/news/2019/08/01/2066966/ iran-uae-sign-mou-on-border-security>. Accessed on January 18, 2022.

33. Ilan Goldenberg and Kaleigh Thomas, op. cit.

34. Will Todman, "The Implications of a Turkish Intervention in Northeastern Syria, Center for Strategic and International Studies (CSIS), October 7, 2019, available at <https://www.csis.org/analysis/implications-turkish-intervention-northeastern-syria>. Accessed on October 17, 2019.

35. Maysam Behravesh, "How Iran Views the Turkish Invasion of Northern Syria," *Middle East Eye*, October 12, 2019, available at <https://www.middleeasteye.net/ news/how-iran-views-turkish-invasion-northern-syria>. Accessed on October 16, 2019.

36. Richard N. Haass, "Evaluating the Trump Administration's Iran Policy," Council on Foreign Relations, January 14, 2020, available at <https://www.cfr.org/ report/evaluating-trump-administrations-iran-policy>. Accessed on December 30, 2020.

37. Simeon Kerr, "Saudi Arabia and Allies to Restore Ties with Qatar," *Financial Times*, January 5, 2021, available at <https://www.ft.com/content/ad2eb477-b8f8-4dae-9e4c-a441759fc897?>. Accessed on January 8, 2021.

38. Nader Entessar and Kaveh L. Afrasiabi, *Trump and Iran*, op. cit., p. 66.

39. Ibid.

40. Ibid., pp. 66–7.

41. Samuel M. Hickey, "A worthless withdrawal: Two years since President Trump abandoned the JCPOA," Center for Arms Control and Non-Proliferation," May 11, 2020, available at <https://armscontrolcenter.org/a-worthless-withdrawal-two-years-since-president-trump-abandoned-the-jcpoa/>. Accessed on December 30, 2020.

42. Ibid.

43. Nader Entessar and Kaveh L. Afrasiabi, *Trump and Iran*, op. cit., p. 67.

44. Ibid.

45. Samuel M. Hickey, op. cit.

46. Ibid.

47. Nader Entessar and Kaveh L. Afrasiabi, *Trump and Iran*, op. cit., pp. 65–6.

48. Seyed Hossein Mousavian and Mohammad Reza Chitsazian, "Iran's Foreign Policy in the Middle East: A Grand Strategy," *Middle East Policy*, Vol. XXVI, No. 3, Fall 2020, pp. 99–114; see especially p. 110.

49. Volker Perthes, "Withdrawing from the nuclear deal is a major blunder—the E-3 must pick up the baton," *The German Times*, October 2018, available at <http://www.german-times.com/withdrawing-from-the-nuclear-deal-is-a-major-blunder-the-e-3-must-pick-up-the-baton/>. Accessed on December 30, 2020.

50. Najmeh Bozorgmehr, "China and Iran Sign 25-Year Agreement to Expand Ties," *Financial Times*, March 27, 2021, available at <https://www.ft.com/content/24393899–909e-4b3f-9e18–06a6951d639d>. Accessed on March 28, 2021.

51. Shi Jiangtao, "China's 25-year deal with Iran marks 'momentous' change as ties with US sour, says former ambassador," *South China Morning Post*, March 28, 2021, available at <https://www.scmp.com/news/china/diplomacy/article/3127346/chinas-25-year-deal-iran-marks-momentous-change-ties-us-sour>. Accessed on March 28, 2021.

52. Ibid.

53. Farnaz Fassihi, "Big Iran Deal Gives Beijing an Oil Supply and Influence," *The New York Times*, March 28, 2021, p. 12.

54. Ibid.

55. Ian McCredi, "Trump's Failure in the Middle East," *Fair Observer*, August 19, 2020, available at <https://www.fairobserver.com/region/north_america/ian-mccredie-donald-trump-us-foreign-policy-middle-east-news-iran-nuclear-deal-jcpoa-world-news-78164/>. Accessed on December 31, 2020.

56. Barbara Slavin, "Five reasons why US 'maximum pressure' on Iran has backfired," *Atlantic Council*, May 14, 2020, available at <https://www.atlanticcouncil.org/blogs/iransource/five-reasons-why-us-maximum-pressure-on-iran-has-backfired/>. Accessed on December 31, 2020.

57. Ian McCredi, op. cit.

58. Jackson Diehl, "Trump's overarching Middle East strategy reaches a disastrous dead end," *The Washington Post*, November 22, 2020; available at <https://www.washingtonpost.com/opinions/global-opinions/trump-middle-east-legacy/2020/11/22/4563bec2-2a7d-11eb-8fa2-06e7cbb145c0_story.html>. Accessed on December 30, 2020.

59. Ibid.

60. Robert A. Pape, "Why Economic Sanctions Do Not Work," in *International Security*, Vol. 22, No. 2, pp. 90–136.

61. Ishaan Tharoor, "Trump's Iran Agenda is About to End in Failure," *The Washington Post*, November 16, 2020, available at <https://www.washingtonpost.com/world/2020/11/17/trump-iran-pressure-biden-nuclear/>. Accessed on December 31, 2020.

62. Nuclear Threat Initiative (NTI), "Nuclear," June 2020, available at <https://www.nti.org/learn/countries/iran/nuclear/>. Accessed on February 5, 2021.

63. Ibid.

64. Richard N. Haass, "Evaluating the Trump Administration's Iran Policy," Council on Foreign Relations, January 14, 2020, available at <https://www.cfr.org/report/evaluating-trump-administrations-iran-policy>. Accessed on December 30, 2020.

65. Ibid.

66. Samantha Vingrod, "Trump's Iran Policy has Failed Across the Board," *CNN.com*, January 3, 2021, available at <https://www.cnn.com/2021/01/03/opinions/trump-pompeo-iran-failed-policy-vinograd/index.html>. Accessed on February 3, 2021.

67. Professor Dane Rowlands is interviewed by Mohammad Mazhari, "Sanctions will hamper Iran's access to medicine and medical equipment: Carleton University professor," *Tehran Times*, October 14, 2020, available at <https://www.tehrantimes.com/news/453558/Sanctions-will-hamper-Iran-s-access-to-medicine-and-medical-equipment>. Accessed on January 1, 2021.

68. Tom Nichols, "Trump Could Still Start a Last-Ditch War With Iran," *The Atlantic*, December 30, 2020, available at <<https://www.theatlantic.com/ideas/archive/2020/12/trump-could-still-start-last-ditch-war-iran/617530/>. Accessed on January 1, 2021.

69. *Euronews*, "US seeks to extend arms embargo on Iran indefinitely in revised UN resolution," December 8, 2020, available at <https://www.euronews.com/2020/08/12/us-seeks-to-extend-arms-embargo-on-iran-indefinitely-in-revised-un-resolution>. Accessed on January 1, 2021.

70. Robert Malley, "10 Conflicts to Watch in 2021: The Year Ahead," *Foreign Policy*, December 29, 2020, available at <https://foreignpolicy.com/author/robert-malley/>. Accessed on January 1, 2021.

71. Daryl G. Kimball, "Trump's Failing Iran Policy," Arms Control Association, June 2019, available at <https://www.armscontrol.org/act/2019–06/focus/trumps-failing-iran-policy>. Accessed on February 2, 2021.

8. THE BIDEN ADMINISTRATION: CHANGE IN THE GEOPOLITICAL WINDS

1. Daniel Larison, "How to Repair the US–Iran Relationship," *The American Conservative*, February 3, 2021, available at <https://www.theamericanconservative.com/articles/how-to-repair-the-u-s-iranian-relationship/>. Accessed on February 6, 2021.

2. Sasan Fayazmanesh, "How to Do 'Regime Change' Correctly: A Blueprint for the Biden Administration," *Counterpunch*, January 29, 2021, available at <https://www.counterpunch.org/2021/01/29/how-to-do-regime-change-correctly-a-blueprint-for-the-biden-administration/>. Accessed on February 6, 2021.

3. Anne Gearan and Karen DeYoung, "Biden Team Exploring How US Might Rejoin Iran Nuclear Deal," *The Washington Post*, February 5, 2021; available at <https://www.washingtonpost.com/politics/biden-iran-deal/2021/02/05/b968154c-67d7–11eb-886d-5264d4ceb46d_story.html>. Accessed on February 6, 2021.

4. William J. Burns, *The Back Channel: A Memoir of American Diplomacy and the Case for Its Renewal*, New York: Random House, 2019, p. 338.

5. Ibid., p. 346.

6. Ibid., p. 350.

7. Ibid., p. 364.

8. Ibid., p. 364.

9. Ibid., pp. 382–3.

10. Ibid., pp. 384–5.

11. Alex Vatanka, The US-Iran-Qatar Triangle," *Middle East Eye*, February 17, 2021, available at <https://www.mei.edu/publications/us-iran-qatar-triangle>. Accessed on March 3, 2021.

12. Ibid.

13. This section is based on unpublished paper by Mahmood Monshipouri and Javad Heiran-Nia, "Biden and Détente with Iran," January 4, 2021.

14. Hamidreza Taraghi, "Are the military a viable option for the presidential election?" October 13, 2020, available at <https://www.isna.ir/news/99072115643>. Accessed on November 20, 2020.

15. Ibid.

16. Ibid.

17. Loveday Morris and Erin Cunningham, "Europe Sees a Narrow Window for Biden to Revive Iran Nuclear Deal," *The Washington Post*, January 17, 2021, available <https://www.washingtonpost.com/world/europe/iran-nuclear-europe-biden/2021/01/16/b0e45352–54f1–11eb-acc5–92d2819a1ccb_story.html>. Accessed on February 6, 2021.

18. "The first military figure officially announced his candidacy for the 2021 elections," www.khabaronline.ir, November 25, 2020, available at <https://www.khabar-online.ir/news/1459101>. Accessed November 26, 2020

19. "The reaction of the fundamentalist and reformist media to Fattah's words", August 12, 2020, available at <https://www.irna.ir/news/83905244>. Accessed on November 20, 2020.

20. "The poverty line in the country is 8 to 10 million Tomans, Iranian society has become completely polarized," www.tahlilbazaar.com, November 9, 2020, available at <https://www.tahlilbazaar.com/news/52856>. Accessed on November 23, 2020.

21. Paul Krugman, "Pax Americana," *The New York Times: Sunday Review*, September 1, 2020, p. SR: 5.

22. Roger Cohen, "America's Word," *The New York Times: Sunday Review*, September 1, 2020, p. SR:5.

23. Paul Wiseman, "From Beijing to Brussels, Trump's Trade Wars at a Glance," *US News and World Report*, October 27, 2020, available at <https://www.usnews.com/news/politics/articles/2020–10–27/from-beijing-to-brussels-trumps-trade-wars-at-a-glance>. Accessed on November 23, 2020.

24. Mahmood Monshipouri, "Upending Trump's Tumultuous Legacy," *Tehran Times*,

329

November 7, 2020, available at <https://www.tehrantimes.com/news/454333/ Upending-Trump-s-tumultuous-legacy>. Accessed on November 7, 2020.

25. Kori Schake, Jim Mattis, Jim Ellis, and Joe Felter, "Defense In Depth: Why U.S. Security Depends on Alliances—Now More than Ever," *Foreign Affairs*, November 23, 2020, available at <https://www.foreignaffairs.com/articles/ united-states/2020-11-23/defense-depth>. Accessed on November 23, 2020.

26. Ibid.

27. Robin Wright, "Will Biden's Iran Diplomacy Become a Shakespearean Tragedy?" *The New Yorker*, February 22, 2021, available at <https://www.newyorker.com/ news/our-columnists/will-bidens-iran-diplomacy-become-a-shakespearean-trag- edy>. Accessed on February 22, 2021.

28. Ibid.

29. Ibid.

30. Ibid.

31. Dan De Luce, Ken Dilanian, Saphora Smith, and Ali Arouzi, "Biden Faces a Race Against the Clock for U.S. to Rejoin Iran Nuclear Deal," *NBCNews.com*, November 21, 2020, available at <https://www.nbcnews.com/politics/national-security/ biden-faces-race-against-clock-u-s-rejoin-iran-nuclear-n1248356>. Accessed on November 26, 2020.

32. Joe Biden, "There is a smarter way to be tough on Iran," *CNN*, Op-ed, September 13, 2020, available at <https://www.cnn.com/2020/09/13/opinions/smarter- way-to-be-tough-on-iran-joe-biden/index.html>. Accessed on November 21, 2020.

33. Parisa Hafezi and Arshad Mohammed, "Analysis: Biden Would Face Uncertain Path to Détente with Wary Iran," *Reuters*, October 28, 2020, available at <https:// www.reuters.com/article/us-usa-election-iran-analysis/analysis-biden-would- face-uncertain-path-to-detente-with-wary-iran-idUSKBN27D1D2>. Accessed on November 21, 2020.

34. Michael Hirsh, "Signaling a New Willingness to Talk, Biden Scrambles to Save Iran Nuclear Deal," *Foreign Policy*, February 18, 2021, available at <https://foreignpol- icy.com/2021/02/18/biden-iran-nuclear-deal-policy/>. Accessed on February 19, 2021.

35. Lara Jakes, Michael Crowley, David E. Sanger, and Farnaz Fassihi, "Biden Administration Formally Offers to Restart Nuclear Talks with Iran," *The New York Times*, February 18, 2021, available at <https://www.nytimes.com/2021/02/18/ us/politics/biden-iran-nuclear.html>. Accessed on February 18, 2021.

36. Parisa Hafezi and Arshad Mohammed, "Analysis: Biden Would Face Uncertain Path to Détente with Wary Iran," *Reuters*, October 28, 2020, available at <https:// www.reuters.com/article/us-usa-election-iran-analysis/analysis-biden-would- face-uncertain-path-to-detente-with-wary-iran-idUSKBN27D1D2>. Accessed on November 21, 2020.

37. David Brennan, "Iran Deal Averts Crisis but Tehran Maintains Red Lines for Joe Biden Talks," *Newsweek*, February 22, 2021, available at <https://www.newsweek.

com/iran-deal-averts-crisis-tehran-maintains-red-lines-joe-biden-talks-1571028>. Accessed on February 22, 2021.

38. Ronen Bergman, Rick Gladstone and Farnaz Fassihi, "Blackout Hits Iran Nuclear Site in What Appears to be Israeli Sabotage," *The New York Times*, April 11, 2021, available at <https://www.nytimes.com/2021/04/11/world/middleeast/iran-nuclear-natanz.html>. Accessed on April 12 2021.

39. Michael Jansen, "After His Own Interests," *Panorama Magazine: Gulf Today*, April 16–22, 2021, pp. 36–7.

40. Javad Heiran-Nia, "Biden and the Persian Gulf security order; the role of Iran and Saudi Arabia," Scientific Research and Middle East Strategic Studies Center, February 1, 2021, available at <https://www.cmess.ir/Page/View/2021–02–01/4642>. Accessed on October 1, 2021.

41. Ibid.

42. Daniel Benaim and Jake Sullivan. "America's Opportunity in the Middle East," *Foreign Affairs*, May 22, 2020, available at <https://www.foreignaffairs.com/node/1126062>. Accessed on August 4, 2021.

43. Gregory Aftandilian, "A Saudi-Iranian Rapprochement Still Has a Long Way to Go," September 21, 2021, available at <https://arabcenterdc.org/resource/a-saudi-iranian-rapprochement-still-has-a-long-way-to-go/>. Accessed on September 30, 2021.

44. *Al-Monitor*, "European Powers Call Iran's Enrichment Plans 'Deeply Worrying,'" December 7, 2020; available at <https://www.al-monitor.com/pulse/originals/2020/12/iran-nuclear-france-germany-uk-e3-inspectors-law-biden-jcpoa.html>. Accessed on December 8, 2020.

45. Loveday Morris and Erin Cunningham, "Europe Sees a Narrow Window for Biden to Revive Iran Nuclear Deal," *The Washington Post*, January 17, 2021, available <https://www.washingtonpost.com/world/europe/iran-nuclear-europe-biden/2021/01/16/b0e45352–54f1–11eb-acc5–92d2819a1ccb_story.html>. Accessed on February 6, 2021.

46. Ibid.

47. "Major General Jafari: There is potential to increase the range of Iranian missiles," *Mashregh News*, October 31, 2017, available at <https://www.mashreghnews.ir/news/793275>. Accessed on November 23, 2020.

48. Javad Heiran-Nia, "Western goals and approach to launching Iran's satellite and missile program", International Peace Studies Center, February 16, 2020, available at <http://peace-ipsc.org/fa/>. Accessed on November 23, 2020.

49. Michael Ellman, "Why Iran's satellite launch does not amount to an ICBM test", The International Institute for Strategic Studies, January 17, 2019, available at <http://peace-ipsc.org/fa/>. Accessed on November 23, 2020.

50. "Fact Sheet: Ballistic vs. Cruise Missiles," The Center for Arms Control and Non-Proliferation, available at <https://armscontrolcenter.org/wp-content/uploads/2017/04/Ballistic-vs.-Cruise-Missiles-Fact-Sheet.pdf>. Accessed on November 23, 2020.

51. "Saudi Arabia Seen to Build Missile Factory," Arms Control Association, available at <https://www.armscontrol.org/act/2019–03/news-briefs/saudi-arabia-seen-build-missile-factory>. Accessed on November 23, 2020.

52. Thomas B. Cochran, "The Relevance of Mordechai Vanunu, Disclosures to Israel's National Security", Natural Resources Defense Council, October 14, 1996, available at <https://fas.org/nuke/cochran/nuc_10149601a_174.pdf>. Accessed on November 23, 2020.

53. Patrick Wintour, "Iran says it would rejoin nuclear deal within an hour of US doing so," *The Guardian*, December 14, 2020, available at <https://www.theguardian.com/world/2020/dec/14/iran-says-rejoin-nuclear-deal-within-hour-us>. Accessed on December 15, 2020.

54. "Iran Foreign Minister Zarif: Full interview with NBC News' Richard Engel," February 15, 2020, available at <https://www.nbcnews.com/video/iran-foreign-minister-zarif-full-interview-with-nbc-news-richard-engel-78791749964>. Accessed on November 23, 2020.

55. "The Hague Code of Conduct against Ballistic Missile Proliferation (HCoC)", February, 2020, available at <https://www.hcoc.at/>. Accessed on November 23, 2020.

56. Javad Heiran-Nia, "Western goals and approach to launching Iran's satellite and missile program," International Peace Studies Center, February 16, 2020, available at <http://peace-ipsc.org/fa/>. Accessed on November 23, 2020.

57. "Resolution 2231 (2015) on Iran Nuclear Issue," United Nations Security Council, available at <https://www.un.org/securitycouncil/content/2231/background>. Accessed on November 23, 2020.

58. Ishaan Tharoor, "Biden's Uphill Battle to Save the Iran Nuclear Deal," *The Washington Post*, January 26, 2021, available at <https://www.washingtonpost.com/world/2021/01/27/biden-iran-nuclear-deal-challenge/>. Accessed on February 9, 2021.

59. Ibid.

60. Julien Barnes-Dacey and Ellie Geranmayeh, "The Narrow Path to Agreement: How Europe Should Support the Iran Nuclear Deal," European Council on Foreign Relations, February 10, 2021, available at <https://ecfr.eu/article/the-narrow-path-to-agreement-how-europe-should-support-the-iran-nuclear-deal/>. Accessed on February 10, 2021.

61. Ibid.

62. Laura Rozen, "Why Biden May Try to Return to Iran Nuclear Deal Before Renegotiating it," *Just Security*, November 22, 2020, available at <https://www.justsecurity.org/73488/why-biden-may-try-to-return-to-iran-nuclear-deal-before-renegotiating-it/>. Accessed on November 25, 2020.

63. Ibid.

64. Ibid.

65. Robert Malley and Stephen Pomper, "Accomplice to Carnage: How America Enables War in Yemen," *Foreign Affairs*, March/April 2021, available at <ile:///C:/

Users/909186933/Documents/Rob Malley How America Enables War in Yemen Foreign Affairs.htm>. Accessed on February 9, 2021.

66. Ibid.

67. Ibid.

68. Barbara Slavin, "A Scorched Earth Strategy on Iran," *The New York Times*, November 26, 2020, available at <https://www.nytimes.com/2020/11/28/opinion/iran-nuclear-scientist-killed.html>. Accessed on November 28, 2020.

69. David E. Sanger, "Iran Pact's Fate Dealt New Blow by Assassination" *The New York Times*, November 29, 2020, pp. 1 and 19.

70. Sam Fraser, "Maximum Pressure on Iran has Failed to Achieve Both Its Stated and Real Goals, Experts Say," *Responsible Statecraft*, June 8, 2020, available at <https://responsiblestatecraft.org/2020/06/08/maximum-pressure-on-iran-has-failed-to-achieve-both-its-stated-and-real-goals-experts-say/>. Accessed on November 21, 2020.

71. Steven A. Cook, "No Exit: Why the Middle East Still Matters to America," *Foreign Affairs*, Vol. 99, No. 6, November/December 2020, pp. 133–42.

72. Seyed Hossein Mousavian, "Fakhrizadeh Killing: How Biden Can Avoid Trap Laid by Opponents of the Iran Nuclear Deal," *Middle East Eye*, November 30, 2020, available at <https://www.middleeasteye.net/opinion/iran-nuclear-scientist-killing-biden-opponents-deal>. Accessed on December 1, 2020.

73. Quoted in Steven Erlanger, "Biden Wants to Rejoin Iran Nuclear Deal, but It Won't Be Easy," *The New York Times*, November 17, 2020, available at <https://www.nytimes.com/2020/11/17/world/middleeast/iran-biden-trump-nuclear-sanctions.html>. Accessed on November 24, 2020.

74. Esfandyar Batmanghelidj and Sahil Shah, "Three Solutions to Biden's Nuclear Stalemate with Iran," *Politico*, February 5, 2021, available at <https://www.politico.com/news/magazine/2021/02/05/biden-nuclear-iran-foreign-policy-466120>. Accessed on February 6, 2021.

75. Ibid.

76. Ibid.

77. Abdolrasool Divsallar, "Why Biden Shouldn't seek to Deprive Iran of Conventional Deterrence," Middle East Institute, February 25, 2021; available at <https://www.mei.edu/publications/why-biden-shouldnt-seek-deprive-iran-conventional-deterrence>. Accessed on February 26, 2021.

78. Ibid.

79. Farnaz Fassihi and David E. Sanger, "Iran Rejects Nuclear Deal Talks With U.S. Proposed by Europe," *The New York Times*, February 28, 2021, available at <https://www.nytimes.com/2021/02/28/world/middleeast/iran-nuclear-talks-united-states.html>. Accessed on February 28, 2021.

80. Kayhan Barzegar, "Aytollah Khamenei's Strategic Thinking," *The Iran Project*, January 17, 2017, available at <https://theiranproject.com/blog/2017/01/17/ayatollah-khameneis-strategic-thinking/>. Accessed on March 23, 2021.

81. Mahmood Sariolghalam, "The Biden Administration and Iran," available at <https://sariolghalam.com/2021/02/24>. Accessed on March 12 2021.

82. Ibid.

83. Ibid.

84. Karen DeYoung and Kareem Fahim, "United States and Iran Warily Circle Each Other over Reactivating Nuclear Deal," *The Washington Post*, March 14, 2021, available at <https://www.washingtonpost.com/national-security/biden-iran-nuclear-deal-talks/2021/03/14/4b020904–8376–11eb-81db-b02f0398f49a_story.html>. Accessed on March 15, 2021.

85. Djavad Salehi-Esfahani, "Iran's Middle Class and the Nuclear Deal," Brookings Institution, April 8, 2021, available at <https://www.brookings.edu/blog/future-development/2021/04/08/irans-middle-class-and-the-nuclear-deal/>. Accessed on April 9, 2021.

86. Ibid.

87. Ibid.

88. Sanam Vakil, "A Regional Security Process for the Middle East," in *US Foreign Policy Priorities*, Chatham House, October 15, 2021, available at <https://www.cha-thamhouse.org/2020/10/us-foreign-policy-priorities/04-regional-security-process-middle-east>. Accessed on February 28, 2021.

89. Ibid.

90. Ibid.

91. Mahmood Monshipouri, *Middle East Politics: Changing Dynamics*, New York: Routledge, 2019, see chapter 12, pp. 295–320.

92. Banafsheh Keynoush, "Prospects for Gulf Engagement with Iran: Opportunities and Challenges," *Inside Arabia*, February 22, 2021, available at <https://insidear-abia.com/prospects-for-gulf-engagement-with-iran-opportunities-and-chal-lenges/>. Accessed on February 22, 2021.

93. Ibid.

94. Abolghasem Bayyenat and Seyed Hossein Mousavian, "How to Make the Iran Nuclear Deal Durable," *The National Interest*, February 28, 2021, available at <https://nationalinterest.org/feature/how-make-iranian-nuclear-deal-dura-ble-178808>. Accessed on February 28, 2021.

95. Garrett Nada, Donald N. Jensen, Gavin Helf, Andrew Scobell, and Tamanna Salikuddin, "How the Region is Reacting to the Taliban Takeover," United States Institute of Peace, August 19, 2021, available at <https://www.usip.org/publi-cations/2021/08/how-region-reacting-taliban-takeover>. Accessed on August 19, 2021.

96. Saheli Roy Choudhury, "From India to China, The Taliban's Return Leaves Afghanistan's Neighbors Scrambling to Adjust," *CNBC*, August 17, 2021, available at <https://www.cnbc.com/2021/08/18/afghanistan-taliban-impact-on-paki-stan-india-china-russia-iran.html>. Accessed on August 19, 2021.

97. Ryan Hass, "How Will China Seek to Profit from the Taliban's Takeover in Afghanistan," *Lawfare*, August 19, 2021, available at <https://www.lawfareblog.

com/how-will-china-seek-profit-talibans-takeover-afghanistan>. Accessed on August 20, 2021.

98. Saheli Roy Choudhury, "From India to China …," op. cit.

99. Mansur Mirovalev, "Does Russia Have a New Strategy for Afghanistan?" *Al Jazeera*, August 16, 2021, available at <https://www.aljazeera.com/news/2021/8/16/whats-russias-strategy-for-afghanistan>. Accessed on August 19, 2021.

100. Saheli Roy Choudhury, "From India to China, …" op. cit.

101. Garrett Nada, Donald N. Jensen, Gavin Helf, Andrew Scobell, and Tamanna Salikuddin, "How the Region is Reacting to the Taliban Takeover," United States Institute of Peace, August 19, 2021, available at <https://www.usip.org/publications/2021/08/how-region-reacting-taliban-takeover>. Accessed on August 19, 2021.

102. Ibid.

103. Helene Cooper, Lara Jakes, Michael D. Shear, and Michael Crowley, "In the Withdrawal from Afghanistan, a Biden Doctrine Surfaces," *The New York Times*, September 5, 2021, p. 9.

104. Ibid.

105. See Thomas L. Friedman's interview with president-elect Joe Biden, "Biden: 'We're Going to Fight Like Hell by Investing in America First,' *The New York Times*, December 2, 2020, available at <https://www.nytimes.com/2020/12/02/opinion/biden-interview-mcconnell-china-iran.html>. Accessed on December 6, 2020.

106. Joby Warrick and Anne Gearan, "Biden has Vowed to Quickly Restore the Iran Nuclear Deal, but that May be Easier Said than Done," *The Washington Post*, December 9, 2020, available at <https://www.washingtonpost.com/politics/2020/12/09/biden-foreign-policy-iran/>. Accessed on December 13, 2020.

107. Assad Rad, "Regime Changers Love to Think Iran Is Always on the 'Brink of collapse,'" *Responsible Statecraft*, February 11, 2021, available at <https://responsiblestatecraft.org/2021/02/11/decades-of-pressure-on-iran-has-failed-time-for-maximum-diplomacy/>. Accessed on February 11, 2021.

108. International Crisis Group, "The Vital but Delicate Task of Reviving the JCPOA," December 10, 2020, available at <https://www.crisisgroup.org/middle-east-north-africa/gulf-and-arabian-peninsula/iran/vital-delicate-task-reviving-jcpoa>. Accessed on December 12, 2020.

109. An Interview with Barbara Slavin, "The State of US–Iran Relations: A Conversation with Barbara Slavin," *Columbia Journal of International Relations*, January 22, 2021, available at <https://jia.sipa.columbia.edu/online-articles/state-us-iran-relations-conversation-barbara-slavin>. Accessed on February 12, 2021.

9. BALANCING THREATS AND INCENTIVES

1. Barbara Slavin, "US Hostility with Iran Only Serves Hardliners on Both Sides," Bourse & Bazaar, November 20, 2020, available at <https://www.bourseandbazaar.com/

articles/2020/11/20/us-hostility-with-iran-only-serves-hardliners-on-both-sides>. Accessed on January 2, 2021.

2. Ibid.

3. John Limbert, "The Obama Administration," in Robin Wright, ed., *The Iran Primer: Power, Politics, and US Foreign Policy*, Washington, DC: United States Institute of Peace Press, 2010, pp. 146–8.

4. Mehrzad Boroujerdi, "Iran," in Ellen Lust, ed., *The Middle East*, Fourteenth Edition, Thousand Oaks, CA: CQ Press, 2017, pp. 455–86; see especially p. 485.

5. Mark Gasiorowski, "Islamic Republic of Iran," in Mark Gasiorowski and Sean Yom, eds., *The Government and Politics of the Middle East and North Africa*, Boulder, CO: Westview Press, 2017, pp. 271–306; see especially pp. 304–5.

6. Mahmood Monshipouri and Jonathan Whooley, "Let's Not Rule Out Diplomacy," *Lobelog.com*, September 26, 2019, available at <https://lobelog.com/tag/mahmood-monshipouri/>. Accessed on January 4, 2021.

7. Mehdi Khalaji, "No War, No Negotiations is Iran's Stance," The Washington Institute for Near East Policy, May 21, 2019, available at <https://www.washingtoninstitute.org/policy-analysis/no-war-no-negotiation-irans-stance>. Accessed on January 4, 2021.

8. Nader Entessar and Kaveh L. Afrasiabi, *Trump and Iran: From Containment to Confrontation*, Lanham, MD: Lexington Books, 2020.

9. Afshin Molavi, "Iran and Gulf States," in Robin Wright, ed., *The Iran Primer: Power, Politics, and US Foreign Policy*, Washington, DC: United States Institute of Peace Press, 2010, pp. 159–62; see especially p. 162.

10. Mehran Kamrava, *Troubled Waters: Insecurity in the Persian Gulf*, Ithaca, NY: Cornell University Press, 2018, pp. 149–50.

11. Mahmood Monshipouri and Manochehr Dooraj, "Iran's Foreign Policy: A Shifting Strategic Landscape," *Middle East Policy*, Vol. XX, No. 4, Winter 2013, pp. 133–47.

12. Mahmood Monshipouri, "The Middle East Post-Petroleum: Averting the Storm," *Middle East Policy*, Vol. XXVI, No. 3, Fall 2019, pp. 77–91.

13. Lara Lakes and Eric Schmitt, "Seeking Fresh Start with Iraq, Biden Avoids Setting Red Lines with Iran," *The New York Times*, February 21, 2021, p. 12.

14. Akan Malici and Stephen G. Walker, *Role Theory and Role Conflict in US–Iran Relations: Enemies of Our Own Making*, New York: Routledge, 2017, p. 176.

15. Seyed Hossein Mousavian and Mohammad Reza Chitsazian, "Iran's Foreign Policy in the Middle East: A Grand Strategy," *Middle East Policy*, Vol. XXVI, No. 3, Fall 2020, pp. 99–114; see especially p. 110.

16. R. K. Ramazani, "The Dilemma of US–Iran Relations: Reflections on a Life's Work," *The University of Virginia Magazine*, available at <https://uvamagazine.org/articles/the_dilemma_of_u.s._iran_relations>. Accessed on January 7, 2021.

17. Mahmood Monshipouri, *Middle East Politics: Changing Dynamics*, New York: Routledge, 2019. See especially Chapter 11.

18. Kenneth Katzman, "Iran Sanctions," Congressional Research Service, November 18,

2020, available at <https://fas.org/sgp/crs/mideast/RS20871.pdf>. Accessed on February 24, 2021.

19. Karen DeYoung and Kareem Fahim, "United States and Iran Warily Circle Each Other over Reactivating Nuclear Deal," *The Washington Post*, March 14, 2021, available at <https://www.washingtonpost.com/national-security/biden-iran-nuclear-deal-talks/2021/03/14/4b020904–8376–11eb-81db-b02f0398f49a_story.html>. Accessed on March 15, 2021.

20. United Nations Human Rights: Office of the High Commissioner, "US Sanctions Violate Human Rights and International Code of Conduct, UN Experts Say," May 6, 2019, available at <https://www.ohchr.org/EN/NewsEvents/Pages/Display News.aspx?NewsID=24566>. Accessed on February 24, 2021.

21. George A. Lopez and David Cortright, "Economic Sanctions and Human Rights: Part of the Problems or Part of the Solution," *International Journal of Human Rights*, Vol. 1, No. 2, Summer 1997, pp. 1–125; see p. 1.

23. Ibid.

24. Ibid.

25. Ibid.

26. Ibid.

27. Human Rights Watch, "Iran: Sanctions Threatening Health," October 29, 2019, available at <https://www.hrw.org/news/2019/10/29/iran-sanctions-threat-ening-health#>. Accessed on February 23, 2021.

28. Seyed Hossein Mousavian, *A New Structure for Security, Peace, and Cooperation in the Persian Gulf*, Lanham, MD: Rowman & Littlefield, 2020, p. 29.

29. Behrooz Ghamari Tabrizi, "Biden and Iran," *Counterpunch*, February 3, 2021, available at <https://www.counterpunch.org/2021/02/03/biden-and-iran/>. Accessed on February 6, 2021.

30. Daniel Benjamin and Steven Simon, "America's Great Satan: The 40-Year Obsession with Iran," *Foreign Affairs*, Vol. 96, No. 5, November/December 2019, pp. 56–66; see especially p. 56.

31. Ibid., p. 58.

32. Ibid., p. 59.

33. Ibid., p. 63

34. Trita Parsi and Tyler Cullis, "The Myth of the Iranian Military Giant," *Foreign Policy*, July 10, 2015, available at <https://foreignpolicy.com/2015/07/10/the-myth-of-the-iranian-military-giant/>. Accessed on February 26, 2021.

35. Ibid.

36. Anthony H. Cordesman and Nicholas Harrington, "The Arab Gulf States and Iran: Military Spending, Modernization, and the Shifting Military Balance," Center for Strategic & International Studies (CSIS), December 12, 2018, available at <https://www.csis.org/analysis/arab-gulf-states-and-iran-military-spending-moderniza-tion-and-shifting-military-balance>. Accessed on February 25, 2021.

37. Ibid.

38. Ibid.

39. Ibid.

40. Mahmood Monshipouri and William Chu, "The Flaws of the Proliferation Cascade Scenario: Iran–Saudi Relations in Perspective," *International Studies Journal*, Vol. 12, No. 3, Winter 2016, pp. 1–14.

41. Ibid.

42. Jonathon Patrick Whooley, *Imagining Iran: Orientalism and the Construction of Security Development in American Foreign Policy*, New York: Peter Lang, 2018.

43. John Limbert, "The Threat From Iran is Overblown," *The New York Times*, January 21, 2016, available at <https://www.nytimes.com/roomfordebate/2016/01/21/does-iran-remain-a-threat/the-threat-from-iran-is-overblown>. Accessed on February 25, 2021.

44. Alex Horton, "I Get the Same Intel: Iran Threat Exaggerated by GOP Hawks, Rep. Gallego Says," *The Washington Post*, May 18, 2019, available at <https://www.washingtonpost.com/politics/2019/05/18/i-get-same-intel-iran-threat-exaggerated-by-gop-hawks-rep-gallego-says/>. Accessed on February 25, 2021.

45. Sayed Hossein Mousavian, "An Iranian Nuclear Business Deal for Trump, Belfer Center, November 1, 2017, available at <https://www.belfercenter.org/index.php/publication/iranian-nuclear-business-deal-trump>. Accessed on February 26, 2021.

46. Robert Hunter, "In a US-Iran Standoff, Biden Must be Willing to Take Some Political Heat," *Responsible Statecraft*, February 9, 2021, available at <https://responsiblestatecraft.org/2021/02/09/in-a-u-s-iran-standoff-biden-must-be-willing-to-take-a-little-political-heat/>. Accessed on February 10, 2021.

47. Ibid.

48. Ibid.

49. Martin Indyk, "Disaster in the Desert: Why Trump's Middle East Plan Can't Work," *Foreign Affairs*, Vol. 98, No. 6, November/December 2019, pp. 10–20; see especially p. 20.

50. Robert F. Worth, "They Break Us or We Break Them," *The New York Times Magazine*, November 4, 2018, pp. 48–57, 69; see especially p. 52.

51. April Longley Alley, "How to End the War in Yemen," *Foreign Policy*, October 15, 2019, available at <https://foreignpolicy.com/2019/10/15/yemen-houthis-saudi-arabia-end-war/>. Accessed on October 24, 2019.

52. Robert Malley, "The Unwanted Wars: Why the Middle East is More Combustive Than Ever," *Foreign Affairs*, Vol. 98, No. 6, November/December 2019, pp. 38–46; see especially p. 46.

53. Shireen T. Hunter, "Persian Gulf Arab States Should Accept Iran's Olive Branch," *LobeLog*, October 4, 2019, available at <https://lobelog.com/persian-gulf-arab-states-should-accept-irans-olive-branch/>. Accessed on October 6, 2019.

54. Mahmood Monshipouri, *Middle East Politics: Changing Dynamics*, New York: Routledge, 2019, p. 221.

55. Laura Wellesley, "Chocking Trade: What the Qatar Crisis Tells Us About Food Supply Risk," *The Arab News*, June 27, 2017, available at <https://www.alaraby.

co.uk/english/comment/2017/6/27/choking-trade-gulf-crisis-reveals-food-supply-risk>. Accessed on September 29, 2018.

56. Abhishek G. Bhaya, "Food Security High on Qatar's Agenda Amid Gulf Crisis," *CGTN.com*, September 16, 2017, available at <https://news.cgtn.com/news/3563444d35557a6333566d54/share_p.html>. Accessed on September 29, 2018.

57. Dina Esfandiari, "No Country for Oversimplifications," The Century Foundation, January 24, 2018, available at <<https://tcf.org/content/report/no-country-oversimplifications/?gclid=Cj0KCQiA88X_BRDUARIsACVMYD_rfMZmNfaNvWburH20vE2kh3kFtcXkJr0G4RvGSh7GXczyKQoH_rQaAs7UEALw_wcB&agreed=1>. Accessed on January 4, 2021.

58. Jon B. Alterman, "The Smart Way out of the Middle East," *The Hill*, February 22, 2021, available at <https://thehill.com/opinion/international/539831-the-smart-way-out-of-the-middle-east>. Accessed on February 22, 2021.

59. Mehran Kamrava, *Troubled Waters: Insecurity in the Persian Gulf*, Ithaca, NY: Cornell University Press, 2018, p. 132.

60. For an illuminating book on this subject, see Seyed Hossein Mousavian, *A New Structure for Security, Peace, and Cooperation in the Persian Gulf*, Lanham, MD: Rowman & Littlefield, 2020.

61. Philip H. Gordon, "The Next Administration Needs a Plan for De-escalation in the Gulf," *Foreign Policy*, October 22, 2020, available at <https://foreignpolicy.com/2020/10/22/election-2020-trump-biden-iran-saudi-arabia>. Accessed on January 20, 2021.

62. Ibid.

63. Abdulaziz Sager and Hossein Mousavian, "We can escape a zero-sum struggle between Iran and Saudi Arabia—if we act now," *The Guardian*, January 31, 2021, available at <https://www.theguardian.com/commentisfree/2021/jan/31/iran-saudi-arabia-joe-biden-cooperation>. Accessed on February 24, 2021.

64. Vali Nasr and Maria Fantappie, "How Iran and Saudi Arabia Can Together Bring Peace to the Middle East," *Foreign Affairs*, August 3, 2021, available at <https://www.foreignaffairs.com/articles/iran/2021–08–03/how-iran-and-saudi-arabia-can-together-bring-peace-middle-east>. Accessed on August 23, 2021.

65. Ibid.

66. Ibid.

67. Hussein Ibish, "Saudi Arabia's New Dialogue with Iran was Long in the Making," The Arab Gulf States Institute in Washington, May 2, 2021, available at <https://agsiw.org/saudi-arabias-new-dialogue-with-iran-was-long-in-the-making/>. Accessed on August 21, 2021.

68. *Tehran Times*, "Saudis May See Opportunity in Raisi Win to Mend Ties with Iran," June 20, 2021, available at <https://www.tehrantimes.com/news/462223/Saudis-may-see-opportunity-in-Raisi-win-to-mend-ties-with-Iran>. Accessed on August 21, 2021.

69. Hussein Ibish, "Saudi Arabia's New Dialogue with Iran …," op. cit.

70. Ibid.

71. *Iran International*, "Iranian Diplomat Says Talks with Saudi Arabia Await Raisi Administration," August 16, 2021, available at <https://iranintl.com/en/iran-in-brief/iranian-diplomat-says-talks-saudi-arabia-await-raisi-administration>. Accessed on August 21, 2021.

72. *Middle East Eye*, "Iran's Raisi Says 'no obstacles' to Restoring Ties with Saudi Arabia," June 21, 2021, available at <https://www.middleeasteye.net/news/iran-saudi-arabia-ebrahim-raisi-no-obstacles-restoring-ties>. Accessed on August 21, 2021.

73. Javad Ershadi, "Masjedi spoke of Iran-Saudi Arabia Talks to Reopen Embassies," *IRNA*, August 16, 2021, available at <https://www.irna.ir/news/84438535>. Accessed on August 23, 2021.

74. *Tehran Times*, "Saudis May See Opportunity in Raisi Win to Mend Ties with Iran," June 20, 2021, available at <https://www.tehrantimes.com/news/462223/Saudis-may-see-opportunity-in-Raisi-win-to-mend-ties-with-Iran>. Accessed on August 21, 2021.

75. Mehran Kamrava, *Troubled Waters*, op. cit., p. 150.

76. Ibid., p. 151.

77. Mahmood Sariolghalam, "Sources of Continuity in Iran's Foreign Policy," in Michael Hudson and Mini Kirk, eds., *Gulf Politics and Economics in a Changing World*, Singapore: World Scientific Publishing Co., 2014, pp. 161–77; see especially p. 176.

78. This section is based on Mahmood Monshipouri and Javad Heiran-Nia, "China's Iran Strategy: What Is at Stake," *Middle East Policy*, Vol. XXVII, No. 4, Winter 2020, pp. 157–72; see especially p. 158.

79. Farnaz Fassihi and Steven Lee Myers, "Defying US, China and Iran Near Trade and Military Partnership," *The New York Times*, July 11, 2020, available at <https://www.nytimes.com/2020/07/11/world/asia/china-iran-trade-military-deal.html>. Accessed on October 4, 2020.

80. Alex Vatanka, "China's Great Game in Iran," *Foreign Policy*, September 5, 2019, available at <https://foreignpolicy.com/2019/09/05/chinas-great-game-in-iran/>. Accessed on October 1, 2020.

81. Ibid.

82. Ibid.

83. Mahmood Monshipouri and Javad Heiran-Nia, "China's Iran Strategy: What Is at Stake," *Middle East Policy*, Vol. XXVII, No. 4, Winter 2020, pp. 157–72; see especially pp. 169–70.

84. Philip H. Gordon, *Losing the Long Game: The False Promise of Regime Change in the Middle East*, New York: St. Martin's Press, 2020, pp. 254–256.

85. Ibid., p. 254.

86. Ibid., pp. 260–3.

87. Ibid., p. 274.

88. Ibid., p. 45.

89. Ibid.

90. Ibid.

91. Vali Nasr, "Trump's Policies Have Convinced Iran to Build a More Advanced

Nuclear Program Before Negotiating," *Foreign Policy*, September 21, 2020, available at <https://foreignpolicy.com/2020/09/21/trumps-policies-have-convinced-iran-to-build-a-more-advanced-nuclear-program-before-negotiating/>. Accessed on February 27, 2021.

92. Ibid.

93. Nicholas L. Miller, "The Lessons of the Past Point to Rejoining the Iran Deal," *War on the Rocks*, January 21 2021, available <https://warontherocks.com/2021/01/the-lessons-of-the-past-point-to-rejoining-the-iran-deal/>. Accessed on February 28, 2021.

10. CONCLUSION: THE PATH FORWARD

1. Colbert C. Held and John Thomas Cummings, *Middle East Patterns: Places, Peoples, and Politics*, Sixth Edition, Boulder, CO: Westview Press, 2014, p. 664.

2. Chas W. Freeman, "Reimagining Relations with Iran," Middle East Policy Council, 2020, available at <https://mepc.org/speeches/reimagining-relations-iran>. Accessed on April 21, 2021.

3. Mahmood Monshipouri and Manochehr Dorraj, "The Resilience of Populism in Iranian Politics: A Closer Look at the Nexus between Internal and External Factors," *Middle East Journal*, Vol. 75, No. 2, Summer 2021, pp. 201–21; see p. 221

4. Chas W. Freeman, "Reimagining Relations with Iran," op. cit.

5. Congressional Research Service, "US Military Withdrawal and Taliban Takeover in Afghanistan: Frequently Asked Questions," Updated August 27, 2021, pp. 1–63; see pp. 17–21; available at <https://crsreports.congress.gov/product/pdf/R/R46879>. Accessed on August 28, 2021.

6. Ibid., p. 22.

7. John Hudson, "CIA Director William Burns Held Secret Meeting in Kabul with Taliban Leader Abdul Ghani Baradar," *The Washington Post*, August 24, 2021, available at <https://www.washingtonpost.com/national-security/burns-afghanistan-baradar-biden/2021/08/24/c96bee5c-04ba-11ec-ba15-9c4f59a60478_story.html>. Accessed on August 28, 2021.

8. Congressional Research Service, op. cit., p. 23.

9. Andrew Parasiliti, Elizabeth Hagedorn, and Joe Snell, "The Takeaway: Iran Can Live with the Taliban Takeover in Afghanistan," *Al-Monitor*, August 18, 2021, available at <https://www.al-monitor.com/originals/2021/08/takeaway-iran-can-live-taliban-takeover-afghanistan>. Accessed on August 24, 2021.

10. *Tehran Times*, "Iran Elaborates on Its Afghanistan Policy," August 25, 2021, p. 3.

11. Shelly Kittleson, "Why Iran Will Welcome the Taliban Takeover in Afghanistan," *Foreign Policy*, August 18, 2021, available at<https://foreignpolicy.com/2021/08/18/why-iran-will-welcome-the-taliban-takeover-in-afghanistan/>. Accessed on August 23, 2021.

12. Dina Esfandiary, "A Practical Policy to Re-Engage and Contain Iran," The Century

Foundation, February 11, 2020, available at <https://tcf.org/content/report/practical-policy-re-engage-contain-iran/?agreed=1>. Accessed on April 21, 2021.

13. See an editorial piece in *The New York Times*, "'Maximum Pressure' on Iran Has Failed," *The New York Times*, April 11, 2021, Sunday Review, p. 6.

14. William Burns and Jeffrey Goldberg, "I worry that we're drifting in the direction of collisions that can escalate very quickly," 2019 Aspen Ideals Festival, available at <https://www.aspenideas.org/sessions/are-we-headed-for-war-with-iran?utm_source=google&utm_medium=adgrant&utm_campaign=World&utm_term=war%20with%20iran&gclid=Cj0KCQjwvYSEBhDjARIsAJMn0lhyRQ3CpyWGJ6N_6U5ZzR6MgaxeznXdecWAwLHj9iOb2Xex9765f_waAt-wHEALw_wcB>. Accessed on April 21, 2021.

15. Seyed Hossein Mousavian and Shahir ShahidSaless, *Iran and the United States: An Insider's View on the Failed Past and the Road to Peace*, New York: Bloomsbury, 2014, p. 289.

16. Mehran Kamrava, *Troubled Waters: Insecurity in the Persian Gulf*, Ithaca, NY: Cornell University Press, 2018, pp. 4–5 and pp. 149–52.

17. Manochehr Dorraj and Hamid Zangeneh, "Mis-opportunities and Political Blunders: The Tale of US–Iran Relations," in Robert E. Looney, ed., *Handbook of US–Middle East Relations*, New York: Routledge, 2009, pp. 484–501.

18. Mahmood Sariolghalam, "The Role of Algorithms in the Persistent US-Iranian Impasse," Middle East Institute, April 16, 2021, available at <https://www.mei.edu/publications/role-algorithms-persistent-us-iranian-impasse>. Accessed on April 21, 2021.

19. Ibid.

20. Ibid.

21. Kareem Fahim, "In leaked audio, Iran's Foreign Minister laments interference by Revolutionary Guard," *The Washington Post*, April 26, 2021, available at <https://www.washingtonpost.com/world/middle_east/iran-nuclear-soleimani-leaked-audio-zarif/2021/04/26/8a7b3672-a64a-11eb-a8a7-5f45ddcdf364_story.html>. Accessed on April 26, 2021.

22. Ibid.

23. Farnaz Fassihi, "Iran's Foreign Minister, in Leaked Tape, Says Revolutionary Guards Set Policies," *The New York Times*, April 25, 2021, available at <https://www.nytimes.com/2021/04/25/world/middleeast/iran-suleimani-zarif.html>. Accessed on April 25, 2021.

24. For more information on this subject, see Mahmood Monshipouri, *Middle East Politics: Changing Dynamics*, New York: Routledge, 2019, pp. 286–9.

25. Shireen T. Hunter, *Iran Divided: The Historical Roots of Iranian Debates on Identity, Culture, and Governance in the Twenty-First Century*, Lanham, MD: Rowman & Littlefield, 2014, p. 256.

26. William D. Hartung and Ben Freeman, "The Saudi Lobby's Scheme to Destroy the Iran Deal," *The American Conservative*, May 23, 2018, available at <https://www.

theamericanconservative.com/articles/the-saudi-lobbys-scheme-to-destroy-the-iran-deal/>. Accessed on August 27, 2021.

27. Catherine Ho, "Pro-Israeli Lobby Groups Have Split Reactions to Iran Deal," *The Washington Post*, July 14, 2015, available at <https://www.washingtonpost.com/news/powerpost/wp/2015/07/14/pro-israel-lobby-groups-have-split-reactions-to-iran-deal/>. Accessed on August 27, 2021.

28. Ibid.

29. Ron Kampeas, "The pro-Israel Iran Dilemma: How to Influence a Policy Biden has Yet to Unveil," *The Times of Israel*, April 24, 2021, available at <https://www.timesofisrael.com/the-pro-israel-iran-dilemma-how-to-influence-policy-biden-has-yet-to-unveil/>. Accessed on August 28, 2021.

30. Brian Katulis and Peter Juul, "Putting Diplomacy First," Center for American Progress, March 12, 2020, available at <https://www.americanprogress.org/issues/security/reports/2020/03/12/481512/putting-diplomacy-first/>. Accessed on March 19, 2021.

31. Philip H. Gordon, *Losing the Long Game: The False Promise of Regime Change in the Middle East*, New York: St. Martin's Press, 2020, p. 274.

32. Nader Entessar, "Permanent War, Elusive Peace: The Evolution of America's Compellence Policy Toward Iran," *Journal of South Asian and Middle Eastern Studies*, Vol. 44 No. 3, Spring 2021, pp. 95–111; see especially p. 109.

33. Adbolrasool Divsallar, "Why Biden Shouldn't Seek to Deprive Iran of Conventional Deterrence," *Middle East Institute*, February 25, 2021, available at <https://www.mei.edu/publications/why-biden-shouldnt-seek-deprive-iran-conventional-deterrence>. Accessed on February 26, 2021.

34. Daniel Benjamin and Steven Simon, "America's Great Satan: The 40-Year Obsession with Iran," *Foreign Affairs*, Vol. 98, No. 6, November/December 2019, pp. 56–66; see especially, p. 59.

35. John Ghazvinian, *America and Iran: A History, 1720 to the Present*, New York: Alfred A. Knopf, 2021, p. 536.

36. Kelsey Davenport and Julia Masterson, "New Iran President May Complicate Nuclear Talks, Arms Control Association, July/August 2021, available at <https://www.armscontrol.org/act/2021–07/news/new-iran-president-may-complicate-nuclear-talks>. Accessed on August 25, 2021.

37. Mohammad Ayatollahi Tabbar, "Iran's War Within," *Foreign Affairs*, Vol. 100, No. 5, September/October 2021, pp. 155–160, 162–8; see especially, pp. 155–6.

38. Alex Vatanka, "Iran and Turkey: Power Dynamics in the South Caucasus," Middle East Institute, February 8, 2021, available at <https://www.mei.edu/publications/iran-and-turkey-power-dynamics-south-caucasus>. Accessed on March 23, 2021.

39. Trita Parsi, "Why Mohammed bin Salman Suddenly Wants to Talk to Iran," *Foreign Policy*, April 29, 2021, available at <file:///C:/Users/909186933/Documents/

Why%20Mohammed%20bin%20Salman%20Suddenly%20Wants%20to%20 Talk%20to%20Iran%20April%2029,%202021.htm>. Accessed on April 29, 2021.

40. "The press conference of the President-elect / Foreign Policy of my government has not started and will not end with the JCPOA," *Fars News Agency*, June 21, 2021, available at <https://www.farsnews.ir/news/14000331000513>. Accessed on August 23, 2021.

41. "Saudi Arabia says it will judge Iran's Raisi by 'reality on the ground'," *Reuters*, June 22, 2021, available at <https://www.reuters.com/world/middle-east/saudi-ara-bia-says-it-will-judge-irans-raisi-by-reality-ground-2021–06–22/>. Accessed on August 23, 2021.

42. Kirsten Fontenrose, "Adding an Ishmael Track to the Abraham Accords: How to Pursue Détente between Iran, Saudi Arabia, and the UAE," *Atlantic Council*, April 29, 2021, available at <https://www.atlanticcouncil.org/blogs/new-atlanticist/ adding-an-ishmael-track-to-the-abraham-accords-how-to-pursue-detente-between-iran-saudi-arabia-and-the-uae/>. Accessed on April 29, 2021.

43. Ibid.

44. Daniel Benjamin and Steven Simon,"America's Great Satan," op. cit., p. 66.

45. Martin Beck, "An International Relations Perspectives on the Iran Nuclear Deal," E-International Relations, August 8, 2018, available at <https://www.e-ir. info/2018/08/08/an-international-relations-perspective-on-the-iran-nuclear-de>. Accessed on October 5, 2021.

46. Mohammad Ayatollahi Tabaar, "Iran's War Within," *Foreign Affairs*, Vol. 100, No. 5, September/October 2021, pp. 155–60, and p. 162–8; see pp. 162–8.

47. For more on this see, Mahmood Monshipouri and Javad Heiran-Nia, "Iran's Security Interests and Policies in the South Caucasus," *Iran and the Caucasus*, Vol. 25, 2021, pp. 284–300.

48. *Investopedia*, The Eurasian Economic Union (EAEU), January 2, 2021; available at <https://www.investopedia.com/terms/e/eurasian-economic-union-eeu.asp>. Accessed on June 10, 2021.

49. Shireen Hunter, "Iran should use the competition of China, Russia and Europe in the Eurasian Union," *Tahlil Bazaar News Agency*, June 9, 2021, available at <https:// www.tahlilbazaar.com/news/92577>. Accessed on June 10, 2021.

50. Martin Beck, "An International Relations Perspectives on the Iran Nuclear Deal," op.cit.

51. Bruce Russett, "Liberalism," in Tim Dunne, Milija Kurki, and Steve Smith, eds., *International Relations Theories: Discipline and Diversity*, Fifth Edition, New York: Oxford University Press, 2021, pp. 68–88; see especially p. 85.

52. Wyn Bowen and Matthew Moran, "Iran's Nuclear Programme: A Case Study in Hedging?" *Contemporary Security Policy*, Vol. 35, No. 1, 2014, pp. 26–52; see espe-cially p. 47.

53. Ibid., p. 49.

54. Barry Buzan, Ole Wæver and Jaap de Wilde, *Security: A New Framework for Analysis*, Boulder, CO: Lynne Rienner Publishers, 1998.

55. Ellie Geranmayeh, "Reviving the Revolutionaries: How Trump's Maximum Pressure is Shifting Iran's Domestic Politics," European Council on Foreign Relations," *Policy Brief*, No. 325, June 2020, pp. 1–2.

56. Ellie Gernmayeh, "Part 3: What Prospects for Diplomacy?" United States Institute of Peace: *The Iran Primer*, July 14, 2020, available at <https://iranprimer.usip.org/blog/2020/jul/14/part-3-what-prospects-diplomacy>. Accessed on August 26, 2021.

57. Mahmood Monshipouri and Manochehr Dorraj, "The Resilience of Populism in Iranian Politics: A Closer Look at the Nexus between Internal and External Factors," *Middle East Journal*, Vol. 75, No. 2, Summer 2021, pp. 201–21.

58. Bilal Y. Saab, "What a New Iran Nuclear Deal Really Requires," *Foreign Policy*, January 27, 2021, available at <https://foreignpolicy.com/2021/01/27/what-a-new-iran-nuclear-deal-really-requires/>. Accessed on April 24, 2021.

59. Joe Sestak, "Joe Sestak: Realistic Diplomacy in Iran," *Pittsburgh Post-Gazette*, March 16, 2021, available at <https://www.post-gazette.com/opinion/Op-Ed/2021/03/16/Realistic-diplomacy-in-Iran-Joe-Sestak/stories/202103160015>. Accessed on March 17, 2021.

60. David Hastings Dunn and Nicholas J. Wheeler, "US-Iranian Relations and the Crisis of Trust," August 1, 2019, available at <https://www.birmingham.ac.uk/news/thebirminghambrief/items/2019/08/us-iranian-relations-and-the-crisis-of-trust.aspx>. Accessed on August 24, 2021.

61. Kim Ghattas, "How America Can Win the Middle East," *The Atlantic*, September 4, 2021, available at <https://www.theatlantic.com/international/archive/2021/09/us-china-middle-east/619977/>. Accessed on September 6, 2021.

62. Ervand Abrahamian, *A History of Modern Iran: Revised and Updated*, New York: Cambridge University Press, 2018, p. 204.

63. Amir-Abdollahian, "The Ukraine crisis is rooted in NATO provocations," TASNIM News Agency, February 24, 2022, available at: <https://www.tasnimnews.com/fa/news/1400/12/05/2670226>. Accessed on March 9, 2022.

64. Hamidreza Azizi, "Ukraine crisis gives rise to hope, concern in Iran," Amwaj Media, March 3, 2022, available at <https://amwaj.media/article/iran-reaction-russian-military-invasion-ukraine>. Accessed on March 9, 2022.

65. Nicole Grajewski, "As the World Shuns Russia over Its Invasion of Ukraine, Iran Strengthens Its Ties with Moscow," *Atlantic Council*, March 7, 2022, available at <https://www.atlanticcouncil.org/blogs/iransource/as-the-world-shuns-russia-over-its-invasion-of-ukraine-iran-strengthens-its-ties-with-moscow%EF%BF%BC/>. Accessed on March 9, 2022.

66. Zvi Bar'el, "Russia's Ukraine Invasion Pushes the U.S. and Iran Together," Haaretz, March 9, 2022, available at <https://www.haaretz.com/israel-news/russia-pushes-to-tie-nuclear-deal-to-ukraine-peace-iran-has-other-plans-1.10655332>. Accessed on March 9, 2022.

67. Abdol-Rahman Fathollahi, "Why did the Raisi government support Putin in the

face of Russian aggression?" Iran Diplomacy, February 26, 2022, available at: <http://irdiplomacy.ir/fa/news/2010152>. Accessed on March 9, 2022.

68. Steven Erlanger, "Iran Nuclear Talks Paused Following Russian Demands to Erase Sanctions," The New York Times, March 11, 2022, available at <https://www.nytimes.com/2022/03/11/world/europe/iran-nuclear-talks-russia.html?referringSource=articleShare>. Accessed on March 11, 2022.

SELECTED BIBLIOGRAPHY

Abrahamian, Ervand, *A History of Modern Iran: Revised and Updated*, New York: Cambridge University Press, 2018.

Adib-Moghaddam, Arshin, "What is Power in Iran? The Shifting Foundations of the *Velayat-e Faqih*," in Mahmood Monshipouri, ed., *Inside the Islamic Republic: Social Change in Post-Khomeini Iran*, New York: Oxford University Press, 2016, pp. 23–36.

Afshari, Reza, *Human Rights in Iran: The Abuse of Cultural Relativism*, Philadelphia: University of Pennsylvania Press, 2001.

Akbarzadeh, Shahram, "Iran Under a Conservative President Still Needs the JCPOA," *Al Jazeera*, June 22, 2021, available at <https://www.aljazeera.com/opinions/2021/6/22/iran-under-a-conservative-president-still-needs-the-jcpoa>. Accessed on August 19, 2021.

Alamdari, Kazem, "The Power Structure of the Islamic Republic of Iran: Transition from Populism to Clientelism, and Militarization of the Government," *Third World Quarterly*, Vol. 26, Issue 8, January 2005, pp. 1285–1301.

Amanat, Abbas, *Iran: A Modern History*, New Haven, CT: Yale University Press, 2017.

Amuzegar, Jahangir, "Ahmadinejad Legacy," *Middle East Policy*, Vol. XX, No. 4, Winter 2013, pp. 124–132.

Ansari, Ali M., *Confronting Iran: The Failure of American Foreign Policy and the Next Great Conflict in the Middle East*, New York: Basic Books, 2006.

Arjomand, Saïd Amir, *After Khomeini: Iran Under His Successors*, New York: Oxford University Press, 2009.

Axworthy, Michael, *Iran: What Everyone Needs to Know*, New York: Oxford University Press, 2017.

Ayoob, Mohammad, "Turkey and Iran in the Era of the Arab Uprisings," in Fawaz A. Gerges, ed., *The New Middle East: Protest and Revolution in the Arab World*, New York: Cambridge University Press, 2014, pp. 402–17.

Barzegar, Kayhan, "Iran's Foreign Policy in Post-Invasion Iraq," *Middle East Policy*, Vol. XV, No. 4, Winter 2008, pp. 47–58.

Bayat, Asef, "The Fire that Fueled the Iran Protests," *The Atlantic*, January 27, 2018, available at <https://www.theatlantic.com/international/archive/2018/01/iran-protest-mashaad-green-class-labor-economy/551690/>. Accessed on August 29, 2021.

Beeman, William, O., "Examining Iran's Ties to Hezbollah," *In These Times*, August 15, 2006, available at <http://www.inthesetimes.com/article/2790/>. Last accessed on July 1, 2010.

Behravesh, Maysam, "How Iran Views the Turkish Invasion of Northern Syria," *Middle East Eye*, October 12, 2019, available at <https://www.middleeasteye.net/news/how-iran-views-turkish-invasion-northern-syria>. Accessed on October 16, 2019.

Benjamin, Daniel and Steven Simon, "America's Great Satan: The 40-Year Obsession With Iran," *Foreign Affairs*, Vol. 98, No. 6, November/December 2019, pp. 56–66.

Bill, James A., *The Eagle and the Lion: The Tragedy of American-Iranian Relations*, New Haven, CT: Yale University Press, 1988.

Boroujerdi, Mehrzad, *Iranian Intellectuals and the West: The Tormented Triumph of Nativism*, Syracuse, NY: Syracuse University Press, 1996.

Bozorgmehr, Najmeh, "China and Iran Sign 25-Year Agreement to Expand Ties," *Financial Times*, March 27, 2021, available at <https://www.ft.com/content/24393899-909e-4b3f-9e18-06a6951d639d>. Accessed on March 28, 2021.

Burns, William Joseph, *The Back Channel: A Memoir of American Diplomacy and the Case for Its Renewal*, New York: Random House, 2019.

Buzan, Barry, Ole Wæver, and Jaap de Wilde, *Security: A new framework for analysis*, Boulder, CO: Lynne Rienner Publishers, 1998.

Chomsky, Noam and Gilbert Achcar, eds., *Perilous Power: The Middle East and U.S. Foreign Policy*, Boulder, CO: Paradigm Publishers, 2007.

Chubin, Shahram, *Iran's Nuclear Ambitions*, Washington, DC: Carnegie Endowment for International Peace, 2006.

Cleveland, William L., and Martin Bunton, *A History of the Modern Middle East*, Sixth Edition, New York: Routledge, 2018.

Cohen, Roger, "Iran: The Tragedy and the Future," *The New York Review of Books*, Vol. LVI, No. 13, August 13, 2009, pp. 7–10.

Congressional Research Service, "US Military Withdrawal and Taliban Takeover in Afghanistan: Frequently Asked Questions," Updated August 27, 2021, pp. 1–63; see pp. 17–21; available at <https://crsreports.congress.gov/product/pdf/R/R46879>. Accessed on August 28, 2021.

Cook, Steven A. "No Exit: Why the Middle East Still Matters to American," *Foreign Affairs*, Vol. 99, No. 6, November/December 2020, pp. 133–142.

Cordesman, Anthony H., *Iran's Developing Military Capabilities*, Washington, DC: Center for Strategic and International Studies, 2006.

Donnelly, Jack and Daniel J. Whelan, *International Human Rights*, Fifth Edition, Boulder, CO: Westview Press, 2018.

Dorraj, Manochehr, "Iranian Populism: Its Vicissitudes and Political Impact," in Dwayne Woods and Barbara Wejnert, eds., *Many Faces of Populism: Current Perspectives*, UK: Emerald Group, 2014, pp. 127–142.

Dorraj, Manochehr and Hamid Zangeneh, "Mis-opportunities and Political Blunders: The Tale of US-Iran Relations," in Robert E. Looney, ed., *Handbook of US-Middle East Relations*, New York: Routledge, 2009, pp. 484–501.

Dunlap, William V., "Iraq: Occupation and Transition," in David P. Forsythe, ed., *Encyclopedia of Human Rights*, Vol. 3, New York: Oxford University Press, 2009, pp. 217–24.

Dunne, Tim, "The English School," in Tim Dunne, Milja Kurki, and Steve Smith, eds., *International Relations Theories: Discipline and Diversity*, Fifth Edition, New York: Oxford University Press, 2021, pp. 108–28.

Ebadi, Shirin, *Until We are Free: My Fight for Human Rights in Iran*, New York: Random House, 2016.

Ehsani, Kaveh and Chris Toensing, "Neo-Conservatives, Hardline Clerics and the Bomb," *Middle East Report*, No. 233, Vol. 34, No. 4, Winter 2004:10–15.

Ehteshami, Anoushiravan, *Dynamics of Change in the Persian Gulf: Political Economy, War, and Revolution*, New York: Routledge, 2013.

Entessar, Nader and Kaveh L. Afrasiabi, *Iran Nuclear Accord and the Remaking of the Middle East*, Lanham, MD: Rowman & Littlefield, 2018.

Entessar, Nader and Kaveh L. Afrasiabi, *Trump and Iran: From Containment to Confrontation*, Lanham, MD: Lexington Books, 2020.

Esfandiari, Haleh, "The Politics of the 'Women's Question' in the Islamic Republic, 1979–1999," in John L. Esposito and R. K. Ramazani, eds., *Iran at the Crossroads*, New York: Palgrave, 2001, pp. 75–92.

Esfandiary, Dina, "A Practical Policy to Re-Engage and Contain Iran," The Century Foundation, February 11, 2020, available at <https://tcf.org/content/report/practical-policy-re-engage-contain-iran/?agreed=1>. Accessed on April 21, 2021.

Esposito, John L., *The Islamic Threat: Myth or Reality?* Third Edition, New York: Oxford University Press, 1999.

Falk, Richard, "A Brief Further Comment on Syria," available at <http://richardfalk.wordpress.com/2012/07/25/a-brief-further-comment-on-syria/>. Accessed on October 14, 2012.

Fassihi, Farnaz and David E. Sanger, "Iran Rejects Nuclear Deal Talks With U.S. Proposed by Europe," *The New York Times*, February 28, 2021, available at <https://www.nytimes.com/2021/02/28/world/middleeast/iran-nuclear-talks-united-states.html>. Accessed on February 28, 2021.

Fayazmanesh, Sasan, *Containing Iran: Obama's Policy of Tough Diplomacy*, Cambridge, UK: Cambridge Scholarly Publishing, 2013.

Forsythe, David P., *Advanced Introduction to The Politics of International Human Rights*, Cheltenham, UK: Edward Elgar Publishing, 2021.

Freeman, Chas W., "Reimagining Relations with Iran," Middle East Policy Council, 2020, available at <https://mepc.org/speeches/reimagining-relations-iran>. Accessed on April 21, 2021.

Fuller, Graham E., "Repairing US–Iranian Relations," *Middle East Policy*, Vol. VI, No. 2, October, 1998, pp. 140–144.

Gasiorowski, Mark, "The Islamic Republic of Iran," in Mark Gasiorowski and Sean L. Yom, eds., *The Government and Politics of the Middle East and North Africa*, Eighth Edition, Boulder, CO: Westview Press, 2017, pp. 271–306.

Gelvin, James L., *The New Middle East: What Everyone Needs to Know*, New York: Oxford University Press, 2018.

Geranmayeh, Ellie, "Reviving the Revolutionaries: How Trump's Maximum Pressure is Shifting Iran's Domestic Politics," European Council on Foreign Relations, *Policy Brief*, No. 325, June 2020.

Ghamari Tabrizi, Behrooz, "Biden and Iran," *Counterpunch*, February 3, 2021, available at <https://www.counterpunch.org/2021/02/03/biden-and-iran/>. Accessed on February 6, 2021.

Ghanea, Nazila, *Human Rights, the UN and the Baha'is in Iran*, The Hague: Kluwer Law International, 2002.

Ghazvinian, John, *America and Iran: A History, 1720 to the Present*, New York: Alfred A. Knopf, 2021.

Giragosian, Richard, "Armenia's Search for Independence," *Current History*, Vol. 113, No. 765, October 2014, pp. 285–89.

Goble, Paul, "Iran Seeks to Expand Its Position in South Caucasus on Wake of Karabakh War," *Eurasia Review*, January 31, 2021; available at <https://www.eurasiareview.com/31012021-iran-seeks-to-expand-its-position-in-south-caucasus-on-wake-of-karabakh-war-oped/>. Accessed on April 19, 2021.

Goldston, Robert, "Iran after Sunset," *Bulletin of The Atomic Scientists*, April 25, 2018, available at <https://thebulletin.org/2018/04/iran-after-sunset/>. Accessed on December 16, 2020.

Gordon, Philip H., *Losing the Long Game: The False Promise of Regime Change in the Middle East*, New York: St. Martin's Press, 2020.

Gordon, Philip and Robert Malley, "Destroy the Iran Deal While Claiming to Save it," *The Atlantic*, January 21, 2018, available at <https://www.

theatlantic.com/international/archive/2018/01/trump-iran-deal-jcpoa/551066/>. Accessed on February 12, 2021.

Haass, Richard N. and Martin Indyk, "Beyond Iraq: A New U.S. Strategy for the Middle East," *Foreign Affairs*, Vol. 88, No. 1, January/February 2009, pp. 41–58.

Heiran-Nia, Javad, "Western goals and approach to launching Iran's satellite and missile program." International Peace Studies Center, February 16, 2020, available at <http://peace-ipsc.org/fa/>. Accessed on November 23, 2020.

Howard, Jane Mary, *Inside Iran: Women's Lives*, Washington, DC: Mage Publishers, 2002.

Hulme, Jr., Derick L., *The Domestic Politics of Terrorism: Lessons from the Clinton Administration*, Lanham, MD: Lexington Books, 2020.

Human Rights Watch, "Iran: Sanctions Threatening Health," October 29, 2019, available at <https://www.hrw.org/news/2019/10/29/iran-sanctions-threatening-health#>. Accessed on February 23, 2021.

Hunter, Robert "In a US-Iran Standoff, Biden Must be Willing to Take Some Political Heat," *Responsible Statecraft*, February 9, 2021, available at <https://responsiblestatecraft.org/2021/02/09/in-a-u-s-iran-standoff-biden-must-be-willing-to-take-a-little-political-heat/>. Accessed on February 10, 2021.

Hunter, Shireen T., *Iran Divided: The Historical Roots of Iranian Debates on Identity, Culture, and Governance in the Twenty-First Century*, Lanham, MD: Rowman & Littlefield, 2014.

Indyk, Martin, "Disaster in the Desert: Why Trump's Middle East Plan Can't Work," *Foreign Affairs*, Vol. 98, No. 6, November/December 2019, pp. 10–20.

Jansen, Michael, "After His Own Interests," *Panorama Magazine: Gulf Today*, April 16–22, 2021, pp. 36–7.

Juneau, Thomas, "Iran's Policy Toward Houthis in Yemen: A Limited Return on a Modest Investment," *International Affairs*, Vol. 92, No. 3, 2016, pp. 647–63.

Kamrava, Mehran, *Troubled Waters: Insecurity in the Persian Gulf*, Ithaca, NY: Cornell University Press, 2018.

Kamrava, Mehran, *Inside the Arab State*, New York: Oxford University Press, 2018.

Katzman, Kenneth, "Iran Sanctions," Congressional Research Service, November 18, 2020, available at <https://fas.org/sgp/crs/mideast/RS20871.pdf>. Accessed on February 24, 2021.

Kaya, Zeynep, "Iran and Armenia: A Symbiotic Relationship," *Review of Armenian Studies*, No. 24, 2011, pp. 153–72.

SELECTED BIBLIOGRAPHY

Keddie, Nikki R., *Modern Iran: Roots and Results of Revolution*, New Haven, CT: Yale University Press, 2003.

Kemp, Geoffrey. "The Reagan Administration," in Robin Wright, ed., *The Iran Primer: Power, Politics, and US Policy*, Washington, DC: United States Institute of Peace Press, 2010, pp. 133–35.

Keohane, Robert O., *After Hegemony: Cooperation and Discord in the World Political Economy*, Princeton: Princeton University Press, 1984.

Keynouch, Banafsheh, "Iran's Regional Dynamics: A Piecemeal Approach," *Middle East Policy*, Vol. XXVII, No. 2, Summer 2020, pp. 94–107.

Khalaji, Mehdi, "No War, No Negotiations Is Iran's Stance," The Washington Institute for Near East Policy, May 21, 2019, available at <https://www.washingtoninstitute.org/policy-analysis/no-war-no-negotiation-irans-stance>. Accessed on January 4, 2021.

Kian-Thiebaut, Azadeh, "Women and the Making of Civil Society in Post-Islamist Iran," in Eric Hooglund, ed., *Twenty Years of Islamic Revolution: Political and Social Transition in Iran Since 1979*, Syracuse, NY: Syracuse University Press, 2002, pp. 56–73.

Kinzer, Stephen, "Diplomacy Is the Best Option for American-Iranian Relations," in Julia Bauder, ed., *Is Iran a Threat to Global Security*, New York: Greenhaven Press, 2006, p. 46–57.

Kouhi-Esfahani, Marzieh, *Iran's Foreign Policy in the South Caucasus: Relations with Azerbaijan and Armenia*, New York: Routledge, 2019.

Kramer, Karen, "Iran Isn't Just a Nuclear File," *Foreign Affairs*, February 2, 2021, available at <https://www.foreignaffairs.com/articles/united-states/2021–02–02/iran-isnt-just-nuclear-file>. Accessed on March 19, 2021.

Krane, Jime, *Energy Kingdoms: Oil and Political Survival in the Persian Gulf*, New York: Columbia University Press, 2019.

Kroenig, Matthew, *A Time to Attack: The Looming Iranian Nuclear Threat*, New York: Palgrave/Macmillan, 2014.

Krugman, Paul, "Pax Americana," *The New York Times: Sunday Review*, September 1, 2020, p. SR: 5.

LaFranchi, Howard, "How Biden's Pick of Wendy Sherman Elevates His Iran Diplomacy," *Christian Science Monitor*, January 28, 2021, available at <https://www.csmonitor.com/USA/Foreign-Policy/2021/0128/How-Biden-s-pick-of-Wendy-Sherman-elevates-his-Iran-diplomacy>. Accessed on February 14, 2021.

Lesch, David, "The Iranian Revolution," in Karl Yambert, ed., *The Contemporary Middle East*, Boulder, CO: Westview Press, 2006, pp. 131–42.

Limbert, John, "The Obama Administration," in Robin Wright, ed., *The Iran Primer: Power, Politics, and US Foreign Policy*, Washington, DC: United States Institute of Peace Press, 2010, pp. 146–48.

SELECTED BIBLIOGRAPHY

Lopez, George A. and David Cortright, "Economic Sanctions and Human Rights: Part of the Problems or Part of the Solution," *International Journal of Human Rights*, Vol. 1, No. 2, Summer 1997, pp. 1–25.

Mahmoudi, Hoda, "Freedom and the Iranian Women's Movement," *Contexts*, Vol. 18, Issue 3, Summer 2019, pp. 14–19.

Malley, Robert, "The Unwanted Wars: Why the Middle East is More Combustive Than Ever," *Foreign Affairs*, Vol. 98, No. 6, November/December 2019, pp. 38–46.

Malley, Robert, "10 Conflicts to Watch in 2021: The Year Ahead," *Foreign Policy*, December 29, 2020, available at <https://foreignpolicy.com/author/robert-malley/>. Accessed on January 1, 2021.

Maloney, Suzanne, "America and Iran: From Containment to Coexistence," The Brookings Institution, August 15, 2001, available at <https://www.brookings.edu/research/america-and-iran-from-containment-to-coexistence/>. Accessed on January 5, 2021.

Maloney, Suzanne, "After Dumping the Nuclear Deal, Trump Has No Strategy for Iran," The Brookings Institution, May 9, 2018, available at <https://www.brookings.edu/blog/order-from-chaos/2018/05/09/after-dumping-the-nuclear-deal-trump-has-no-strategy-for-iran/>. Accessed on February 1, 2021.

Mamedov, Eldar, "Iran's delicate balancing act in the South Caucasus," *Responsible Statecraft*, October 9, 2020, available at <https://responsiblestatecraft.org/2020/10/09/irans-delicate-balancing-act-in-the-south-caucasus/>. Accessed on March 24, 2021.

Mattair, Thomas R. *Global security watch—Iran: A Reference Handbook*, Westport, CT: Praeger, 2008.

Mayer, Ann Elizabeth, *Islam and Human Rights: Tradition and Politics*, Boulder, CO, Westview Press, 1991.

Mazzetti, Mark, "U.S. Reports Says Iran Halted Nuclear Weapon Program in 2003," *The New York Times*, December 3, 2007, available at <https://www.nytimes.com/2007/12/03/world/americas/03iht-cia.5.8573960.html>. Accessed on December 16, 2020.

Menashri, David, *Post-Revolutionary Politics in Iran: Religion, Society, and Power*, London: Frank Cass Publishers, 2001.

Messari, Nizar, "Identity and Foreign Policy: The Case of Islam in U.S. Foreign Policy," in Vendulka Kubalkova, ed., *Foreign Policy in a Constructed World*, Armonk, NY: M. E. Sharpe, 2001, pp. 227–46.

Milani, Abbas, "Pious Populist," *Boston Review*, November–December 2007, pp. 7–14.

Milani, Farzaneh, "A Revolution Within Two Revolutions: Women and Literature in Contemporary Iran," in Mahmood Monshipouri, ed., *Inside the Islamic Republic: Social Change in Post-Khomeini Iran*, New York: Oxford University Press, 2016, pp. 113–31.

Milani, Mohsen M., "Tehran's Take: Understanding Iran's US Policy," *Foreign Affairs*, Vol. 88, No. 4, July/August 2009, pp. 46–62.

Milani, Mohsen, "Is US–Iran Détente Possible," *Current History*, Vol. 12, Issue 758, December 2013, pp. 345–48.

Mir-Hosseini, Ziba, "Religious Modernists and the 'Woman Question'," in Eric Hooglund, ed., *Twenty Years of Islamic Revolution: Political and Social Transition in Iran Since 1979*, Syracuse, NY: Syracuse University Press, 2002, pp. 74–95.

Moaveni, Azadeh and Ali Vaez, "US Maximum Pressure on Iran Hurts the Women It Claims to Help," *International Crisis Group*, March 6, 2020, available at <https://www.crisisgroup.org/middle-east-north-africa/gulf-and-arabian-peninsula/iran/us-maximum-pressure-iran-hurts-women-it-claims-help>. Accessed on March 26, 2021.

Moghadam, Valentine M., "Islamic Feminism and Its Discontents: Toward a Resolution of the Debate," *Journal of Women in Culture and Society*, Vol. 27, No. 41, Summer 2002, pp. 1135–71.

Mohammad-Nia, Mahdi, "Understanding Iran's Foreign Policy: An Application of Holistic Constructivism," *World Affairs*, Vol. 15, No. 2, Summer 2011, pp. 196–238.

Mokhtari, Shadi and Neda Nazmi, "The Politics of Human Rights in Iran Since the Green Movement," in Anthony Tirado Chase, ed., *Routledge Handbook on Human Rights and the Middle East and North Africa*, New York: Routledge, 2017, pp. 116–28

Molavi, Afshin, "Iran and Gulf States," in Robin Wright, ed., *The Iran Primer: Power, Politics, and US Foreign Policy*, Washington, DC: United States Institute of Peace Press, 2010, pp. 159–62.

Monshipouri, Mahmood, ed., *Inside the Islamic Republic: Social Change in Post-Khomeini Iran*, New York: Oxford University Press, 2016.

Monshipouri, Mahmood, *Middle East Politics: Changing Dynamics*, New York: Routledge, 2019.

Monshipouri, Mahmood, and Ali Assareh, "The Islamic Republic and the 'Green Movement': Coming Full Circle," *Middle East Policy*, Vol. XVI, No. 4, Winter 2009, pp. 27–46.

Monshipouri, Mahmood and William Chu, "The Flaws of the Proliferation Cascade Scenario: Iran-Saudi Relations in Perspective," *International Studies Journal*, Vol. 12, No. 3, Winter 2016, pp. 1–14.

Monshipouri, Mahmood and Manochehr Dorraj, "The Resilience of Populism in Iranian Politics: A Closer Look at the Nexus between Internal and External Factors," *Middle East Journal*, Vol. 75, No. 2, Summer 2021, pp. 201–20.

Monshipouri, Mahmood and Javad Heiran-Nia, "China's Iran Strategy: What Is at Stake," *Middle East Policy*, Vol. XXVII, No. 4, Winter 2020, pp. 157–72.

Monshipouri, Mahmood and Javad Heiran-Nia, "Iran's Security Interests and Policies in the South Caucasus," *Iran and the Caucasus*, Vol. 25, 2021, pp. 284–300.

Monshipouri, Mahmood and Mehdi Zakerian, "The State of Human Rights in Iran," in Mahmood Monshipouri, ed., *Inside the Islamic Republic: Social Change in Post-Khomeini Iran*, New York: Oxford University Press, 2016, pp. 151–75.

Mortazavi, Negar, "US Sanctions on Iran are 'Limiting Import of Life-Saving Medicine,'" *Independent*, October 29, 2019, available at <https://www. independent.co.uk/news/world/americas/iran-sanctions-us-medicine-imports-hospital-disease-a9178246.html>. Accessed on October 30, 2019.

Mousavian, Seyed Hossein, *A New Structure for Security, Peace, and Cooperation in the Persian Gulf*, Lanham, MD: Rowman & Littlefield, 2020.

Mousavian, Seyed Hossein and Mohammad Reza Chitsazian, "Iran's Foreign Policy in the Middle East: A Grand Strategy," *Middle East Policy*, Vol. XXVII, No. 3, Fall 2020, pp. 99–114.

Mozaffari, Mehdi, "Rushdie Affair," in John L. Esposito, ed., *The Oxford Encyclopedia of the Modern Islamic World*, New York: Oxford University Press, 1995, pp. 443–45.

Murray, Donette, *US Foreign Policy and Iran: American-Iranian Relations Since the Islamic Revolution*, Oxon, UK: Routledge, 2010.

Nasr, Vali, *The Shi'a Revival: How Conflict Within Islam Will Shape the Future*, New York: W. W. Norton & Company, 2006.

Nasr, Vali, "Trump's Policies Have Convinced Iran to Build A More Advanced Nuclear Program Before Negotiating," *Foreign Policy*, September 21, 2020, available at <https://foreignpolicy.com/2020/09/21/trumps-policies-have-convinced-iran-to-build-a-more-advanced-nuclear-program-before-negotiating/>. Accessed on February 27, 2021.

Osanloo, Arzoo, "Women and Criminal Law in Post-Khomeini Iran," in Mahmood Monshipouri, ed., *Inside the Islamic Republic: Social Change in Post-Khomeini Iran*, New York: Oxford University Press, 2016, pp. 91–112.

Osiewicz, Przemyslay, *Foreign Policy of the Islamic Republic of Iran: Between Ideology and Pragmatism*, New York: Routledge, 2020.

Pape, Robert A., "Why Economic Sanctions Still Do Not Work," *International Security*, Vol. 22, No. 2, Fall 1997, pp. 90–136.

Parsa, Misagh, *Democracy in Iran: Why It Failed and How It Might Succeed*, Cambridge, MA: Harvard University Press, 2016.

Parsi, Trita, "Why Did Iran Diplomacy Work this Time Around?" *Insight Turkey*, Vol. 16, No. 3, Summer 2014, pp. 47–54.

Parsi, Trita and Bijan Khajehpur, "How to Make Iran Trust a New Nuclear

Deal," *Foreign Policy*, August 15, 2021, available at <https://foreign-policy.com/2021/08/17/iran-nuclear-deal-talks-biden-raisi/>. Accessed on August 18, 2021.

Pesaran, Evaleila, *Iran's Struggle for Economic Independence: Reform and Counter-reform in the Post-revolutionary Era*, New York: Routledge, 2011.

Ramazani, Rouhollah K., *Revolutionary Iran: Challenge and Response in the Middle East*, Baltimore, MD: The Johns Hopkins University Press, 1986.

Ramazani, Rouhollah K., "Ideology and Pragmatism in Iran's Foreign Policy," *Middle East Journal*, Vol. 58, No. 4, Autumn 2004, pp. 549–59.

Rieffer-Flanagan, Barbara Ann, "Addressing Religious Intolerance in an Increasingly Illiberal World," in Mahmood Monshipouri, ed., *Why Human Rights Still Matter in Contemporary Global Affairs*, New York: Routledge, 2020, pp. 285–302.

Sadegh Zadeh, Kaweh, "Iran's Strategy in the South Caucasus," *Caucasian Review of International Affairs*, Vol. 2, Nol. 1, Winter 2008, pp. 1–7.

Salehi-Isfahnai, Djavad, "The Iranian Family in Transition," in Mahmood Monshipouri, ed., *Inside the Islamic Republic: Social Change in Post-Khomeini Iran*, New York: Oxford University Press, 2016, pp. 133–50.

Salehi-Isfahani, Djavad, "Iran's Middle Class and the Nuclear Deal," The Brookings Institution, April 8, 2021, available at <https://www.brook-ings.edu/blog/future-development/2021/04/08/irans-middle-class-and-the-nuclear-deal/>. Accessed on April 9, 2021.

Sanasarian, Eliz, *Religious Minorities in Iran*, Cambridge, UK: Cambridge University Press, 2000.

Sanger, David E., "US Ending a Few of the Sanctions Imposed on Iran," *The New York Times*, March 18, 2000, available at <https://www.nytimes.com/2000/03/18/world/us-ending-a-few-of-the-sanctions-imposed-on-iran.html>. Accessed on December 27, 2020.

Sariolghalam, Mahmood, "Sources of Continuity in Iran's Foreign Policy," in Michael Hudson and Mini Kirk, eds., *Gulf Politics and Economics in a Changing World*, Singapore: World Scientific Publishing Co., 2014, pp. 161–77.

Sariolghalam, Mahmood, "The Role of Algorithms in the Persistent US-Iranian Impasse," *Middle East Institute*, April 16, 2021, available at <https://www.mei.edu/publications/role-algorithms-persistent-us-iranian-impasse>. Accessed on April 21, 2021.

Seyedrazaghi, Ali, "US Sanctions Against Iran Embolden Its Hardliners," in Avery Elizabeth Hurt, ed., *US—Iran Relations*, New York: Greenhaven Publishing, 2018, pp. 104–09.

Sherman, Wendy R., "Iran Assassination Highlights Biden's National Security Challenge: His Team is up to it," *USA Today*, November 30,

2020, available at <https://www.usatoday.com/story/opinion/2020/11/30/iran-assassination-biden-national-security-team-crises-column/6456169002/>. Accessed on February 14, 2021.

Sick, Gary, "The Carter Administration," in Robin Wright, ed., *The Iran Primer: Power, Politics, and US Policy*, Washington, DC: United States Institute of Peace Press, 2010, pp. 129–132.

Slavin, Barbara, "34 Years of Getting to No With Iran," *Politico Magazine*, November 19, 2013, available at <https://www.politico.com/magazine/story/2013/11/a-failure-to-communicate-100052>. Accessed on October 15, 2019.

Slavin, Barbara, "Five reasons why US 'maximum pressure' on Iran has backfired," *Atlantic Council*, May 14, 2020, available at <https://www.atlanticcouncil.org/blogs/iransource/five-reasons-why-us-maximum-pressure-on-iran-has-backfired/>. Accessed on December 31, 2020

Tabaar, Mohammad Ayatollahi, "Iran's War Within," *Foreign Affairs*, Vol. 100, No. 5, September/October 2021, pp. 155–60, 162–8.

Tajbakhsh, Kian, "Who Wants What from Iran Now? The Post-Nuclear Deal U.S. Policy Debate," *The Washington Quarterly*, Vol. 41, No. 3, Fall 2018, pp. 41–61.

Takeyh, Ray, *Hidden Iran: Paradox and Power in the Islamic Republic*, New York: Times Books, 2006.

Telhami, Shibley, "The Contemporary Middle East: Some Questions, Some Answers," in Karl Yambert, ed., *The Contemporary Middle East: A Westview Reader*, Second Edition, Boulder, CO: Westview Press, 2010, pp. 355–65.

Tohidi, Nayereh, "Women's Rights and Feminist Movements in Iran," *International Journal on Human Rights*, Issue 24, December 2016, available at <https://sur.conectas.org/en/womens-rights-feminist-movements-iran/>. Accessed on February 28, 2021.

Treviño, Rusty, "Is Iran an Offensive Realist or a Defensive Realist? A Theoretical Reflection on Iran Motives for Creating Instability," *Journal of Strategic Security*, Vol. 6, No. 3, Fall 2013, pp. 382–92.

Vakil, Sanam, "A Regional Security Process for the Middle East," in *US Foreign Policy Priorities*, Chatham House, October 15, 2021, available at <https://www.chathamhouse.org/2020/10/us-foreign-policy-priorities/04-regional-security-process-middle-east>. Accessed on February 28, 2021.

Vatanka, Alex, "The Saudis and Iran's Moderates," *Middle East Institute*, September 21, 2015, available at <https://www.mei.edu/publications/saudis-and-irans-moderates>. Accessed on December 23, 2020.

Waltz, Kenneth N., "Why Iran Should Get a Bomb," *Foreign Affairs*, Vol. 91, No. 4, July/August 2012, pp. 2–5.

SELECTED BIBLIOGRAPHY

Whooley, Jonathon Patrick, *Imagining Iran: Orientalism and the Construction of Security Development in American Foreign Policy*, New York: Peter Lang, 2018.

Wright, Robin, "Will Biden's Iran Diplomacy Become a Shakespearean Tragedy?" *The New Yorker*, February 22, 2021, available at <https://www.newyorker.com/news/our-columnists/will-bidens-iran-diplomacy-become-a-shakespearean-tragedy>. Accessed on February 22, 2021.

Zakaria, Fareed, *From Wealth to Power: The Unusual Origins of America's World Role*, Princeton, NJ: Princeton University Press, 1999.

Zunes, Stephen, "Iran's History of Civil Insurrections," *The Huffington Post*, August, 4, 2009, available at <http://www.huffingtonpost.com/stephen-zunes/irans-history-of-civil-in_b_217998.html>. Last accessed on August 6, 2009.

INDEX

INDEX